BOULDERS BEYOND BELIEF:
AN EXPLORER'S HIKING GUIDE TO AMAZING BOULDERS AND NATURAL ROCK FORMATIONS OF THE ADIRONDACKS

Russell Dunn

BOULDERS BEYOND BELIEF

Published by John Haywood Photography

First Edition Paperback 2018
Copyright © 2018 by C. Russell Dunn

Without limiting the rights under copyright above, no part of this publication may be reproduced, stored in or introduced into a retrieval system, or transmitted, in any form, by any means (electronic, mechanical, photocopying, recording, or otherwise), without the prior written permission of the publisher of this book.

ISBN-13:978-1724937155

CAUTION: Outdoor recreational activities are by their very nature potentially hazardous and contain risk. See Caution: Safety Tips, p. 35.

Front cover: Goliath Rock. Photograph by Christy Butler.
Back cover: Balanced Rock on Bald Bluff. Photograph by Barbara Delaney.

Maps created by Russell Dunn & John Haywood using TOPO! Software @ 2006 National Geographic Maps. To learn more, visit nationalgeographic.com/topo.

Photographs by the author unless otherwise noted.

Printed in the USA

10 9 8 7 6 5 4 3 2 1

BOULDERS BEYOND BELIEF

To Richard Delaney, my dear brother-in-law, whose devotion to grammar and syntax has made me a better writer.

BOULDERS BEYOND BELIEF

CONTENTS

Regional Maps	10
Introduction	19
No two rocks are alike	20
Delineating boulders and rock formations	23
Rocks have infiltrated the English language	28
Boulders and the theory of glaciation	30
GPS Coordinates	32
Delorme NYS Atlas & Gazetteer	33
Areas covered	33
Caution: Safety Tips	35
The Adirondacks	38

Section One: Northern Adirondacks   41

1. Poke-O-Moonshine Boulder (Deerhead) — 41
2. Ausable Chasm (Ausable Chasm) — 44
3. Lyon Mountain Boulder (Lyon Mountain) — 47
4. Bald Peak Boulder (New Russia) — 49
5. Mount Gilligan Rocks (New Russia) — 51
6. Johnson Pond Road Boulders (North Hudson) — 53
7. Cheney Mountain Boulders (Port Henry) — 54
8. North Fork Boulder & Potholes (Euba Mills) — 56
9. Solitary Rock (Euba Mills) — 58
10. Whale Rock (Euba Mills) — 59
11. Rock of Gibraltar (Euba Mills) — 61
12. Giant of the Valley Rocks (St. Huberts) — 62
13. Giant Mountain Boulders (St. Huberts) — 65
14. Boulders across Road from Chapel Pond Parking Area (St. Huberts) — 67
15. Roaring Brook Boulder (St. Huberts) — 69
16. East Trail Boulders (St. Huberts) — 71
17. Gill Brook Rock-Shelter (St. Huberts) — 75
18. Balancing Rock: Gothics (St. Huberts) — 76
19. Deer Brook Shelter Cave (St. Huberts) — 77
20. Rooster Comb Rock (Keene Valley) — 79
21. Split Rock: Keene Valley (Keene Valley) — 80

BOULDERS BEYOND BELIEF

22. First Brother Rock-Shelter (Keene Valley)	82
23. Phelps Trail Boulders (Keene Valley)	83
24. Slant Rock (Keene Valley)	85
25. Blueberry Mountain Boulder (Keene/Keene Valley)	87
26. Little Crow Boulders (Keene)	88
27. Jackrabbit Trail Boulders: Alstead Hill Road Approach (Keene)	90
28. Jackrabbit Trail Boulders: Mountain Lane Approach (North Elba)	93
29. Jay Boulder (Jay)	95
30. Stagecoach Rock (North Elba)	97
31. Balanced Rocks: Pitchoff Mountain (North Elba)	100
32. Cascade Mountain Boulders (North Elba)	103
33. Porter Mountain Boulder (North Elba)	105
34. Grant Rock (Heart Lake)	106
35. Mt. Jo Trailhead Boulder (Heart Lake)	108
36. Indian Pass Boulders (Heart Lake & Tahawus)	110
37. Whiteface Brook Boulders (Lake Placid)	116
38. High Falls Gorge Pothole (Wilmington)	119
39. West Branch Boulders, Ausable River (Wilmington)	122
40. Whiteface Mountain Summit Rocks (Wilmington)	124
41. John Brown's Boulders (North Elba)	125
42. Scarface Mountain Boulder (Ray Brook)	128
43. McKenzie Pond Boulders (Saranac Lake)	131
44. Pulpit Rock: Lake Placid (Lake Placid)	134
45. Additional Boulders & Rocks in the High Peaks Region	136
46. Split Rock: Harrietstown (Harrietstown)	145
47. St. Regis Mountain Boulders (Paul Smiths)	147
48. Historic Sinkhole (Vermontville)	151
49. Ampersand Mountain Rocks (Saranac Lake)	152
50. Second Pond Boulders (Saranac Lake)	155
51. Gull Rock and Bluff Island Cliff-Wall (Lower Saranac Lake)	158
52. Fernow Forest Boulder (Wawbeek)	160
53. Captain Peter's Rock (Tupper Lake)	162
54. Mount Arab Boulder (Piercefield)	163
55. Tooley Pond Road Boulders (Cranberry Lake)	166
56. Gumdrop Boulder (Clare)	168
57. Reuben Wood Rock (Cranberry Lake)	170
58. Stoner's Cave (Cranberry Lake)	172

BOULDERS BEYOND BELIEF

59. Bear Mountain Boulders (Cranberry Lake)	174
60. Ranger School Trail Boulder (Wanakena)	176
61. Haystack Rock (Stark)	177
62. Sunday Rock (South Colton)	180
63. The Pinnacle (Santa Clara)	183
64. Azure Mountain Balanced Rock (Santa Clara)	185
65. Jumbo Rock (Lake Ozonia)	189
66. Croghan Rock (Croghan)	192
67. Natural Bridge Caverns (Natural Bridge)	193
68. Bonaparte's Cave (Harrisville)	196
69. Pulpit Rock (Oxbow)	201
70. Am's Rock (Unknown)	204
71. Cooper's Falls Pothole (DeKalb)	206
72. Indian Kettle: Morristown (Morristown)	208
73. Devil's Oven (Devil's Oven Island)	210

Section Two: Central Adirondacks

74. Hough's Cave (Martinsburg)	213
75. Deerlick Rock (Glenfield)	214
76. Sugar River Unique Bedrock, Potholes, & Glacial Boulder (Boonville)	217
77. Elk Lake Road Boulder (North Hudson)	219
78. Balancing Rock: Blue Ridge Road (Boreas River)	220
79. Rich Lake Boulder (Newcomb)	222
80. Adirondack Hotel Rock (Long Lake)	224
81. Buttermilk Falls Boulder (Deerland)	226
82. Castle Rock (Blue Mountain Lake)	228
83. Leviathan Rock (Blue Mountain Lake)	229
84. Sawyer Mountain Boulder (Indian Lake)	231
85. Balanced Rock: Little Sawyer Mountain (Indian Lake)	233
86. Split Rock: Lewey Lake (Lewey Lake)	236
87. Snowy Mountain Boulders (Sabel)	237
88. Chimney Formation & Chimney Mountain Ice Caves (Wilderness Lodge)	240
89. Blue Mountain Lake Boulder (Blue Mountain Lake)	245
90. Hodge's Rock (Utowana Lake)	246
91. Utowana Lake Rock (Utowana Lake)	248

BOULDERS BEYOND BELIEF

92. Arnold's Rock (Seventh Lake)	250
93. Battleship Rock (Seventh Lake)	252
94. Natural Rock Dam (Inlet)	254
95. Fern Park Recreation Area Boulder (Inlet)	257
96. Neodak Split Rock (Inlet)	258
97. Roosevelt Rock & Martin Road Boulders (Big Moose)	260
98. Balanced Rock: Bald Mountain (Old Forge)	263
99. Chain Pond Trail Boulders (Eagle Bay)	267
100. Middle Settlement Lake Rocks (Thendara)	269
101. Flatrock Boulders (Thendara)	275
102. Putt's Monument (White Lake – Woodgate)	277
103. Monument Park Boulders (Atwell)	280
104. Peaked Mountain Boulders (North River)	282
105. Severance Hill Boulder (Severance)	284
106. Hoffman Notch Boulders (Schroon Lake)	285
107. Gull Pond Boulders (Gull Pond)	288
108. Crown Point Pothole (Crown Point)	291
109. Natural Stone Bridge & Caves (Pottersville)	293

Lake George Area

110. Elephant Rock (Graphite)	298
111. Split Rock: Hague (Hague)	300
112. Indian Kettles (Hague)	302
113. Rogers Rock Boulders (Hague)	305
114. North Bolton Boulders (North Bolton)	308
115. Buck Mountain Boulder (Pilot Knob)	310

Section Three: Southern Adirondacks

116. High Rock (Northville)	312
117. Tory Rock (Brooks Bay – Great Sacandaga Lake)	314
118. Manville Rock (Lake Desolation)	316
119. Irving Pond Rocks (Wheelersville)	318
120. Lily Lake Rocks (Canada Lake)	320
121. Pinnacle Boulders (Wheelersville)	322
122. Green Lake Boulders (Green Lake)	324
123. Green Lake Rockwall (Green Lake)	326
124. Prison Rock (Green Lake)	328

125. Pine Lake Boulders (Pine Lake) — 330
126. Nine Corner Lake Boulders (Canada Lake) — 332
127. West Lake Trail Boulders (Canada Lake) — 334
128. East Stoner Lake Outlet Stream Rock & Rock-Shelter (East Stoner Lake) — 336
129. Sherman Mountain Balanced Rock & Boulders (Arietta) — 339
130. Good Luck Cliffs Boulders & Talus Caves (Arietta) — 340
131. Stallion Boulder (Averys Place) — 343
132. Northville-Placid Trail Glacial Erratic (Piseco) — 344
133. Couch Rock & Square Rock (Piseco Lake) — 345
134. West Branch Boulders (Whitehouse) — 347
135. Bidwell's Hotel Rock (Gilmantown) — 349
136. Indian Face and Roadside Boulders (Speculator) — 351
137. Camp-of-the-Woods Boulder (Speculator) — 353
138. Kunjamuk Cave (Speculator) — 355
139. Pig Rock (Speculator) — 358
140. Hadley Mountain Boulders (Hadley) — 360
141. Griffin Falls & Auger Falls Boulders (Griffin) — 363
142. Dean Mountain Road Rock (Hadley – Lake Luzerne) — 365
143. Potash Mountain Boulder #1 (Fourth Lake) — 367
144. Potash Mountain Boulder #2 (Fourth Lake) — 368
145. Boulderwoods & Natural Bridge: Crane Mountain (Garnet Lake) — 370
146. Paint Mine Boulders (Garnet Lake) — 375
147. Schaefer Trail Boulders (North Creek) — 378
148. Paul Schaefer Boulder (Bakers Mills) — 381
149. Blind Rock (North Glens Falls) — 382
150. High Rock (Warrensburg) — 384
151. Pack Forest Rock (Warrensburg) — 386
152. Wilkie Reservoir Split Rock (Glens Falls) — 388
153. Cooper's Cave (South Glens Falls) — 389
154. Additional Boulder References — 393

Books & websites on Adirondack bouldering & rock climbing — 400
Articles on bouldering — 401
Acknowledgments — 402
Other books by the author — 403
Index — 405

BOULDERS BEYOND BELIEF

Joe Quinn, Metin Ozisik, & Andrew Canavan pause for a moment by a large boulder between Skylight and Mount Marcy. Photograph by Aidan Canavan.

BOULDERS BEYOND BELIEF

REGIONAL MAPS

1. Poke-O-Moonshine Boulder (Map 1)
2. Ausable Chasm (Map 1)
3. Lyon Mountain Boulder (Map 1)
4. Bald Peak Boulder (Map 1)
5. Mount Gilligan Rocks (Map 1)
6. Johnson Pond Road Boulders (Map 4)
7. Cheney Mountain Boulders (Map 1)
8. North Fork Boulder & Potholes (Map 1)
9. Solitary Rock (Map 1)
10. Whale Rock (Map 1)
11. Rock of Gibraltar (Map 1)
12. Giant of the Valley Rocks (Map 1)
13. Giant Mountain Boulders (Map 1)
14. Boulders across Road from Chapel Pond Parking Area (Map 1)
15. Roaring Brook Boulder (Map 1)
16. East Trail Boulders (Map 1)
17. Gill Brook Rock-Shelter (Map 1)
18. Balancing Rock: Gothics (Map 1)
19. Deer Brook Shelter Cave (Map 1)
20. Rooster Comb Rock (Map 1)
21. Split Rock: Keene Valley (Map 1)
22. First Brother Rock-Shelter (Map 1)
23. Phelps Trail Boulders (Map 1)
24. Slant Rock (Map 1)
25. Blueberry Mountain Boulder (Map 1)
26. Little Crow Boulders (Map 1)
27. Jackrabbit Trail Boulders: Alstead Hill Road Approach (Map 1)
28. Jackrabbit Trail Boulders: Mountain Lane Approach (Map 1)
29. Jay Boulder (Map 1)
30. Stagecoach Rock (Map 1)
31. Balanced Rocks: Pitchoff Mountain (Map 1)
32. Cascade Mountain Boulders (Map 1)
33. Porter Mountain Boulder (Map 1)
34. Grant Rock (Map 1)
35. Mt. Jo Trailhead Boulder (Map 1)
36. Indian Pass Boulders (Map 1)
37. Whiteface Brook Boulders (Map 1)
38. High Falls Gorge Pothole (Map 1)
39. West Branch Boulders, Ausable River (Map 1)
40. Whiteface Mountain Summit Rocks (Map 1)
41. John Brown's Boulders (Map 1)
42. Scarface Mountain Boulder (Map 1)
43. McKenzie Pond Boulders (Map 1)
44. Pulpit Rock: Lake Placid (Map 1)
45. Additional Boulders & Rocks in the High Peaks Region
46. Split Rock: Harrietstown (Map 1)
47. St. Regis Mountain Boulders (Map 1)

BOULDERS BEYOND BELIEF

48. Historic Sinkhole (Map 1)
49. Ampersand Mountain Rocks (Map 1)
50. Second Pond Boulders (Map 1)
51. Gull Rock and Bluff Island Cliff-Wall (Map 1)
52. Fernow Forest Boulder (Map 1)
53. Captain Peter's Rock (Map 2)
54. Mount Arab Boulder (Map 2)
55. Tooley Pond Road Boulders (Map 2)
56. Gumdrop Boulder (Map 2)
57. Reuben Wood Rock (Map 2)
58. Stoner's Cave (Map 2)
59. Bear Mountain Boulders (Map 2)
60. Ranger School Trail Boulder (Map 2)
61. Haystack Rock (Map 2)
62. Sunday Rock (Map 2)
63. The Pinnacle (Map 2)
64. Azure Mountain Balanced Rock (Map 2)
65. Jumbo Rock (Map 2)
66. Croghan Rock (Map 6)
67. Natural Bridge Caverns (Map 3)
68. Bonaparte's Cave (Map 3)
69. Pulpit Rock (Map 3)
70. Am's Rock (Unknown)
71. Cooper's Falls Pothole (Map 3)
72. Indian Kettle: Morristown (Map 3)
73. Devil's Oven (Map 3)
74. Hough's Cave (Map 6)
75. Deerlick Rock (Map 6)
76. Sugar River Unique Bedrock, Potholes, & Glacial Boulder (Map 6)
77. Elk Lake Road Boulder (Map 4)
78. Balancing Rock: Blue Ridge Road (Map 4)
79. Rich Lake Boulder (Map 4)
80. Adirondack Hotel Rock (Map 5)
81. Buttermilk Falls Boulder (Map 5)
82. Castle Rock (Map 5)
83. Leviathan Rock (Map 5)
84. Sawyer Mountain Boulder (Map 5)
85. Balanced Rock: Little Sawyer Mountain (Map 5)
86. Split Rock: Lewey Lake (Map 5)
87. Snowy Mountain Boulders (Map 5)
88. Chimney Formation & Chimney Mountain Ice Caves (Map 5)
89. Blue Mountain Lake Boulder (Map 5)
90. Hodge's Rock (Map 5)
91. Utowana Lake Rock (Map 5)
92. Arnold's Rock (Map 5)
93. Battleship Rock (Map 5)
94. Natural Rock Dam (Map 5)
95. Fern Park Recreation Area Boulder (Map 5)
96. Neodak Split Rock (Map 5)
97. Roosevelt Rock & Martin Road Boulders (Map 5)
98. Balanced Rock: Bald Mountain (Map 5)
99. Chain Pond Trail Boulders (Map 5)
100. Middle Settlement Lake Rocks (Map 5)
101. Flatrock Boulders (Map 5)
102. Putt's Monument (Map 6)

103. Monument Park Boulders (Map 5)
104. Peaked Mountain Boulders (Map 4)
105. Severance Hill Boulder (Map 4)
106. Hoffman Notch Boulders (Map 4)
107. Gull Pond Boulders (Map 4)
108. Crown Point Pothole (Map 4)
109. Natural Stone Bridge & Caves (Map 4)
110. Elephant Rock (Map 4)
111. Split Rock: Hague (Map 4)
112. Indian Kettles (Map 4)
113. Rogers Rock Boulders (Map 4)
114. North Bolton Boulders (Map 4)
115. Buck Mountain Boulder (Map 4)
116. High Rock (Map 4)
117. Tory Rock (Map 4)
118. Manville Rock (Map 4)
119. Irving Pond Rocks (Map 5)
120. Lily Lake Rocks (Map 5)
121. Pinnacle Boulders (Map 5)
122. Green Lake Boulders (Map 5)
123. Green Lake Rockwall (Map 5)
124. Prison Rock (Map 5)
125. Pine Lake Boulders (Map 5)
126. Nine Corner Lake Boulders (Map 5)
127. West Lake Trail Boulders (Map 5)
128. East Stoner Lake Outlet Stream Rock & Rock-Shelter (Map 5)
129. Sherman Mountain Balanced Rock & Boulders (Map 5)
130. Good Luck Cliffs Boulders & Talus Caves ((Map 5)
131. Stallion Boulder (Map 5)
132. Couch Rock & Square Rock (Map 5)
133. Northville-Placid Trail Glacial Erratic (Map 5)
134. West Branch Boulders (Map 5)
135. Bidwell's Hotel Rock (Map 5)
136. Indian Face and Roadside Boulders (Map 5)
137. Camp-of-the-Woods Boulder (Map 5)
138. Kunjamuk Cave (Map 5)
139. Pig Rock (Map 5)
140. Hadley Mountain Boulders (Map 4)
141. Griffin Falls & Auger Falls Boulders (Map 5)
142. Dean Mountain Road Rock (Map 4)
143. Potash Mountain Boulder #1 (Map 4)
144. Potash Mountain Boulder #2 (Map 4)
145. Boulderwoods & Natural Bridge: Crane Mountain (Map 4)
146. Paint Mine Boulders (Map 4)
147. Schaefer Trail Boulders (Map 4)
148. Paul Schaefer Boulder (Map 4)
149. Blind Rock (Map 4)
150. High Rock (Map 4)
151. Pack Forest Rock (Warrensburg)
152. Wilkie Reservoir Split Rock (Map 4)
153. Cooper's Cave (Map 4)

BOULDERS BEYOND BELIEF

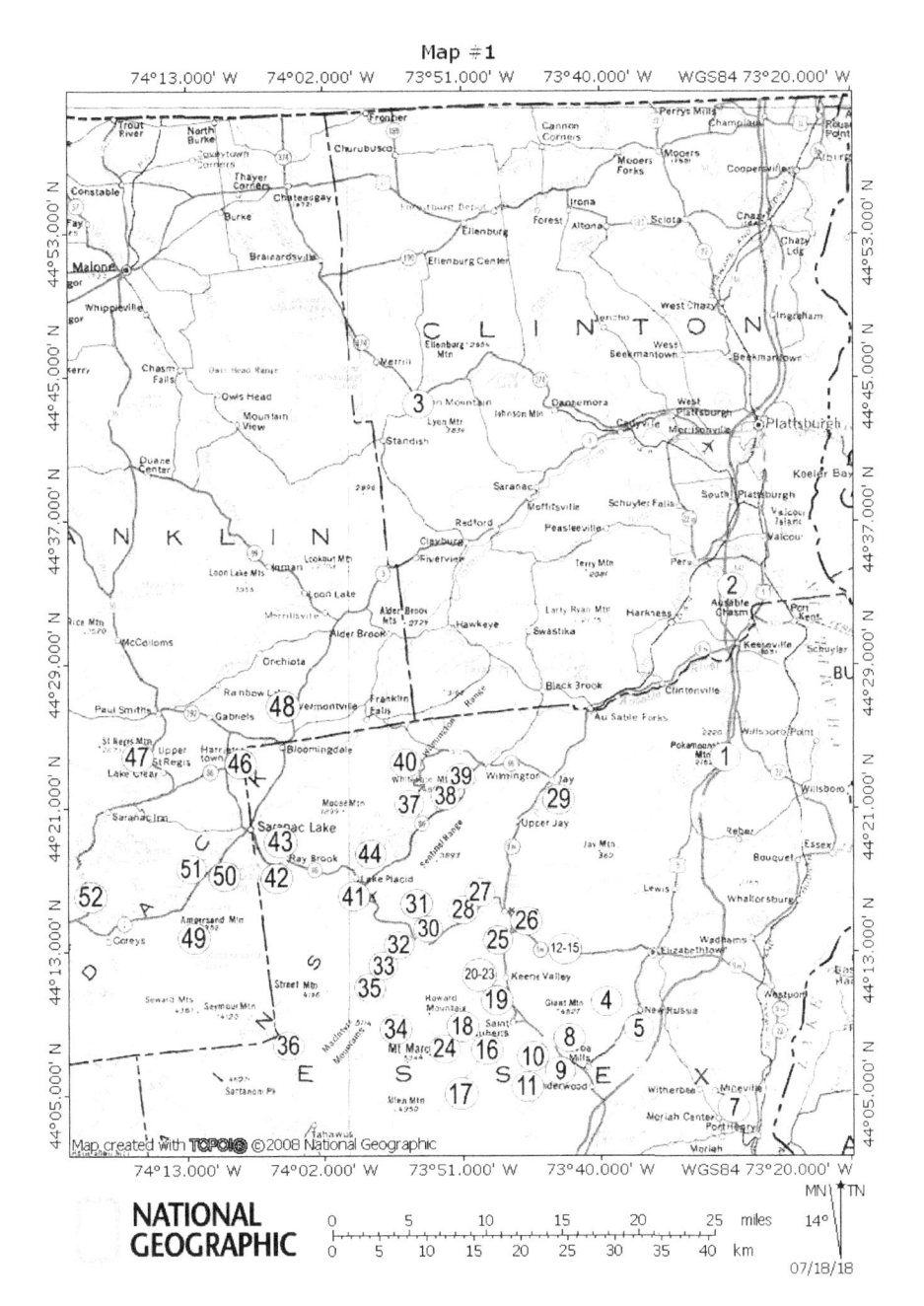

Map #1

BOULDERS BEYOND BELIEF

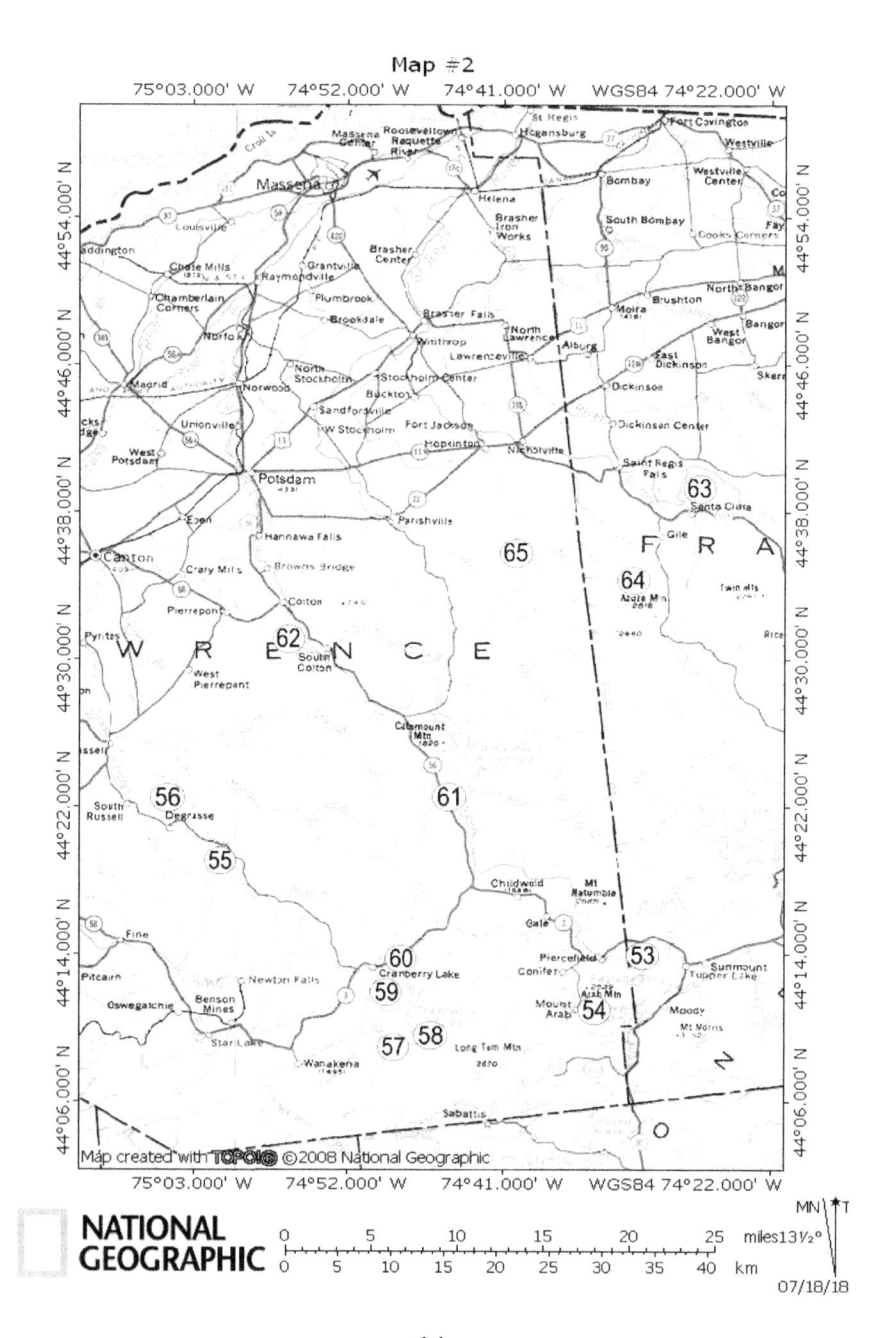

Map #2

BOULDERS BEYOND BELIEF

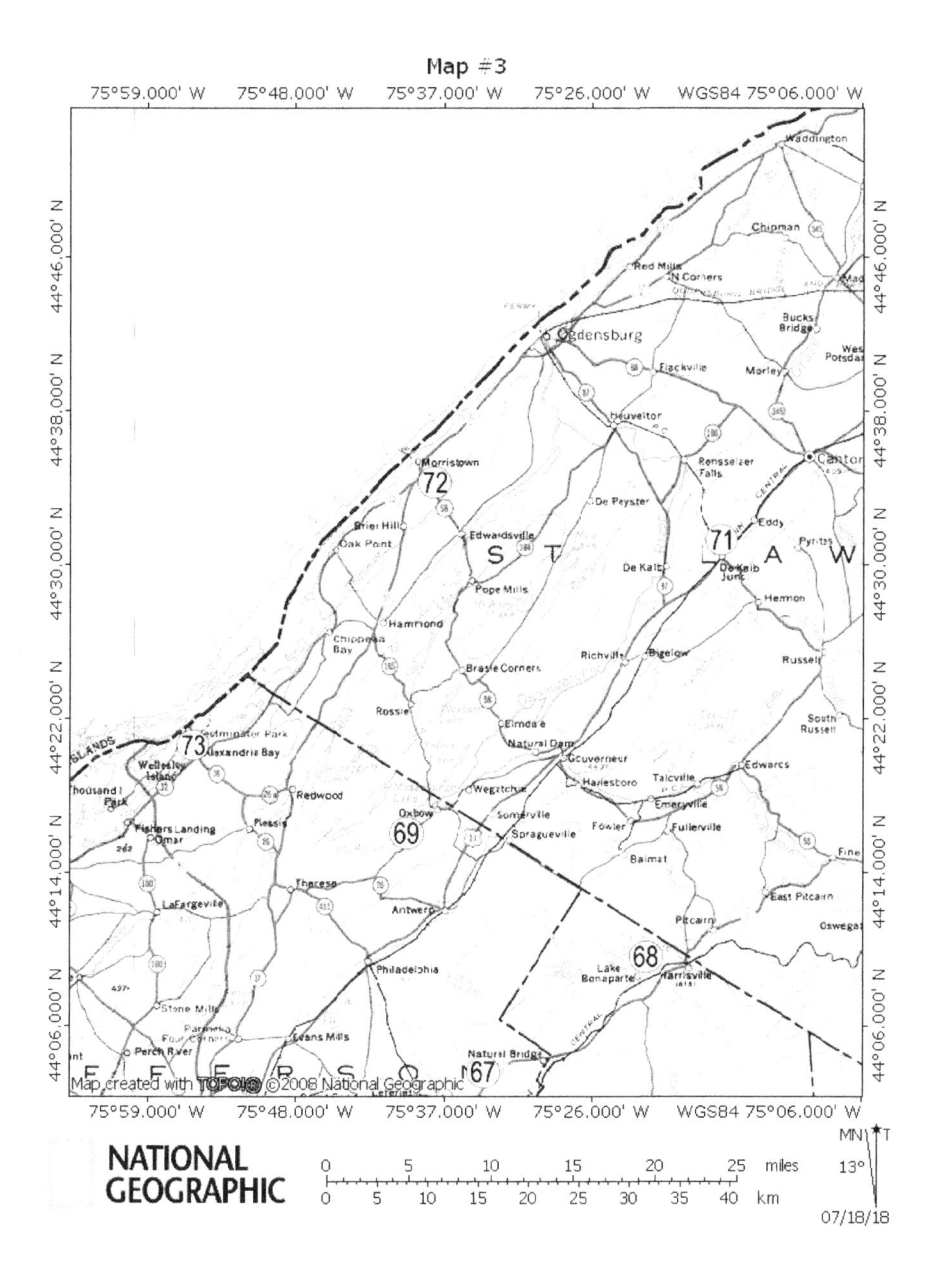

Map #3

BOULDERS BEYOND BELIEF

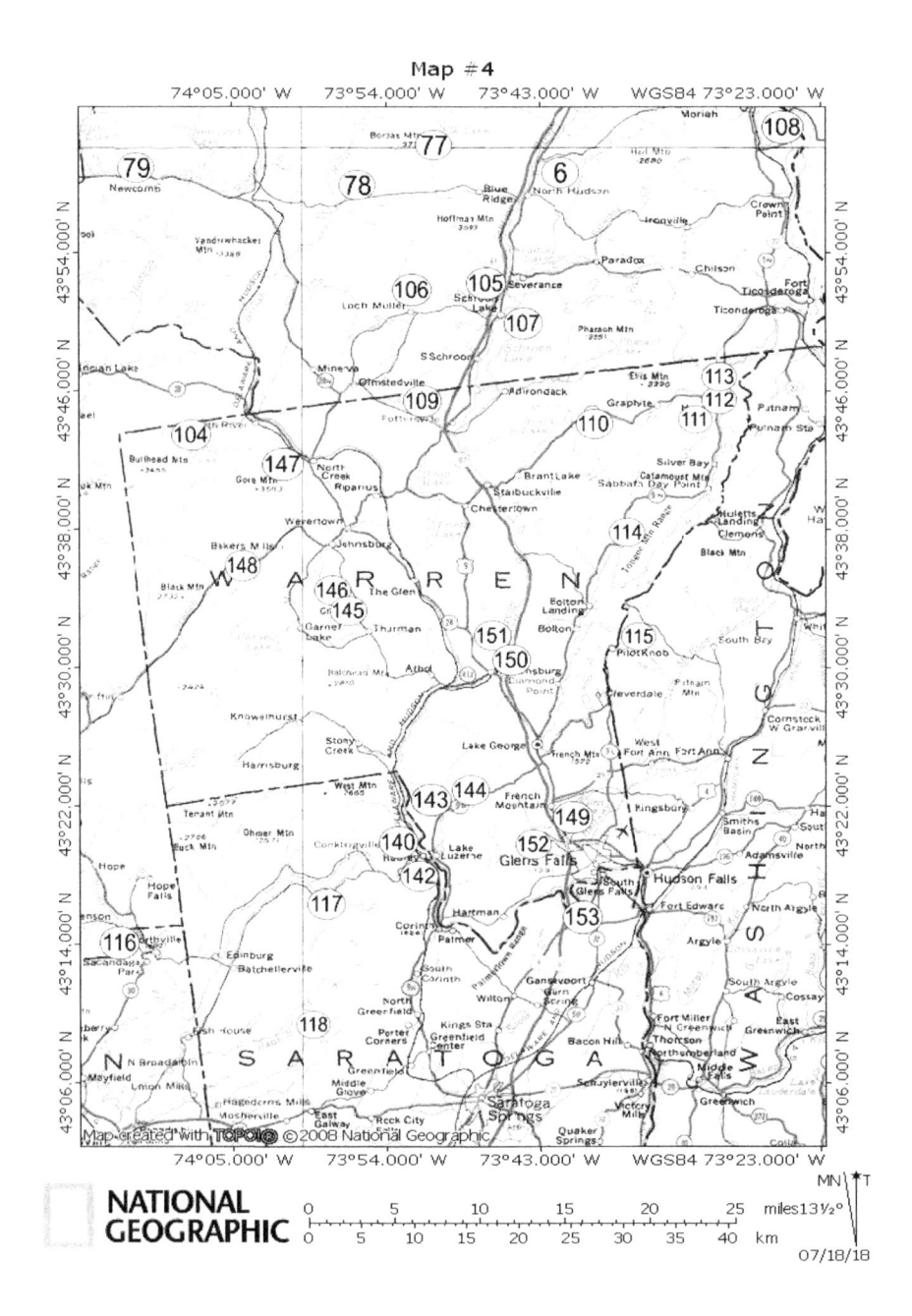

Map #4

BOULDERS BEYOND BELIEF

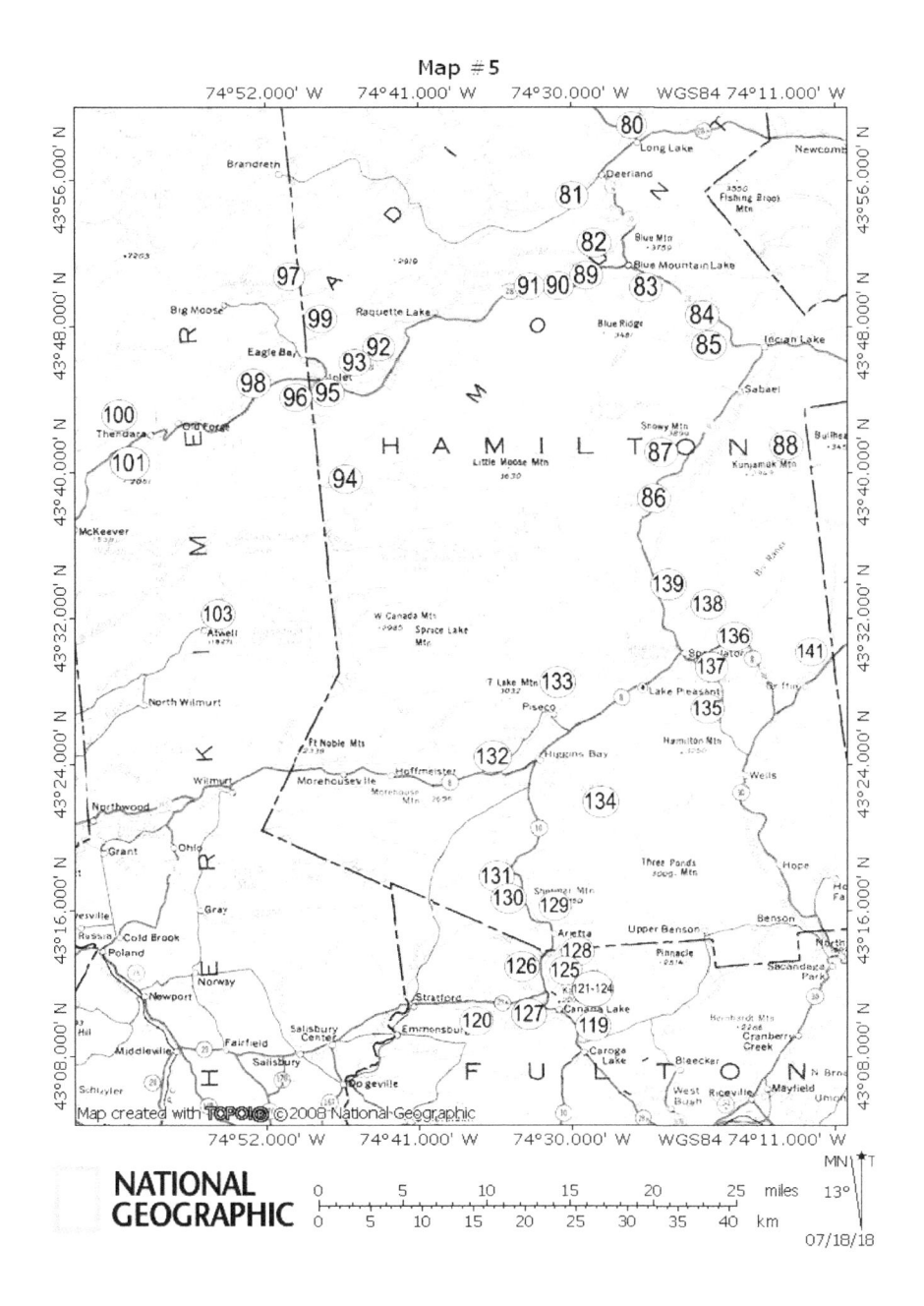

Map #5

BOULDERS BEYOND BELIEF

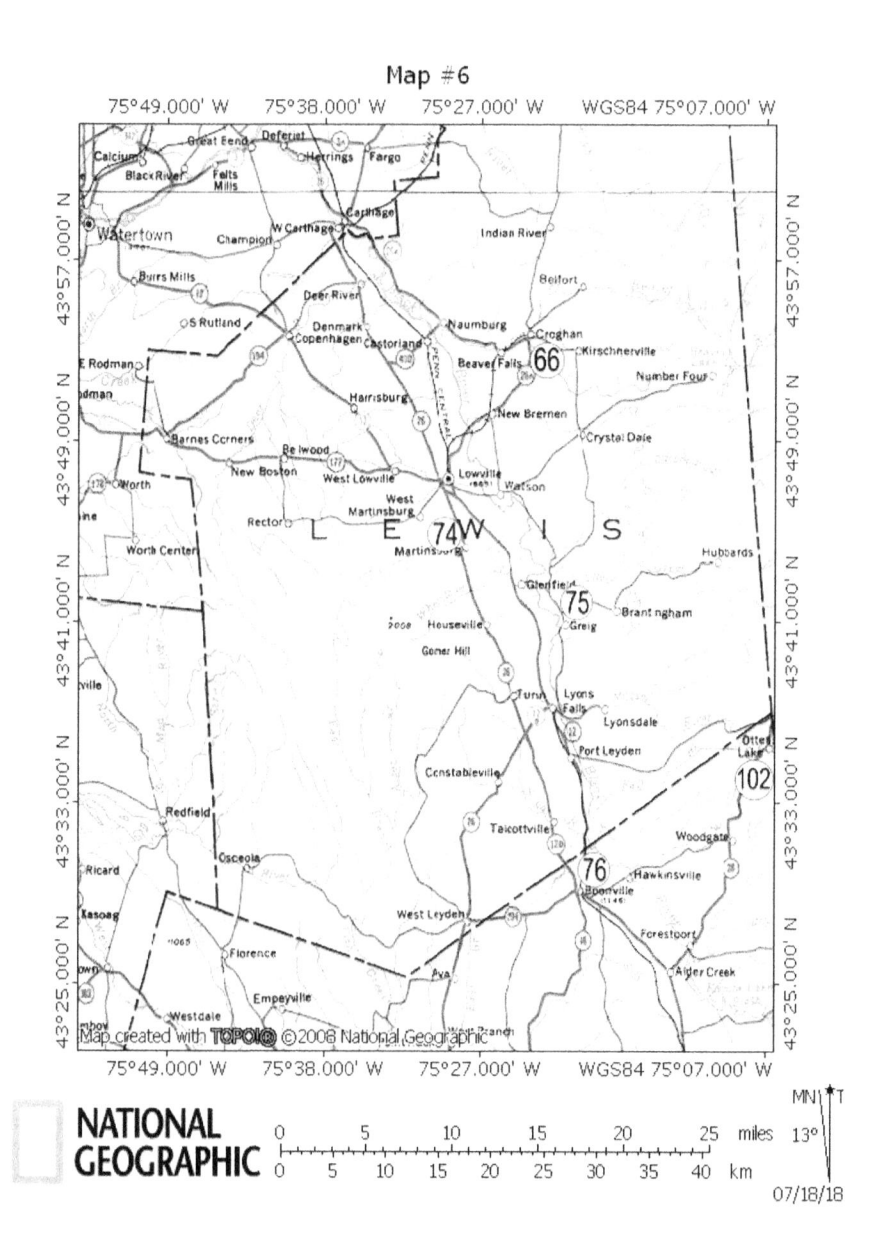

Map #6

BOULDERS BEYOND BELIEF

INTRODUCTION

Rocks are literally everywhere around us. Walk out your door and you are instantly standing on the bedrock of the Earth, solid and unyielding. Paddle on a river, pond, lake, or ocean, and below you, the water is supported by the inescapability of bedrock. Stroll along a sandy beach, and your feet are pressing down against the residue of shattered rocks. Rocks even rain down on us from the sky as meteorites—not to mention the moon, which is one huge rock that continuously sweeps across the sky.

So why write a book about rocks when everything around us is rock?

To be sure, there would be no reason to write a book about rocks were rocks uniform in composition and unaffected by the erosive forces of wind, rain, snow, ice, and life itself. After all, what would there be to say about a landscape that is eternal and unchanging?

As it turns out, the bedrock around us is anything but uniform and eternal. It is constantly reforming and reshaping. It is for this reason that *Boulders Beyond Belief* came into existence—a book about hiking to massive glacial boulders called glacial erratics (meaning rocks that don't fit in with their surroundings) and unusual rock formations, including rock profiles, painted rocks, rock-shelters, balanced rocks, talus rocks, perched rocks, potholes, sinkholes, and natural bridges. What all of these phenomenon share in common is that they are not commonly found.

Nor are they easily found! I have written eight regional waterfall guidebooks, and have come to the inescapable conclusion that waterfalls are easier to find than unusual rocks for the simple reason that they are formed on streams (and streams, at least, show up on topo maps). In addition, waterfalls produce noise, becoming readily audible in the early spring when rivers and streams are fully engorged with snow-melt. Boulders and rock formations, however, are silent and impassive. They give away no sign of their presence until you are almost upon them. Likewise, Forest Ranger Scott Van Laer knows something about this matter, given that his passion has been to seek out lost airplane crash sites in the Adirondacks that also reveal very little of where they are located.

Because New York State was over-ridden by glaciers, which not only reshaped the land, but left behind untold number of boulders, it is blessed with an abundance of rocks that invite exploration. Geologists believe that

BOULDERS BEYOND BELIEF

glaciers may even have come close to covering New York State's highest mountain—Mount Marcy (5,343')—as it advanced southward.

Glaciers have carried boulders over incredible distances. This was born out in the 1930s when the Brooklyn Botanic Garden set up an exhibit showcasing twenty-eight boulders, with a bronze plaque on each one stating their probable point of origin. The boulder that made the longest journey came from the southeast Adirondacks, a distance of 250 miles.

Boulder on Goodnow Mountain. Photograph by Robert Stone.
Lisa Densmore Ballard, in "Best Easy Day Hikes: Adirondacks," writes, "Its roots sprawl down the sides of the rock like a giant octopus reaching its tentacles towards the ground."

No two rocks are alike.

There are three main types of rock that you will encounter when hiking in the Adirondacks:

Sedimentary Rocks, which are eroded fragments of other rocks, or the calcium-rich skeletons of living creatures, that have become compacted under enormous pressures over eons of time. Think of limestone as an example of a sedimentary rock.

Metamorphic Rocks come into being when sedimentary or igneous rocks are subjected to extreme heat and pressure inside the Earth's interior, causing them to recrystallize. Marble, which is limestone recrystallized, and slate, which is shale recrystallized, are fine examples of a metamorphic rocks.

Igneous Rocks are created when molten rock is brought up to the Earth's surface and solidifies. Granite is an example of an igneous rock. So is anorthosite. In fact, a great deal of the Adirondacks is composed of this kind of rock.

Lone hiker on Owls Head. Photograph by Barbara Delaney.

For purposes of this book, the words rock, stone, and boulder are used interchangeably even though each word has its own individual meaning. *Stone* comes from the Latin word *stilla*, which means "drop." These are stones that have been dropped on the Earth's surface, generally by retreating glaciers, or have formed in streambeds where energetic waters have rolled and polished them.

BOULDERS BEYOND BELIEF

Boulder is derived from the old Norse word *bullersten*, meaning "noise stone." It is easy to imagine the grinding sound that rocks produce when being crushed under the massive weight of glaciers. The kind of boulders described in this book are not tiny ones, but boulders so large that they cannot be moved or lifted by even a gang of humans working in unison. To be sure, some of the big rocks described are not technically boulders, but rather blocks that have broken off from cliff-faces (talus), or sections of bedrock that have survived after the surrounding rock has been eroded away.

Rock, strictly speaking, does not refer to a specific object, but rather is a general classification to describe the material out of which most of the crust on the Earth is made.

Cracked boulder at Diamond Point: Great Sacandaga Lake.

You will find that rock and water tend to co-exist, for water in motion has tremendous power to reshape rock. When you visit Natural Stone Bridge & Caves in Pottersville, for example, you will see what Trout Brook has accomplished over eons of time [see chapter on Natural Stone Bridge & Caves]. Glaciers are simply a solid version of the power of moving water.

BOULDERS BEYOND BELIEF

Delineating boulders and rock formations –
Balanced Rocks and Perched Rocks – Balanced Rocks are large boulders that have come to rest on top of an equally large or larger boulder.

Perched Rocks are boulders that rest on a mound of bedrock.

In both instances, the boulder "appears" to be delicately balanced, and likely to tumble if given a sufficient prod.

"Appears" to be is the operative word here, for no boulder that is so precariously balanced can endure for long without being quickly toppled—often by pesky humans. Fortunately, not all large, precariously balanced rocks have vanished. Some are so massive that they have resisted the combined effort of dozens of puny humans to topple them, and have held onto their existence for future generations to enjoy. One example is the Balanced Rock on Bald Mountain [see chapter on Balanced Rock: Bald Mountain].

There are huge balanced rocks scattered about our planet, to be sure—Idol Rock [54°04.816'N 01°41.103'W] in Yorkshire, UK; Ruggesteinen Balanced Rock [58°21.020'N 06°20.613'E] in Norway; and Big Balanced Rock at Chiricahua National Monument Park [32°00.783'N 109°20.457'W] in Arizona. These represent just a few of many. There may even be balanced rocks on other worlds. One such rock, dubbed the Ballerina Rock, was sighted on Comet 67P/Churyumov-Gerasimenko by a European Space Agency landing probe.

Bill Delaney & Tom Delaney hike past the base of a mammoth slide along the Dix Mountain Trail.

BOULDERS BEYOND BELIEF

A word of advice goes a long way here. If you feel that you and your friends must test your might by trying to destabilize a balanced rock—DON'T. What makes these rocks so unique and precious is the fact that they are balanced!

There are large perched rocks as well, such as Krishna's Butter Ball [12°37.145'N 80°11.541'E] in Mahabalipuram, India, and the Devil's Marbles [20°30.000'S 134°14.000'E] in Australia.

Large boulders – This is one case where size does matter. Who hasn't been astonished when coming across a boulder the size of an automobile, or house, or barn? In *Boulders Beyond Belief,* you will encounter boulders exceeding 30 feet in height.

Huntley Pond Boulder near Moravia.

How big can a massive boulder get? The largest free-standing boulder in the United States—perhaps even in the world—is located in the Mojave Desert near Landers, California. It's called (not surprisingly) Giant Rock and it stands over seven stories high (34°19.970'N 116°23.325'W).

Many of the large rocks described in this book are glacial erratics. In *Guide to the Geology of the Lake George Region,* D. H. Newland & Henry

BOULDERS BEYOND BELIEF

Vaughan define what a glacial erratic is: "Glacial boulders, or erratics, noticeable from the fact that they differ in nature from the local country rocks, are widely scattered. They occur isolated or massed together, just as they were dropped from their positions within or on the ice. They often have their corners and edges rounded by abrasion or their sides polished and grooved by the same process as they were swept along in the ice current."

To be sure, not all large rocks are glacial erratics. Some, for instance, have been calved off from canyon walls and have fallen into piles at the base of a cliff. The large rocks in the massive gorge at Good Luck Cliffs in the southern Adirondacks is a great example of this phenomenon [See chapter on Good Luck Cliffs Boulders].

Saddleback Mountain Boulder.

Rock Profiles – Our brains are hardwired to look at chaotic scenes and, from seeming randomness, extract recognizable patterns. Over eons, this has proven to be of enormous significance. Early humans, gazing across a varied savannah, were alerted to the presence of a hidden tiger by pattern recognition. Our survival as a species depended upon this ability.

As all children know while lying on their backs to watch cumulus clouds floating by, indefinite shapes and patterns emerge, and then disappear— visages of monsters, elves, dragons, faces, and images conjured up by the mind.

We are particularly predisposed to see faces, undoubtedly because facial recognition is imperative for facilitating infants bonding with parents, and then later in negotiating the complex social interactions that our species have developed. For this reason, a fair amount of anthropomorphism takes place when rock profiles are encountered. The most famous facial rock profile of them all in the northeast United States was New Hampshire's Old-Man-of-the-Mountain until it came crashing down unexpectedly in May of 2003.

While some of the profiles are so striking as to appear intentionally created, a simple experiment will show that this is not the case, and that nature has not contrived to purposefully astonish humans. Stand in front of a recognizable rock profile, walk a short distance to your right or left, and you will observe that the recognizable features readily disappear. This is because the components creating the profile depend upon a particular alignment. Take away the alignment, and the components—unlike those of a true sculptured profile—fall into randomness, and the illusion is destroyed.

Stopping to pause on the summit of Round Mountain.

The famous (or, perhaps more infamous) "Face on Mars" (science.nasa.gov/science-news/science-at-nasa/2001/ast24may_1/) is a perfect example of people seeing what they want to see.

Another point worth making about rock profiles is that they are very short-lived. Fully exposed to the ravages of wind, rain, snow, ice, and water, they are constantly being eroded and swept away. It doesn't take long for

BOULDERS BEYOND BELIEF

nature to remove enough rock so that the illusion is permanently destroyed. This is especially true for ocean-side rock formations, where the rocks are not only subjected to all the normal erosive processes, but to the effect of salty air and waves as well.

Rock-Shelters, aka rockhouses, crepuscular caves, abris, and bluff shelters – These natural shelters are formed by overhanging rock at the base of a cliff or bluff. Some of the shelters were occupied by prehistoric peoples who took refuge from the elements under their protective ledges. Many represent wonderful archaeological sites.

Some of the best known rock-shelters in the United States are the Meadowcroft Rock-shelter [40°17.186'N 80°29.326'W] in Pennsylvania, Big Rock Rock-Shelter [35°03.694'N 80°49.643'W] in Charlotte, North Carolina, and the Weis Rock-shelter in the Nez Perde National Historic Park [46°26.851'N 116°49.364'W] in Idaho.

Talus Caves -- These formations typically result when large sections of bedrock break off from a cliff-face and, coming together below, form a maze of passageways and enclosures. The Adirondacks possess one of the largest talus cave systems in the world, if not the largest.

Tectonic Caves, aka Fissure Caves – Tectonic Caves are non-solutional caves created when the bedrock splits apart, forming a crack, crevice, or crevasse. Virtually all tectonic caves are the result of some kind of ground movement.

Potholes -- Potholes serve as vivid reminders of the erosive power of fast moving water and its capability to carve out deep gorges and chasms given eons of time. Potholes in bedrock develop when whirlpools and eddies in a fast-moving stream capture stones, swirling them around and deepening depressions in the bedrock.

Large glacial erratic near Lindsay Brook. Photograph by Jayne Bouder.

27

BOULDERS BEYOND BELIEF

Potholes can be seen in abundance at Natural Stone Bridge and Caves in Pottersville [see chapter on Natural Stone Bridge & Caves], at High Falls Gorge near Wilmington [see chapter on High Falls Gorge], and at Ausable Chasm near Keeseville [see chapter on Ausable Chasm]—three of the Adirondacks' most wondrous commercial attractions.

Natural Bridges -- Natural Bridges are few and far between in the northeast, being considerably more common out west, e.g., Natural Bridges National Monument in Utah. The most famous Natural Bridge in the east is 215-foot-high Natural Bridge in Rockbridge County, Virginia, but we have our own natural bridge too at Natural Stone Bridge & Caves [see chapter on Natural Stone Bridge & Caves], and it too is a beauty!

The largest natural bridge in the world is the Xianren Bridge, aka Fairy Bridge [24°41.199′N 106°48.569′E], in the Northwest Guangxi Province of China.

Natural Dams – Natural Dams are waterfalls that look like artificial dams. They typically extend across the full length of the river and are of unvarying height. Not only is one hamlet in the Adirondacks called Natural Dam for its natural formation, there is also a natural dam near Inlet that can be hiked to as a destination [see chapter on Natural Rock Dam].

Historic Boulders – Occasionally, large rocks become significant through association with a particular historical event, e.g., Plymouth Rock, or, serve as rock faces that plaques have been affixed to in order to commemorate a historical event. Sunday Rock is such an example [see chapter on Sunday Rock].

Painted Rocks – The defacement of rocks should never be encouraged, no matter how expertly done nor how wonderful the image may be. Still, some painted rocks have become so much a part of the Adirondack landscape today that they have been grand-fathered in, so to speak, and allowed to remain. Pig Rock, near Speculator, is an example of such a painted rock. [See chapter on Pig Rock].

Rock have infiltrated the English language –

So much that we are barely aware of their influence until someone points it out.

We talk of someone who acts foolish or dumb as having rocks in his or her head.

BOULDERS BEYOND BELIEF

The 1950s and 1960s inaugurated a new kind of music called Rock and Roll.

When a girl shows off an impressive engagement ring, we reflexively exclaim "What a rock!"

Old time religion carries the mantle of "Rock of Ages."

When relationships begin to fall apart, we say that they are "on the rocks."

When we are experiencing tough times, we talk about the road ahead being a rocky one.

When we have fallen into despair and things can't get any worse, we say that we have hit rock bottom.

When we wish to give encouragement to others we often say "Rock On!"

One of our most lovable movie icons is Sylvester Stallone's Rocky.

Even the Beatles have gotten into the act with their song Rocky Raccoon.

Algonquin Peak boulders. Photograph c. 1976 by John Hughes.

We owe much of who we are today to rocks. Civilization has literally raised itself up from primitive bands of hunters and gatherers by using rocks. Many early cities were built on rocky hills and fortified by defending rock walls. By the twelfth century, the use of stone blocks allowed builders to raise structures up even higher, one story on top of another, and cities became vertical as well as horizontal.

The pyramids, constructed out of enormous limestone blocks, have survived for over 3,000 years, and will undoubtedly last for another 3,000. They are the only one of the original Seven Wonders of the World to have survived into modern times—all thanks to the durability of rock.

The Great Wall of China, which began to take shape in the seventh century B. C., is reputedly the only human-made object that can be seen from an orbital space station. And it too is constructed out of rock

Christy Butler waits to hitch a ride on Freight Train Rock.

Boulders and the theory of glaciation

I find it interesting to read about how some nineteenth-century geologists accounted for the virtually endless number of large and small boulders that dotted the landscape. The theory they embraced was a biblical one—that Noah's Great Flood had caused boulder-bearing ice-sheets to break off from the Arctic Circle, and that as these icebergs moved south and melted, they dropped their load into the deep waters of a then-flooded Earth. After Noah's Flood ended and the deep waters mysteriously vanished, the boulders were literally left high and dry.

Geologists were not terribly happy with this theory. It seemed inconceivable to most that so many boulders could have been carried south on icebergs. Thousands?—maybe. But trillions? And how did all of these boulders get on top of the icebergs to begin with? Furthermore, many of these same boulders seemed to have been transported relatively short distances, tens to hundreds of miles—not thousands of mile as you would have expected if they came from the Arctic Circle.

With the proposal of glacial theory, the inexplicable presence of so many large boulders was demystified. The new understanding postulated that during a planetary winter, glaciers bulldozed their way south, loosening and scooping up bedrock in the process, and then ultimately releasing their titanic loads as they melted and retreated north. It is profoundly sobering when you visualize in your mind the power of these glacial advances.

Peaked Mountain. Look for a large boulder partially hidden by trees on the left.

Many articles have been written about the theory of glaciation and boulders. One excellent piece that appeared in a regional magazine is William P. Ehling's "The Not So Erratic History of Erratics," in the February/March, 1984 issue of *Adirondac*, pages 4–7, & 35.

BOULDERS BEYOND BELIEF

GPS Coordinates –

Many of the GPS coordinates were taken right on the spot using a hand-held Garmin etrex 12 channel GPS unit.

An equal number were taken right off of Google Earth.

After a while, I began to realize that the two sets of GPS coordinates didn't necessarily match up every single time. In a number of instances, discrepancies between the two versions could be as much as 0.05 mile off. No doubt, this was partially due to how large Google maps are created by stitching together smaller maps as seamlessly as possible.

Glacial erratics. Postcard c. 1900.

There were times when I simply was forced to make compromises.

In a certain number of cases where I hadn't personally visited the site, or had failed to take a reading at the opportune moment when at the site, or had been at the site earlier when I wasn't taking GPS readings, or when the unit momentarily quit on me, I did my best to come up with a GPS reading, which are listed as "Estimated GPS Coordinates."

I also found that during my series of hikes in the Old Forge area, some of the GPS readings I had taken looked questionable when viewed later—so I had to rely on Google Earth to come up with something that looked more reasonable, once again forcing me to improvise, arriving, at best, at an intelligent guesstimate.

In a few cases, such as Am's Rock, it was impossible to come up with even a guesstimate, since even the general location of the rock was unknown to me.

Delorme NYS Atlas & Gazetteer –

For each chapter, two sets of Delorme Atlas & Gazetteer coordinates have been provided. The reason for this has to do with the fact that Delorme reversed the numerical sequence of its maps in its latest edition, so that, for instance, what was page 96 for the High Peaks Region on the old maps is now page 30 on the new map. All you need to do is to make sure that you use, of the two Delorme Atlas & Gazetteer coordinates listed, the one that corresponds to the edition you are using.

In the two sections of the book where additional boulder and rock formations are listed, but are not given their own chapters, the Delorme Coordinates provided indicate the general location of the rock formation, not where the trailhead is.

Areas covered --

Somewhat arbitrarily, the book is divided into three sections: The Northern Adirondacks, Central Adirondacks, and Southern Adirondacks. Most of the chapters fall within the blue line of the Adirondack Park, but not necessarily all.

The fact that not every hike has been fully explored is what makes this book not only a hiker's guide, but also an explorer's guide. Here is the chance for you to set out on a number of treks without advanced knowledge of all the possible conditions and contingencies that you will meet and need to overcome.

Boulders Beyond Belief is a unique book, but not the first of its kind. In 2016, Christy Butler and I coauthored a book entitled *Rockachusetts: An Explorer's Guide to Amazing Boulders of Massachusetts*; and as far as we know, this is the first book that treated boulders and natural rock formations as hiking destinations, and not merely objects to be climbed on, or as side-diversions.

BOULDERS BEYOND BELIEF

Earlier this year I published *Rambles to Remarkable Rocks*, which focused on the Greater Capital Region, Catskills, and Shawangunks. *Boulders Beyond Belief* follows in this tradition.

While I've been busily at work on *Boulders Beyond Belief* and earlier, *Rambles to Remarkable Rocks*, Christy Butler has been equally as productive. His book, *Erratic Wandering*, published in 2018, features large boulders and rock formations in the states of Vermont, New Hampshire, and Maine, a prodigious undertaking by any measure. Truly, Christy is the foremost proponent of boulder hikes in this part of the country.

We love rocks. There's no two ways about it.

So rock it is.

—Rock on!

You're golden on the Mount Colden Boulder.

BOULDERS BEYOND BELIEF

CAUTION: SAFETY TIPS

Nature is inherently wild, unpredictable, and uncompromising. Outdoor recreational activities are by their very nature potentially hazardous and contain risk. All participants in such activities must assume the responsibility for their own actions and safety. No book can replace good judgment. The outdoors is forever changing. The author and the publisher cannot be held responsible for inaccuracies, errors, or omissions, or for any changes in the details of this publication, or for the consequences of any reliance on the information contained herein, or for the safety of people in the outdoors.

Remember: the destination is not the boulder, rock formation, or the mountain summit. The destination is home, and the goal is getting back there safely.

1. Always hike with two or more companions so that should one member becomes incapacitated, a second member can stay back with the victim while the rest go for help.

2. Make it a practice of bringing along a day pack complete with emergency supplies, compass, whistle, flashlight, dry matches, raingear, power bars, extra layers, gorp, duct tape, lots of water (at least twenty-four ounces per person), mosquito repellent, emergency medical kit, sunblock, and a device for removing ticks.

3. Your skin is the largest organ in your body. To protect it, wear sunblock when exposed to sunlight for extended periods of time, especially during the long days of summer, and apply repellents when you know that you are going into an area brimming with mosquitoes, black flies, and other insects that view you as meal time. A substitute for applying repellents is to pack a leafy branch that you can swish around you to keep the annoying insects at bay.

Wearing a hat with a wide brim to keep out the sun is always helpful, too. Remember that even on a cloudy day, you can get burned. Wear long pants and a long sleeve shirt to protect yourself from both the sun and biting insects.

4. Hike with ankle-high boots—always! High-ankle boots provide traction, gripping power, and ankle support that your sneakers and shoes

cannot provide. People who head out into the woods wearing loafers or flip-flops are especially asking for trouble.

5. Be cognizant of the risk of hypothermia and stay dry. The air temperature doesn't have to be near freezing for you to become over-chilled.

Equally of concern is the danger of hyperthermia (overheating). Be sure to drink plenty of water when the weather is hot and muggy. Also, stay in the shade whenever possible, and use a nearby stream, if there is one, to cool off in if you begin to overheat.

Always be mindful of where you are.

6. Stay out of the woods during hunting season where hunters are present. If you do enter the woods during hunting season, wear an orange-

colored vest and make periodic loud noises to draw attention to the fact that you are a human and not a fleeing animal.

7. Unless you are proficient in orienteering, stay on trails whenever possible to avoid becoming disoriented and lost. Off-trail hiking causes more damage to the environment. This is particularly true in summit areas of the High Peaks where there are rare plants and mosses.

8. Be flexible and adaptive to a wilderness environment that can change abruptly. Trails described in this book can become altered by blowdown, beaver dams, avalanches, mudslides, and forest fires.

9. Always let someone know where you are going, when you will return, and what to do if you have not shown up by the designated time.

10. Avoid any creature acting erratically. If an advancing animal cannot be frightened off, assume that it is either rabid or operating in a predatory mode.

11. Use good judgment, something that is easier said than done. Unless you are in a sudden crisis and need to react immediately and decisively, stop for a moment and think through what your options are.

The old sports adage "the best offense is a good defense" applies to hiking. It's far better to defuse a problem early on than to wait until it has reached crisis proportions.

12. Leave early in the morning if you are undertaking a long hike. A late start could cause you to be caught out in the woods with daylight dwindling and a long ways still to go. Allow for even more extra time if the hike is in the winter, where night arrives hours earlier than it does in the summer.

13. Be mindful of ticks, which have become increasingly prevalent and virulent as their range expands. Check yourself thoroughly after every hike and remove any tick immediately. The longer the tick remains in contact with your skin, the greater the risk that you will contract a disease such as Lyme.

BOULDERS BEYOND BELIEF

THE ADIRONDACKS

The Adirondacks constitute an enormous, six million-acre patchwork of public and private lands that include New York State's highest mountains (the High Peaks), over three thousand bodies of water, as well as thousands of miles of streams. There are still parts of the Adirondacks that are so wild and inaccessible that no human has yet to set foot. Readers should remember that once you leave the main areas where most day hikers gather, i.e., along Route 73, wilderness is but a step away.

From Wright Peak, trees look like inverted ice cones.

The Adirondacks have always exerted an irresistible pull on hikers, drawing them in from near and far. They are more heavily visited than either the Catskills or Shawangunks, despite these two downstate areas being considerably closer to vast centers of population.

The Adirondack Mountains were formed when a 160-mile-wide, one-mile-high dome of bedrock called the Laurentian/Canadian Shield was pushed up some five million years ago. The rock in this dome constitutes some of the oldest on Earth, dating back to over one billion years ago when it was formed under intense pressure and heat fifteen miles beneath the planet's surface.

The rock specifically underlying most of the High Peaks region is called anorthosite, or moon-rock, because it is also found in abundance on the Moon.

The infamous Pig Rock. Photograph by Barbara Delaney.

Elizabeth Jesse and Howard Jesse, in *Geology of the Adirondack High Peaks*, write, "A very large mass of anorthosite called the Marcy Massif underlies all of the High Peaks Region of the Adirondacks." Other parts of the Adirondacks are formed out of different kinds of rocks, but mostly some form of gneiss. And contrary to popular belief, the Adirondacks are not geologically related to the Appalachians.

The work of glaciers is evident everywhere in the Adirondacks—in its mountain passes, its enormous cirques (like the one on Giant Mountain where a glacier stalled), and, of course, in its vast deposits of large boulders. Indeed, the last glacial advance, called the Wisconsin (or Laurentide) Glaciation, left behind the Adirondacks much as it looks today

Bradford B. Van Diver, in *Roadside Geology of New York*, writes, "Summit regions have been further steepened by alpine glaciers that coursed down their sides in the closing stages of the Ice Age. Had these persisted long enough, they would have carved Matterhorn-like peaks out of the domes." It's a sobering thought to realize how less accessible the High Peaks would be today and how fewer boulders would have congregated on their summits and slopes had the Ice Age lasted longer and sharpened the peaks to pointy spires.

According to Elizabeth Jesse and Howard Jesse, "Erratics have been found as high as 4,600 feet on Mount Marcy, so we can say that the last ice sheet covered the lower peaks of the Adirondacks."

In the section on the Northern Adirondacks, we have included only a handful of the possible boulders on mountain summits, generally describing those that are accessible from Route 73.

Resources: Elizabeth Jesse & Howard Jesse, *Geology of the Adirondack High Peaks* (Glens Falls, NY: Adirondack Mountain Club, Inc., 1986), 10 & 320.
Jeff Chiarenzelli, "The Bedrock beneath our Boots," *Adirondac* (January-February 2016), 20–25. Professor Chiarenzelli provides a detailed account of how the Adirondacks came to be, and of their uniqueness.
apa.ny.gov/About_Park/geology.htm.
wildadirondacks.org/adirondack-geology.html.
James C. Dawson, "The Geology of the Adirondack High Peaks Region," *Adirondack 46ers: Of the Summits, of the Forests* (Morrisonville, NY: Adirondack 46ers, 1991), 172–177.

BOULDERS BEYOND BELIEF

SECTION ONE: NORTHERN ADIRONDACKS

1. POKE-O-MOONSHINE BOULDER

Type of Formation: Large Boulder; Talus Cave
WOW Factor: 6
Location: Deerhead (Essex County)
Tenth Edition, NYS Atlas & Gazetteer: p. 31, A7; **Earlier Edition NYS Atlas & Gazetteer**: p. 97, A5–6
Estimated Parking GPS Coordinates: 44º24.229N 73º30.156'W
Poke-O-Moonshine Boulder GPS Coordinates: 44º24.453'N 73º30.153'W
Accessibility: 100-foot walk
Degree of Difficulty: Easy
Additional Information: Friends of Poke-O-Moonshine, pokeomoonshine.org/index.html

Poke-O-Moonshine. Postcard c. 1910.

Description: A number of large rocks, primarily composed of granite gneiss (a coarse-grained rock), can be found at the base of Poke-O-Moonshine Mountain. The most striking boulder is a 25-foot-high rock that is used for bouldering, a fact that becomes immediately apparent when you move in closer for a look and see the chalk marks on its vertical surface.

Other significant rocks lie nearby, making this truly a treasure trove for explorers of large rocks.

Lisa Denmore Ballard, in *Hiking the Adirondacks*, writes that the trail up Poke-O-Moonshine passes by "several large glacial erratics."

Poke-O-Moonshine Boulder. Photograph by Barbara Delaney

History: Although the mountain's name may sound quaint and old-fashion, Poke-O-Moonshine is reputedly a corruption of the Algonquin words *pohqui*, meaning "broken," and *moosie*, meaning "smooth." Informally, Poke-O-Moonshine is called Poke-O by hikers and rock-climbers.

For those approaching from the north, Poke-O-Moonshine is considered to be the 'Gateway to the Adirondacks." The mountain's nearly 1,000-foot-high cliffs, close to the Adirondack Northway, irresistibly draw in the eye.

The boulders, rocks, and mountain are part of the discontinuous 53,280-acre Taylor Pond Management complex. Verplanck Colvin, the nineteenth-century, Adirondack surveyor, used the summit of Poke-O-Moonshine (station #26) as one of his benchmark posts.

The 25-site Poke-O-Moonshine Campground that was built at the base of Poke-O-Moonshine in 1930 has been closed since 2009.

Take note that the cliffs at Poke-o-Moonshine are a favorite place for Peregrine falcons and avoid disturbing the birds during nesting season.

BOULDERS BEYOND BELIEF

Directions: Heading north on the Adirondack Northway (I-87), get off at Exit 32 and head west on Stowersville Road (Route 12) for 1.7 miles. Turn right onto Route 9 and then proceed north for ~9.3 miles. The abandoned campground is to your left.

Heading south on the Adirondack Northway (I-87), get off at Exit 33, turn left onto Route 22, and then, after going under the Adirondack Northway, turn right and proceed south on Route 9 for ~2.9 miles. The former campground is to your right.

Resources: Barbara McMartin, *Fifty Hikes in the Adirondacks* (Woodstock, VT: Backcountry Publications, 1988), 125–127.
Dennis Aprill, *Paths Less Traveled* (Mt. Kisco, NY: Pinto Press, 1998), 23–27.
en.wikipedia.org/wiki/Poke-O-Moonshine_Mountain.
Dennis Conroy, James C. Dawson, & Barbara McMartin, *Discover the Northeastern Adirondacks* (Woodstock, VT: Backcountry Publications, 1987), 199–203.
Rhonda & George Ostertag, *Hiking New York* (Guilford, CT: The Globe Pequot Press, 2002), 47–49.

Blocks of talus form perfect hideaways.

Tony Goodwin (editor), *Adirondack Trails: High Peaks Region. 13th Edition* (Lake George, NY: Adirondack Mountain Club, Inc., 2004), 196.
Hardie Truesdale, *Adirondack High: Images of America's First Wilderness* (Woodstock, VT: Countryman Press, 2005). A winter shot of huge talus blocks at the base of Poke-O-Moonshine is shown on page 19.
Lisa Densmore Ballard, *Hiking the Adirondacks. Second Edition* (Guilford, CT: Falcon Guides, 2017), 243.
Rose Rivezzi & David Trithart, *Kids on the Trails! Hiking with children in the Adirondacks* (Lake George, NY: Adirondack Mountain Club, 1997), 60. "Rock falls have produced 'caves' of considerable size."
adirondacknaturalist.blogspot.com/2012/08/poke-o-moonshine.html.

BOULDERS BEYOND BELIEF

2. AUSABLE CHASM

Types of Formation: Rock Profile; Pothole; Cave
WOW Factor: 9–10
Location: Ausable Chasm (Essex County)
Tenth Edition, NYS Atlas & Gazetteer: p. 23, D8; **Earlier Edition NYS Atlas & Gazetteer**: p. 103, D6
Visitor Center GPS Coordinates: 44º31.478'N 73º27.679'W
Fee: Admission charged
Accessibility: Up to 0.5-mile hike
Degree of Difficulty: *Elephant Head* – Easy; visible from the rim of the Chasm
   Jacob's Well, Hydes Cave, and *Devil's Oven* – Moderately easy; visible from the Inner Sanctum Trail.
Additional Information: Ausable Chasm, 2144 Route 9, Ausable Chasm, NY 12911; (518) 834-7454; ausablechasm.com.

Elephant's Head. Postcard c. 1950.

Description: *Elephant Head* consists of a tall, vertical, stone column that resembles the head and trunk of a large, onrushing elephant. The broad, upper part of the column represents the elephant's forehead; the lower part, which gradually tapers, is its sinewy trunk.

Jacobs Well is a 20-foot-deep, 6-foot-wide pothole that was created higher up on the sidewall of the gorge when the Ausable River had yet to cut itself deeper into the Chasm.

Closer to the river is a larger, but shallower, pothole; only partially developed. It's called the *Punch Bowl*.

Hydes Cave consists of a notch worn into the sidewall. It was named after a nineteenth-century, Philadelphia man who descended to the cave from the canyon's rim by rope in 1871.

According to Duane Hamilton Hurd, in *History of Clinton and Franklin Counties, New York*, Hydes Cave "…is a crevasse leading off at right angles from the main fissure towards the west, and continues on the opposite side by a similar opening." Hurd further states that

BOULDERS BEYOND BELIEF

"Hyde's Cave is one hundred and fifty feet back, and perhaps thirty above the river—a continuation of one of the grand side openings of the gorge."

Devil's Oven is described by Clay Perry, a mid-twentieth-century author, newspaperman, and amateur caver, as "… a deep, cavernous recess in the rock of one steep bank…."

In *The Adirondacks Illustrated*, Seneca Ray Stoddard writes that "The cave known as the 'Devil's Oven' is a hole in the rock about thirty feet deep by twenty feet high…"

Duane Hamilton Hurd, in *History of Clinton and Franklin Counties, New York*, writes that "It is simply a hole in the rock, perhaps twenty feet in diameter at its mouth, and thirty feet deep."

Many descriptions have been written up about the Chasm's geological features, of which these selected formations are but a few.

Jacob's Well. Nineteenth-century stereoview by Seneca Ray Stoddard. Take note of the man climbing out of the well.

History: Ausable Chasm has been called, rightfully so, the "Grand Canyon of the East" and a "Yosemite in Miniature." It opened in 1870 and has been in continuous operation ever since, making it the longest, continuously operating natural attraction in the United States.

The bedrock out of which Ausable Chasm formed was laid down some 520 million years ago. The Chasm itself is a byproduct of the last Ice Age, created when the Ausable River was fed by the prodigious meltwaters of a retreating, mile-high glacier. At the head of the two-mile-long Chasm can be seen the chisel that Nature used (and still uses) to carve out the chasm—70-foot-high Rainbow Falls.

BOULDERS BEYOND BELIEF

There are a number of other famous and historic natural features in the Chasm, including Mystic Gorge, Point-of-Rocks, Post-Office, Hanging-Garden, Table Rock, Devil's Pulpit, Grand Flume, Sentry Box, Broken Needle, Pulpit Rock, and Jacob's Ladder.

Ausable Chasm. Postcard c. 1940.

Directions: From the Adirondack Northway (I-87) going north, get off at Exit 34 for Keeseville-Ausable Forks and turn right onto Route 9N. Head northeast for 1.3 miles into the village of Keeseville, continuing straight at the first traffic light (a 4-way intersection), and then turn left onto Route 9 at the second traffic light. Proceed north on Route 9 for 1.5 miles and, as soon as you cross over the Ausable Chasm Bridge, turn left into the entrance for Ausable Chasm.

From the Adirondack Northway going south, get off at Exit 35 for Peru/Port Kent and turn left onto Bear Swamp Road (Route 442). After driving east for 2.9 miles, turn right onto Route 9 and head south for 3.7 miles. Then, turn right into the entrance for Ausable Chasm.

To learn more about Ausable Chasm, its geological history, and its natural formations, be sure to pick up a copy of *Ausable Chasm in Pictures and Story* while at the Visitor Center.

BOULDERS BEYOND BELIEF

Resources: Russell Dunn, John Haywood, & Sean Reines, *Ausable Chasm in Pictures and Story* (Albany, NY: John Haywood Photography, 2015).
Clay Perry, *Underground Empire: Wonders and Tales of New York Caves* (New York: Stephen Daye Press, 1948), 163.
C. R. Roseberry, *From Niagara to Montauk* (Albany, NY: State University of New York Press, 1982), 177–179.
Seneca Ray Stoddard, *The Adirondacks Illustrated* (Albany, NY: Weed, Parsons & Co., Printers, 1874), 45–51.
Charles E. Resser, *Ausable Chasm in Pictures and Story* (Ausable Chasm, NY: Ausable Chasm Company. Reprinted from *Scientific Monthly*, January 1942, Vol. LIV).
Eleanor Early, *Adirondack Tales* (Boston: Little, Brown and Company, 1939), 90–109.
Unnamed author, *Ausable Chasm* (Chicago, ILL: (Curt Teich & Co., 1967).
Duane Hamilton Hurd, *History of Clinton and Franklin Counties, New York* (Philadelphia: J. W. Lewis & Co., 1880), 206.
Russell Dunn & John Haywood, *Ausable Chasm in 3D* (John Haywood Photography, 2015).
Richard B. Frost, *One Foot Forward: Walks in Upstate New York* (Peru, NY: Bloated Toe Publishing, 2008), 7.
Seneca Ray Stoddard, *The Northeastern Caver* Vol. XXXIV. No. 2 (June 2003). On the cover is an interesting c. 1890 photograph taken by Seneca Ray Stoddard while looking up from the interior of Jacob's well.
Arthur S. Knight (editor), *Adirondack Northway Guide* (Lake George, NY: Adirondack Resorts Press, Inc., 1964), 360–365.
Dennis Conroy, James C. Dawson, & Barbara McMartin, *Discover the Northeastern Adirondacks* (Woodstock, VT: Backcountry Publications, 1987), 176 & 177.

3. LYON MOUNTAIN BOULDER

Type of Formation: Large Boulder; Rock-Shelter
WOW Factor: Not determined
Location: Lyon Mountain (Clinton County)
Tenth Edition, NYS Atlas & Gazetteer: p. 22, B3; **Earlier Edition NYS Atlas & Gazetteer**: p. 102, C2—3
Parking GPS Coordinates: 44º43.430'N 73º50.504'W
Estimated Destination GPS Coordinates: Not determined
Accessibility: ~1.5 miles
Degree of Difficulty: Moderate

BOULDERS BEYOND BELIEF

Additional Information: Map created by Andy Arthur can be seen at cnyhiking.com/LyonMountain.htm.

Description: In *Hiking the Adirondacks*, Lisa Densmore Ballard writes about a "...large glacial erratic on right side of the trail. The huge boulder has a cleft in its side, creating a shallow overhang."

History: Lyon Mountain (3,840'), as well as the hamlet of Lyon Mountain, is named after Nathaniel Lyon who moved to the base of the mountain in 1803.

The new trail was created in 2009, extending the hike by about a mile, but eliminating the unnecessary erosion that was happening to the more steeply inclined old section of the trail.

Directions: From the hamlet of Lyon Mountain (junction of Routes 374 & 1/Standish Road), drive northeast on Route 374 for 3.6 miles. When you come to Chazy Lake Road near the west side of Chazy Lake, turn right, and proceed south for 1.7 miles. Then turn right onto a seasonal dirt road (called Lowenburg Road at an earlier time), and drive west for 0.9 mile to the road's end, where the trailhead begins.

Follow the red-blazed trail southwest for somewhere around 1.5 miles. I'm forced to be imprecise here because I have not actually hiked up Lyon Mountain. From the chapter on Lyon Mountain in Lisa Densmore Ballard's *Hiking the Adirondacks*, it is clear that the boulder is somewhere between 1.0 and 2.5 miles up the trail. I figure that ~1.5 miles might be about right.

The 3.4-mile-long trail continues up to the summit where a 35-foot-high, restored 1917 fire tower extends the view farther.

Resources: Lisa Densmore Ballard, *Hiking the Adirondacks. Second Edition* (Guilford, CT: Falcon Guides, 2017), 46.
en.wikipedia.org/wiki/Lyon_Mountain,_New_York.
summitpost.org/lyon-mountain/456239.
Lisa Densmore Ballard, *Best Easy Day Hikes. Adirondacks. Second Edition* (Guilford, CT: Falcon Guides, 2017), 55.
cnyhiking.com/LyonMountain.htm.
bigelowsociety.com/slic/lyon1.htm.

BOULDERS BEYOND BELIEF

4. BALD PEAK BOULDER

Type of Formation: Large Boulder
WOW Factor: 8
Location: New Russia (Essex County)
Tenth Edition, NYS Atlas & Gazetteer: p. 31, D6; **Earlier Edition NYS Atlas & Gazetteer**: p. 97, CD5
Parking GPS Coordinates: 44°08.985′N 73°37.589′W
Bald Peak Boulder GPS Coordinates: 44º09.552′N 73º40.097′W
Accessibility: 3.9-mile hike; ~2,400-foot elevation gain
Degree of Difficulty: Difficult

*Craig LeRoy lends a hand to Connie LaPorta at the Bald Peak Boulder.
Photograph by Chuck Porter.*

Description: This 15-foot-high boulder, standing on its end like an upright potato, is poised at the edge of an escarpment just downhill from the summit of Bald Peak (3,060′).

James R. Burnside, in *Exploring the Adirondack 46 High Peaks*, writes that "…one gigantic boulder balances on end, seemingly ready to topple at the first whisper of the wind."

BOULDERS BEYOND BELIEF

In *Discover the Northeastern Adirondacks*, Dennis Conroy & etc. state that "...on the climb up to Bald Peak, you have no doubt been tantalized by a large balanced rock, resembling a shark's fin that sits atop the ridge."

History: The Bald Peak Boulder is typically seen by hikers as they make their way up and over Bald Peak to reach Rocky Peak Ridge or Giant Mountain from the Route 9 trailhead near New Russia. The approach from Route 9 is one of the longer, more demanding hikes in this book, but it is also one of the more visually enjoyable treks for those who relish stupendous, uninterrupted vistas along exposed ridge lines. The trail was constructed by New York State in 1968.

A number of other large boulders have come to rest in the general area as can be seen in Jerome Wycroff's *The Adirondack Landscape*.

Rocky Ridge's absence of trees is the result of a forest fire in 1913.

Directions: From Euba Mills (junction of Routes 9 & 73), drive north on Route 9 for ~4.7 miles and turn left into the parking area for the "Giant Mountain Wilderness. East Trail to Giant Mountain."

From the parking area, hike west, climbing constantly uphill for nearly 4.0 miles to just past the relatively flat summit of Bald Peak

Resources: James R. Burnside, *Exploring the Adirondack 46 High Peaks* (Schenectady, NY: High Peaks Press, 1996), 61.
adk.org/bald-peak.
Den Linnehan, *Adirondack Splendor* (NY: Linnehan Press, 2004). A photograph of the giant boulder is shown on page 92.
Jerome Wycroff's *The Adirondack Landscape, Its Geology & Landforms: A Hiker's Guide* (Gabriels, NY: Adirondack Mountain Club, 1967). Two large glacial boulders are shown on page 46.
Gary Randorf, "Is Forever Wild in Danger?" *The Conservationist* (September/October, 1980). On page 8 is a photograph taken by Randorf of a triangle-shaped rock on Rocky Ridge.
Phil Brown, "My day in the sun," *Adirondack Explorer* Vol. 8, No. 5 (September/October, 2006). On page 17, a hiker can be seen bouldering a large glacial erratic near the summit of Bald Peak. On page 17, Brown talks about one boulder being a "15-foot-tall curiosity."
Tony Goodwin (editor), *Adirondack Trails: High Peaks Region. 13th Edition* (Lake George, NY: Adirondack Mountain Club, Inc., 2004), 200. Goodwin mentions "a huge glacial erratic at 4.0 mi."

BOULDERS BEYOND BELIEF

5. MOUNT GILLIGAN ROCKS

Type of Formation: Large Talus Block; Talus Cave
WOW Factor: 6
Location: New Russia (Essex County)
Tenth Edition, NYS Atlas & Gazetteer: p. 36, D6; **Earlier Edition NYS Atlas & Gazetteer**: p. 97, CD6
Parking GPS Coordinates: 44º08.083'N 73º38.393'W
Talus Rock Field GPS Coordinates: 44º08.113'N 73º38.186'W
Accessibility: 0.1-mile hike & 100-foot bushwhack
Degree of Difficulty: Easy

Huge blocks of talus have gathered at the base of Mount Gilligan.

Description: *Talus Rocks* – At the bottom of a 90–100-foot-high cliff is an assortment of automobile-sized blocks of talus that have broken off from the cliff face. Near the center of this field, a grouping of huge blocks have nestled together, creating a talus cave.

BOULDERS BEYOND BELIEF

Round Rock -- Farther up the trail, over halfway to the summit, a large, rounded boulder is reported to be near trailside.

Rock Overhang -- In *Adirondack Trails: High Peaks Region. 13th Edition*, Tony Goodwin mentions "...an interesting overhung rock..." that is encountered near the summit.

History: Mount Gilligan (1,420') was previously known as Sunrise Mountain. For this reason, the trail leading to the mountain's summit is called the Sunrise Trail.

Directions: From Euba Mills (junction of Routes 9 & 73), drive north on Route 9 for 3.4 miles and turn right onto Schriver Road (a dirt road) that leads in 100 feet to a fishing access parking area to your right just before the bridge spanning the Boquet River is crossed.

Walk across the bridge and proceed east for less than 0.05 mile, turning left at the trailhead to Gilligan Mountain next to the lawn of a private residence.

The huge rocks come into view within 0.1 mile, just as the trail begins to ascend steeply. Leave the trail and bushwhack south for 100 feet until you come to the bottom of a towering, 100-foot-high cliff. An enormous field of boulders lies at its base.

If you continue following the trail uphill, a large, rounded boulder is reached at 0.6 mile.

In 0.8–0.9 mile, a rock overhang is encountered.

The top of the mountain is reached in 1.1 miles.

Resources: Tony Goodwin (editor) & Neal Burdick (series editor), *Adirondack Trails: High Peaks Region. 13th Edition* (Lake George, NY: Adirondack Mountain Club, Inc., 2004), 202.
Bruce Wadsworth, *Day Hikes For All Seasons: An Adirondack Sampler* (Lake George, NY: Adirondack Mountain Club, 1996), 74.
Dennis Conroy, James C. Dawson, & Barbara McMartin, *Discover the Northeastern Adirondacks* (Woodstock, VT: Backcountry Publications, 1987), 76–78.
lakechamplainregion.com/hiking/mount-gilligan.
Rose Rivezzi & David Trithart, *Kids on the Trails! Hiking with children in the Adirondacks* (Lake George, NY: Adirondack Mountain Club, 1997), 105.
Brochure – *Champlain Area Trails. Saving Land. Making Trails. 2017–2018. Trail Map.*

BOULDERS BEYOND BELIEF

6. JOHNSON POND ROAD BOULDERS

Type of Formation: Large Boulder
WOW Factor: 3–4
Location: North Hudson (Essex County)
Tenth Edition, NYS Atlas & Gazetteer: p. 38, A5; **Earlier Edition NYS Atlas & Gazetteer**: p. 88, A4
Parking GPS Coordinates: 43º57.314′N 73º43.107′W
Accessibility: 150-foot bushwhack involving a small stream crossing
Degree of Difficulty: Moderately easy

Description: A numbers of boulders ranging in size from a height of 4 to 12 feet can be found on the downslope below a small cliff-face that has calved off the rocks.

What's appealing about this site is that the ground is covered with pine needles, and can be easily traversed both uphill, downhill, and laterally without encountering major obstructions.

Directions: From the Adirondack Northway, get off at Exit 29 and drive east on Blue Ridge Road for 0.3 mile.

One of several 12-footers.

Turn left onto Route 9 and head north for 0.3 mile. Then turn right onto Johnson Pond Road and proceed east for 0.4 mile. Park on the north (left) side of the road just before you reach a 30 mph sign, turning the car around to face west. Walk down the slope and across a small stream to reach the boulder field, less than 200 feet away.

Johnson Pond Road connects North Hudson with Paradox via Letsonville Road

Resources: communitywalk.com/map/list/299298.
communitywalk.com/location/johnson_pond/info/2808715.

BOULDERS BEYOND BELIEF

7. CHENEY MOUNTAIN BOULDERS
Town of Moriah Property

Type of Formation: Large Boulder
WOW Factor: *Resting Rock* – 1; *Leaning Potato* -- 5; *Perched Rock* -- 3
Location: Port Henry (Essex County)
Tenth Edition, NYS Atlas & Gazetteer: p. 31, DE8; **Earlier Edition NYS Atlas & Gazetteer**: p. 97, D6
Parking GPS Coordinates: 44º04.816'N 73º28.955'W
Destination GPS Coordinates: *Resting Rock & Leaning Potato* -- 44º04.504'N 73º28.653'W; *Perched Rock* -- 44º04.279'N 73º28.516'W
Accessibility: *Resting Rock & Leaning Potato* – 0.6-mile hike; *Perched Rock* --0.9-mile hike; 500-foot elevation gain
Degree of Difficulty: Moderate
Additional Information -- cnyhiking.com/CheneyMountain.htm – The website contains a trail map.

Description: *Leaning Potato* is a unique, substantial-sized boulder that is shaped like a tilted potato; hence, its name. One end of the boulder rises up 10 feet, where a 6-foot-deep shelter cave has formed. The rock is 15–20 feet long.

Resting Rock is a 1-foot-high, 3-foot-long flat rock that was named by "CNY Hikers" who noticed that its shape and location provided a convenient resting spot for hikers.

Perched Rock is a 3–4-foot-high boulder that is about the size of a young hiker.

Kid-sized Perched Rock on Cheney Mountain.

History: The boulders are located on Cheney Mountain (1,347'), a sizeable piece of property owned by the Town of Moriah, and containing one of several hikes that are part of the Champlain Area Trails (CATS). Some contend that the mountain is shaped like a loaf of bread.

I couldn't help but wonder if the mountain is named after the famous Adirondack guide John Cheney.

BOULDERS BEYOND BELIEF

The trail opened in June 2012 and was cut by a group of volunteers from Port Henry, Mineville, Moriah, Crown Point, Westport, and Wadhams, coordinated by Moriah Town Councilman Timothy Garrison.

Leaning Potato Rock.

Directions: From Port Henry (junction of Route 9N/22 & Main Street), drive north on Route 9N/22 for 3.0 miles. Turn left onto Pilfeshire Road and head west for 1.5 miles, turning left again into the trailhead parking area for Cheney Mountain.

From the parking area, walk across the landfill and enter the woods, following a well-marked trail. Climbing gradually uphill, bear right when you arrive at a trail junction. At 0.6 mile, you will come to Resting Rock, in the middle of the trail.

From Resting Rock, bushwhack left into the woods for ~70 feet to reach the Leaning Potato. You will need to tromp around to the east end of the boulder to see its unusual feature.

BOULDERS BEYOND BELIEF

From Resting Rock, continue uphill, following the path as it then levels off and even begins descending slightly. At the next junction (0.8 mile), bear left, and follow the path for 0.1 mile to its end, where a small, child-sized, perched boulder can be seen.

Resources: Brochure – *Champlain Area Trails. Saving Land. Making Trails. 2017–2018. Trail Map.*
cnyhiking.com/CheneyMountain.htm.
lakeplacid.com/blog/2013/03/cheney-mountain-–-quick-jaunt.
champlainareatrails.com.
offonadventure.com/2015/01/cheney-mountain-moriah-ny-11715.html.

8. NORTH FORK BOULDER & POTHOLES

Type of Formation: Large Boulder; Pothole
WOW Factor: *Boulder* – 5; *Potholes* -- 3
Location: Euba Mills (Essex County)
Tenth Edition, NYS Atlas & Gazetteer: p. 30, D5; **Earlier Edition NYS Atlas & Gazetteer**: p. 96, CD4
Parking GPS Coordinates: 44°06.844′N 73°42.581′W
North Fork Boulder & Potholes GPS Coordinates: 44º06.796′N 73º42.518′W
Accessibility: 300-foot walk & 50-foot downhill scramble
Degree of Difficulty: Moderate

North Fork Pothole.

Description: These two geological features lie next to the Chasm Cascade, aka Flume Falls—a small waterfall that lies at the head of a chasm formed on the North Fork of the Boquet River

Large Boulder – This large, fairly oval-shaped boulder stands 15 feet high and, unlike other nearby boulders, doesn't actually rest in the streambed. Its appearance would be greatly enhanced, however, were it more out in the open instead of being confined by brush, trees, and the steep slope of the embankment.

BOULDERS BEYOND BELIEF

Potholes – A series of potholes, graceful arcs and contours, and even a water chute have been created at the mouth of Chasm Cascade by the energetic action of the North Fork waters. The effect is as though a master sculptor took chisel in hand to render a highly polished work of art.

Directions: From Euba Mills (junction of Routes 73 & 9), drive northwest on Route 73 for 1.4 miles. Park to your right in a wide pull-off as soon as you cross over the bridge spanning the Boquet River's North Fork.

North Fork Boulder. Photograph by Christy Butler.

Walk back along Route 73 for several hundred feet, crossing over the North Fork bridge, and continue southeast along the east side of the guardrail for another hundred feet. Follow a short path to your left that takes you down a steep, 30-foot-high embankment, first to the boulder; then to the flume and potholes.

Use caution while walking along Route 73. This is a heavily-traveled, high-speed highway.

BOULDERS BEYOND BELIEF

9. SOLITARY ROCK

Type of Formation: Large Boulder
WOW Factor: 5
Location: Euba Mills (Essex County)
Tenth Edition, NYS Atlas & Gazetteer: p. 30, D5; **Earlier Edition NYS Atlas & Gazetteer**: p. 96, CD4
Parking GPS Coordinates: 44°06.844′N 73°42.581′W
Solitary Rock GPS Coordinates: 44º06.752′N 73º42.543′W
Accessibility: 200-foot trek from road
Degree of Difficulty: Easy

For a brief moment, Solitary Rock is no longer solitary while rock man Christy Butler embraces it.

Description: Solitary Rock is a 15-foot-high boulder that stands alone next to a wide, open, camping area that overlooks the North Fork of the Boquet River.

Directions: From Euba Mills (junction of Routes 73 & 9), head northwest on Route 73 for ~1.4 miles. As soon as you cross over the bridge spanning the North Fork of the Boquet River, park to your right.

Walk over to the north side of the road, cross the bridge spanning the North Fork of the Boquet River and, as soon as the guardrail ends, follow a path uphill that leads to an open area used by campers. The boulder is 20 feet into the woods from the south side of the open area.

BOULDERS BEYOND BELIEF

10. WHALE ROCK

Type of Formation: Large Boulder
WOW Factor: 4
Location: Euba Mills (Essex County)
Tenth Edition, NYS Atlas & Gazetteer: p. 30, D5; **Earlier Edition NYS Atlas & Gazetteer**: p. 96, CD4
Parking GPS Coordinates: 44°06.844'N 73°42.581'W
Whale Rock GPS Coordinates: 44º06.663'N 73º43.103'W
Accessibility: 0.7-mile hike
Degree of Difficulty: Moderate

Description: Whale Rock (a name given to it by Christy Butler) is a large, 12-foot-high, 40-foot-long boulder located next to Twin Pond Brook (the outlet stream from Twin Pond), just upstream from the creek's confluence with the North Fork of the Boquet River. Interestingly, Twin Pond Brook follows along the full length of the boulder, its channel kept straight and true by the shape of the rock.

Close to Whale Rock is an 8-foot-high boulder that is fairly undistinguished.

History: Twin Pond Brook got its name from Twin Pond, which is the fraternal twin—not identical twin—of Round Pond.

The boulder is frequently passed by hikers making their way to the upper falls on the Boquet River and, beyond that, the Dix Mountain range.

Directions: From Euba Mills (junction of Routes 73 & 9), head northwest on Route 73 for ~1.4 miles. As soon as you drive over the bridge spanning the North Fork of the Boquet River, park to your right.

Walk over to the north side of the bridge and follow a path that leads upriver along the north bank for several hundred feet. Then turn right onto a path that heads steeply uphill, a vigorous climb that will require a moment or two of effort to accomplish. Once you are at the top, continue southwest following the trail along the north rim of the gorge for around 0.6 mile. Along this distance, the path will take you up and down in places, but never to the level of the river.

After 0.6 mile, the trail finally descends to a lower, near-river level where you come to a "T" junction. Turn right (northwest), following a well-worn, earlier established trail. In 0.1 mile, you will come to Twin Pond Brook where a large boulder can be seen on your right, literally at the junction of the stream and trail.

Whale Rock. Photograph by Christy Butler. Look for the tiny figure near the right end of the rock.

Additional Site –

By continuing southwest from Whale Rock, following the trail for another 0.05 mile, you will come to Shoebox Falls, which can be accessed by a steep path leading downhill, left, for 75 feet. The trail proceeds to the top of the waterfall from where you can see countless 6–8-foot-high boulders next to and downstream from the waterfall. Shoebox Falls itself is a monstrosity of exposed bedrock, named for a rectangular-shaped swimming hole at its base.

BOULDERS BEYOND BELIEF

11. ROCK OF GIBRALTAR

Type of Formation: Large Boulder
WOW Factor: 5
Location: Euba Mills (Essex County)
Tenth Edition, NYS Atlas & Gazetteer: p. 30, D5; **Earlier Edition NYS Atlas & Gazetteer**: p. 96, CD4
Parking GPS Coordinates: 44°06.844'N 73°42.581'W
Estimated Rock of Gibraltar GPS Coordinates: 44º05.257'N 73º44.754'W
Accessibility: 3.1-mile hike
Degree of Difficulty: Moderately difficult

Description: The Rock of Gibraltar (if, indeed, the formation listed on topo maps is the boulder described here and not just a huge rock outcrop) is a 12–15-foot-high, triangular shaped boulder that receives occasional visits from hikers heading up towards Dix Mountain (4,857') and Grace Peak (4,026').

Adam Maurer at the Rock of Gibralta.
Photograph by Melissa Fox.

History: The name is taken from the famous Rock of Gibraltar at the southernmost point of the Iberian Peninsula. Perhaps the right-angle shape of the rock, similar to that of the Rock of Gibraltar, suggested its name.

Directions: Follow directions given to Whale Rock in the previous chapter.

Cross over Twin Pond Brook and continue heading southwest. At 1.2 miles from Route 73, the trail takes you down to the North Fork of the Boquet and crosses over the stream. At 1.4 miles, the trail then crosses over a tributary to the North Branch.

BOULDERS BEYOND BELIEF

In another 0.9 mile (or 2.3 miles from the start), the South Fork of the Boquet is reached. From here, the path follows the east bank of the river, frequently high above the South Fork. The Rock of Gibraltar is reached, to your left, at 3.1 miles, 0.2 mile before arriving at a tributary that flows down from Dix Mountain.

Resources: 46peaks.wordpress.com/2014/01/14/east-dix-south-dix-macomb – This site contains a photograph of the rock taken by Melissa Fox.
Tony Goodwin (editor), *Adirondack Trails: High Peaks Region. 13th Edition* (Lake George, NY: Adirondack Mountain Club, Inc., 2004), 204.

12. GIANT OF THE VALLEY ROCKS

Type of Formation: Large Boulder; Rock-Shelter
WOW Factor: 9
Location: St. Huberts (Essex County)
Tenth Edition, NYS Atlas & Gazetteer: p. 30, D5; **Earlier Edition NYS Atlas & Gazetteer**: p. 96, CD4
Parking GPS Coordinates: 44º08.220'N 73º44.548'W
Giant of the Valley Rocks GPS Coordinates: 44°08.133'N 73º44.587'W
Accessibility: 200-foot trek
Degree of Difficulty: Easy

Description: A number of enormous rocks have come together at the base of Round Mountain, just southeast of Chapel Pond. One rock in particular (the largest in the group) rises to a height of over 30 feet and lies on top of another boulder, forming an enormous rock-shelter. Boulderers call the rock slab Goliath Rock.
   The first rock encountered on the way in is called, not surprisingly, Gateway Boulder.

History: Chapel Pond, which lies nearby, is arguably the most picturesque, roadside pond or lake in all of the Adirondacks. It is framed to the southwest by towering cliffs that rise up steeply from the water's edge, forming the east shoulder of Round Mountain, and, to the northeast, by the awesome verticality of Giant Mountain. The pond remains a magical oasis of water in an otherwise rolling landscape of riotous mountains and precipitous valleys.

BOULDERS BEYOND BELIEF

Goliath Rock. Photograph by Christy Butler.

BOULDERS BEYOND BELIEF

While there are other groupings of large boulders in the Adirondacks, none are so close to roadside and so near a pond as gorgeous as Chapel Pond.

Heidi Mosley jumps for joy in front of Goliath Rock. Photograph by John Haywood.

Direction: From Euba Mills (junction of Routes 73 & 9), head northwest on Route 73 for 3.9 miles until you cross over Beede Brook and immediately come to the first pull-off on your right for Giant Mountain.

From the parking area, cross over the road, and then follow the guardrail south for a hundred feet. At the end of the guardrail, turn right and follow a well-defined path to the boulders. During early spring and late fall, the rocks are clearly visible from roadside.

Although no official trails lead through this boulder field, there are informal paths, making it easy enough to navigate your way around and over the enormous litter of rocks.

Additional site --

Talus field near Round Pond Parking Area – Driving northwest along Route 73 from Euba Mills (junction of Routes 73 & 9), you will pass by a sloping field of large rocks to your right [44°07.831'N 73°43.731'W] approximately 0.1 mile before reaching the Round Pond Parking Area [44°07.923'N 73°40.923'W]. This towering, >0.2-mile-long field of boulders along a fairly steep slope can be explored at your leisure. Just be mindful of fast-moving traffic when walking along Route 73.

The boulders along this section of the road have been written up extensively in Justin Sanford's *New York Adirondack Park Bouldering*. Some of the rocks have been given colorful names, such as Mousetrap, Battleship, Cribbage, and Twister. The first big rock encountered walking southeast from the Round Pond parking area is called Balderdash.

Resources: Justin Sanford, *New York Adirondack Park Bouldering* (Broadalbin, NY: Southern Adirondack Climber, LLC, 2015). Refer to pages 216–225 for the Chapel Pond boulders, and pages 202–215 for Zones A-D of the Round Pond Boulders.
Den Linnehan, *Adirondack Splendor* (NY: Linnehan Press, 2004). Several photographs of the boulders can be seen on page 98.
mountainproject.com/area/111334237/chapel-pond-bouldering.
mountainenthusiast.com/2011/10/chapel-pond.html.

13. GIANT MOUNTAIN BOULDERS

Type of Formation: Large Boulder
WOW Factor: 6–7
Location: St. Huberts (Essex County)
Tenth Edition, NYS Atlas & Gazetteer: p. 30, D5; **Earlier Edition NYS Atlas & Gazetteer**: p. 96, CD4
Parking GPS Coordinates: 44°08.309'N 73°44.621'W
Upper Boulder GPS Coordinates: 44°09.305'N 73°43.527'W
Accessibility: *Ledge Boulder* – 1.2-mile hike; *Upper Boulder* -- ~2.5-mile hike
Degree of Difficulty: Difficult

Description: *Ledge Boulder* -- Tony Goodwin, in *Adirondack Trails: High Peaks Region. 13th Edition*, mentions "…a large boulder on the ledge…" that is encountered 1.2 miles into the hike.

Upper Boulder -- This 15–20-foot-high, near-trailside boulder is appropriately positioned on a mountain where everything is oversized and larger-than-life. The rock's broad back, tipped at a 45 degree angle, makes for an inviting slide (but only if you're willing to risk injury).

BOULDERS BEYOND BELIEF

History: Giant Mountain (4,627'), aka Giant of the Valley during the late nineteenth century, is very accessible due to its proximity to Route 73, but also very difficult to ascend due to its relentless uphill climb. The mountain is the namesake of the 23,100-acre Giant Mountain Wilderness. Giant Mountain is listed as the twelfth highest of the Adirondack High Peaks.

Directions: From Euba Mills (junction of Routes 73 & 9), drive northwest on Route 73 for 4.1 miles and park on either side of the road. The Zander Scott Trail to the summit of Giant Mountain begins from the northeast side of Route 73.

Follow the Zander Scott Trail as it takes you constantly uphill. You will pass by the Giants Nubble Trail, on your left, at 1.0 mile, and then come to the *Ledge Boulder* at 1.2 miles. The Roaring Brook Trail enters on your left at 2.2 miles. From here, it is only 0.2 –0.3 mile further until you come to the *Upper Boulder* on your left, only 20 feet from the trail, but somewhat difficult to see during the summer.

Aidan Canavan & Luciano Fiore stop along their hike up Giant Mountain. Photograph by Andrew Canavan.

Thanks go to Andrew Canavan & Aidan Canavan (Siena College track stars) for bringing the Upper Boulder to my attention.

It is another 0.5 mile, if you wish, to continue up to the summit.

Resources: Barbara McMartin, *Fifty Hikes in the Adirondacks* (Woodstock, VT: Backcountry Publications, 1988), 232–236.
Tim Starmer, *Five-Star Trails in the Adirondacks: A Guide to the Most Beautiful Hikes* (Birmingham, AL: Menasha Ridge Press, 2010), 252–256.
James R. Burnside, *Exploring the 46 Adirondack High Peaks* (Schenectady, NY: High Peaks Press, 1996), 44–57.

BOULDERS BEYOND BELIEF

Adirondack Mountain Club, *Adirondack 46ers: Of the Summits, of the Forests* (Morrisonville, NY: Adirondack 46ers, 1991), 49–51.
Tony Goodwin (editor) & Neal Burdick (series editor), *Adirondack Trails: High Peaks Region. 13th Edition* (Lake George, NY: Adirondack Mountain Club, Inc., 2004), 98.
lakeplacid.com/do/hiking/giant-mountain.
Lisa Densmore Ballard, *Hiking the Adirondacks. Second Edition* (Guilford, CT: Falcon Guides, 2017), 103. The author refers to "a large boulder on your left" at >2.4 miles.

14. BOULDERS ACROSS ROAD FROM CHAPEL POND PARKING AREA

Type of Formation: Large Boulder
WOW Factor: 4
Location: Chapel Pond (Essex County)
Tenth Edition, NYS Atlas & Gazetteer: p. 30, D4–5; **Earlier Edition NYS Atlas & Gazetteer**: p. 96, CD4
Parking GPS Coordinates: 44°08.432'N 73°44.796'W
Boulder GPS Coordinates: 44º08.446'N 73º44.790'W
Accessibility: 50–100-foot-trek from guardrail
Degree of Difficulty: Easy

Guardrail Boulder along Route 73.

Description: *Roadside Boulders* – There are two large rocks across from the Chapel Pond parking area. The boulder to your right, slightly in the woods, is 8 feet high and 12 feet wide. The boulder to your left, directly behind the guardrail, is 15 feet tall. Its smooth rock face contains vertical grove lines, indicative that part of the boulder was blasted away to make room for Route 73.

Trailside Boulders – A number of large blocks of talus and boulders have formed on the downslope across Route 73 from Chapel Pond. The main

BOULDERS BEYOND BELIEF

boulder is 15 feet high and 20 feet long, and is the easiest one to reach. Nearby, are clusters of rocks covered with moss and growth, considerably harder to reach. Two talus caves can be seen.

One of several large boulders opposite Chapel Pond.

Directions: From Euba Mills (junction of Routes 73 & 9), drive northwest on Route 73 for 4.1 miles and turn left into the parking area for Chapel Pond.

Roadside Boulders -- Two roadside boulders can be seen directly across Route 73 from the parking area.

Trailside Boulders -- To access the trailside boulders, walk across Route 73 and then follow a path into the woods between the two roadside boulders that leads diagonally downhill. Within 50 feet, you will pass by a boulder to your right that is best seen from below. Continue down the path for another 20 feet and then bushwhack over to the base of the rock. A number of other big rocks will be visible in this area, mostly clumped together, interspersed with much brush and growth, and not all that inviting.

BOULDERS BEYOND BELIEF

Additional site to explore –

From the parking area at Chapel Pond, drive northwest on Route 73 for 0.2 mile and turn right into a narrow pull-off next to the road [44º08.575′N 73º45.035′W]. A kiosk is visible nearby in the woods.

Step over the guardrail, walk past the kiosk, and follow a short path northeast for less than hundred feet to a large clearing from where excellent views of a huge talus field on the southwest slope of Giant Mountain can be obtained. At one time this clearing served as a parking area until it was closed off years ago.

Talus field near the base of Giant Mountain.

15. ROARING BROOK BOULDER

Type of Formation: Large Boulder
WOW Factor: 4–5
Location: St. Huberts (Essex County)
Tenth Edition, NYS Atlas & Gazetteer: p. 30, D4; **Earlier Edition NYS Atlas & Gazetteer**: p. 96, C3–4
Parking GPS Coordinates: 44º09.030′N 73º46.051′W
Estimated Roaring Brook Boulder GPS Coordinates: 44º09.074′N 73º45.632′W
Accessibility: 0.5-mile hike with steady uphill climb
Degree of Difficulty: Moderate

BOULDERS BEYOND BELIEF

Description: Roaring Brook Boulder is a giant, standalone rock some 20 feet high and 30 feet long. Hikers unfailingly pass by it on their uphill climb along the Roaring Brook Falls/Giant Mountain trail, but few probably take notice of it in their excitement to reach the top of 325-foot-high Roaring Brook Falls and its fantastic panoramic views of the Great Range. The waterfall is one of the most popular Adirondack ice-climbing routes in the deep freeze of winter.

An often overlooked boulder along the Roaring Brook Falls Trail.

In *Discover the Northeastern Adirondacks*, Dennis Conroy & etc. mention that "There is a very large rock on the left, one of many signs you will see of glacial action," but no description of the boulder is provided. Hopefully, the rock will receive the consideration it has long deserved now that attention has been drawn to it.

Directions: From Euba Mills (junction of Routes 73 & 9), drive northwest on Route 73 for 5.5 miles. Turn right into the parking area for Roaring Brook Falls. Follow the main trail northeast for less than 0.1 mile. When the path divides, go left, heading steadily uphill for another 0.3–0.4 mile. Look for the boulder to your left, 50 feet from the trail. If you continue uphill from the boulder, the trail quickly leads to a spur path that will take you to the top of Roaring Brook Falls.

Resources: Dennis Conroy, James C. Dawson, & Barbara McMartin, *Discover the Northeastern Adirondacks* (Woodstock, VT: Backcountry Publications, 1987), 88.
mountainproject.com/route/106263580/roaring-brook-falls.
Tony Goodwin (editor) & Neal Burdick (series editor), *Adirondack Trails: High Peaks Region. 13th Edition* (Lake George, NY: Adirondack Mountain Club, Inc., 2004), 95.

16. EAST TRAIL BOULDERS

Type of Formation: Large Boulder
WOW Factor: *Cottage Boulder* – 3; *Footbridge Boulder* – 3; *Colossus Rock* -- 6
Location: St. Huberts (Essex County)
Tenth Edition, NYS Atlas & Gazetteer: p. 30, D4; **Earlier Edition NYS Atlas & Gazetteer**: p. 96, C3–4
Parking GPS Coordinates: 44°08.962'N 73°44.951'W
East Trail Boulders GPS Coordinates: *Cottage Boulder* -- 44°08.992'N 73º46.888'W; *Footbridge Boulder* -- 44º09.041'N 73º45.57.3'W; *Colossus Rock* -- 44º07.931'N 73º48.739'W
Accessibility: 0.8-mile hike from parking area to gatehouse and trailhead. Starting from gatehouse:
    Cottage Boulder – Next to gatehouse (0.8 mile in total)
    Footbridge Boulder -- <0.1 mile down connecting path to East River Trail (0.9 mile in total)
    Colossus Rock – ~2.0 mile-hike (2.8 miles in total)
Degree of Difficulty: *Cottage Boulder* & *Footbridge Boulder* – *Moderately easy*; *Colossus Rock* – Moderately difficult

Description: *Cottage Boulder* is a substantial-sized boulder, 10–12 feet high, occupying a strategic position at the start of the Lake Road. Unfortunately, it typically goes unnoticed as hikers, hurrying along, are driven by visions of what lies ahead—not by what lies close at hand.

Footbridge Boulder is a 15–20-foot high, rectangular shaped boulder, standing upright on its end on a sloping embankment above the start of the East River Trail, a short distance downriver from a footbridge crossing.

BOULDERS BEYOND BELIEF

Colossus Rock is a 15–20-foot-high, 40-foot-long boulder that is either one large boulder that has split into two, side-by-side pieces, or two large boulders that have been pushed together by the action of the stream (most likely the latter). The rocks lay along the bank of the East Branch of the Ausable River, partially in and partially out of the water.

Cottage Boulder stands directly across from the gatehouse.

History: *Cottage Boulder* is an integral part of the Ausable Club's history. Many years ago, Scott Brown, an attorney and postmaster from Elizabethtown, built a camp by the boulder and called his dwelling Boulder Cottage. When a fire started in the Boquet River area and swept over Noonmark Mountain, the Brown family reputedly immersed some of their possessions in Laundry Brook—the tiny creek that runs adjacent to the boulder—to protect their heirlooms from the fire. Fortunately, the fire was averted before it reached the Ausable Club area, and the camp was spared—but only temporarily. It subsequently burned down at a later date, leaving little behind other than the boulder.

Eventually, a second camp was erected, also named Boulder Cottage, which is the camp that you see near the boulder today.

BOULDERS BEYOND BELIEF

Directions: From Euba Mills (junction of Routes 73 & 9), drive northwest on Route 73 for ~5.5 miles and turn left onto Ausable Road. Park immediately in a large area to your left. Take note that parking is not allowed anywhere along the Ausable Club Road.

Colossus Rock as seen from the West River Trail.

From the parking area, walk west, proceeding uphill for 0.6 mile along a partially dirt road to reach the Ausable Club. When you arrive at the tennis courts, turn left, and follow the road southwest for 0.2 mile until you come to the gatehouse. Straight ahead is the 3.5-mile-long Lake Road, listed in the ADK guidebook as the Lake Road Trail.

Sign in at the trail register located at the gatehouse.

The *Cottage Boulder* is located right next to the gatehouse. In fact, the trail leading down to the East Branch of the Ausable River runs directly past the boulder, only 50 feet away.

BOULDERS BEYOND BELIEF

Footbridge Boulder – From the gatehouse, follow the connecting path downhill that leads to the start of the East River Trail. The path parallels Laundry Brook, to your right, where medium-sized boulders can be seen in the streambed just up from Laundry Brook's confluence with the East Branch of the Ausable River.

The Footbridge Boulder is virtually at the junction of Laundry Brook and the East Branch of the Ausable River, several hundred feet downriver from the where the footbridge crosses the East Branch.

Colossus Rock – There are two ways of accessing this large boulder. *Option #1*: From the gatehouse, follow the East River Trail southwest for ~2.0 miles. Look for the boulder on your right, just downhill from the trail.

Option #2: Follow the Lake Road (a private road/foot travel only), for ~1.7 miles. Turn right onto a connecting trail that leads west in 0.4 mile to the East River Trail. Then turn right, and follow the East River Trail northeast for ~0.3 mile. The boulder will be to your left next to the river.

A 20-footer near the footbridge.

Colossus Rock is also visible from the West River Trail at 44°07.920'N 73°48.763'W.

Additional Attraction –

If you decide to take the East River Trail to its south end at the Lower Ausable Lake Dam, cross over a footbridge to the west side of the East Branch, and then continue west for 0.2 mile to reach Rainbow Falls—a spectacular 150-foot-high waterfall contained in a box canyon. On the way in to the falls, you will pass by and through a number of medium-sized boulders, as well as larger ones in the interior of the canyon.

Resources: Edith Pitcher, *Up the Lake Road* (Keene, NY: Centennial Committee for the Trustees of the Adirondack Mountain Reserve, 1987), 33–34. A photo of the cottage next to the boulder can be seen on page 34.

BOULDERS BEYOND BELIEF

17. GILL BROOK ROCK-SHELTER

Type of Formation: Rock-Shelter
WOW Factor: 4–5
Location: St. Huberts (Essex County)
Tenth Edition, NYS Atlas & Gazetteer: p. 30, D4; **Earlier Edition NYS Atlas & Gazetteer**: p. 96, C3–4
Parking GPS Coordinates: 44°08.962'N 73°44.951'W
Estimated Rock-Shelter GPS Coordinates: 44º07.514'N 73º48.530'W
Accessibility: 1.2-mile hike up Gill Brook Trail (or a total of nearly 4.0 miles from the parking area)
Degree of Difficulty: Difficult if you take into account the 0.8-mile walk along Ausable Club Road and the 1.8-mile walk along the Lake Road just to reach the Gill Brook trailhead

Gill Brook Rock-Shelter along the Gill Brook Trail.

Description: The *Gill Brook Rock-Shelter* consists of a 12-foot-high boulder with a 6-foot overhang. It provides a convenient shelter for hikers.

Along the way on the Gill Brook Trail, you will also encounter a grouping of 15-foot-high boulders near one of the scenic spur-trails.

BOULDERS BEYOND BELIEF

To be sure, the main reason for doing the Gill Brook Trail is to see its many waterfalls, a fact that I am perfectly aware of, having written up Gill Brook in my recent *Keene Valley Region Waterfall Guide*. This is one of those instances when the boulders are truly secondary.

History: Gill Brook was heavily visited during the nineteenth century by artists who painted scenes of mountains, rivers, and waterfalls. There is no evidence, however, that they painted any of the boulders along Gill Brook.

Directions: Follow the directions given in the chapter on the "East Trail Boulders" to reach the gatehouse at the start of the Lake Road/Trail.

From the gatehouse, head south on the Lake Road/Trail for 1.8 miles. When you come to the red-blazed Gill Brook trail, turn left and follow the trail southwest for ~1.2 miles, paralleling Gill Brook. The rock-shelter is on your left as soon as you pass by the Indian Head Trail junction and cross over a tributary to Gill Brook.

18. BALANCING ROCK: GOTHICS

Type of Formation: Balanced Rock
WOW Factor: 8
Location: Saint Huberts (Essex County)
Tenth Edition, NYS Atlas & Gazetteer: p. 30, D3; **Earlier Edition NYS Atlas & Gazetteer**: p. 96, CD3
Parking GPS Coordinates: 44°08.962'N 73°44.951'W
Destination GPS Coordinates: Not taken
Accessibility: 4.2 miles from the Lake Road Gatehouse (5.0 miles from parking area)
Degree of Difficulty: Difficult

Description: Lisa Densmore Ballard in *Hiking the Adirondacks*, describes a "...large glacial erratic (boulder) balanced on another rock on your right. The two boulders form a slanting shallow cave, about 10 feet tall at its mouth."

Directions: Follow the directions given in the chapter on the "East Trail Boulders" to reach the gatehouse at the start of the Lake Road/Trail. Sign in at the trail register located at the gatehouse.

BOULDERS BEYOND BELIEF

Follow the connecting trail next to the gatehouse that leads gradually downhill west to the East Branch of the Ausable River in 0.2 mile. Walk over the footbridge and turn left to begin hiking on the West River Trail, which parallels the East Branch as you head upriver. In 2.5 miles, you will come to Beaver Meadow Falls.

Just past Beaver Meadow Falls, turn right onto the blue-marked Gothics-Armstrong Trail, which starts with a ladder climb and continues uphill steeply. At ~1.7 miles from the start of this trail you will encounter the balancing rock to your right.

Resources: Lisa Densmore Ballard, *Hiking the Adirondacks. Second Edition* (Guilford, CT: Falcon Guides, 2017), 110. A spectacular photograph of the balanced rock is included, with a hiker sitting under a huge space created where the rock has been levered upward by natural forces.
Tony Goodwin (editor), *Adirondack Trails: High Peaks Region. 13th Edition* (Lake George, NY: Adirondack Mountain Club, Inc., 2004), 79. A large balanced rock on your right is indicated.

19. DEER BROOK SHELTER CAVE

Type of Formation: Shelter Cave
WOW Factor: 3
Location: St. Huberts (Essex County)
Tenth Edition, NYS Atlas & Gazetteer: p. 30, CD4; **Earlier Edition NYS Atlas & Gazetteer**: p. 96, C3–4
Parking GPS Coordinates: 44°09.891′N 73°46.764′W
Estimated Deer Brook Shelter Cave GPS Coordinates: 44º09.855′N 73º47.333′W
Accessibility: 0.7-mile trek
Degree of Difficulty: Moderately difficult

Description: The Deer Brook Shelter Cave is quite unusual for an Adirondack cave. Unlike most of the rock-shelters and talus caves that you will encounter in the High Peaks, this one was created when a huge section of rock and earth slid out from underneath the more rocky, solid upper part of the sidewall. The opening is 3–4 feet high and leads into a chamber roughly 25 feet long and 15 feet high. The floor of the cave rises at an appreciable angle so that when you reach the back of the cave, you are touching the ceiling.

BOULDERS BEYOND BELIEF

According to experts I have spoken with, the cave developed along a fault zone.

Along the way through Deer Brook Gorge, you will encounter some pretty large boulders (especially near the end of the gorge) as well as a succession of attractive cascades.

Deer Brook Falls, an 80-foot-high cascade, is farther upstream, beyond the gorge.

Deer Brook Cave is near the head of Deer Brook Gorge.

Directions: From Euba Mills (junction of Routes 73 & 9), drive northwest on Route 73 for ~6.6 miles. Park to your right after crossing over the bridge spanning the Ausable River's East Branch.

From Holt's Corner (junction of Routes 73 & 9N South), drive south on Route 73 for ~4.8 miles. Park to your left just before crossing over the bridge spanning the East Branch.

The trailhead is on the west side of Route 73, ~0.05-mile north of the bridge.

The hike to Deer Brook Cave takes you through Deer Brook Gorge following a trail (or what remains of one due to the repeated assaults of tropical storms) indicated by green ATIS markers that crosses the stream at least four times and takes you past one cascade after another.

In less than 0.7 mile, you will encounter the Deer Brook Shelter Cave to your right just before the last stream crossing after which the trail steeply exits from the gorge.

Resources: Russell Dunn, "Deer Brook Cave," *Northeastern Caver* (Vol. XLI, no. 2 (June 2001), 52.

BOULDERS BEYOND BELIEF

Barbara McMartin, *Discover the Adirondack High Peaks* (Canada Lake, NY: Lake View Press, 1989), 206.

Rose Rivezzi & David Trithart, *Kids on the Trails! Hiking with children in the Adirondacks* (Lake George, NY: Adirondack Mountain Club, 1997), 108. "The flume…is often quite steep and narrow as it winds through large boulders…There's a huge cave to the right."

20. ROOSTER COMB ROCK

Type of Formation: Large Boulder
WOW Factor: 6–7
Location: Keene Valley (Essex County)
Tenth Edition, NYS Atlas & Gazetteer: p. 30, C4; **Earlier Edition NYS Atlas & Gazetteer**: p. 96, C3
Parking GPS Coordinates: 44º11.123' 73º47.195'W
Estimated Rooster Comb Rock GPS Coordinates: 44º10.349'N 73º48.530'W
Accessibility: 2.0-mile hike
Degree of Difficulty: Moderately difficult; 1,750-foot ascent

View of Giant Mountain from summit of Rooster Comb.

Description: This large rock is described by Phil Brown & Tom Woodman in *12 Short Hikes Near Keene Valley* as "…a garage-sized boulder." Lisa Densmore Ballard, in *Best Easy Day Hikes. Adirondacks. Second Edition*, also mentions it when she writes, "The path goes around an enormous glacial erratic" as does

BOULDERS BEYOND BELIEF

Tony Goodwin in *Adirondack Trails: High Peaks Region. 13th Edition* when he states that the "…Rooster Comb Trail passes under a mammoth boulder…"

History: Rooster Comb's name arose when an early hiker or settler saw a series of sub-High Peaks along the ridge line and thought that they resembled the comb of a roster.

Rooster Comb Mountain rises to an elevation of 2,788 feet.

Directions: From Euba Mills (junction of Routes 73 & 9), drive northwest of Route 73 for ~8.2 miles. Just before entering the hamlet of Keene Valley, turn left into a large parking area for Rooster Comb Mountain. Follow the trail across a boardwalk through a marshy area, around a pond, and then begin heading uphill. In 0.7 mile, you will come to a junction. Bear right, following the Sachs Trail as it heads south initially, and then southwest, paralleling Flume Brook (to your left).

At over 2.0 miles, you will come to a junction with the Hedgehog Mountain Trail, where a giant boulder comes into view.

Resources: Phil Brown & Tom Woodman, *12 Short Hikes Near Keene Valley* (Saranac Lake, NY: Adirondack Explorer, 2015), 27. The authors write about a "garage size boulder."
Phil Brown, "The good Old Route, *Adirondack Explorer* (September/October, 2015), 18 A photograph on top of Rooster Comb shows a few small boulders.
Lisa Densmore Ballard, *Best Easy Day Hikes. Adirondacks. Second Edition* (Guilford, CT: Falcon Guides, 2017), 45.
Tony Goodwin (editor) & Neal Burdick (series editor), *Adirondack Trails: High Peaks Region. 13th Edition* (Lake George, NY: Adirondack Mountain Club, Inc., 2004), 60.
Lisa Densmore Ballard, *Hiking the Adirondacks. Second Edition* (Guilford, CT: Falcon Guides, 2017), 215. The rock is described as an "enormous glacial erratic."

21. SPLIT ROCK: KEENE VALLEY

Type of Formation: Split Rock
WOW Factor: 4
Location: Keene Valley (Essex County)
Tenth Edition, NYS Atlas & Gazetteer: p. 30, C4; **Earlier Edition NYS Atlas & Gazetteer**: p. 96, C3

BOULDERS BEYOND BELIEF

Split Rock GPS Coordinates: 44º11.373′N 73º47.912′W
Accessibility: Roadside

Description: This large boulder has been seen through thousands of windshields as hikers drive up to The Garden—a main point of access into the interior of the High Peaks Region.

The boulder is 12–15 feet high and 25 feet long with a wide fracture near its middle. Over time, a tree has taken root and sprouted up between the two halves, forcing them even farther apart, much like a wedge. A rocky overhang on the south side of the boulder has produced a tiny shelter cave.

Split Rock, further wedged apart by an expanding tree.

History: In 1871, Eli Montgomery Crawford erected a saw mill near the boulder, not far downstream from where the current bridge crosses Johns Brook.

Directions: From Euba Mills (junction of Routes 73 & 9), drive northwest on Route 73 for 8.6 miles until you reach the center of Keene Valley. Turn left onto Adirondack Street (which becomes Johns Brook Lane) and drive south for 0.6 mile.

BOULDERS BEYOND BELIEF

Look for the split rock on the right side of the road, just before Johns Brook Lane crosses over Johns Brook.

Take note that although the land is posted, the rock can be fully viewed from roadside.

Resources: theadirondacker.com/2018/02/11/amazing-boulders-of-the-adirondacks.

22. FIRST BROTHER ROCK-SHELTER

Type of Formation: Rock-Shelter
WOW Factor: 4–5
Location: Keene Valley (Essex County)
Tenth Edition, NYS Atlas & Gazetteer: p. 30, C4; **Earlier Edition NYS Atlas & Gazetteer**: p. 96, C3
Parking GPS Coordinates: 44°11.376′N 73°48.975′W
Estimated Rock-Shelter GPS Coordinates: 44°11.380′N 73°50.007′W
Fee: Modest fee charged to park
Accessibility: 1.5-mile hike; 1,437 foot ascent.
Degree of Difficulty: Moderately difficult

Description: In *12 Short Hikes Near Keene Valley*, Phil Brown & Tom Woodman write, "Just before reaching the summit, you pass a natural shelter—a humungous boulder with a roof that sticks out like an awning."

The ADK publication, *Adirondack Trails: High Peaks Region*, also describes it as a "natural rock-shelter."

In *Exploring the Adirondack 46 High Peaks*, James R. Burnside writes, "Just beyond and below the summit, a house-sized lump of rock leans close to an exposed cliff to form a snug shelter. There is obviously much to see on top of the First Brother."

History: The First Brother is one of three mountain peaks called, collectively, The Brothers. The Second Brother (3,120′) is reached at 1.8 miles; the Third Brother (3,681′) at 2.6 miles.

The Garden was built in 1970 and acquired its name from a private landowner's vegetable garden that the parking lot replaced.

BOULDERS BEYOND BELIEF

Directions: From Euba Mills (junction of Routes 73 & 9), continue northwest on Route 73 for 8.6 miles until you reach the center of Keene Valley. Turn left onto Adirondack Street (which becomes Johns Brook Lane) and drive south. The Garden—a respectable-sized parking area—is reached at the end of the road after a drive of 1.6 miles. Take note that the Garden fills up quickly with cars during busy weekends. In the event that you arrive and there is no parking room left, you will have to return to the village and either come back on foot (adding on another 1.6 miles each way to your hike) or catch a shuttle if one is operating on the day of your visit. No parking is allowed along the road leading up to The Garden.

From the kiosk at the west end of the parking area, follow the Big Slide Trail northwest for 0.2 mile. At a junction, bear left and continue following the Big Slide Trail west for another 1.3 miles to reach the summit of the First Brother.

Resources: Phil Brown & Tom Woodman, *12 Short Hikes Near Keene Valley* (Saranac Lake, NY: Adirondack Explorer, 2015), 32.
Tony Goodwin (editor) & Neal Burdick (series editor), *Adirondack Trails: High Peaks Region. 13th Edition* (Lake George, NY: Adirondack Mountain Club, Inc., 2004), 56.
James R. Burnside, *Exploring the Adirondack 46 High Peaks* (Schenectady, NY: High Peaks Press, 1996), 92.

23. PHELPS TRAIL BOULDERS

Type of Formation: Large Boulder
WOW Factor: 4–5
Location: Keene Valley (Essex County)
Tenth Edition, NYS Atlas & Gazetteer: p. 30, C4; **Earlier Edition NYS Atlas & Gazetteer**: p. 96, C3
Parking GPS Coordinates: 44°11.376′N 73°48.975′W
Grandfather Rock GPS Coordinates: 44°10.362′N 73°50.447′W
Fee: Modest parking fee charged
Accessibility: Up to 1.6 miles of hiking
Degree of Difficulty: Moderate

Description: A number of large boulders can be seen along the Phelps Trail between The Garden and the Interior Outpost Ranger Station. The boulders

BOULDERS BEYOND BELIEF

came to their present position either through the action of glaciers, or as rockfall from The Brothers (a series of sub-High Peaks). Boulderers refer to this smorgasbord of rocks as the Valleyland Boulders.

History: The Phelps Trail, aka Northside Trail and Johns Brook Trail, was established by Ed Phelps, son of Orson Scofield (Old Mountain) Phelps.

One of several large boulders along the Phelps Trail.

Directions: See "First Brother Rock-Shelter" chapter for directions to The Garden.

From The Garden, walk southwest. In 0.3–0.4 mile, you will pass between two medium-sized rocks, the one on the left being about 8 feet high [44°11.154′N 73°49.203′W]. I am calling them the Sentinel Rocks because of the way they seemingly keep guard over the trail.

At 0.5 mile, the junction with the now abandoned Southside Trail, to your left, is passed. From this point on, you will repeatedly encounter large rocks, some of respectable size.

BOULDERS BEYOND BELIEF

At around 0.9 mile, you will see, to your right, a large, 15-foot-high square-shaped boulder next to a tiny brook. Two other decent-sized boulders are just slightly upstream from the first one.

At 1.3 mile, you will cross over Deer Brook via two railed footbridges.

In less than 0.1 mile from Deer Brook, a litter of boulders is reached. In *Adirondack Trails: High Peaks Region. 13th Edition*, Tony Goodwin writes, "…the trail passes three large boulders on the R and comes to a small stream at 1.5 mi." The largest boulder is only 50 feet from the trail, and stands 20 feet high. Just beyond is a 15-foot-high trailside boulder with a pronounced overhang that creates a rock-shelter.

The next large boulder, to your left, is what I have named Grandfather Rock, because it is the largest boulder along the Phelps Trail (undoubtedly, it is known by another name by boulderers). The boulder is 25 feet high and, by far, the most massive of the trailside boulders. Multiple fissures have formed in it, and at some point the cracks will assuredly cause the rock to break apart into smaller pieces.

Resources: mountainproject.com/v/valleyland/110508114.
Tony Goodwin (editor) & Neal Burdick (series editor), *Adirondack Trails: High Peaks Region. 13th Edition* (Lake George, NY: Adirondack Mountain Club, Inc., 2004), 37.
mountainproject.com/area/110508114/valleyland.
mountainproject.com/area/110508271/kings-valley.
James R. Burnside, *Exploring the Adirondack 46 High Peaks* (Schenectady, NY: High Peaks Press, 1996). On page 233 is a hiker pushing against the underbelly of a huge, 20-foot-high boulder that lies along the Phelps Trail.

24. SLANT ROCK

Type of Formation: Leaning Rock
WOW Factor: 5–6
Location: Keene Valley (Essex County)
Tenth Edition, NYS Atlas & Gazetteer: p. 30, C4; **Earlier Edition NYS Atlas & Gazetteer**: p. 96, C3
Parking GPS Coordinates: 44°11.376'N 73°48.975'W
Estimated Slant Rock GPS Coordinates: 44º07.616'N; 73º53.963'W
Fee: Parking fee is charged
Accessibility: ~6.8-mile hike from The Garden

BOULDERS BEYOND BELIEF

Degree of Difficulty: Difficult due to length

Description: Slant Rock is a huge, triangular-shaped boulder that has served for many decades as a way-point for hikers along the Phelps Trail. What distinguishes the rock is not only its size—15 feet at its highest point and over 20 feet across along its base—but that it leans at a perilous angle, forming a rock-shelter. This precipitous lean has caused at least one hiker to fret while camping under it. In 1909, Billy Burger, who stayed overnight beneath the rock before summiting Mount Marcy, wrote, "And as I turned over to go to sleep [I wondered] if by any chance the rock might roll over on my mate and me while we're in slumberland."

Slant Rock with its slanted tree.

History: It is said that the rock was named by none other than Orson Scofield Phelps (Old Mountain Phelps) who used it as a stop-over when guiding sports up his trail to the summit of Mt. Marcy

In Sandra Weber's book, *Mount Marcy: The High Peak of New York*, the author states that Slant Rock served as a base camp for Dr. Walter Lowrie (a noted Alpinist) for a number of years. In order to make the rock hospitable during his stay, Lowrie covered the two sides with logs to fashion an impromptu Adirondack Lean-to.

Directions: See "First Brother Rock-Shelter" chapter for directions to The Garden.

From The Garden, follow the yellow-blazed Johns Brook Trail southwest for ~6.8 miles until you reach Slant Rock, on your left near the junction with the trail leading up to Mount Haystacks and Basin Mountain. Along the way, Johns Brook Lodge is passed at 3.5 miles—virtually the halfway point.

Resources: James R. Burnside, *Exploring the 46 Adirondack High Peaks* (Schenectady, NY: High Peaks Press, 1996), 336. A photo of the rock, unidentified, can be seen on page 233.
Sandra Weber, *Mount Marcy: The High Peak of New York* (Fleischmanns, NY: Purple Mountain Press, Ltd., 2001), 109. Photos of the boulder can be seen on pages 104 and 106, the former taken circa 1920s, and the latter in 2000 by William L. Weber, III.
"The Adirondacker Up Mount Marcy in 1909," Record-Post (Ausable Forks, NY: April 2, 1942).
Jared Gange, *100 Classic Hikes of the Northeast* (Burlington, VT: Huntington Graphics, 2005), 80. A photograph of Slant Rock and the Slant Rock lean-to is shown.
Tony Goodwin (editor), *Adirondack Trails: High Peaks Region. 13th Edition* (Lake George, NY: Adirondack Mountain Club, Inc., 2004), 38. Mention is made that "This large rock, which forms a natural shelter, was a famous early camping spot. The lean-to that formerly faced the rock was replaced in 2001."
Susanne Lance, *Heaven Up-h'isted-ness! The history of the Adirondack Forty-sixers and the High Peaks of the Adirondacks* (Cadyville, NY: The Adirondack Forty-sixers, Inc., 2011), 510 & 511. A brief history of Slant Rock is recounted, telling how it was found, and then re-found.
Mary Arakelian, *Doc: Orra A. Phelps, MD* (Utica, NY: North Country Books, 2000), 173. Dr. Phelps visited Slant Rock in June of 1937 and wrote an article about it for *High Sports*.

25. BLUEBERRY MOUNTAIN BOULDER

Type of Formation: Large Boulder
WOW Factor: 5
Location: Keene/Keene Valley (Essex County)
Tenth Edition, NYS Atlas & Gazetteer: p. 30, C4; **Earlier Edition NYS Atlas & Gazetteer**: p. 96, C3
Parking GPS Coordinates: 44º13.267'N 73º44.971'W
Blueberry Mountain Boulder GPS Coordinates: 44º13.053'N 73º49.049'W
Accessibility: 2.4-mile hike; 1,900-foot ascent
Degree of Difficulty: Moderately difficult

BOULDERS BEYOND BELIEF

Description: In *12 Short Hikes Near Keene Valley*, Phil Brown & Tom Woodman write that "The summit is crowned by a large boulder, a ten-by-fifteen-foot rectangle some eight feet high in the middle of the rock clearing." In *Discover the Adirondack High Peaks*, Barbara McMartin describes it as "…a broad, flat, rocky field with a huge boulder in the middle."

History: Blueberry Mountain (2,910') is named for the plethora of blueberries that can be seasonally picked by hikers along its slope.

Directions: From the trailhead parking at Marcy Airport (1.1 miles south of the junction of Routes 73 & 9N South), follow the red-blazed Porter Mountain Trail west for 2.4 miles, an ascent of 1,900 feet. (Note: Blueberry Mountain is along part of the route that leads up to the summit of Porter Mountain). The boulder is located near Blueberry Mountain's summit.

Resources: Phil Brown & Tom Woodman, *12 Short Hikes near Keene Valley* (Saranac Lake, NY: Adirondack Explorer, 2015), 40.
Barbara McMartin, *Discover the Adirondack High Peaks* (Canada Lake, NY: Lake View Press, 1989), 214.
Den Linnehan, *Adirondack Splendor* (NY: Linnehan Press, 2004). A photograph of the boulder is shown on page 73.
peakbagger.com/peak.aspx?pid=6029.
– This website mentions "…a unique summit, which sits atop an 8-foot erratic."
Tony Goodwin (editor), *Adirondack Trails: High Peaks Region. 13th Edition* (Lake George, NY: Adirondack Mountain Club, Inc., 2004), 59. The author identifies "…a large boulder at the summit of Blueberry Mt. at 2.4 mi…"
Phil Brown, "Porter's quiet side," *Adirondack Explorer* Vol. 4, no. 8 (July/August 2002), 37. A giant glacial erratic on Blueberry Mountain is mentioned.

26. LITTLE CROW BOULDERS

Type of Formation: Medium-sized Boulder
WOW Factor: 3–4
Location: Keene (Essex County)
Tenth Edition, NYS Atlas & Gazetteer: p. 30, B4; **Earlier Edition NYS Atlas & Gazetteer**: p. 96, BC4
Parking GPS Coordinates: 44º15.541'N 73º45.293'W
Lower Boulder GPS Coordinates: 44º15.721'N 73º45.225'W

BOULDERS BEYOND BELIEF

Upper Boulder GPS Coordinates: 44º15.762'N 73º45.240'W
Accessibility: 0.2-mile hike to boulders; 0.9-hike mile to summit
Degree of Difficulty: Moderate

Description: According to Bruce Wadsworth in *Day Hikes For All Seasons: An Adirondack Sampler*, "You pass a large boulder, a huge U-shaped rock, and an immense oak tree."

The first boulder, which lies next to the trail, is 10 feet in height. The second boulder, 50 feet off-trail, is 8 feet high and 12 feet long.

Neither boulder warrants a special trip unless you are planning to climb to the summit of Little Crow anyhow.

View from the Crows.

History: Little Crow Mountain (2,450') is the lesser of the two contiguous peaks known as The Crows. Big Crow Mountain rises up to an elevation of 2,800 feet, making it higher by 350 feet.

BOULDERS BEYOND BELIEF

Directions: From Keene (junction of Routes 73 & 9N North), drive southeast on Route 73 for 0.1 mile and turn left onto Hurricane Road (Route 13). Proceed steadily uphill, heading east, for ~2.0 miles.

The trailhead starts from the left side of Hurricane Road, but can be extremely easy to miss given the fact that there is no parking area by it, nor is the trail marked by a kiosk or large sign.

What I can tell you is that the trail starts up an embankment, and is marked by a tiny cross with a red trail marker on it. It sounds like it should be easy to spot but it isn't. You may need to drive back and forth a couple of times until you spot it (I had to). Park off to the side of the road in a narrow pull-off about 100 feet southwest of the trailhead. Be sure not to block a driveway.

Follow the red-blazed trail northeast as it wends its way between two homes. After 0.2 mile, you will come to the first boulder to your left, which the trail goes in front of it, and then veers around, heading uphill. The second (upper) boulder is less than 0.05 mile farther up the trail, 50 feet off in the woods to your left.

Resources: Bruce Wadsworth, *Day Hikes For All Seasons: An Adirondack Sampler* (Lake George, NY: Adirondack Mountain Club, 1996), 83 & 84.
offonadventure.com/2014/07/big-crow-little-crow-nun-da-ga-o-range.html.
mountainproject.com/area/113501427/little-crow-mountain.
Tony Goodwin (editor) & Neal Burdick (series editor), *Adirondack Trails: High Peaks Region. 13th Edition* (Lake George, NY: Adirondack Mountain Club, Inc., 2004), 190.

27. JACKRABBIT TRAIL BOULDERS: ALSTEAD HILL ROAD APPROACH

Type of Formation: Large Boulder
WOW Factor: 5
Location: Keene (Essex County)
Tenth Edition, NYS Atlas & Gazetteer: p. 30, B3; **Earlier Edition NYS Atlas & Gazetteer**: p. 96, BC2–3
Parking GPS Coordinates: 44°15.998'N 73°51.048'W
Destination GPS Coordinates: *Trailside Boulder* -- 44º15.704'N 73°51.799'W; *Stand-alone Boulder & Boulder Field* -- 44º15.029'N 73º51.837'W; *Meadow Boulders* -- 44º15.602'N 73º52.024'W

BOULDERS BEYOND BELIEF

Accessibility: *Trailside Boulder* – 0.7-mile walk; *Stand-alone Boulder and Boulder Field* – 0.8-mile hike; M*eadow Boulders* -- 1.0-mile hike
Degree of Difficulty: Moderately easy

Description: *Trailside Boulder* is a 10-foot-high boulder with a smaller rock directly behind it.

Stand-alone Boulder is a massive, 20-foot-high, 25-foot-long boulder that rests at the bottom of a sloping field of boulders. The rock is used extensively for bouldering.

The flat-top Stand-alone Boulder.

Meadow Boulders consists of a grouping of medium-sized boulders, the four largest being 8–10 feet high. They can be found in a huge meadow created by beavers. A field of smaller rocks has to be crossed to get to them.

In *Discover the Northern Adirondacks* Barbara McMartin, etc. write, talking about the meadow, "The pond is filled with stumps and dead trees, a number of boulders, and a beaver lodge."

History: The Old Military Road (now a trail) was constructed in the late eighteenth century for intended troop movement between Lake Champlain and Lake Ontario, as well as to assist Revolutionary War Vets in accessing tracts of land that were set up by New York State to compensate them for their military service.

The road was made somewhat famous or at least historically notable by John Brown, who traveled back and forth on it in his struggle to win the fight against slavery. It's quite possible that it was via this route that John Brown's body and his entourage made their way back to North Elba from Elizabethtown after Harper's Ferry.

By the 1950s, the road was totally unusable for automobile travel, having been made obsolete by the much handier and more forgiving Cascade Pass Road to the west of Pitchoff Mountain (later to become Route 73).

Today, the Old Military Road is part of the Jackrabbit Trail—a cross-country ski route founded in 1986. It was named in honor of Herman "Jack Rabbit" Johannsen, a Norwegian who was one of the first people to introduce the sport of cross-country skiing to North America.

Scholars believe that the famous poem called "Allen's Bear Fight Up In Keene," written in 1846 by an anonymous poet, took place, if it actually did, along the Jackrabbit Trail. One line goes "Against the rock with giant strength/He held her out at his arm's length./"Oh God!" he cried in deep despair,/If you don't help me, don't help the bear." Tony Goodwin, in *Adirondack Trails: High Peaks Region. 13th Edition*, states that "Hikers must still guess, however, as to which of the several large boulders is the one referred to by the lines in the poem."

It's also quite possible that the boulder may be one of the rocks mentioned in the next chapter.

Directions: From Keene (junction of Route 73 & 9N North), drive north on Route 73 for 0.8 mile. Turn right onto Alstead Hill Road and head west for 2.8 miles. Along the way, you will pass by the Bark Eater Inn [barkeater.com] at 0.4 mile, which was originally a stagecoach stop at an old, family farm. Park at the drivable end of Alstead Hill Road, next to Rock & River [a lodge and guide service located at 616 Alstead Hill Lane, Keene 12942. (518) 576-2041].

The trail from the parking area starts on the non-drivable part of the Old Military Road which, having formerly been a road, is both wide and well-graded as it heads uphill.

BOULDERS BEYOND BELIEF

Trailside Boulder -- At 0.8 mile, a wooden bridge takes you over Nichols Brook—a medium-sized stream that, up until now, has been to your left. Just before crossing the brook, you will see, to your right, the Trailside Boulder.

Stand-alone Boulder and upper boulder field -- After crossing Nichols Brook via a footbridge, look for a cairn on your left at 44º15.660'N 73º51.866'W. Follow a worn path from here that leads across two brooks (which can be tricky to cross in the spring) and up to a massive boulder at the bottom of an extensive field of medium-sized boulders along the side of a mountainous slope.

Meadow Boulders -- At ~0.9 mile, the Jackrabbit Trail comes out to an open field that contains a beaver pond at its center. To your right, a couple of hundred feet across the field, are a cluster of medium-sized boulders.

Resources: Jim Bailey, "The Jackrabbit Trail," *Adirondac* (January, 1988), 9–11.
rockclimbing.com/routes/North_America/United_States/New_York/Adirondack_park/Cascade_Lakes.
jackrabbittrail.org.
Tony Goodwin (editor) & Neal Burdick (series editor), *Adirondack Trails: High Peaks Region*. 13th *Edition* (Lake George, NY: Adirondack Mountain Club, Inc., 2004), 167.
Barbara McMartin, Patricia Collier, James C. Dawson, Phil Gallos & Peter O'Shea, *Discover the Northern Adirondacks* (Woodstock, VT: Backcountry Publications, 1988), 22.

28. JACKRABBIT TRAIL BOULDERS: MOUNTAIN LANE APPROACH

Type of Formation: Large Boulder
WOW Factor: 5–6
Location: North Elba (Essex County)
Tenth Edition, NYS Atlas & Gazetteer: p. 30, C3; **Earlier Edition NYS Atlas & Gazetteer**: p. 96, BC2–3
Parking GPS Coordinates: 44º14.205'N 73º53.771'W
Destination GPS Coordinates: *First Large Boulder* -- 44º14.249'N 73º53.563'W
Accessibility: *First large boulder* – 0.2-mile hike
    Second large boulders – 0.5-mile hike
    Shelter Rock -- -0.7-mile hike
Degree of Difficulty: Moderate

BOULDERS BEYOND BELIEF

Description: *Trailside Boulders* -- Several large boulders are encountered on the hike along the Mountain Lane Trail to a beaver-created pond, as well as along the informal path that bypasses the pond. All are in the 15–25-foot-high range.

Shelter Rock -- In *Discover the Northern Adirondacks*, Barbara McMartin, etc., write "…just below the cliffs, is gargantuan Shelter Rock. This huge boulder has fallen from the rock wall of Pitchoff." The authors go on to add that hikers would often stop to "…enjoy a picnic on the rock. From it you have a wonderful view of the pass and of the mountain; you can even spot the place on the flanks of Pitchoff from which the boulder fell."

Jackrabbit Trail Boulder via Mountain Lane. Photograph by B. Delaney.

Directions: From Keene (junction of Routes 73 & 9N North), drive west on Route 73 for 8.6 miles and turn right onto Mountain Lane.

From Lake Placid (junction of Routes 73 & 86), drive southwest on Route 73 for 5.5 miles and turn left onto Mountain Lane.

BOULDERS BEYOND BELIEF

Proceed northeast on Mountain Lane for ~0.9 mile to the drivable end of the road where there is room for several cars.

Take note of the 8-foot-high, 15-foot-long boulder next to the cement barrier at the start of the hike.

As you hike along the trail (an abandoned, old road), you will see a number of medium-sized boulders scattered here and there. The first really big boulder is reached at ~0.2 mile, on the left side of the trail.

At around 0.5 mile, the road seemingly runs directly into a pond and disappears. The pond was created by beavers years ago, and was not part of the original road design. Take note of a rugged, informal path to the left that follows around the northwest side of the pond. While on this trail, you will see two, 20–25-foot-high boulders to your left, separated by 200 feet.

After bypassing the beaver pond at 0.7 mile, you will soon come to Shelter Rock on your right.

Resources: Tony Goodwin (editor) & Neal Burdick (series editor), *Adirondack Trails: High Peaks Region. 13th Edition* (Lake George, NY: Adirondack Mountain Club, Inc., 2004), 167.
Barbara McMartin, Patricia Collier, James C. Dawson, Phil Gallos & Peter O'Shea, *Discover the Northern Adirondacks* (Woodstock, VT: Backcountry Publications, 1988), 24.

29. JAY BOULDER

Type of Formation: Large Boulder
WOW Factor: 3–4
Location: Jay (Essex County)
Tenth Edition, NYS Atlas & Gazetteer: p. 30, A5; **Earlier Edition NYS Atlas & Gazetteer**: p. 96, AB4
Parking GPS Coordinates: 44°22.396'N 73°43.528'W
Accessibility: Roadside; 50-foot walk to covered bridge
Degree of Difficulty: Easy

Description: This large boulder rests in the streambed of the Ausable River's East Branch, just upstream from the 175-foot-long, historic Jay Covered Bridge.

BOULDERS BEYOND BELIEF

Readers should be prepared for the possibility that this massive boulder is periodically moved along the East Branch of the Ausable River's riverbed during times of heavy flow and may already be repositioned since my last visit.

Jay Boulder, upriver from the Jay Covered Bridge.

History: The Jay (covered) Bridge, built in 1857, was removed from its abutments in 1997 for restoration. It was remounted in 2007, fully restored.

The town of Jay is named after John Jay, governor of New York State when the town was formed.

Directions: From Keene (junction of Routes 9N North & 73), drive north on Route 9N for ~9.6 miles. At the center of Jay, turn right onto John Fountain Road (Route 22) and drive southeast for less than 0.2 mile. Then turn right onto a short, dead-end street, and park by the north end of the Jay Covered Bridge.

The boulder can be seen from the Jay Covered Bridge as well as from the east side of the river.

Resources: coveredbridgesite.com/ny/jay.html.

BOULDERS BEYOND BELIEF

30. STAGECOACH ROCK

Type of Formation: Historic Rock
WOW Factor: 2
Location: North Elba (Essex County)
Tenth Edition, NYS Atlas & Gazetteer: p. 30, C3; **Earlier Edition NYS Atlas & Gazetteer**: p. 96. BC2–3
Roadside GPS Coordinates: 44º13.241'N 73º53.118'W
Accessibility: Roadside

Description: Stagecoach Rock is a medium-sized boulder containing the image of a stagecoach, including the driver and a team of horses. The rock is considered to be so special that a pull-off alongside Route 73 was created for it.

Stagecoach Rock.

Stagecoach Rock is contained in Cascade Pass, which features Lower and Upper Cascade Lakes. Elizabeth Jesse & Howard Jesse, in *Geology of the Adirondack High Peaks*, point out that "The rock [in the pass] on the Cascade Mountain side is anorthosite, and the Pitchoff side, syenite." Anorthosite, is a plutonic rock composed primarily of calcic plagioclase; syenite is a coarse-grained, intrusive, igneous rock, very similar to granite.

History: In the late 1930s, Donald Rogers, a district engineer, noticed the presence of a large boulder that had fallen downhill from the shoulder of Pitchoff Mountain onto, or close to, the road. Rather than demolishing the rock or casting it aside, Rogers, and Bill Petty from Conservation, decided to create a monument to celebrate the vital role played by stagecoaches in Adirondack history. Louis Brown, a monument designer from Carnes Granite Co., Inc., made a sketch of the stagecoach and then Wilfred Carnes, using Brown's sketch, sandblasted the image onto the boulder.

Cascade Lake Boulder.

Directions: From Keene (junction of Routes 73 & 9N North), drive northwest, then southwest, on Route 73 for ~6.4 miles (or 4.3 miles from Adirondack Loj Road). Turn into the pull-off on your right, just before the trailhead parking areas for Cascade Mountain, on your left, begin.

BOULDERS BEYOND BELIEF

From Lake Placid (junction of Routes 73 & 86), drive southeast on Route 73 for ~7.8 miles. The pull-off for Stagecoach Rock is on your left, just after the trailhead parking for Cascade Mountain.

Additional Boulders --

#1 – On the drive up on Route 73 from Keene to the Cascade Lakes, look for a fairly large rock that juts out from Lower Cascade Lake near its northeast end [44º14.237'N 73º51.699'W], roughly 4.8 miles from Keene. It is easy to see from the second pull-off on your left. A photograph of a large boulder in the Cascade Lakes, possibly of this one, with Jenny and Peter Taylor scrambling up to the top in the rain with their wedding attire on, appeared in the Adirondack Life Magazine's *2018 Guide to the Great Outdoors.*

#2 Continuing southwest for another 0.2 mile (or 5.0 mile from Keene), a tall, 15–20-foot-high boulder can be seen on your right, literally hanging over the highway. The side facing the road has been sheared off, as if cleaved by an enormous hatchet, and maybe was partially destroyed when the new road was created

Pull into the fourth parking area on your left [44º14.121N 73º51.892W] if you wish to see this rock in a more leisurely fashion. It lies several hundred feet farther down the road at 44º14.094'N 73º51.938'W. However, there is no opportunity to park in front of the rock due to the narrowness of the road and guardrails.

Resources: Phil Brown, *Longstreet Highroad Guide to the New York Adirondacks* (Marietta, Georgia: Longstreet Press, Inc., 1999), 23.
adirondackview.blogspot.com/2008/07/stagecoach-rock.html (blogger) references an article by Jeffrey G. Kelly in the February 1986 issue of *Adirondack Life*.
Lee Manchester (editor), *The Plains of Abraham: A History of North Elba and Lake Placid. Collected Writings of Mary MacKenzie* (Utica, NY: Nicholas K. Burns, 2007), 44—46.
theadirondacker.com/2018/02/11/amazing-boulders-of-the-dirondacks.
Laura Viscome, "Precious Waters, Saving Waters," *The Conservationist* (May-June 1985). A pretty photo of the rock can be seen on page 41.
Bruce Wadsworth, *Day Hikes For All Seasons: An Adirondack Sampler* (Lake George, NY: Adirondack Mountain Club, 1996), 80—82. A photograph of the rock is shown on page 82.
Elizabeth Jesse & Howard Jesse, *Geology of the Adirondack High Peaks* (Glens Falls, NY: Adirondack Mountain Club, Inc., 1986), 306.

BOULDERS BEYOND BELIEF

31. BALANCED ROCKS: PITCHOFF MOUNTAIN

Type of Formation: Balanced Rock
WOW Factor: 7
Location: North Elba (Essex County)
Tenth Edition, NYS Atlas & Gazetteer: p. 30, C3; **Earlier Edition NYS Atlas & Gazetteer:** p. 96, BC2–3
Parking GPS Coordinates: 44º13.138'N 73º53.247'W
Balanced Rock #1 GPS Coordinates: 44º13.747'N 73º52.691'W
Accessibility: *Balanced Rock #1 and Wind Tunnel* -- 1.6-mile hike; *Balanced Rock #2 & South Summit* – 2.0-mile hike; 1,300' ascent
Degree of Difficulty: Difficult

Description: *Balanced Rocks #1* -- There are two massive boulders on Pitchoff Mountain that loom near the edge of a precipice. The larger one has cracked into two large pieces, with one of the halves resting above a large rift in the bedrock.

Bruce Wadsworth, in *Day Hikes For All Seasons: An Adirondack Sampler*, writes, "Void of any vegetation, the two great balanced rocks perch at the extreme point of the ridge, seemingly ready to fall into the great abyss below. Giant eroded joint patterns in the rock floor give the whole scene an appearance of being ready to collapse at any moment...."

In *By Foot in the Adirondacks*, Phil Gallos writes that "The Balanced Rocks, as seen from the vicinity of North Country School and the Van Hoevenberg Road, look like two small houses perched on the very edge of the dizzying precipice at the end of the ridge." Gallos continues, describing some of the geological features associated with the boulders. "It is apparent that this end of the ridge has received brutal treatment from the forces of nature. There are gaping crevices all around; and, below the Rocks, there is a place where a very large, wedge-shaped piece of the mountain has been removed, leaving an extremely overhung zone, which is several yards deep."

Susanne Lance, in *Heaven Up-h'isted-ness! The history of the Adirondack Forty-sixers and the High Peaks of the Adirondacks*, describes "...a group of reddish boulders perched on rocks ledges. The boulder embellishment continues to the top. Two boulders positioned by a long-gone glacier are poised on the summit as well. Indeed, the mammoth slabs of rock perch precariously, as if dropped from the hand of some giant onto the open peak."

BOULDERS BEYOND BELIEF

Lance goes on to mention that, in his book *Indian Pass*, Alfred Billings Street asserts that Pitchoff Mountain took its name from one of the large boulders precariously perched near the "northeast corner of its crest."

Wind Tunnel – Just below the Balanced Rocks is a cleft in the rock that leads to a shelter cave that some have named the Wind Tunnel.

Balanced Rock #2 --In *Adirondack Trails: High Peaks Region. 13th Edition*, a second boulder is described as a "...balanced boulder at the south summit of Pitchoff Mt. at 2.0 mi (3.2km)."

Balanced Rock. Photograph by Peter Fedorick

History: Pitchoff Mountain looms above the Cascades Lakes at a height of 3,500 feet. The mountain is appropriately named, for once you gain altitude and start following the ridge line you can literally pitch a rock or, inadvertently, yourself over the side of the mountain (but don't do either except in your imagination).

BOULDERS BEYOND BELIEF

Balanced Rock #1 has been a favorite side-diversion for hikers climbing up to the summit of Pitchoff Mountain. As a point of interest, the boulder is featured in an ad run by the Nature Conservancy. One example can be seen in the September/October 2016 issue of the *Adirondack Explorer*. It shows a young woman sprinting along on top of the boulders.

Directions: From Keene (junction of Routes 73 & 9N North), drive southwest on Route 73 for ~6.6 miles and park on your left at the trailhead for Pitchoff Mountain, Cascade Mountain, and Porter Mountain.

From Lake Placid (junction of Routes 86 & 73), drive northwest, then southeast, on Route 73 for ~7.5 miles and park to your right.

Note: There is also an east trail up to Pitchoff Mountain, but it involves a much greater ascent due to its lower trailhead elevation.

Walk to the north side of Route 73 to pick up the west trail to Pitchoff Mountain's summit. Follow the red-blazed trail, mostly an uphill climb, for 1.5 miles. Then turn right onto a spur path that leads across relatively flat terrain to the boulders in 0.1 mile.

Continue uphill for another 0.5 mile to reach the second balanced rock, which is located on the south summit, at 2.0 miles.

Resources: Bruce Wadsworth, *An Adirondack Sampler: Day Hikes For All Seasons* (Lake George, NY: Adirondack Mountain Club, 1996), 79 & 80.
Tim Starmer, *Five-Star Trails in the Adirondacks: A Guide to the Most Beautiful Hikes* (Birmingham, AL: Menasha Ridge Press, 2010), 58.
Hardie Truesdale, *Adirondack High: Images of America's First Wilderness* (Woodstock, VT: Countryman Press, 2005). A photo of the boulders is shown on page 23.
Gary A. Randorf, *The Adirondacks: Wild Island of Hope* (Baltimore: The John Hopkins University Press, 2002). On page 135 is a photo of a man standing on top of one of the large boulders.
Phil Gallos, *By Foot in the Adirondacks* (Saranac Lake, NY: Adirondack Publishing Company, Inc., 1972), 20–23.
Cliff Reiter, *Witness the Forever Wild: A Guide to Favorite Hikes around the Adirondack High Peaks* (Lulu.com, 2008). On page 37 is a view looking out from the cave under the balanced rocks.
Susanne Lance, *Heaven Up-h'isted-ness! The history of the Adirondack Forty-sixers and the High Peaks of the Adirondacks* (Cadyville, NY: The Adirondack Forty-sixers, Inc., 2011), 413.

BOULDERS BEYOND BELIEF

Tony Goodwin (editor) & Neal Burdick (series editor), *Adirondack Trails: High Peaks Region. 13th Edition* (Lake George, NY: Adirondack Mountain Club, Inc., 2004), 165.
lakeplacid.com/blog/2013/05/balanced-rocks -- Wind Tunnel.
Adirondack Life: Annual Guide to the Adirondacks. 1993 (Vol. XXIV. No. 4). A large photo of Balanced Rocks by Nathan Farb can be seen on page 40/41.
Gary Randorf, "Is Forever Wild in Danger?" *The Conservationist* (September-October, 1980). On page 8 is a photo taken by the author of the view from under the balanced rocks.
Barbara McMartin, "Adirondack High Peaks: More than Marcy," *New York State Conservationist* (December 1995). On page 4 is a photograph taken in the winter by Gary Randorf showing a hiker standing on top of one of the large boulders.
lakeplacid.com/do/hiking/balanced-rocks.
Adirondack Explorer (September/October 2016), 50.
Paul Schaefer, *Adirondack Cabin County* (York State Books, 1993), 138. A photograph shows Paul Schaefer's four children—Monica, Francis ("Cub"), Evelyn, and Mary—presumably sitting on top of one of the large boulders.
Rose Rivezzi & David Trithart, *Kids on the Trails! Hiking with children in the Adirondacks* (Lake George, NY: Adirondack Mountain Club, 1997), 103.
James Kraus, *Adirondack Moments* (Buffalo, NY: Firefly Books, 2009), 29. A photo of the boulders is shown.
Lisa Densmore Ballard, *Best Easy Day Hikes. Adirondacks. Second Edition* (Guilford, CT: Falcon Guides, 2017), 40. "…A curious boulder that seems to defy gravity."

32. CASCADE MOUNTAIN BOULDERS

Type of Formation: Large Boulder
WOW Factor: 5
Location: North Elba (Essex County)
Tenth Edition, NYS Atlas & Gazetteer: p. 30, C3; **Earlier Edition NYS Atlas & Gazetteer**: p. 96, BC2–3
Parking GPS Coordinates: 44º13.180′N 73º53.155′W
Estimated Destination GPS Coordinates: *Trailside Boulder* --44º12.742′N 73º52.456′W; *Summit Boulder* -- 44º13.120′N 73º51.609′W
Accessibility: *Trailside Boulder* -- ~1.4 mile-hike; *Summit Boulder* – 2.4-mile hike; 1,940′ ascent
Degree of Difficulty: *Trailside Boulder* -- Moderately difficult; *Summit Boulder* -- Difficult

BOULDERS BEYOND BELIEF

Description: *Trailside Boulder* -- A large boulder is encountered along the trail up to Cascade Mountain and Porter Mountain.

Summit Boulder – A photograph of one of the large boulders can be seen in Gary A. Randorf's *The Adirondacks: Wild Island of Hope*.

The rocky summit of Cascade Mountain.

History: Cascade Mountain (4,098') and the Cascade Lakes were named for the 200-foot-high cascade that drops down from above near the isthmus between the two Cascade Lakes.

The mountain's rocky dome is due to a forest fire in 1903 that not only swept the top of the mountain, but also destroyed an earlier version of the Adirondack Loj by Heart Lake, some miles away.

Directions: See previous chapter for parking directions.

Follow the red-blazed Cascade Mountain/Porter Mountain Trail, ascending continuously, until you come to a large boulder at 1.4 miles, roughly 0.7 mile before the Cascade Mountain/Porter Mountain junction is reached at 2.1 miles.

Medium-to large-sized boulders also awaits atop Cascade Mountain after a hike of 2.4 miles.

BOULDERS BEYOND BELIEF

Resources: Barbara McMartin, *Discover the Adirondack High Peaks* (Canada Lake, NY: Lake View Press, 1989), 244.
Gary A. Randorf, *The Adirondacks: Wild Island of Hope* (Baltimore: The John Hopkins University Press, 2002). A photo of a large boulder on top of Cascade Mountain is shown on page 22.

33. PORTER MOUNTAIN BOULDER

Type of Formation: Large Boulder
WOW Factor: 6
Location: North Elba (Essex County)
Tenth Edition, NYS Atlas & Gazetteer: p. 30, C3; **Earlier Edition NYS Atlas & Gazetteer**: p. 96, BC2–3
Parking GPS Coordinates: 44º13.180'N 73º53.155'W
Estimated Porter Mountain Boulder GPS Coordinates: 44º12.736'N 73º51.300'W
Accessibility: 2.7-mile hike; 1,900' ascent
Degree of Difficulty: Difficult

Dan Ziegler at the nearly buried trail junction sign.

Description: This large boulder is found less than 0.1 mile from the summit of Porter Mountain. In *Discover the Adirondack High Peak*, Barbara McMartin writes that "From the top of this rock, you can look straight down into Railroad Notch and the westmost pair of the four beaver ponds of the Little Meadows area."

History: Porter Mountain is named for Noah Porter (president of Yale University from 1871 to 1886) who made the first recorded ascent of the mountain in 1875.

BOULDERS BEYOND BELIEF

Directions: See chapter on "Balanced Rocks: Pitchoff Mountain" for parking directions.

From the parking area, follow the red-blazed Cascade Mountain/Porter Mountain Trail, heading uphill south, then east, for 2.1 miles. At the junction with the Cascade Mountain Trail (0.3 mile before the summit of Cascade Mountain), take the trail right that leads to Porter Mountain. In 0.2 mile from the junction you will descend to a col between the two mountains. Then, after ascending for 0.4 mile (or a total of 0.6 mile from the junction), you will come to a large boulder, 0.1 mile from the summit. A faint path leads left to the top of the rock.

Resources: Barbara McMartin, *Discover the Adirondack High Peaks* (Canada Lake, NY: Lake View Press, 1989), 245.
summitpost.org/cascade-mountain-and-porter-mountain/840096.
adirondackexperience.com/recreation/cascade-mountain-overlook – website shows two hikers standing next to some mid-sized boulders.
Tony Goodwin (editor) & Neal Burdick (series editor), *Adirondack Trails: High Peaks Region. 13th Edition* (Lake George, NY: Adirondack Mountain Club, Inc., 2004), 164. Mention is made that a large boulder is encountered 0.6 mile from the junction with the Cascade Mountain trail.
summitpost.org/cascade-mountain-and-porter-mountain/840096.
cnyhiking.com/PorterMountain.htm.

34. GRANT ROCK

Type of Formation: Boulder or Rock Outcrop
WOW Factor: Unknown
Location: Heart Lake (Essex County)
Tenth Edition, NYS Atlas & Gazetteer: p. 30, C2; **Earlier Edition NYS Atlas & Gazetteer**: p. 96, C2
Parking GPS Coordinates at High Peaks Information Center: 44º10.975'N 73º57.8152'W
Destination GPS Coordinates: Unknown
Fee: Modest parking fee
Accessibility: Unknown
Degree of Difficulty: Unknown

BOULDERS BEYOND BELIEF

Description: Unknown

History: President Ulysses S. Grant, on his hike up to the summit of Mount Marcy is reputed to have climbed up to the top of this rock along the way; hence, the name, Grant Rock. Not only did Grant attain the highest office in the nation then, but also the highest peak in New York State.

Grant lived in New York at the end of his career, dying unfortunately from throat cancer at his home, now the Grant Cottage State Historic Site, which is on the slope of Mt. McGregor in Wilton.

The Finest Square Mile.

I have been unable to find additional historical references to Grant Rock other than what happens to be mentioned in Lana Fennessy's book, *The History of Newcomb*. For now, this is all there is to tell.

Perhaps you may have an opinion as to which rock is Grant Rock. The person I would ask if given the opportunity is retired NYS Forest Ranger Pete Fish, who has ascended Mount Marcy more than 707 times (and that was as of 2009!).

Directions: From Lake Placid (junction of Routes 73 & 86), drive southeast on Route 73 for ~3.3 miles and turn right onto Adirondack Loj Road.

From Keene (junction of Routes 9N & 73), drive south on Route 73 for ~10.7 miles and turn left onto Adirondack Loj Road.

Coming from either direction, proceed south on Adirondack Loj Road for 4.8 miles and turn left into the parking area by the High Peaks Information Center. There is parking for about 200 cars. On a busy weekend, this entire area for parking can be filled to the brim!

BOULDERS BEYOND BELIEF

Note: Parking is not allowed on the final mile of Adirondack Loj Road—obviously an attempt to limit the number of hikers in an area that often seems to exceed capacity.

Follow the blue-blazed trail that leads to the summit of Mount Marcy. At some point along the trek is Grant's Rock, but as to which rock, boulder, or outcrop is the rock, your guess is as good as mine.

Roadside Rock along Route 73 –

Just before you turn left onto Adirondack Loj Road from Keene, take notice of a large, distinctive looking rock on your right jutting out from the shoulder of Route 73 (44°14.608'N 73°57.2652'W). Given the rock's prominence, it's been seen by many thousands of hikers driving into the Heart Lake area, but I suspect that few have actually pulled over to the side of the road to take a closer look at it. The rock probably the product of Route 73 being widened.

Resources: Lana Fennessy, *The History of Newcomb* (Newcomb, NY: 1996), 13 & 14.

35. MT JO TRAILHEAD BOULDERS

Type of Formation: Medium-sized Boulder
WOW Factor: 2
Location: Heart Lake (Essex County)
Tenth Edition, NYS Atlas & Gazetteer: p. 30, C2; **Earlier Edition NYS Atlas & Gazetteer**: p. 96, C2
Parking GPS Coordinates: 44°10.975'N 73°57.8152'W
Estimated Mount Jo Trailhead Boulders GPS Coordinates: 44°11.069'N 73°58.0272'W
Fee: Modest parking fee
Accessibility: 0.1–0.2-mile walk
Degree of Difficulty: Easy

Description: According to Anne Diggory in an article entitled "Sketching the Mt. Jo Trail", "Just a few feet past the [Mount Jo] trail register are two large boulders that become a visual event because they are larger than typical human size and they stand out from the visual chaos of the woods."

BOULDERS BEYOND BELIEF

History: The Mount Jo Trail leads to the summit of 700-foot-high Mount Jo—a name given to the mountain in the 1870s by Henry Van Hoevenberg to honor his fiancée, Josephine Schofield, who died during their engagement. The mountain was originally called Bear Mountain.

It's very possible that Anne Diggory may be the first Adirondack author to have written an article about glacial boulders as objects worthy of artistic rendition.

Heidi Mosley is beginning to realize that summer's a long way off near the Mt. Jo trailhead.

Directions: Follow the directions provided in the previous chapter on Grant Rock to reach the parking area by the High Peaks Information Center.

Starting from the parking area, walk back towards the entrance booth. Look for the sign that says Mount Jo and Indian Pass and begin there, initially following along the shoreline of Heart Lake until you come to the Mount Jo trail register.

The boulders are just beyond the register. One is near the trail; the other, slightly into the woods. Were it not for the fact that they have been written up and drawn in detail, they would not have been included in this book.

While in the area, you may wish to do the "Rock Garden Trail" up to the summit of Mt. Jo, which involves a hike through a boulder field.

Resources: Anne Diggory, "Sketching the Mt. Jo Trail," *Adirond*ac Vol. LXVIII, no. 4 (July/August 2004), 12–17. The article includes several sketches of the Mount Jo Trailhead Boulders, as well as guidelines on how to draw glacial boulders. summitpost.org/mt-jo/154479.

BOULDERS BEYOND BELIEF

36. INDIAN PASS BOULDERS

Type of Formation: Large Boulder
WOW Factor: 10
Location: Indian Pass (Essex County)

HEART LAKE APPROACH (FROM THE NORTH)
Tenth Edition, NYS Atlas & Gazetteer: p. 30, C2; **Earlier Edition NYS Atlas & Gazetteer**: p. 96, C2
Parking GPS Coordinates at High Peaks Information Center: 44º10.975'N 73º57.8152'W
Generalized GPS Boulder Coordinates: 44°08.150'N 74°02.027'W
Fee: Modest parking fee charged
Accessibility: 6.0-mile hike
Degree of Difficulty: Difficult due to length of hike

TAHAWUS APROACH (FROM THE SOUTH)
Tenth Edition, NYS Atlas & Gazetteer: p. 30, D1; **Earlier Edition NYS Atlas & Gazetteer**: p. 96, D1
Parking GPS Coordinates at Tahawus: 44º05.335'N 74º03.381'W
Generalized GPS Boulder Coordinates: 44°08.150'N 74°02.027'W
Accessibility: >5.0-mile hike
Degree of Difficulty: Difficult due to length of hike

Description: Indian Pass is filled with enormous, house-sized rocks and boulders. Of these, the largest by far is *Megalith* which is 60 feet high and 150 feet long. It is part of the Henodowada Megalith Cave system that was "discovered" by spelunker Robert Carroll in 1975. Like the other large rocks, it lies at the base of the towering cliff on Wallface Mountain.

In "A Hiker Observes Glacial Clues," Douglas Ayres Jr. writes, "Glacial erratics plucked from Wallface Mountain and the McIntyre range and dropped in Indian Pass in Essex County, were moved a very short distance. These boulders are massive, angular chunks of the bedrock, fifteen feet high or so, about 20 feet long, lying in a jumbled mass along the trail….A cluster of these boulders, with shapes reminiscent of the prow of a ship, are adjacent to the Indian Pass Trail."

BOULDERS BEYOND BELIEF

Summit Rock is a huge rock that marks the southern edge of the pass. Contrary to expectations, however, it is not the highest point along the trail in the pass. That still lies 0.5 mile ahead if you are hiking in from Tahawus.

Indian Pass rocks.

History: If there were Seven Wonders of the Northeastern United States, then most assuredly Indian Pass, also called the Adirondack Pass, would be at the top of the list—and for three good reasons. First, it lies at the base of Wallface Mountain, the highest vertical cliff-face in the northeast. Second, it contains the largest talus cave system in the Northeast and, quite possibly, the world—The TSOD (Touchy Sword of Damocles), that totals over 13,000 feet of passageways. Third, its tiny creek, Indian Pass Brook, is the stream source of the Hudson River, New York State's largest river.

But there are even more pedigree credentials associated with Indian Pass. Unlike other passes in the Adirondacks that are essentially river valley systems devoid of glacial debris, Indian Pass has no large stream running through its length. It is filled with boulders. In *A History of the Adirondacks*, Alfred L. Donaldson describes Indian Pass as possessing a "...large number of huge boulders, often plumed with trees, that seem balanced in precarious poises, yet are found to be securely rooted against the powerful dislodging agents that attack them." Charles Ingham, a New York City artist, painted the

BOULDERS BEYOND BELIEF

Indian Pass. Photograph by Barbara Delaney.

BOULDERS BEYOND BELIEF

pass, entitling it "The Great Adirondack Pass—Painted on the spot" and began exhibiting it in 1837.

In *The Military and Civil History of the County of Essex, New York* (1869), Winslow C. Watson writes that the pass "… occupies a narrow ravine, formed by a rapid acclivity of Mount McMartin on one side, rising at an angle of forty-five degrees, and on the opposite by the dark naked wall of a vertical precipice, towering to an altitude of eight hundred to one thousand two hundred feet from its base, and extending more than a mile in length….The deep and appalling gorge is strewn and probably occupied for several hundred feet, with gigantic fragments hurled into it from the impending cliffs, by some potent agency. The elements still advance the process."

Early explorers were awed by Indian Pass's gargantuan boulders and towering cliffs, recesses where thunderstorms would boom through, echoing like cannon-fire. The first known white men to go through the pass were David Henderson and Duncan McMartin, along with a manservant. Indian Pass finally made it onto a map in the 1830s when it was surveyed by Professor Ebenezer Emmons.

According to Alfred Billings Street, Native Americans called the pass variously *He-No-do-as-da*, meaning "path of thunder," *Os-ten-wanne*, or "Great Rock," and *Otne-yar-heh* for "Stonish Giants."

Geologists believe the reason why Indian Pass wasn't swept clear of boulders during the last glacial snowmelt was because an enormous block of ice lingered in the pass well past this initial deluge. Later, when the ice block melted, all of the boulders in it fell into the gorge, leaving the pass boulder-strewn.

At one time there was some discussion about building a highway through Indian Pass to connect Newcomb with Lake Placid. Thankfully, no action was ever taken on this proposal.

Directions: *North Approach from High Peaks Information Center*—Follow the directions provided in the chapter on Grant Rock to reach the parking area by the High Peaks Information Center.

From the parking area, follow the red-blazed trail southwest for 5.5 miles to reach the height of land in Indian Pass. Summit Rock is another 0.5 mile beyond (or a total of 6.0 miles). The immense conglomeration of boulders is generally to your right.

BOULDERS BEYOND BELIEF

South Approach from Tahawus—From the Adirondack Northway, get off at Exit 29 for North Hudson and drive west on Route 84/Blue Ridge Road for over 17 miles. When you come to Route 25, turn right and head north for nearly 10 miles until you come to the parking area at the end of the road.

Indian Pass. Photograph by Barbara Delaney.

BOULDERS BEYOND BELIEF

From here, follow the yellow-blazed, gravel road/trail north for 1.5 miles. Continue straight ahead, the trail now being marked by red markers, and proceed northeast for another 2.9 miles. Summit Rock is reached at a total of 4.4 miles. The actual height of land in the pass is achieved at 4.9 miles. The immense conglomeration of boulders will generally be to your left.

Resources: Barbara McMartin, *Fifty Hikes in the Adirondacks* (Woodstock, VT: Backcountry Publications, 1988), 237–241.
Russell Dunn, "Great Grottoes!" *Adirondack Life: Annual Guide to the Adirondacks* (1994), 74–79.
Russell Dunn & Barbara Delaney, *Adirondack Trails with Tales: History Hikes through the Adirondack Park and the Lake George, Lake Champlain & Mohawk Valley Region* (Hensonville, NY: Black Dome Press, 2009), 141–155.
Michael Nardacci (editor-in-chief), *Guide to the Caves and Karst of the Northeast: 50th Anniversary SSS Convention* (Huntsville, Alabama: National Speleological Society, 1991), 11.
Tony Goodwin (editor) & Neal Burdick (series editor), *Adirondack Trails: High Peaks Region. Thirteenth Edition* (Lake George, NY: Adirondack Mountain Club, Inc., 2004), 137–137 and 232 & 233.
Alfred L. Donaldson, *A History of the Adirondacks* (Mamaroneck, NY: Harbor Hill Books, 1977), 164–167.
Den Linnehan, *Adirondack Splendor* ((NY: Linnehan Press, 2004), 49.
Rhonda & George Ostertag, *Hiking New York* (Guilford, CT: The Globe Pequot Press, 2002), 63–67.
C. R. Roseberry, *From Niagara to Montauk* (Albany, NY: State University of New York Press, 1982), 147–151.
Nathaniel Sylvester, *Northern New York and the Adirondack Wilderness* (Harrison, NY: Harbor Hill Books, 1973 reprint), 58–60.
John Evans, etc. (editors), *An Introduction to Caves of the Northeast* (National Speleological Society, 1979), 63 & 64.
Douglas Ayres, Jr., "A Hiker Observes Glacial Clues," *Adirondac* (February/March 1984), 3 & 29.
Jim Bailey, "Through Indian Pass, with Backward Glances," *Adirondac* (October/November, 1989), 19–21.
adkhighpeaks.com/forums/forum/hiking/adirondack-trip-reports/481575-indian-pass-talus-caves-tsod-and-henadoawda-2017-november-4. This site contains a number of beautiful photographs of some of the rocks and talus caves.
Warwick Stevens Carpenter, *The Summer Paradise in History* (Albany, NY: The Delaware and Hudson Company, 1914), 81. The author describes "…a mass of titanic boulders that have been hurled from the mountain-sides or dropped there by the grinding glaciers that once covered the country."

Tim Starmer, *Five-Star Trails in the Adirondacks: A Guide to the Most Beautiful Hikes* (Birmingham, AL: Menasha Ridge Press, 2010), 257–262.
Hardie Truesdale, *Adirondack High: Images of America's First Wilderness* (Woodstock, VT: Countryman Press, 2005). A photograph of a talus cave is shown on page 72.
Phil Brown, "Climbing the Wall," *Adirondack Explorer 2018 Annual Outings Guide*, 87. "The valley below the trail is clogged with humongous boulders. We pass one that is big as a house."

37. WHITEFACE BROOK BOULDERS

Type of Formation: Large Boulder; Perched Rock
WOW Factor: 3–4
Location: Lake Placid (Essex County)
Tenth Edition, NYS Atlas & Gazetteer: p. 30, B2; **Earlier Edition NYS Atlas & Gazetteer**: p. 96, B2
Parking GPS Coordinates: 44º18.522′N 73º56.185′W
Whiteface Brook Boulder & Perched Rock GPS Coordinates: 44º20.723′N 73º55.643′W
Accessibility: 3.5-mile hike (1.0-mile long if you arrive by boat on Lake Placid to Whiteface Landing)
Degree of Difficulty: Moderate due to length

Description: Two notable rocks are in very close proximity to the Whiteface Brook Shelter:
    Perched Rock is a medium-sized boulder, seemingly balanced precariously atop a half-buried rock.
    Whiteface Brook Boulder is a sizable, oblong-shaped rock, roughly 8 feet high and 25 feet long.

History: The rocks by the Whiteface Brook Shelter have been glimpsed in passing by many hikers heading up the trail to the summit of Whiteface Mountain. Undoubtedly, those who have camped at the shelter are more familiar with the rocks, having had a chance to explore the immediate area in a more leisurely fashion.

Directions: From Lake Placid (junction of Routes 86 & 73), drive northeast on Route 86 for 2.9 miles. Turn left onto Connery Pond Road (presently a dirt

BOULDERS BEYOND BELIEF

road) and proceed northwest for 0.6 mile to a small parking area at the drivable end of the road. If the parking area is full, then park at one of the pull-offs along the way.

Perched rock near Whiteface Shelter.

Follow the red-blazed trail (an abandoned logging road that was used to clean up debris from the "Big Blowdown of 1950") north for 2.5 miles. The first 0.3 mile is a bypass route, keeping hikers away from a private residence on the lake. For virtually the entire distance to Whiteface Landing, the trail is wide and well-trodden, with little change in elevation. It makes for a very easy hike. Don't be concerned about the lack of red-blaze trail markers once you leave the Connery Pond area. There is no way to get lost on this trail. You will know that you have reached the 2.5 mile mark when you come to a junction where the sign reads, "Whiteface Landing 0.1 mile. Whiteface Brook Lean-to 1.0 mile. Whiteface Mountain 3.0 miles."

Whiteface Landing is 0.05 mile ahead. It provides a scenic view of the northeast end of Lake Placid, complete with a dock and campfire pit. Evidently, many people start the hike up Whiteface Mountain from this point after arriving by boat.

From the trail junction, head northeast, following the red-blazed Whiteface Mountain Trail as it slowly heads uphill. After ~0.6 mile, the trail comes up to Whiteface Brook where a series of small cascades can be seen.

Although the Whiteface Mountain Trail no longer crosses back and forth across Whiteface Brook three times as it once did (having caused untold problems for hikers, I'm sure), you will still have to ford a sizeable tributary coming in from the east, and this can be tricky to accomplish in the early spring or during times of high water. Fortunately, this is the only stream crossing you will have to make.

You will reach the Whiteface Brook Lean-to at ~1.0 mile from the junction, where a commanding 8-foot-high, 25-foot-long, oblong-shaped boulder near the lean-to and a perched rock behind the shelter can be seen.

Additional boulders –

For those so inclined, a small boulder field can be explored between the lower slabs and upper sections of the Whiteface Brook Slide [44º21.817'N 73º54.646'W]—a hike from the trail that involves a fairly demanding bushwhack.

Phil Brown writes up an account about climbing the slide in "Life on the slide," which appeared in both the September/October 2009 issue of *Adirondack Explorer* and the *Adirondack Explorer 2018 Annual Outings Guide*.

Resources: Tony Goodwin (editor), *Adirondack Trails: High Peaks Region. 13th Edition* (Lake George, NY: Adirondack Mountain Club, Inc., 2004), 152 & 153.
summitpost.org/whiteface-brook-slide/231574.
adirondackexplorer.org/outtakes/climbing-the-whiteface-slide.

BOULDERS BEYOND BELIEF

38. HIGH FALLS GORGE POTHOLES

Type of Formation: Pothole
WOW Factor: 5–6
Location: Wilmington (Essex County)
Tenth Edition, NYS Atlas & Gazetteer: p. 30, A3; **Earlier Edition NYS Atlas & Gazetteer**: p. 96, AB2–3
Parking GPS Coordinates: 44º20.834′N 73º52.670′W
Fee: Admission charged
Accessibility: 0.05-mile walk
Degree of Difficulty: Easy
Additional Information: High Falls Gorge, 4761 Route 86, Wilmington, NY 12997; (518) 946-2278; highfallsgorge.com. highfallsgorge.com/trail-map-hiking-walking-wheelchairs-lake-placid-ny.php – Trail map

A plethora of potholes can be seen at High Falls Gorge.

Description: High Fall Gorge's master pothole, measuring 7 feet wide and 35 feet deep, rests some 50 feet above the present level of the river—irrefutable proof that the Ausable River's West Branch has carved its way through the bedrock over the eons, deepening the gorge in the process.

Multiple potholes are visible in the sidewall of the gorge as well. According to Bradford B. Van Diver in *Roadside Geology of New York*, "The gorge is a great place to see potholes. These are rounded and polished hollows carved by the swirling of sand and gravel against bedrock in stream

BOULDERS BEYOND BELIEF

In the Gorge at High Falls,
Wilmington Notch,
Adirondack Mountains, N. Y.

eddies. Many of those you see high above the river now are really still active, being carved deeper each spring when the water may rise 10 feet or more."

History: The High Falls Gorge commercial attraction has been accommodating tourists since ~1890, utilizing a series of catwalks and stairways that allow ready access into the interior of the gorge. Were it not for the presence of this vital commercial attraction, High Falls Gorge would be essentially inaccessible.

According to Adeline F. Jaques in *Echoes from Whiteface Mountain: A Brief History of Wilmington*, Dick and Josephine Washer ran the business in the 1920s, leasing it from the Rogers Company of Ausable Forks.

Historically, during the days of lumbering there were terrible log jams in the gorge, necessitating that dynamite be used to break up the bottleneck. Fortunately, no damage was done to the gorge in the process.

Ironically, High Falls Gorge is an oasis of private entrepreneurmanship surrounded by Forever Wild New York State lands.

Directions: From Lake Placid (junction of Routes 86 & 73), drive northeast on Route 86 for ~7.6 miles. Turn left into the parking area for High Falls Gorge.

From Wilmington (junction of Routes 86 & 431), drive south on Route 86 for ~4.5 miles and turn right into the parking area.

The tour of High Falls Gorge is a self-guided one, allowing you to proceed at your own pace, lingering to take in the sights and sounds of the Ausable River's West Branch as it rushes over towering waterfalls.

The master pothole lies next to the interior gorge walkway, just downstream from "Mini Falls" and the middle steel footbridge. Farther downstream are a series of potholes worn into the sidewall, visible from the lower footbridge.

While visiting, be sure to look for the huge anorthosite boulder on display near the start of the trail after you cross over the upper footbridge from the Visitor Center.

Resources: Bradford B. Van Diver, *Routes and Routes of the North Country, New York* (Geneva, NY: W. F. Humphrey Press, Inc., 1976), 103.
Bradford B. Van Diver, *Roadside Geology of New York* (Missoula, MT: Mountain Press Publishing Company, 1985), 317.
C. R. Roseberry, *From Niagara to Montauk: The Scenic Pleasures of New York State* (Albany, NY: State University of New York Press, 1982), 163–166.

highfallsgorge.com/rates-hours-schedule-outdoor-recreation-lake-placid-ny.php.
adirondack.net/business/high-falls-gorge-8918.
Richard B. Frost, *One Foot Forward: Walks in Upstate New York* (Peru, NY: Bloated Toe Publishing, 2008), 9. "Formed by the scouring action of sand and small rocks over eons of time, this cavity [the pothole] plunges thirty-five feet through a basalt dike."
Arthur S. Knight (editor), *Adirondack Northway Guide* (Lake George, NY: Adirondack Resorts Press, Inc., 1964), 330 & 331.
Elizabeth Jesse & Howard Jesse, *Geology of the Adirondack High Peaks* (Glens Falls, NY: Adirondack Mountain Club, Inc., 1986), 317.
Adeline F. Jaques, *Echoes from Whiteface Mountain: A Brief History of Wilmington, New York* (Author, 1980), 30 & 31.

39. WEST BRANCH BOULDERS, AUSABLE RIVER

Type of Formation: Large Boulder
WOW Factor: 3–4
Location: Wilmington (Essex County)
Tenth Edition, NYS Atlas & Gazetteer: p. 30, A3; **Earlier Edition NYS Atlas & Gazetteer**: p. 96, AB2–3
Parking GPS Coordinates: 44º21.229'N 73º51.581'W
West Branch Boulders GPS Coordinates: *West Branch Boulders* -- 44º21.235'N 73º51.607'W; *Nature Trailhead Boulder* – 44º21.107'N 73º51.791'W
Accessibility: *West Branch Boulders* – 50-foot walk from parking area
   Nature Trailhead Boulder – 0.2-mile trek from parking area
Degree of Difficulty: Easy to moderately easy

Description: *West Branch River Boulders* – These two large boulders have been seen by innumerable people as they walk over the Whiteface Ski Center Bridge that spans the West Branch of the Ausable River. A plaque on the bridge points out that the West Branch's water level has been high enough periodically to completely engulf the boulders.

Bradford B. Van Diver, in *Roadside Geology of New York*, describes this section of the West Branch as "...a clear, bouldery mountain stream, with bedrock banks, frequent rapids, waterfalls, and quiet pools that attract many trout fishermen in season."

BOULDERS BEYOND BELIEF

Nature Trailhead Boulder – This 8-foot-high boulder, like a silent sentinel, guards the entry point to the red-blazed West Branch Nature Trail, a 1.9-mile-long loop.

Boulders along the West Branch of the Ausable River. Photograph by John Haywood.

Directions: From Lake Placid (junction of Routes 86 & 73), drive northeast on Route 86 for ~8.8 miles. Turn left into the Whiteface Mountain Ski Center.

From Wilmington (junction of Routes 86 & 431), drive south on Route 86 for ~3.0 miles and turn right into the Whiteface Mountain Ski Center.

Coming from either direction, drive downhill, heading west, for 0.1 mile, and turn into in a large parking area on your right just before crossing over the West Branch of the Ausable River.

West Branch River Boulders -- Walk over to the bridge spanning the West Branch and look upstream to view the large boulders in the river below.

Trailhead Boulder -- At the end of the bridge, turn left and follow a path upriver behind the ski center. You will immediately come out by a ski-tow. Stay far away when the tow is in operation. Continue south, with the river to your left, following another ski-tow that parallels the West Branch. In less than 0.2 mile, you will come to the end of the ski-tow. Walk over to a shed where a large, 8-foot-high glacial boulder can be seen at the start of the West Branch Nature Trail.

Wilmington Notch Falls, on the West Branch of the Ausable River, is only a short distance away.

BOULDERS BEYOND BELIEF

40. WHITEFACE MOUNTAIN SUMMIT ROCKS

Type of Formation: Medium-sized Boulder
WOW Factor: 2
Location: Wilmington (Essex County)
Tenth Edition, NYS Atlas & Gazetteer: p. 30, A3; **Earlier Edition NYS Atlas & Gazetteer**: p. 96, AB2–3
Summit parking GPS Coordinates: 44º22.035'N 73º54.332'W
Fee: Admission charged to use toll-road
Accessibility: Short walk up to summit
Degree of Difficulty: Easy
Additional Information: Whiteface Mountain Veterans Memorial Highway (518) 946-7175. During the regular season, the highway is open daily from 8:45 am to 5:15 pm.

For more specific information, check out Whiteface Mountain's website at whiteface.com/activities/whiteface-veterans-memorial-highway.

Approaching the summit of Whiteface Mountain. Postcard c. 1910.

Description: For those who would like to see small-to medium-sized glacial boulders on top of one of the Adirondack's High Peaks, but don't feel up to undertaking the climb involved, then there is an easy way to resolve the matter. Take the 5.0-mile-long automobile road up to the summit of Whiteface Mountain.

BOULDERS BEYOND BELIEF

History: The paved, 5.0-mile-long highway to the summit of Whiteface Mountain (4,867')—the fifth highest peak in the Adirondacks—opened in 1936, seven years after being dedicated to Governor Franklin D. Roosevelt in 1929. It involves an altitude gain of over 2,300 feet.

In *Adirondack Trails: High Peaks Region. 13th Edition*, Tony Goodwin mentions that the anorthosite granite of Whiteface Mountain came from a different source than the rest of the High Peaks and that "…mountain glaciers clung to its higher slopes long enough in the aftermath of the last Ice Age to create the most distinct alpine features to be found on any Adirondack peak."

Directions: From Wilmington (junction of Routes 431 & 86), drive west on Route 431 for 2.9 miles. At a fork, continue straight ahead on Route 431 for another 0.2 mile until you come to the alpine-style tollhouse and the beginning of the Whiteface Veteran's Memorial Highway.

From the tollhouse, drive up the toll road for ~5.0 miles to reach the parking area near the summit. From here, you can either walk up the 0.2-mile long nature trail to the summit (an area called the Castle), or use the elevator if it is in operation.

Resources: Wilmington Historical Society, *Images of America: Wilmington and the Whiteface Region* (Charleston, SC: Arcadia Publishing, 2013), 26. An 1883 photo shows Victorian hikers on top of Whiteface Mountain next to a bunch of 3–4-foot high boulders.
whiteface.com/activities/whiteface-veterans-memorial-highway.
en.wikipedia.org/wiki/Whiteface_Mountain.
Tony Goodwin (editor), *Adirondack Trails: High Peaks Region. 13th Edition* (Lake George, NY: Adirondack Mountain Club, Inc., 2004), 151.

41. JOHN BROWN'S BOULDERS
John Brown Farm State Historic Site

Type of Formation: Historic Boulder; Large Boulder
WOW Factor: 3–4
Location: North Elba (Essex County)
Tenth Edition, NYS Atlas & Gazetteer: p. BC1–2; **Earlier Edition NYS Atlas & Gazetteer**: p. 96, BC2
Parking GPS Coordinates: 44º15.124'N 73º58.314'W

BOULDERS BEYOND BELIEF

Destination GPS Coordinates: *Graveside Rock* -- 44º15.121'N 73º58.268'W; *Barn Boulder* -- 44º15.067'N 73º58.289'W
Fee: None to tour the grounds; modest fee to enter John Brown's House (a must-do when you are visiting).
Accessibility: *Gravesite Rock*—Roadside
    Barn Boulder—0.05-mile walk
Additional Information: John Brown Farm State Historic Site, 115 John Brown Road, Lake Placid, NY 12946; (518) 523-3900.

John Brown's Gravesite Rock. Postcard c. 1900.

Description: There are two boulders that command attention—one, for its historical significance; the other, for its size and bulk.

Gravesite Rock -- The first boulder is distinguished by a plaque affixed to its face in 1941 that lists the names of all the Brown family members buried here. It is part of a fenced-in gravesite. The boulder is massive, irregular-shaped, and partially buried in the ground. It stands over 8 feet high.

In *Northern New York and the Adirondack Wilderness*, Nathaniel Sylvester writes, "Above the little grassy enclosure, towers the mighty rock, almost as high as the house, and on its summit is cut in massive granite characters the inscription 'John Brown, 1859'."

BOULDERS BEYOND BELIEF

Barn Boulder -- The second boulder is partially buried in the earth near the corner of John Brown's barn, just past the pond and barn. It is 8 feet high at its highest and 15 feet long.

Barn Boulder.

History: John Brown is one of the most historically significant figures to have emerged from the Civil War era. In fact, many contend that the Civil War might not have erupted as it did, or have been delayed, were it not for the actions taken by Brown.

Brown was an abolitionist who believed passionately that slavery was morally wrong and should be abolished, even if taking action to accomplish this goal meant the loss of lives, including his own. In an unsuccessful attempt to seize armory supplies at Harpers Ferry, John Brown was captured, tried for treason, found guilty, and hanged. Later, his body was returned to his homestead in North Elba, New York, for burial, where it now lies interred.

BOULDERS BEYOND BELIEF

New York State acquired Brown's 270-acre farm in 1896. It is presently operated as a museum by the New York State Office of Parks, Recreation and Historic Preservation.

The John Brown Memorial statue in the middle of the cul-de-sac was unveiled in 1935.

Directions: From Lake Placid Village (junction of Routes 73 & 86), drive southeast on Route 73 for over 1.5 miles. Turn right onto John Brown Road, cross over Old Military Road (Route 35), and continue southwest for less than 0.7 mile until you reach the end of the road at a large cul-de-sac. Park off to the side of the road, or in a nearby parking area.

The boulder closest to the road is part of the gravesite that lies adjacent to the cul-de-sac. The second boulder is only a scant 0.05-mile walk from the cul-de-sac, near the corner of John Brown's barn, just past the pond.

Resources: Russell Dunn & Barbara Delaney, *Adirondack Trails with Tales: History Hikes through the Adirondack Park and the Lake George, Lake Champlain & Mohawk Valley Region* (Hensonville, NY: Black Dome Press, 2009), 121–131.
lakeplacid.com/do/hiking/john-brown-farm-state-historic-site.
parks.ny.gov/historic-sites/29/details.aspx.
pdfhost.focus.nps.gov/docs/NHLS/Text/72000840.pdf.
Evan Carton, *Patriotic Treason: John Brown and the South of America* (New York: Free Press, 2006).
Paul Schneider, *The Adirondacks: A History of America's First Wilderness* (New York: Henry Holt & Company, Inc., 1997), 107–113.
Nathaniel Sylvester, *Northern New York and the Adirondack Wilderness* (Harrison, NY: Harbor Hill Books, 1973 reprint), 139.
Martin V. Ives, *Through the Adirondacks in Eighteen Days* (Harrison, NY: Harbor Hill Books, 1985). An old photograph of the grave rock is shown on page 45.

42. SCARFACE MOUNTAIN BOULDER
Saranac Lakes Wild Forest

Type of Formation: Medium-sized Boulder
WOW Factor: 2
Location: Ray Brook (Essex County)
Tenth Edition, NYS Atlas & Gazetteer: p. 29, B10; **Earlier Edition NYS Atlas & Gazetteer**: p. 96, B1

BOULDERS BEYOND BELIEF

Parking GPS Coordinates: 44º17.885'N 74º05.015'W
Boulder at Clearing GPS Coordinates: 44º17.013'N 74º05.447'W
Accessibility: *Boulder* -- 1.2 mile-hike; *Summit* – 3.8-mile hike
Degree of Difficulty: B*oulder* – Moderate; *Summit* -- Difficult
Additional Information: trail map at alltrails.com/trail/us/new-york/scarface-mountain

Description: Although described as a large rock in a clearing in Bruce Wadsworth's *Day Hikes For All Seasons: An Adirondack Sampler*, the boulder actually turns out to be modest in size, roughly 4 feet high and 10 feet long. What the rock does provide, however, is a comfortable rest stop.

The large clearing next to the boulder is interesting in itself, for at its center is a huge cement slab that must have once supported a structure of considerable size.

Although I did continue on the trail for another mile or so, turning sharply left at one point, and then following along a stream that ultimately had to be crossed, I saw no further rocks of any significance.

My turn-around point was at 44º16.597'N 74º05.290'W near a 6-foot-high, 30–35-foot-long rock embedded in the hill to my left (it really isn't as impressive as it sounds).

The hike brought to mind the reality that sometimes in pursuit of large boulders, you end up chasing ghosts. At what point do you give up the ghost and turn around empty handed? At what point do you ignore the irresistible pull to look around just one more bend or hillock to see what lies ahead, knowing that you may miss out on something of real interest as a result? These are questions that have no answers.

History: Scarface Mountain (3,088') is one of six sub-High Peaks surrounding the village of Saranac Lake that have been dubbed the Saranac Lake 6-ers.

The bench encountered just before the bridge is dedicated to Paul John McKay, a 31-year old Australian soldier who died on the mountain in 2014 from hypothermia. It is believed that McKay, who suffered from PTSD, may have committed suicide.

BOULDERS BEYOND BELIEF

The footbridge crossing Ray Brook is of incredible length. One can only imagine the amount of labor that must have gone into its creation. Without it, there would be no way of fording Ray Brook.

Footbridge across Ray Brook.

Directions: From Ray Brook (junction of Routes 86 & 33), drive east on Route 86 for <0.2 mile and turn right onto Ray Brook Road, opposite "NYS Offices Ray Brook, NY." Proceed southwest for 0.1 mile and turn left into the small parking area for Scarface Mountain.

Follow the red-marked trail, heading south. You will cross over railroad tracks and then, at 0.5 mile, a footbridge spanning Ray Brook. From here, the trail climbs up to higher ground and then stays relatively flat until you reach the boulder and clearing.

Keep your expectations low on this one. I would recommend making the summit of Scarface your destination to justify the effort.

However, in all fairness to Bruce Wadsworth who mentions "a large boulder" in a clearing, I later noticed that the mileage he indicated to the clearing was 0.7 mile, which I passed through early on in the hike. All I can say is that I saw nothing distinctive along the trail until I reached the clearing and boulder I have written up. On the other hand, I vaguely do remember seeing a medium-sized boulder to my right in the woods with a large tree leaning against it, partially obscuring it from view. Perhaps that's the boulder being referred to. If so, the clearing has pretty much vanished

Resources: Bruce Wadsworth, *Day Hikes For All Seasons: An Adirondack Sampler* (Lake George, NY: Adirondack Mountain Club, 1996), 88. Wadsworth mentions coming to a clearing at 0.7 mile into the hike up Scarface Mountain "…where a large boulder is the center of attention."

BOULDERS BEYOND BELIEF

Tony Goodwin (editor), *Adirondack Trails: High Peaks Region.* 13th *Edition* (Lake George, NY: Adirondack Mountain Club, Inc., 2004), 179.
lakeplacid.com/do/hiking/scarface-mountain.
saranaclake.com/hiking/scarface-mountain.

43. MCKENZIE POND BOULDERS

Type of Formation: Large Boulder
WOW Factor: 8–9
Location: Saranac Lake (Essex County)
Tenth Edition, NYS Atlas & Gazetteer: p. 29, B10; **Earlier Edition NYS Atlas & Gazetteer** p. 96, B1
Parking GPS Coordinates: 44º18.295'N 74º05.705'W
McKenzie Pond Boulder Zone #1 GPS Coordinates: 44º18.303'N 74º05.627'W
Accessibility: >0.1-mile trek to visit all four sites
Degree of Difficulty: Moderately easy

McKenzie Pond Boulders comprise what is called a "rock city."

Description: The McKenzie Pond Boulders consists of four distinct zones of large rocks separated by short distances. Most of the boulders are in the 10–20-foot height range. Some rock enthusiasts have described the site as a village made out of boulders—literally a rock city.

BOULDERS BEYOND BELIEF

Boulderers have given the rocks such colorful names as Sweet Pea, Makaia, Pathogen, Super Slab, Far East, Swamp, Satellite, and others too numerous to list.

History: Without a doubt, this is one of the best and oldest sites for bouldering in the Adirondack Park.

As strange as it may sound, during early days, the site was not appreciated for its large rocks but rather was used for rendering fat for industrial purposes after it was collected from local hotels. The stone-lined pits from this past activity still remain partially visible today.

Bouldering is a new form of rock climbing. Photograph by John Haywood.

In 2013, the Essex County Highway Department constructed the current parking pull-off.

The most famous rock city in New York State is Rock City Park in Olean, Cattaraugus County, near the border with Pennsylvania (42º01.041'N 78º28.596'W).

BOULDERS BEYOND BELIEF

Directions: From west of Lake Placid (junction of Routes 86 & 35), drive west on Route 86 for 3.1 miles.

Turn right onto McKenzie Pond Road (Route 33), and drive northwest for 0.6 mile. Park to your left at a roadside pull-off between designated "parking area" signs. From here, walk back up the road for over 100 feet (past the yellow 25 mph sign on the right side of the road), and then follow a well-worn path into the woods from the north side of the road that leads to the first set of boulders in a couple of hundred feet. The very first large boulder encountered has been dubbed "The Front" by boulderers.

From the first set of boulders, keep following the path as it leads on from one stupendous grouping of massive boulders to the next.

The boulders are located on state land but border private property to the south. Please be respectful of the neighbors and stay on the sites that have been developed by the emerging bouldering community.

Big rocks are the norm at McKenzie Pond Boulders.

Resources:
Justin Sanford, *Adirondack Park Bouldering* (Broadalbin, NY: Southern Adirondack Climber, LLC, 21015), 226.
Tim Kemple, *New England Bouldering* (New Castle, CO: Wolverine Publishing, 2004), 142–151.
mountainproject.com/area/107414193/mckenzie-pond-boulders.
adirondackdailyenterprise.com/page/content.detail/id/538720.html.
saranaclake.com/blog/2016/09/village-boulders.
static1.squarespace.com/static/53228caae4b0182e183bdd11/t/535cfaf8e4b039ef276cbda8/1398602488222/McKensieGuide.pdf -- This is the site for the *McKenzie Pond Bouldering Guide* by Kippy, Groover, and friends of McKenzie Pond.

44. PULPIT ROCK: LAKE PLACID

Type of Formation: Rocky Bluff; Rock Profile
WOW Factor: 3–4
Location: Lake Placid (Essex County)
Tenth Edition, NYS Atlas & Gazetteer: p. 30, B2; **Earlier Edition NYS Atlas & Gazetteer**: p. 96, B2
Launch Site Parking GPS Coordinates: 44º17.870'N 73º58.728'W
Estimated Pulpit Rock GPS Coordinates: 44º18.742'N 73º58.076'W
Accessibility: 1.2-mile paddle
Degree of Difficulty: Moderately easy

Pulpit Rock. Postcard c. 1910.

Description: Pulpit Rock is a 50-foot-high cliff that has both attracted rock climbers and swimmers as well as creating some notoriety in the early 1960s. The rock-face is quite distinctive looking and, at least in old postcard reproductions, seems to show the image of a face.

BOULDERS BEYOND BELIEF

According to George Christian Ortloff in *A Lady in the Lake*, "Pulpit Rock's sheer cliffs plunge to a depth of about 90 feet, then a rock ledge slopes gently down into a layer of silt approximately four feet down."

Although not technically a boulder or unusual rock formation, the cliff wall's inclusion seems justifiable due to its unusual history [read on below].

History: The unusual history goes back to 1963, when divers inadvertently found the body of 56 year old Mabel Smith Douglass near Pulpit Rock below 100 feet of water. She had been missing for thirty years. Despite the passage of three decades, her body was surprisingly well preserved—mummified, if you will—by the cold, deep waters of the lake; so well preserved, in fact, that authorities initially thought that the body was of a recent drowning victim.

The account led George Christian Ortloff to write a book in 1994 entitled *A Lady in the Lake: The True Account of Death and Discovery in Lake Placid*.

In his book, Ortloff writes that Pulpit Rock "...was named for an unusual formation about ten feet above the water, resembling a preacher's pulpit, worn out of the cliff by untold centuries of falling, dropping water."

Directions: From Lake Placid (junction of Routes 86 & 73), drive north on Route 86 (Main Street) for 0.9 mile. When Route 86 turns sharply left uphill, continue straight ahead, now on Mirror Drive, and proceed northeast for 0.5 mile. Turn left into the public DEC boat launch site.

From the boat launch, paddle north for 1.2 miles, staying close to the shoreline. After passing by a long series of camps (there are 225 on the lake), you will come to an area on your right not populated by camps and cottages, where Pulpit Rock, a sheer cliff, can be seen.

Resources: Dean S. Stansfield, *Lake Placid: Images of America* (Charleston, SC: Arcadia Press, 2002), 35. A very fuzzy image of Pulpit Rock is shown in a ~1905 postcard.
George Christian Ortloff, *A Lady in the Lake: The True Account of Death and Discovery in Lake Placid* (Lake Placid, NY: With Pipe and Book, 1985), 8, 34 & 34..
townsandtrails.com/pulpit-rock-lake-placid.
mountainproject.com/photo/111974578/pulpit-rock-lake-placid-ny.
mountainproject.com/area/111972906/pulpit-rock.

BOULDERS BEYOND BELIEF

45. ADDITIONAL BOULDERS & ROCKS IN THE HIGH PEAKS REGION

Large boulders on or near mountain summits in the High Peaks Region are fairly common. In writing this book, we are literally just scratching the surface.

The following is a selection of additional large rocks and boulders in the High Peaks Region that have been mentioned or photographed in Adirondack-related books and articles:

Lower Ausable Lake. Postcard c. 1910.

Nippletop Mountain -- James R. Burnside, *Exploring the Adirondack 46 High Peaks* (Schenectady, NY: High Peaks Press, 1996). *Tenth Edition, NYS Atlas & Gazetteer:* p. 30, D4; *Earlier Edition NYS Atlas & Gazetteer:* p. 96. CD3. A photograph of a huge, flat-topped boulder on top of Nippletop Mountain (4,610') can be seen on page 202.

Pisgah Mountain -- Linda M. Champagne (editor), *Wilderness and People: The Future of the Adirondack Park* (Schenectady, NY: The Association for the Protective Future of the Adirondacks, 1993). *Tenth Edition, NYS Atlas & Gazetteer:* p. 29, A10; *Earlier Edition NYS Atlas & Gazetteer:* p. 95, B7. On page 55 is a photograph of three boys sitting near the top of a large glacial boulder. The caption reads, "Glacial Boulder in Meadow on Pisgah Mountain," an area just north of Saranac Lake.

BOULDERS BEYOND BELIEF

Saddleback Mountain -- Nathan Farb, *100 Views of the Adirondacks* (NY: Rizzoli International Publications, Inc., 1989). *Tenth Edition, NYS Atlas & Gazetteer:* p. 30, D3; *Earlier Edition NYS Atlas & Gazetteer:* p. 96, CD2–3. A photo of a large boulder on Saddleback Mountain (4,528') is shown on page 36.

Hardie Truesdale, *Adirondack High: Images of America's First Wilderness* (Woodstock, VT: Countryman Press, 2005). On page 52 is a photograph of a perched boulder on Saddleback Mountain.

Split Rock. Postcard c. 1900.

Haystacks -- Tony Goodwin (editor), *Adirondack Trails: High Peaks Region. 13th Edition* (Lake George, NY: Adirondack Mountain Club, Inc., 2004), 51. *Tenth Edition, NYS Atlas & Gazetteer:* p. 30, D3; *Earlier Edition NYS Atlas & Gazetteer:* p. 96, CD2. By following the yellow-marked Shorey Short Cut Trail from the State Range Trail, a "large boulder" is passed after >0.2 mile.

Algonquin Peak -- Gary A. Randorf, *The Adirondacks: Wild Island of Hope* (Baltimore: The John Hopkins University Press, 2002). *Tenth Edition, NYS Atlas & Gazetteer:* p. 30, D2; *Earlier Edition NYS Atlas & Gazetteer:* p. 96, CD2. A photograph of a large boulder on the summit of Algonquin Peak (5,115') can be seen on page 103.

Grace Peak -- Gary A. Randorf, *The Adirondacks: Wild Island of Hope* (Baltimore: The John Hopkins University Press, 2002). *Tenth Edition, NYS Atlas & Gazetteer:* p. 30, E4; *Earlier Edition NYS Atlas & Gazetteer:* p. 96, D4. On page 51 is a photograph of a large boulder on Grace Peak (4,012'), a mountain peak formerly known as East Dix Mountain.

Susan Bibeau, "Amazing Grace," *Adirondack Explorer* (September/October, 2014). On page 49 can be seen a photograph of a large rock with a commemorative sign affixed to it that reads "Grace Peak."

Cascade Lake. Postcard c. 1900.

Avalanche Pass -- Tony Goodwin (editor), *Adirondack Trails: High Peaks Region. 13th Edition* (Lake George, NY: Adirondack Mountain Club, Inc., 2004), 127. *Tenth Edition, NYS Atlas & Gazetteer:* p. 30, D2; *Earlier Edition NYS Atlas & Gazetteer:* p. 96, CD2. Many large boulders are passed while negotiating the climb through Avalanche Pass.

BOULDERS BEYOND BELIEF

Hurricane Mountain -- Annie Stoltie & Elizabeth Ward (editors), *Dog Hikes in the Adirondacks* (Westport, NY: Shaggy Dog Press, 2009). *Tenth Edition, NYS Atlas & Gazetteer:* p. 30, C5; *Earlier Edition NYS Atlas & Gazetteer:* p. 96, BC4. On page 26 is a photograph of a woman and her dogs next to a 6–8-foot-high boulder on Hurricane Mountain (3,678′).

Little Marcy -- Hardie Truesdale, *Adirondack High: Images of America's First Wilderness* (Woodstock, VT: Countryman Press, 2005). *Tenth Edition, NYS Atlas & Gazetteer:* p. 30, D2–3; *Earlier Edition NYS Atlas & Gazetteer:* p. 96, CD2. A photograph of a boulder on Little Marcy (4,718′) is displayed on page 63.

Cold River. Postcard c. 1910.

Little Porter Mountain -- Barbara McMartin, *Discover the Adirondack High Peaks* (Canada Lake, NY: Lake View Press, 1989). *Tenth Edition, NYS Atlas & Gazetteer:* p. 30, C3–4; *Earlier Edition NYS Atlas & Gazetteer:* p. 96, C3. On page 212 is a photograph of a large boulder on Little Porter Mountain (2,822+′).

Phil Brown & Tom Woodman, *12 Short Hikes Near Keene Valley* (Saranac Lake, NY: Adirondack Explorer, 2015), 35. At around 1.7 miles, "you pass by a large boulder" on Little Porter Mountain.

BOULDERS BEYOND BELIEF

Noonmark Mountain -- Nathan Farb, *Adirondack Wilderness* (New York: Rizzoli, 2009), 34/35, and Neal Burdick, "The Art of Nathan Farb," *Adirondack Explorer* Vol. 7, No. 1 (January/February, 2005). *Tenth Edition, NYS Atlas & Gazetteer:* p. 30, D4; *Earlier Edition NYS Atlas & Gazetteer:* p. 96, CD3–4. A medium-sized glacial rock atop Noonmark Mountain (3,556') is shown on page 28.

Mount Colvin -- *Adirondac* Vol. 48, no. 1 (January 1984). *Tenth Edition, NYS Atlas & Gazetteer:* p. 30, D4; *Earlier Edition NYS Atlas & Gazetteer:* p. 96, CD3. A line drawing by Herbert Kates of an enormous boulder along the trail to Mount Colvin (4,057') can be seen on page 15. Of particular interest is the pup tent in the drawing that is sheltered by the rock overhang.

Mountain Lake near Paul Smith's. Postcard c. 1900.

West Mill Brook -- Dennis Conroy, James C. Dawson, & Barbara McMartin, *Discover the Northeastern Adirondacks* (Woodstock, VT: Backcountry Publications, 1987), 48. *Tenth Edition, NYS Atlas & Gazetteer:* p. 30, E5; *Earlier Edition NYS Atlas & Gazetteer:* p. 96, D4. In the chapter on West Mill Brook, "two large erratics" twenty feet to the left of the trail are mentioned, probably ~1.3 miles into the hike.

Silver Lake Mountain -- Ray Fadden, "Rare Pottery Discovered on Silver Lake Mountain," *North Country Life* Vol. 14, no.1 (Winter 1960), 21–23 & 49. *Tenth Edition, NYS Atlas & Gazetteer:* p. 22, D3; *Earlier Edition NYS Atlas &*

BOULDERS BEYOND BELIEF

Gazetteer: p. 102, D3. Fadden talks about a rock-shelter on the upper side of Silver Lake Mountain (934′) where a 300 year old bowl was found and later donated to the Six Nation Indian Museum at Onchiota.

Norton Mountain -- Glyndon Cole, "The Mystery of the Lost Cave," *New York Tradition* Vol. 27, no. 1 (Winter 1973), 22–27. *Tenth Edition, NYS Atlas & Gazetteer:* p. 22, C2; *Earlier Edition NYS Atlas & Gazetteer:* p. 102, CD2. After Captain E. E. Thomas wrote about discovering a cave on Norton Mountain (2,874′) that rivaled Mammoth Cave in Kentucky in size, Glyndon Cole went out to look for it and only managed to find a deep depression, some five feet wide, which went down for a considerable depth.

Barbara McMartin, Patricia Collier, James C. Dawson, Phil Gallos & Peter O'Shea, *Discover the Northern Adirondacks* (Woodstock, VT: Backcountry Publications, 1988), 211–214. The authors discuss a 1.9-mile-long bushwhack to the summit of Norton Mountain and its caves, which are formed by a 250-foot-long rift that is 20 feet deep and 20 feet wide.

Canoeing the Adirondacks. Postcard c. 1910.

Giant Mountain -- Dennis Conroy, James C. Dawson, & Barbara McMartin, *Discover the Northeastern Adirondacks* (Woodstock, VT: Backcountry Publications, 1987), 98 & 99. *Tenth Edition, NYS Atlas & Gazetteer:* p. 30, CD5; *Earlier Edition NYS Atlas & Gazetteer:* p. 96, C4. In a section entitled "The Slides

BOULDERS BEYOND BELIEF

on Giant Mountain," a map shows a very large boulder in a gully which is then described on the next page as "...a house-sized boulder lying in the bottom of the gully. For twenty years after the massive slide of 1963, this block threatened hikers from a perch thirty feet higher on the left side of the gully, before finally breaking loose on a dry summer day to settle into its present location."

Gothics -- Tony Goodwin (editor), *Adirondack Trails: High Peaks Region. 13th Edition* (Lake George, NY: Adirondack Mountain Club, Inc., 2004), 46. *Tenth Edition, NYS Atlas & Gazetteer:* p. 30, D3; *Earlier Edition NYS Atlas & Gazetteer:* p. 96, CD2–3. Following the blue-marked Orebed Trail up towards Gothics from near the DEC Interior Outpost, "a huge boulder on the right" is passed at 1.5 miles, and then, at 2.6 miles, "several large boulders."

Boulder Bend. Saranac River. Postcard c. 1910.

Beaver Meadow Brook -- Jerome Wyckoff, *The Adirondack Landscape* (Glens Falls, NY: Adirondack Mountain Club, 1967). *Tenth Edition, NYS Atlas & Gazetteer:* p. 31, D6; *Earlier Edition NYS Atlas & Gazetteer:* p. 97, CD5. On page 36 is a photograph of a large pothole on Beaver Meadow Brook. I presume that the Beaver Meadow Brook that Wyckoff is referring to is the one that flows into the east bank of the Boquet River near New Russia—not the one above Beaver Meadow Falls.

BOULDERS BEYOND BELIEF

Catamount Mountain -- Tony Goodwin (editor), *Adirondack Trails: High Peaks Region. 13th Edition* (Lake George, NY: Adirondack Mountain Club, Inc., 2004), 158. *Tenth Edition, NYS Atlas & Gazetteer:* p. 22, E3; *Earlier Edition NYS Atlas & Gazetteer:* p. 96, A2–3. Mention is made of a balanced rock on Catamount Mountain (3,168') at 1.3 miles. The Chimney climb is reached at 1.4 miles.

Mt. Marcy summit. Postcard c. 1920.

Carey's Rock -- Jeanne Reynolds & Bessie DeCosse, *Two Towns…Two Centuries* (Gouverneur, NY: Mrs. Press, 1976). A dark photo of Carey's Rock resting between an unidentified lake and road is shown on page 168. The rock looks to be 8–10 feet high. The lake may be Star Lake. So far, I have not been able to find any reference to Carey's Rock other than this one source.

Mt. Colden -- Tony Goodwin (editor) & Neal Burdick (series editor), *Adirondack Trails: High Peaks Region. 13th Edition* (Lake George, NY: Adirondack Mountain Club, Inc., 2004), 130. *Tenth Edition, NYS Atlas & Gazetteer:* p. 30, D2; *Earlier Edition NYS Atlas & Gazetteer:* p. 96, CD2. On the red-marked trail up Mt. Colden from Lake Colden, "the trail passes under two huge boulders" at 1.3 miles. Then, after another 0.2 mile, a "large balanced boulder on the left" is reached.

Sawteeth -- Tony Goodwin (editor) & Neal Burdick (series editor), *Adirondack Trails: High Peaks Region. 13th Edition* (Lake George, NY: Adirondack Mountain

Club, Inc., 2004), 82. *Tenth Edition, NYS Atlas & Gazetteer:* p. 30, D3; *Earlier Edition NYS Atlas & Gazetteer:* p. 96, CD3. Mention is made of a spectacular view of Lower Ausable Lake from "a ledge with a boulder 250 ft. above the lake," 1.0 mile along the trail leading up to Sawteeth.

Barbara Delaney explores the McKenzie Pond Boulders.

Bluff Mountain -- Dennis Conroy, James C. Dawson, & Barbara McMartin, *Discover the Northeastern Adirondacks* (Woodstock, VT: Backcountry Publications, 1987), 157 & 158. *Tenth Edition, NYS Atlas & Gazetteer:* p. 31, A6; *Earlier Edition NYS Atlas & Gazetteer:* p. 97, B4–5. This is a fairly demanding hike, initially following a trail southeast from the end of Lincoln Hill Road, and then requiring a bushwhack north to reach Bluff Mountain whose summit is "...distinguished by a couple of large, balanced rocks."

Cranberry Lake -- Peter O'Shea, *Guide to Adirondack Trails: Northern Region* (Woodstock, VT: Backcountry Publications, 1988), 167. *Tenth Edition, NYS Atlas & Gazetteer:* p. 28, D2; *Earlier Edition NYS Atlas & Gazetteer:* p. 94, CD2. From the southwest end of South Bay at West Flow (Cranberry Lake) follow the Sixmile Creek Trail for ~0.4 mile to reach the Sliding Rock Trail, where an amazing 15-foot-high, 50-foot-long cascade, called Sliding Rock Falls, can be seen. Hikers use it as a waterslide for recreation. Then, at 2.9 miles, "a huge glacial erratic with young birch and polypod fern growing on it" is passed.

Algonquin Peak/Iroquois Peak -- Lisa Densmore Ballard, *Hiking the Adirondacks. Second Edition* (Guilford, CT: Falcon Guides, 2017). *Tenth Edition, NYS Atlas & Gazetteer:* p. 30, D2; *Earlier Edition NYS Atlas & Gazetteer:* p. 96, CD2. On page 63 is a photograph of a large boulder with other rocks visible in the distance, located in an alpine zone between Algonquin Peak and Iroquois Peak.

46. SPLIT ROCK: HARRIETSTOWN

Type of Formation: Split Rock
WOW Factor: 4–5
Location: Harrietstown (Franklin County)
Tenth Edition, NYS Atlas & Gazetteer: p. 29, A9–10; **Earlier Edition NYS Atlas & Gazetteer**: p. 95, A7
Parking GPS Coordinates: 44º24.912′N 74º09.326′W
Split Rock GPS Coordinates: 44º24.921′N 74º09.254′W
Accessibility: View from roadside

Split Rock: Harrietstown.

Description: Split Rock is a 15-foot-high, 30-foot-long boulder that has split into two halves. The huge gap between the two pieces of rock would be easy to walk through were it not for the huge amount of brush that has grown up between them. Barbara McMartin, and etc., in *Discover the Northern Adirondacks*, describe the rock as an "enormous split erratic in the field beside the road." That it is!

BOULDERS BEYOND BELIEF

History: In *The Place Names of Franklin County, New York*, Kelsie Harder & Carol Payment Poole talk about a "very large rock which is more than 6 feet in height, and is split into two parts, sitting a few hundred feet off the road."

The boulder was a significant enough land-feature for a nearby road to be named after it.

Split Rock in mid-winter: Harrietstown.

Directions: From Saranac Lake (junction of Routes 86 & 186), drive north on Route 86 for 1.7 miles. Turn right onto Split Rock Road and head north for 0.2 mile. Look to your right to see the boulder in a field just before reaching Balsam Lane.

Unfortunately, the wide split that developed in Split Rock, and which gave the rock its name, faces Balsam Lane (a private road), making it somewhat difficult to view the boulder in its entirety from Split Rock Road.

Resources: Kelsie Harder & Carol Payment Poole, *The Place Names of Franklin County, New York* (Brushton, NY: Teach Services, Inc., 2008), 308. A photograph of the rock can be seen on page 307.
Barbara McMartin, Patricia Collier, James C. Dawson, Phil Gallos & Peter O'Shea, *Discover the Northern Adirondacks* (Woodstock, VT: Backcountry Publications, 1988), 53.

BOULDERS BEYOND BELIEF

47. ST. REGIS MOUNTAIN BOULDERS

Type of Formation: Large Boulder; Balancing Rock
WOW Factor: Boulders – 8–9; Summit Rocks -- 5–6
Location: Paul Smiths (Franklin County)
Tenth Edition, NYS Atlas & Gazetteer: p. 21, E8; **Earlier Edition NYS Atlas & Gazetteer**: p. 95, A6
Parking GPS Coordinates: 44º25.926'N 74º18.006'W
Destination GPS Coordinates: *Boulder* -- 44º25.753'N 74º18.104'W; *Summit* -- 44º24.519'N 74º19.777'W
Accessibility: 0.4-mile hike to boulder; 3.4-mile hike to summit; 1,250-foot ascent
Degree of Difficulty: *Boulders* – Moderately easy; *Rocks near summit* -- Difficult due to length of hike
Additional Information: cnyhiking.com/StRegisMountain.htm – Trail map

St. Regis Mountain Fire Tower.

Description: A number of large boulders can be seen along the way up St. Regis Mountain. In *Fifty Hikes in the Adirondacks*, Barbara McMartin writes, "Huge erratics of Marcy anorthosite with large blue crystals of labradorite edge the trail as it begins a short descent and then climbs a small hill."

The principal boulders are encountered near the beginning of the hike shortly after passing by a tiny pond. These are truly massive rocks. The main boulder is 30 feet high, and easily as long. It is partially balanced on a 4-foot-high rock that has been pushed into the earth by the greater weight of its upper companion. This arrangement has created a small shelter cave where the large boulder has been tilted upward. On the opposite side of the boulder is a huge overhang where a substantial sized shelter cave has formed. The campfire pit under the overhang is sufficient proof that the shelter has been put to good use on occasion.

BOULDERS BEYOND BELIEF

At least three massive rocks surround the main boulder, much like satellites orbiting a planet. To the east is a 15-foot-high, 8-foot-wide, triangular-shaped boulder. Its smooth, vertical face suggests that it was originally part of the larger boulder until it fractured off. To the west is a 15-foot-high, 30-foot-long boulder with a 10-foot overhang. There is sufficient space to crawl under the overhang, but not so much room that you would want to linger for long. The side of this rock facing away from the main boulder looks like a long, polished wall.

House-sized boulder near St. Regis Mountain Trail.

In front of the main boulder is an 8-foot-high, 15-foot-long boulder as well as an 8-foot-high rock. There is much to see here!

According to Tim Starmer in *Five-Star Trails in the Adirondacks*, a couple of miles beyond as you near the summit, the trail takes you past "...a large balancing rock on your left and another boulder directly to your right."

BOULDERS BEYOND BELIEF

History: St. Regis Mountain rises to an elevation of 2,874 feet with a 35-foot-tall fire tower providing panoramic views of more than 30 lakes. It is one of six mountains surrounding the Saranac Lakes. The fire tower was erected in 1918 by the NYS Conservation Commission.

Directions: From Paul Smiths (junction of Routes 30 & 86), proceed north on Route 30 for 100 feet and turn left onto Keese Mill Road. Head west for nearly 2.6 miles and park in the area to your left.

The hike up to the summit of St. Regis Mountain is 3.4 miles long if you choose to go the entire distance.

St. Regis Mountain grows large rocks.

The trek begins by crossing a bridge that spans the St. Regis River and following a dirt road south. Within 0.1 mile, a trail leads off to your right from the road into the woods. After a few minutes, a small pond is passed on your left, after which the trail turns sharply right and begins climbing. Within moments you are paralleling a huge rock face to your left. Just before the rock face comes to an end, look to you right to see a grouping of large boulders in the woods. Bushwhack 70 feet south from the trail to reach the cluster of large rocks.

Later, at 3.2 miles into the hike, a number of large boulders are encountered near the summit, including a balanced rock.

Although my wife and I climbed St. Regis Mountain many years ago, we were not thinking about boulders then, and so have no memory of any big rocks we might have seen. On my recent trek, I continued west from the large boulders for another 0.3 mile before turning around after seeing nothing more. I wasn't being lazy. I simply was trying not to overdo a recovering fractured left femur and recent surgery for a left torn meniscus.

I suspect from accounts that there are other large rocks along the trail before the summit is reached.

Resources: Tim Starmer, *Five-Star Trails in the Adirondacks* (Birmingham, AL: Menasha Ridge Press, 2010), 225.
Barbara McMartin, *Fifty Hikes in the Adirondacks* (Woodstock, VT: Backcountry Publications, 1988), 112.
aranaclake.com/hiking/st-regis-mountain.
lakeplacid.com/do/hiking/st-regis-mountain – mentioned on this web- site are "areas of giant glacial errata."
theoutbound.com/new-york/hiking/hike-st-regis-mountain.
John Freeman with Wesley H. Haynes, *Views from on High: Fire Tower Trails in the Adirondacks and Catskills* (Lake George, NY: Adirondack Mountain Club, Inc., 2001).
Peter V. O'Shea (editor & Neal Burdick (series editor), *Guide to Adirondack Trails: Northern Region. Second Edition* (Lake George, NY: Adirondack Mountain Club, Inc., 2000), 81. "At 3.2 mi, the trail passes enormous boulders."
Norm Landis & Bradly A. Pendergraft, *Adirondack Mountain Club Western Trails. First Edition* (Lake George, NY: Adirondack Mountain Club, Inc., 2016), 193.
Lisa Densmore Ballard, *Hiking the Adirondacks. Second Edition* (Guilford, CT: Falcon Guides, 2017), 50–55.

BOULDERS BEYOND BELIEF

48. HISTORIC SINKHOLE

Type of Formation: Sinkhole
WOW Factor: Unknown
Location: Vermontville (Franklin County)
Tenth Edition, NYS Atlas & Gazetteer: p. 22, E1; **Earlier Edition NYS Atlas & Gazetteer**: p. 96, A1
Possible Sinkhole GPS Coordinates: 44º28.460'N 74º03.160'W

Description: There must be something of extraordinary interest north of Vermontville if a Delorme NYS Atlas & Gazetteer map indicates the presence of a "sinkhole" near a road. I can't recall coming across anything like it before.

With this in mind, I recently drove up past Vermontville and went back and forth along Sink Hole Road—a paved, 1.6-mile-long backcountry road north of Vermontville—to look for a large depression in the earth. I saw no evidence of one (or at least what I expected a large sinkhole to look like).

However, by good fortune, I did get to talk to one of the homeowners on Sink Hole Road who happened to be out in her front yard as I passed by. She stated that she had been told some time ago that the sinkhole is located in a section of the road where a small creek periodically floods, covering the road with water and silt. This is roughly 0.5 mile along Sinkhole Road from its south end, just past a tiny bridge, and at a definite low-point. A sign here warns of flooding, and indeed, a fair amount of sediment was visible along the road on the day of my visit. The homeowner furthermore stated that an 8-foot-wide sinkhole had recently formed on her property, leading me to believe that this type of incident is not an uncommon event in this area.

But where was the sinkhole? All I saw was a marshland created by a small stream.

I left the area scratching my head. I'm not really sure if what the lady said was accurate. On the NYS Atlas & Gazetteer, the word sink hole is placed along the left (west) side of the road, near its south end. I could see nothing there while driving by, nor does anything show up on Google Earth.

History: According to an article that appeared in the *Syracuse Post Standard* in 1932, "From the time of horse-drawn transportation over the years, a large 30-to 40-acre sinkhole developed. In 1932 the sinkhole was filled with tree trunks cut from both sides of the road and then covered with layers of earth…"

BOULDERS BEYOND BELIEF

Route 3 was subsequently rerouted to avoid the sinkhole. However, that didn't stop houses from being built along a section of the old road. The road, despite all, is still being maintained, even though the sinkhole is said to be anything but dormant.

Sinkholes, to be sure, come in all sizes, and this one is by no means a particularly large one. Near Cairo, Egypt is the Qattara sinkhole, which measures 50 miles long and 75 miles wide.

Directions: From Bloomingdale (junction of Routes 3 & 18), drive northeast on Route 3 for ~5.0 miles, passing through Vermontville in the process. Turn left onto Sink Hole Road which re-enters Route 30 a mile and a half farther north.

The challenge is to locate the sinkhole, which maps show to be on the left side of the road. I'm not sure if I really met this challenge.

Resources: Kelsie Harder & Carol Payment Poole, *The Place Names of Franklin County, New York* (Brushton, NY: TEACH Services, Inc., 2008), 301.
(Newspaper) *Syracuse Post Standard*, June 31, 1932.

49. AMPERSAND MOUNTAIN ROCKS

Type of Formation: Large Boulder; Split Rock
WOW Factor: 5–6
Location: Saranac Lake (Franklin County)
Tenth Edition, NYS Atlas & Gazetteer: p. 29, BC9; **Earlier Edition NYS Atlas & Gazetteer**: p. 95, BC7
Parking GPS Coordinates: 44º15.104′N 74º14.360′W
Boulders GPS Coordinates: Not taken; **Summit GPS Coordinates**: 44º14.075′N 74º12.202′W
Accessibility: *Boulders* – 2.4-mile hike; *Split Rock* – 2.5-mile hike; *Summit* -- 2.7-mile hike; 1,775′ ascent
Degree of Difficulty: Moderately difficult

Description: Along the hike up to the summit of Ampersand Mountain, you will pass through an area of jumbled boulders, some the size of garages and small houses. Passageways can be followed between some of the larger rocks, where rock-shelters have formed.

BOULDERS BEYOND BELIEF

In *Discover the Northern Adirondacks*, Barbara McMartin, etc., write, "The final approach to the summit is gorgeous. To your left are massive rocks; a huge split rock on the right invites exploring. Enough people have left the trail here to explore the rocks and crevices that you will find a number of small herd paths."

Peter W. Kick, in *Discover the Adirondacks*, talks about a "sheer and cavernous split rock on your right as the trail bears left."

At the summit of Ampersand Mountain.

History: Ampersand Mountain (3,352') takes its name from nearby Ampersand Creek, which, in turn, was named for its twists and turns, much like the Ampersand symbol (&).

Directions: From Saranac Lake (junction of Routes 3 & 86), drive southwest on Route 3 for ~8.0 miles. Pull into a parking area on the right side of the road, opposite from the trailhead.

From Tupper Lake (junction of Routes 30 & 3 South), drive east on Route 30/3 for 5.5 miles. Then continue east on Route 3 for another 6.9 miles to reach the parking area for Ampersand Mountain on your left.

Follow the well-marked, heavily-used trail for 2.4 miles to reach the boulder area. From here, it is another 0.3 mile to the summit.

BOULDERS BEYOND BELIEF

Barbara Delaney gets ready to explore the mountain's nooks & crannies.

Resources: Barbara McMartin, *Fifty Hikes in the Adirondacks* (Woodstock, VT: Backcountry Publications, 1988), 191.
saranaclake.com/hiking/ampersand-mountain.
tupperlake.com/activities/ampersand-mountain.
Tim Starmer, *Five-Star Trails in the Adirondacks: A Guide to the Most Beautiful Hikes* (Birmingham, AL: Menasha Ridge Press, 2010). A photograph of a narrow passageway is shown on page 234.
Bruce Wadsworth, *Day Hikes For All Seasons: An Adirondack Sampler* (Lake George, NY: Adirondack Mountain Club, 1996), 86. "An extremely large rock overhang is passed under" at 2.4 miles into the hike.
Tony Goodwin (editor), *Adirondack Trails: High Peaks Region. 13th Edition* (Lake George, NY: Adirondack Mountain Club, Inc., 2004), 181. Goodwin mentions that a "large split boulder" is encountered on the right at 2.5 miles.
Barbara McMartin, Patricia Collier, James C. Dawson, Phil Gallos & Peter O'Shea, *Discover the Northern Adirondacks* (Woodstock, VT: Backcountry Publications, 1988), 83.
Peter W. Kick, *Discover the Adirondacks* (Boston, MA: Appalachian Mountain Club Books, 2012), 39. There is a "…sheer and cavernous split rock on your right as the trail bears left."

BOULDERS BEYOND BELIEF

Lisa Densmore Ballard, *Hiking the Adirondacks. Second Edition* (Guilford, CT: Falcon Guides, 2017), 147. The author talks about a "...huge boulder on the right. Yellow arrows point the way through this interesting narrow chasm. The boulders that form a wall next to the trail probably split apart during the last ice age." A photograph of one of the boulders is seen on page 145.

50. SECOND POND BOULDERS

Monster Rock with its rock-shelter.

Type of Formation: Large Boulder
WOW Factor: 7–8
Location: Saranac Lake (Franklin County)
Tenth Edition, NYS Atlas & Gazetteer: p. 29, B9; **Earlier Edition NYS Atlas & Gazetteer**: p. 95, B7
Parking GPS Coordinates: 44º17.353′N 74º10.840′W
Destination GPS Coordinates: *Rosetta Stone* -- 44º17.474′N 74º10.649′W; *Monster Rock* -- 44º17.387′N 74º10.736′W; *Boulder #2* -- 44º17.397′N 74º10.703′W

BOULDERS BEYOND BELIEF

Accessibility: 0.05–0.1-mile bushwhack
Degree of Difficulty: Moderate

Description: Three large glacial erratics are located not far from roadside.

Northwest side of road – A boulder called the *Rosetta Stone*—a name given to it by boulderers for reasons that elude me—is a massive glacial erratic, 25 feet high and 15–20 feet long. It is partially surrounded by several smaller boulders; smaller, of course, being a relative term.

The Rosetta Stone, looking a bit mysterious in the early morning mist.

An old, cement highway post juts out of the ground next to the huge rock. It marks the start of an abandoned road, now heavily overgrown, which passes by near the boulder, paralleling Route 3 for some distance.

BOULDERS BEYOND BELIEF

The Rosetta Stone lies so close to Route 3 that it can be readily seen through the woods while driving southwest, providing, of course, you know where to look.

Southeast side of road -- Monster Rock is a 25-foot-high, 25–30-foot-long, massive boulder that stands alone, lying on a gentle slope. A 6-foot overhang is prominent at one end. Unlike the Rosetta Stone, it has no companions.

Boulder #2 stands 15 feet high, and is 20 feet long. Like Monster Rock, it also lies on a gentle slope. Undoubtedly, boulderers have given a name to it, but for the moment I only know it as Boulder #2.

History: The Second Pond Boulders are one of two bouldering sites near Second Pond. The second site is between Second Pond and Oseetah Lake.

Will Roth and Joel Brandt were the first boulderers to document climbing routes on these boulders in 2007.

Directions: From Saranac Lake (junction of Routes 3 East & 86 West), drive southwest on Route 3 for ~3.8 miles. Pull over to your right, off-road, just past the end of the guardrail.

From Tupper Lake (junction of Routes 30 & 3 South), drive north on Route 30/3 for ~5.5 miles. At a junction, continue straight on Route 3 for another ~11.0 miles (or a total of ~16.5 miles). After crossing the bridge between First Pond and Second Pond, continue northeast for >0.3 mile; then turn around so that the car is facing southwest, and park off-road at the end of the guardrail.

Rosetta Stone – From the roadside pull-off, walk northeast down the road for less than 100 feet and turn left into the woods. You will immediately come to the Roseatta Stone, which is a mere 50 feet from the road.

Monster Rock – From where you have parked, walk across Route 3 and then up and embankment into the woods. You will come to Monster Rock slightly to your right, less than 80 feet into the woods.

Boulder #2 – From Monster Rock, bushwhack southwest through the woods, paralleling Route 3. You will come to Boulder # 2 in >0.1 mile. It also lies near the top of the embankment, close to the road.

Resources: Justin Sanford, *Adirondack Park Bouldering* (Broadalbin, NY: Southern Adirondack Climber, LLC, 21015), 252–272.

BOULDERS BEYOND BELIEF

51. GULL ROCK & BLUFF ISLAND CLIFF-WALL

Type of Formation: Large Boulder; Cliff-Wall
WOW Factor: 5
Location: Lower Saranac Lake (Franklin County)
Tenth Edition, NYS Atlas & Gazetteer: p. 29, B9; **Earlier Edition NYS Atlas & Gazetteer**: p. 95, BC7
Parking GPS Coordinates: 44º17.197'N 74º11.147'W
Destination GPS Coordinates: *Bluff Island Cliff-Wall* -- 44º17.858'N 74º11.802'W; *Gull Rock* -- 44º17.796'N 74º12.296'W
Accessibility: *Bluff Island Cliff-Wall* – 1.1-mile trek by water; *Gull Rock* -- ~1.5-mile trek by water
Degree of Difficulty: Easy by motorboat; moderately easy by paddle
Additional Information: A map of the Saranac Lakes is shown at -- dec.ny.gov/docs/permits_ej_operations_pdf/saranaclakeisl2016.pdf.

Gull Rock, complete with a gull on top of the boulder.

Description: The *Cliff-Wall* at Bluff Island consists of a vertical, 70-foot-high wall of rock that rises up from the lake. Daredevils have jumped from its heights, but this is not a stunt for the faint-of-heart, nor one to be taken lightly, for potential risks are involved.

Gull Rock is a 6–7-foot-high boulder that rests on a shallow mound of bedrock. Paddlers often glide up to the rock for a closer look. Boaters need to

BOULDERS BEYOND BELIEF

be more cautious, for the waters get shallow here, and props can be damaged if they are not raised out of the water.

On the day of our visit—surprise! surprise!—a gull was seated on top of the boulder.

History: Gull Rock was named for its colony of gulls.

Bluff Island was named for its 70-foot-high, vertical cliff-wall that rises up from the water on the southeast side of the island. In a memorable scene in *The Perils of Pauline*—a melodramatic film-serial that premiered in 1914—the cliff-wall is on full display as a rider on horseback leaps off the precipice into the waters below.

Lower Saranac Lake is one of three Saranac Lakes on the Saranac River—the other two being Middle Saranac Lake and Upper Saranac Lake.

View from Bluff Island. Photograph c. 1936.

Directions: From the village of Saranac Lake (junction of Routes 3 West, 3 East & 86 West), head southwest on Route 3 for 4.3 miles. As soon as you cross over the Saranac River between First Pond and Second Pond, turn left into the Second Pond Boat Launch, aka State Bridge Boat Launch.

From the boat launch, paddle or motor northwest for 1.1 miles. You will come out onto Lower Saranac Lake, roughly opposite Bluff Island, which features an enormous, 70-foot-high cliff-wall.

After looking at the towering bluff on Bluff Island, bear left and proceed west for 0.4 mile to reach Gull Rock, just west of Partridge Island.

Resources: adirondackexplorer.org/outtakes/adirondack-cliff-jumping.
stephenesherman.com/65-jumps-the-lake.
localwiki.org/hsl/Bluff_Island – This website contains past history of Bluff Island as well as a map of the island.
mountainproject.com/area/111942228/bluff-island.

BOULDERS BEYOND BELIEF

52. FERNOW FOREST BOULDER
Fernow Experimental Forest /Saranac Lakes Wild Forest

Type of Formation: Large Boulder
WOW Factor: 3
Location: Wawbeek (Franklin County)
Tenth Edition, NYS Atlas & Gazetteer: p. 29, BC7; **Earlier Edition NYS Atlas & Gazetteer**: p. 95, BC6
Parking GPS Coordinates: 44º14.983'N 74º20.786'W
Fernow Forest Boulder GPS Coordinates: 44º15.120'N 74º20.779'W
Accessibility: >0.2-mile hike
Degree of Difficulty: Easy

Fernow Boulder. Photograph by Barbara Delaney.

Description: An impressive 10–11-foot high, 15-foot-long glacial boulder is part of the Fernow Experimental Forest, directly next to Station #3. A plaque on the rock reads, in part, "This forest plantation and trail dedicated to Bernard E. Fernow 1851–1923…."

BOULDERS BEYOND BELIEF

A number of smaller glacial boulders are scattered about the plantation, visible through the woods. One of the more noticeable rocks is encountered just after Station #6, where a 4-foot-high boulder can be seen seventy feet from the trail. I mention this because Station #6 seems to direct your attention to a large tree that was struck by lightning. A split runs down its trunk, and most of its upper section is burnt. Both the tree and boulder are worth a quick look.

History: The forest preserve is named after Bernard E. Fernow, whom some consider to be the father of modern forestry. The preserve was established in 1934 to address water quantity, water quality, and timber quality issues. It is presently operated by the U.S. Forest Service's Northern Research Station.

The walk through this forest, essentially on pine needles, is very pleasant and the trees are old-timers that tower above you at a great height.

Directions: From Tupper Lake (junction of Routes 30 & 3 South), drive east on Route 30/3 for 5.5 miles. At a junction, turn left onto Route 30 and drive northeast for 0.7 mile. Then turn left into the roadside parking area for Fernow Forest.

From the parking area, follow the short, yellow-blazed, 0.8-mile long, self-guided nature trail to Station 3, where the main boulder can be seen. It is located on the right side of the path just before you reach the loop section, a hike of less than 0.3 mile.

Resources: Dennis Aprill, *Short Treks in the Adirondacks and Beyond* (Utica, NY: Nicholas K. Burns Publishing, 2005), 119. A winter photograph of the boulder is also shown on page 119.
nrs.fs.fed.us/ef/locations/wv/fernow.
cnyhiking.com/FernowForestNatureTrail.htm – The site contains a picture of the plaque on the rock.
Robert F. Hall, *Pages from Adirondack History* (Fleischmanns, NY: Purple Mountain Press, 1992), 7.
Barbara McMartin, Patricia Collier, James C. Dawson, Phil Gallos & Peter O'Shea, *Discover the Northern Adirondacks* (Woodstock, VT: Backcountry Publications, 1988), 88. "Various glacial erratics are noted."

BOULDERS BEYOND BELIEF

53. CAPTAIN PETER'S ROCK

Type of Formation: Large Boulder
WOW Factor: 1–2
Location: Tupper Lake (Franklin County)
Tenth Edition, NYS Atlas & Gazetteer: p. 28/29, C6; **Earlier Edition NYS Atlas & Gazetteer**: p. 95, BC4–5
Boat Launch site GPS Coordinates: 44º11.754'N 74º29.029'W
Captain Peter's Rock GPS Coordinates: 44º13.931'N 74º30.260'W
Accessibility: 5.0-mile trek by boat
Degree of Difficulty: Moderate

Description: Captain Peter's Rock is described by Kelsie Harder and Carol Payment Poole in *The Place Names of Franklin County, New York* as "…a huge rock jutting out of the Raquette River just below the Underwood bridge."

History: According to Frederick J. Seaver in *Historical Sketches of Franklin County and its Several Towns*, "The legend is that Captain Peter once jumped from the rock to the shore, a distance of sixteen feet." Captain Peter was Peter Sabattis (c.1750–1861), an Abenaki chief who also was a member of an 1812 surveying party.

Perhaps it was possible to leap the distance from the rock to the shore during the nineteenth century (although 16 feet requires quite a stretch of the imagination), but not so today—the rock is dozens of feet away from the shoreline and has been since the lake was created.

Another rock has also come to be associated with Captain Peter and is known as Peter's Rock. In an article by Curt Stager called *Hidden Heritage*, the author writes, "Directly across from [Paul Smith's] campus, smooth gray anorthosite juts into the water near the outlet to the St. Regis River. Peter's Rock is a popular campsite maintained by the college…" This Peter's Rock, a rock outcropping, is located at the end of a peninsula on Lower St. Regis Lake at a GPS of 44º25.782'N 74º15.594'W.

Directions: From Tupper Lake (junction of Routes 30 & 3 South), drive southwest on Route 30 for 2.6 miles and turn right into the parking area for the DEC Tupper Lake Boat Launch.

From the south end of Tupper Lake (junction of Routes 30 & 421), head north on Route 30 for 6.1 miles and turn left into the boat launch site.

BOULDERS BEYOND BELIEF

Head northwest by boat or canoe/kayak for ~5.0 miles to reach the Underwood Railroad Bridge and then continue west for another 0.1 mile to Captain Peter's Rock. It lies 1.2 miles upstream from the Setting Pole Dam (named for how boatmen would set poles in the river bed and then push off in order to advance their boat through the rapids).

There may be a legal way of accessing this rock by land, but I have not explored that option. Possibly, the rock could be accessed by following the railroad tracks (but not on them) from Gull Pond Road south of Piercefield, to the railroad bridge, a walk of over 3.0 miles.

In "Coming down the Raquette—Setting Pole rapids to Sunday Rock," Paul Jamieson writes, "The Town of Altamont maintains a small camping and picnic area at the dam and rapids, accessible by a woods road from Route 3" at a GPS reading of roughly 44°14.064'N 74°31.782'W. The problem here, however, is that you're on the opposite shore of the river, and over one mile downriver from the rock.

Resources: Kelsie Harder & Carol Payment Poole, *The Place Names of Franklin County, New York* (Brushton, NY: Teach Services, Inc., 2008), 52.
adirondacklifemag.com/blogs/2017/10/05/hidden-heritage – The part of this article written by Curt Stager pertaining to Captain Peter is near the end of the piece.
Frederick J. Seaver, *Historical Sketches of Franklin County and its Several Towns* (Albany, NY: J. B. Lyon Company, 1918), 134.
compelledtoact.com/Involvement_pages/PSC/Photos_PSC.htm.
Paul Jamieson, Coming down the Raquette—Setting Pole rapids to Sunday Rock," *The Quarterly*, Vol. XXXIII, no. 4 (October 1978), 6.

54. MOUNT ARAB ROCK

Location: Piercefield (St. Lawrence County)
Tenth Edition, NYS Atlas & Gazetteer: p. 28, C4; **Earlier Edition NYS Atlas & Gazetteer**: p. 94, C4
Parking GPS Coordinates: 44°12.816'N 74°35.771'W
Destination GPS Coordinates: *Off-trail Boulder* -- 44°12.713'N 74°35.576'W; *Picture Rock* -- 44°12.564'N 74°35.534'W
Accessibility: *Off-trail Boulder* -- 0.3-mile hike; *Picture Rock* – 0.7-mile hike; *Summit* -- 1.0-mile hike; 744-foot ascent
Degree of Difficulty: Moderate

BOULDERS BEYOND BELIEF

Additional Information: Friends of Mount Arab, PO Box 185, Piercefield, NY 12973; friendsofmtarab.org.
Donations are welcomed in an on-site locked box.

Off-Trail Boulder. Photograph by Barbara Delaney.

Description: *Off-trail Boulder* – Of the two boulders described, this is the one that I found to be the more impressive. The boulder stands at a height of 10 feet, and is 15 feet long. It lies only 25 feet from the trail. No path leads to it, which suggests that the rock is rarely visited.

Picture Rock is 7 feet high, and shaped like a softball. The boulder's photo-popularity was personally born out when I saw a couple stop to take a selfie of themselves next to the rock.

History: Mount Arab, aka Arab Mountain, contains a 1918, forty-foot fire tower on its summit that was rehabilitated in 1999.

According to a sign at the trailhead, "The 1.0 mile Mount Arab Trail begins on private working land owned by Rayonier [a global forest products company] subject to a conservation easement with New York State, then continues onto NYS land to the fire tower on the 2,539 foot summit."

BOULDERS BEYOND BELIEF

Directions: From Tupper Lake (junction of Routes 3 & 30), drive west on Route 3 for 6.8 miles. Turn left onto Route 62 (Conifer Road), and drive southwest for nearly 1.8 miles. Then turn left onto Mount Arab Road and proceed southeast for 0.8 mile. Pull into a large parking area on your right.

From the parking area, cross over the road, and follow the Mount Arab Trail uphill. In ~0.3 mile, you will pass by the *Off-trail Boulder* to your right. In ~0.7 mile, you will come to *Picture Rock* after ascending a flight of wooden stairs. The boulder is directly next to the trail on your right. You can't miss it.

Picture Rock.

From Picture Rock, continue up to the summit if you wish (why not?—you're almost there), a total distance of ~1.0 mile.

Resources: cnyhiking.com/MountArab.htm.
bing.com/images/search?q=blog+picture+rock+mount+arab+ny -- A photograph of the boulder, with two children sitting on top, can be seen on this site. It was from this blog that I got the name Picture Rock.
Evan Williams, "An oasis on Mount Arab," *Adirondack Explorer: 2014 Outings Guide*, 53. A hike up Mount Arab is described, but no mention is made of the boulder along the way.
Peter W. Kick, *Discover the Adirondacks* (Boston, MA: Appalachian Mountain Club Books, 2012), 59–62.
Norm Landis & Bradly A. Pendergraft, *Adirondack Mountain Club Western Trails. First Edition* (Lake George, NY: Adirondack Mountain Club, Inc., 2016), 174 & 175.
Susan Omohundro, "Mount Arab Fire Observation Tower," *The Quarterly* Vol. LVI, no. 4 (2011), 14 & 15.

BOULDERS BEYOND BELIEF

55. TOOLEY POND ROAD BOULDERS

Tooley Pond Road is a 17-mile-long, backcountry road that was constructed in 1864, originally to serve as a stage coach route. It connects the hamlets of Cranberry Lake and Degrasse, generally following along the South Branch of the Grass River. Its name comes from Tooley Pond, which is 5.8 miles northwest of the hamlet of Cranberry Lake.

Tooley Pond Road's main features, in addition to its pond, are its seven off-road waterfalls, these being in consecutive order, heading northwest: Copper Rock Falls, Rainbow Falls, Bulkhead Falls, Stewart's Rapids, Twin Falls, Sinclair Falls, and Basford Falls. With the exception of Twin Falls, all can be readily accessed from the road.

In addition, two more unnamed falls are reported to be 0.2 mile upstream from Copper Rock Falls. This is a very waterfall rich area, indeed.

The land along Tooley Pond Road is in the Northern River Flow-Tooley Pond Tract.

Location: Cranberry Lake/Degrasse (St. Lawrence County)
Tenth Edition, NYS Atlas & Gazetteer: p. 28, C1— 27, A8–9; **Earlier Edition NYS Atlas & Gazetteer**: p. 94, C2 —93, B7

Directions: From Sevey Corners (junction of Routes 3 & 65), drive west on Route 3 for 9.3 miles. Just before crossing the Oswegatchie River, turn right onto Tooley Pond Road.

Resources: Randi Minetor, *Hiking Waterfalls in New York* (Guilford, CT: Falcon Guides, 2014), 234–236.
hikingthetrailtoyesterday.wordpress.com/2017/01/19/toohley-pond-road-waterfalls.
Steven Bailey, "The Waterfall Road," *Adirondac* Vol. LXVII, no. 3 (Summer 2003), 16 & 17.
Mark Bowie, "A cascade of riches: Waterfall hopping in the Tooley Pond Tract, *Adirondack Explorer* Vol. 6, no. 4 (July/August 2004), 48 & 49.
Bill Ingersoll, "Grass Routes: A half-dozen walks to hidden waterfalls," *Adirondack Life Annual Guide 2002*, 100–107.

BOULDERS BEYOND BELIEF

PEACE SIGN ROCK

Type of Formation: Large Boulder
WOW Factor: 4
Estimated Peace Sign Rock GPS Coordinates: 44°19.785'N 75°00.522'W
Accessibility: Roadside
Degree of Difficulty: Easy

Description: This 10-foot-high, 12-foot-long roadside boulder is distinguished by a peace sign that has been painted on the side facing the road.

Directions: The Peace Sign Boulder is reached at ~12.6 miles. It is located on the right side of the road.

BULKHEAD BOULDERS

Type of Formation: Large Boulder
WOW Factor: 6–7
Parking GPS Coordinates: 44°19.889'N 75°01.117'W
Bulkhead Boulders GPS Coordinates: 44°19.807'N 75°01.097'W
Accessibility: 0.1-mile hike
Degree of Difficulty: Moderate

Description: There are a number of impressive, 12-foot-high boulders next to and downstream from Bulkhead Falls, one of the largest being 25 feet long.

History: Bulkhead Falls is also known as Adrenaline Falls, a name given to it by whitewater paddlers.

Directions: The trailhead for Bulkhead Falls is reached at 13.3 miles. Look for a faint path on the left side of the road that begins next to a yellow "No motor vehicles" sign. It leads to upstream views of Bulkhead Falls and the boulders in 0.1 mile.

BOULDERS BEYOND BELIEF

The path to Bulkhead Falls appears to be noticeably less used than the other paths that lead to waterfalls on the South Branch of the Grass River.

Bulkhead Boulders.

Resources: Norm Landis & Bradly A. Pendergraft, *Adirondack Mountain Club Western Trails. First Edition* (Lake George, NY: Adirondack Mountain Club, Inc., 2016), 224 & 225.
nnywaterfalls.com/grassriver/bulkheadfalls.

56. GUMDROP BOULDER
Lampson Falls

Type of Formation: Large Boulder
WOW Factor: 5–6
Location: Clare (St. Lawrence County)
Tenth Edition, NYS Atlas & Gazetteer: p. 27, A9; **Earlier Edition NYS Atlas & Gazetteer**: p. 93, A7
Parking GPS Coordinates: 44º24.289'N 75º03.706'W
Lampson Falls Boulder GPS Coordinates: 44º24.340'N 75º04.232'W
Accessibility: 0.4-mile walk
Degree of Difficulty: Moderately easy

BOULDERS BEYOND BELIEF

Description: Gumdrop Boulder (a name given to the rock by my wife) is 12 feet high and shaped like...well...a gumdrop.

Gumdrop Rock overlooks Lampson Falls—a 30-foot high, two-tiered, broad waterfall that is one of the Adirondack's most heavily visited.

Gumdrop Boulder overlooks Lampson Falls.

Directions: From the junction of Tooley Pond Road and Clare Road/Route 27, drive north on Clare Road/Route 27 for 3.9 miles and pull into the parking area for Lampson Falls on your left.

The hike to Lampson Falls follows an old road and is flat enough and free of obstacles to allow wheelchair access. Near the end of the road, a trail to the left descends via a wood-lined, zig-zagging walkway that leads to an overlook of the falls. Along the way, Gumdrop Boulder is passed, on your right.

Resources: Scott A. Ensminger, David J. Schryver, & Edward M. Smathers, *Waterfalls of New York* (Buffalo, NY: Firefly Books Ltd., 2012), 206 & 207.
Phil Brown, "Lampson Falls," *Adirondack Explorer* Vol. 2, no. 8 (May 2000), 37.
Paul Jamieson, "Lampson Falls," *Adirondack Life* (March/April 1980), 10.
Barbara McMartin & Bill Ingersoll, with Lee M. Brenning, William P. Ehling & Peter O'Shea, *Discover the Northwestern Adirondacks* (Canada Lake, NY: Lake View Press, 1990), 209.

57. REUBEN WOOD ROCK
Cranberry Lake

Type of Formation: Medium-sized Boulder
WOW Factor: 1–2
Location: Cranberry Lake (St. Lawrence County)
Tenth Edition, NYS Atlas & Gazetteer: p. 28, C1; **Earlier Edition NYS Atlas & Gazetteer**: p. 94, C2
Parking GPS Coordinates: 44º13.227'N 74º50.741'W
Reuben Wood Rock GPS Coordinates: 44º09.261'N 74º47.858'W
Accessibility: ~5.5-mile trek by water
Degree of Difficulty: Easy-moderately difficult depending upon whether your boat is motorized

Description: Reuben Wood Rock is a medium-sized boulder, ~5–6 feet in height (above the water?), which rests partially in water at the shoreline.

History: The boulder is named after Reuben Wood, a world champion fly caster who lived from 1822 to 1888. In 1895, his friends had the following inscription chiseled into the boulder: "In memory of Reuben Wood, a genial gentleman and great fisherman who was fond of these solitudes."

The Cranberry Lake Biological Station is located nearby on Barber Point.

Cranberry Lake was named for an extensive cranberry bog that flourished when the lake was much smaller in size. The lake's size changed dramatically after 1865 when the first log crib dam was built next to today's launch site, effectively doubling the lake's surface area.

BOULDERS BEYOND BELIEF

Slightly farther south at the mouth of Chair Rock Creek is tiny *Chair Rock Island* which, according to Barbara McMartin, Bill Ingersoll, etc., in *Discover the Northwestern Adirondacks*, was "...named for a rock formation..." on the island.

REUBEN WOOD ROCK
CRANBERRY LAKE

Directions: From Sevey Corners (junction of Routes 3 & 56), drive southwest on Route 3 for ~9.5 miles. As soon as you cross over the Oswegatchie River, turn left onto Columbian Road and head east for over 0.3 mile. Then turn left into the boat launch area located next to the Cranberry Lake Hydro-dam at the northwest end of the lake. The parking area can accommodate up to 55 cars and trailers.

From the launch site, paddle east and then southeast, passing by the east side of Joe Indian Island (named after an Ogdensburg barrister named Joe Naughton who camped on the island) and then, from Buck Island, east toward the Cranberry Lake Biological Station. The rock is near the mouth of Sucker Brook in a cove just southeast of Buck Island.

Resources: Susan Thomas Smeby, *Cranberry Lake and Wanakena. Postcard Historical Series* (Charleston, SC: Arcadia Press, 2008). A photograph of the rock can be seen on page 55.

BOULDERS BEYOND BELIEF

Phil Brown (editor), *Bob Marshall in the Adirondacks* (Saranac Lake, NY: Lost Pond Press, 2006). A photograph of Reuben Wood Rock at the mouth of Sucker Brook is shown on page 167.
en.wikipedia.org/wiki/Cranberry_Lake -- "A large rock on Barber Point near the Biological Station bears an engraved memorial for international fly casting champion of the late 1800s, Reuben Wood, designer of the Reub Wood fishing flies."
Donald G. Pasko, "Cranberry Lake: A New Role for a One-Time Famous Brook Trout Water," *The Conservationist* (June-July, 1961), 16–18.
Barbara McMartin & Bill Ingersoll, with Lee M. Brenning, William P. Ehling & Peter O'Shea, *Discover the Northwestern Adirondacks* (Canada Lake, NY: Lake View Press, 1990), 173.
Albert Vann Fowler (editor), *Cranberry Lake 1845–1959: An Adirondack Miscellany* (Blue Mountain Lake, NY: Adirondack Museum, 1959), 33–44. For those interested in knowing more about Wood, "A summer vacation with Reuben Wood" is recounted.
Kelsie B. Harder & Mary H. Smallman (editors*), Claims to Name: Toponyms of St. Lawrence County* (Utica, NY: North Country Books, Inc., 1992), 39 & 127.
Paul Jamieson & Donald Morris, *Adirondack Canoe Waters: North Flow. Third Edition* (Glens Falls, NY: The Adirondack Mountain Club, Inc., 1988), 31–35.

58. STONER'S CAVE
Cranberry Lake

Type of Formation: Shelter Cave
WOW Factor: 5
Location: Cranberry Lake (St. Lawrence County)
Tenth Edition, NYS Atlas & Gazetteer: p. 28, C1; **Earlier Edition NYS Atlas & Gazetteer**: p. 94, C2
Boat Launch GPS Coordinates: 44º13.227'N 74º50.741'W
Estimated Stoner's Cave GPS Coordinates: 44º09.564'N 74º45.710'W
Accessibility: 6.0-mile paddle; 1.0-mile hike
Degree of Difficulty: Difficult
Additional Information: Trail map -- tupperlake.com/hiking/sucker-brook-road-curtis-pond

Description: Stoner's Cave, aka Willy's Cave, is formed by a massive boulder that rests against another rock. In *Cave for Kids in Historic New York*, Patricia Edwards Clyne writes, "This shelter, now known as Stoner's Cave, was formed by the tip of one massive boulder being tilted into position on top of another by glacial action." A photograph of the cave suggests that the opening is at least 10 feet high.

History: The cave is named after Nick Stoner, the famous frontiersman and Indian fighter who lived in the Canada Lake region and whose exploits are well documented. It is alleged that Stoner hid out in this cave in order to evade a pursuing war party.

In the *Adirondack Life 2011 Annual Guide to the Great Outdoors*, Neal Burdick writes, "Those souvenirs of the last Ice Age [glacial erratics] reach epic proportions out here. A garden of them between Curtis Pond and East Inlet is littered with specimens that suggest the prow of a ship. A couple even have names: there's 'Sleeping Turtle' and house-size 'Willy's Cave.' Nineteenth-century backwoodsman Nick Stoner is said to have lived in the latter for half a year."

Today, the cave is still favored, only now by hikers.

Directions: See directions given for Reuben Wood Rock to reach the Cranberry Lake launch site.

From the launch site, paddle south for over 3.5 miles to reach Joe Indian Island. Turn left here, and head straight east for another 2.5 miles into the southeast end of East Inlet, where a large shoreline boulder can be seen [Estimated GPS Coordinates: 44º10.039′N 74º46.351′W].

From the large boulder, follow a trail, heading southeast that leads to Curtis Pond in less than 1.0 mile. The cave is found near the trail, approximately 150 feet from the pond.

Resources: Patricia Edwards Clyne, *Cave for Kids in Historic New York* (Monroe, NY: Library Research Associates, 1980), 143–151. A photograph of the cave can be seen on page 144.
tupperlake.com/hiking/sucker-brook-road-curtis-pond.
Barbara McMartin & Bill Ingersoll, *Discover the Northwest Adirondacks* (Canada Lake, NY: Lake View Press, 1990), 147.
Neal Burdick, *Adirondack Life 2011 Annual Guide to the Great Outdoors* (Vol. XLII, no.4), 20. This article can also be viewed at blog site adirondacklifemag.com/blogs/2014/07/24/cranberry-50/#x.

BOULDERS BEYOND BELIEF

59. BEAR MOUNTAIN BOULDERS
Cranberry Lake

Type of Formation: Large Boulder
WOW Factor: 5
Location: Cranberry Lake (St. Lawrence County)
Tenth Edition, NYS Atlas & Gazetteer: p. 28, C2; **Earlier Edition NYS Atlas & Gazetteer**: p. 94, C2
Estimated Parking GPS Coordinates: 44º12.295'N 74º49.572'W
Estimated Summit GPS Coordinates: 44º11.748'N 74º48.739'W
Fee: Day-use fee to enter campground
Accessibility: 1.2-mile hike
Degree of Difficulty: Moderate
Additional Information: Cranberry Lake Campground & Day Use Area, 243 Lone Pine Road, Cranberry Lake, NY 12927; (315) 848-2315; Open May 19th – October 9th.

Photograph of Bear Mountain Boulder from tupperlake.comhikingbear-mountain.

BOULDERS BEYOND BELIEF

Description: Rose Rivezzi & David Trithart, in *Kids on the Trails! Hiking with children in the Adirondacks*, write, "Two large boulders offer scrambling and photo opportunities, but no views. Behind and beneath the boulder on the right (west) side is a bivouac site. As with much Adirondack rock, these boulders are rough, with interesting banding." The boulders are 12–15 feet high.

History: The Cranberry Lake Campground began in 1935 when the Civilian Conservation Corps (CCC) erected fifteen campsites. Expansions were made in the 1960s and 1970s. The campground now contains 173 campsites.

Cranberry Lake doubled its size in 1867 when a log crib dam was built at the village end of the lake. The present concrete dam was erected in 1916.

Directions: From just east of the hamlet of Cranberry Lake on Route 3, drive south on Lone Pine Road for ~1.5 miles and park near camp #27 or at whatever new area has been created for day hikers. A kiosk and trail register are right at the parking area. Be sure to pick up a map at the gate which will give you specific directions on how to get to the nearby trailhead.

Follow the red-blazed Bear Mountain Trail southeast for 1.2 miles to reach the boulders.

Resources: Rose Rivezzi & David Trithart, *Kids on the Trails! Hiking with children in the Adirondacks* (Lake George, NY: Adirondack Mountain Club, 1997), 70.
alltrails.com/trail/us/new-york/bear-mountain-trail-from-cranberry-lake-campground.
tupperlake.com/hiking/bear-mountain – This website shows a photograph of a hiker making his way up one of the boulders.
hikingthetrailtoyesterday.wordpress.com/2018/03/21/bear-mountain-at-cranberry-lake – This site includes a fair amount of history of the area.
Barbara McMartin & Bill Ingersoll, with Lee M. Brenning, William P. Ehling & Peter O'Shea, *Discover the Northwestern Adirondacks* (Canada Lake, NY: Lake View Press, 1990), 143.
dec.ny.gov/outdoor/24460.html.

BOULDERS BEYOND BELIEF

60. RANGER SCHOOL TRAIL BOULDER

Type of Formation: Large Boulder
WOW Factor: 5
Location: Wanakena (St. Lawrence County)
Tenth Edition, NYS Atlas & Gazetteer: p. 27, CD10; **Earlier Edition NYS Atlas & Gazetteer**: p. 94, C1
Parking GPS Coordinates: 44º09.394'N 74º55.442'W
Estimated Large Rock GPS Coordinates: Not determined
Accessibility: *Large Boulder* – 1.2 miles
Degree of Difficulty: Moderate
Additional Information: cnyhiking.com/CathedralRock.htm – trail map.

Description: *Boulder* – This hulking boulder lies next to the trail/road. It has been described as a large glacial erratic.
   Cathedral Rock is described by Barbara McMartin, Bill Ingersoll, & etc. in *Discover the Northwestern Adirondacks*, as "...an imposing cliff that forms a natural amphitheater with huge angular towers of rock strewn around the bottom of the bowl." I have not been to it.

History: The sign at the gated barrier along Route 3 states "These lands are managed by the SUNY College of Environmental Science and Forestry (ESF) for forestry and scientific research."

BOULDERS BEYOND BELIEF

The fire tower on Cathedral Rock was originally on Tooley Pond Mountain and brought to its present location in 1970.

Directions: From Sevey Corners (junction of Routes 3 & 56), drive southwest on Route 3 for ~15.6 miles and park on your left next to a gated barrier, approximately 0.6 mile before Wanakena Road/Route 61 at Wanakena.

Proceeding on foot, head southeast for 0.2 mile. At a junction, bear right and follow the road/trail for another 1.0 mile to reach a large glacial erratic on your left.

If you continue following the road/trail, you will eventually come to the Latham Trail which, if taken, will lead up to the fire tower on top of Cathedral Rock (a large buttress of rock).

Resources: Barbara McMartin & Bill Ingersoll, with Lee M. Brenning, William P. Ehling & Peter O'Shea, *Discover the Northwestern Adirondacks* (Canada Lake, NY: Lake View Press, 1990), 136.
Susan Thomas Smeby, *Cranberry Lake and Wanakena. Postcard Historical Series* (Charleston, SC: Arcadia Press, 2008). On page 123 is a photograph of Cathedral Rock.
cnyhiking.com/CathedralRock.htm.
John P. Freeman with Wesley H. Haynes, *Views from on High: Fire Towers in the Adirondacks and Catskills* (Lake George, NY: Adirondack Mountain Club, Inc., 2001). Pages 60–62 deal with Cathedral Rock, with a nice map of the area on page 61.
hikingthetrailtoyesterday.wordpress.com/2017/12/05/cathedral-rock-fire-tower.

61. HAYSTACK ROCK

Type of Formation: Large Boulder
WOW Factor: 6–7
Location: Stark (St. Lawrence County)
Tenth Edition, NYS Atlas & Gazetteer: p. 28, A2; **Earlier Edition NYS Atlas & Gazetteer**: p. 94, A2–3
Haystack Rock GPS Coordinates: 44º24.329′N 74º45.976′W
Accessibility: Roadside
Degree of Difficulty: Easy

BOULDERS BEYOND BELIEF

Description: Haystack Rock, aka College Rock, is a large, 20-foot-high boulder with an enormous base that looms invitingly by roadside, its triangular shape further enhanced by colorful graffiti that has (unfortunately) accumulated on virtually all of its surfaces except for the backside where nothing can be seen anyway from roadside.

Haystack Rock as it looked in the early 2000s.

For a brief period of time, Haystack Rock showed its patriotic side when a large American Flag was painted on the rock, covering up the underlying graffiti, at least momentarily. Sometime in the 1970s, the name Haystack Rock was painted on the boulder, which is how the rock is known today.

BOULDERS BEYOND BELIEF

Haystack Rock is part of a corridor of glacial debris that has been scattered over a length of 0.1 mile next to Route 3. A number of 8–10-footers can be seen, but many are in the woods where the land is posted.

History: According to the Colton Historical Society in *Colton, New York: Story of a Town, II*, "…the Indians used its distinctive shape and size as a landmark to guide them to the series of cold, boiling springs near which they camped. History tells us that Indian council fires burned beside it." Furthermore, "When the white man came, he too, used its 20 feet height and its shape, so much like a haystack, to orient himself…."

As a point of interest, the biggest Haystack Rock in North America, considered by some to be the third tallest intertidal structure in the world, is a 235-foot-high sea stack at Cannon Beach, Oregon [45º53.066'N 123º58.102'W].

Directions: From Sevey Corners (junction of Routes 56 & 3), drive north on Route 56 for ~9.0 miles. Haystack Rock is on the right side of the road, partitioned off by guardrails.

Additional Site –

Roughly 1.4 miles north of Haystack Rock, looming large on the east side of Route 3 near Cold Pond, is a large mound of rock (not a boulder) that is very distinctive looking [44º25.354'N 74º46.747'W], and well worth an appreciative glance as you drive by.

Resources: Colton Historical Society, *Colton, New York: Story of a Town, II* (Baltimore, MD: Gateway Press, Inc., 1993), 157 & 158. A photograph of the rock can be seen on page 157.
Kelsie B. Harder & Mary H. Smallman (editors), *Claims to Name: Toponyms of St. Lawrence County* (Utica, NY: North Country Books, Inc., 1992), 106.
John Vesty, *Adirondack Treks: Placers and People in the Adirondacks* (Indian Lake, NY: Crossroads Publication, 1990). A photograph of Haystack Rock appears on page 241.

BOULDERS BEYOND BELIEF

62. SUNDAY ROCK

Type of Formation: Large Boulder; Historic Rock
WOW Factor: 5
Location: South Colton (St. Lawrence County)
Tenth Edition, NYS Atlas & Gazetteer: p. 20, D1; **Earlier Edition NYS Atlas & Gazetteer**: p. 100, D1
Sunday Rock GPS Coordinates: 44º30.589'N 74º53.651'W
Accessibility: Roadside
Degree of Difficulty: Easy

Description: Sunday rock, aka Big Rock, is an 11-foot-high, 64,000-pound, rectangular-shaped boulder that has served as a local landmark for centuries. According to legend, the boulder once marked the boundary between civilization and wilderness.

A plaque reads "Sunday Rock/ Preserved by/ The Sunday Rock Association/ 1925." This was the year that the rock was scheduled to be destroyed by highway engineers who needed to widened and straightened out Route 56. At that time, the rock sat directly in the middle of the road, and really posed a nuisance. In the end, however, the engineers were redirected in their efforts by the Sunday Rock Association, a group of fervent individuals who rose up to save the rock by insisting that it be relocated despite the additional costs involved.

Nevertheless, even after it was relocated, the rock still was not out of the woods, so to speak. For a second time, Sunday Rock had to be relocated due to further modernization of Route 56.

BOULDERS BEYOND BELIEF

Sunday Rock has been at its present location since 1965, and it would appear that this is the rock's final resting place. The location is ideal for the rock—close to the road for maximum visibility, with bucolic farmlands in the background.

Sunday Rock as viewed on a Saturday.

History: In 1941 the boulder appeared in Ripley's *Believe or Not*, its amazing story recounted for what would prove to be not the last time.

In 2010, the boulder was added to the National Register of Historic Places through the efforts of Sally Thomas, a longtime member of the Adirondack Mountain Club. A new sign was added that reads, "Welcome to Sunday Rock. An Adirondack Landmark and Legend. This glacial boulder, twice preserved by local citizens, marks the gateway to the 'Great South Woods.' In the frontier days it was said there was no law or no Sunday beyond this point. May all who pass this way continue to enjoy the beauty of the mountains."

BOULDERS BEYOND BELIEF

Directions: From Colton (junction of Routes 56 & 68), drive southeast on Route 56 for ~3.7 miles. Look for Sunday Rock on your right.

From the center of South Colton (junction of Route 56 & Windmill Road), drive west on Route 56 for over 0.3 mile and turn left into the parking area for the boulder

BELIEVE IT OR NOT By Ripley

HOW MUCH IS A PIECE ? Answer Tomorrow

SUNDAY ROCK
South Colton, N.Y.
SO NAMED BY A HARD WORKING LUMBERMAN WHO MAINTAINED THAT BEYOND THIS ROCK — ALL DAYS WERE THE SAME – NO SUNDAYS!

Resources: Lisa Crosby Metzger, "Rock's Role Recognized," *Adirondac* Vol. LXXV, no. 6 (November-December 2011), 26 & 27.
Flora Smith Miller, "Sunday Rock," *North Country Life* Vol. 7, no. 4 (Fall 1953), 31–33. A photograph of the rock is on page 31.
Christopher Angus, *Reflections from Canoe Country: Paddling the Waters of the Adirondacks and Canada* (Syracuse, NY: Syracuse University Press, 1997), 3.
sundayrock.com.
Lawrence P. Gooley – adirondackalmanack.com/2016/11/sunday-rock-a-historic-adirondack-landmark-part-1.html.
Lawrence P. Gooley -- adirondackalmanack.com/2016/12/sunday-rock-historic-adirondack-landmark-conclusion.html.
Paul Jamieson, *Adirondack Pilgrimage* (Glens Falls, NY: Adirondack Mountain Club, Inc., 1986), 218.
Colton Historical Society, *Colton, New York: Story of a Town, II* (Baltimore, MD: Gateway Press, Inc., 1993), 155–157. A photograph of the rock is shown on page 126, surrounded by a group of people.

BOULDERS BEYOND BELIEF

Susan Omohundro, "Sunday Rock," *The St. Lawrence County Historical Society Quarterly* (Vol. LVI, no. 1, 2001), 22 & 23. Photographs of Sunday Rock, both at its original location and at its final location, are shown.
"South of Sunday Rock," *The St. Lawrence County Historical Society Quarterly* Vol. LIV, no. 2, (2009). A photograph of the rock taken by Louise A. Bixby is shown on page 4.
The St. Lawrence County Historical Society Quarterly (Vol. XXXIII, no. 4, October, 1978). On page 50 is a photograph of the rock taken by Dwight Church.
northcountryfolklore.org/rvsp/index.php?id=129.
Kelsie B. Harder & Mary H. Smallman (editors), *Claims to Name: Toponyms of St. Lawrence County* (Utica, NY: North Country Books, Inc., 1992), 232.
Bruce Wadsworth, *Day Hikes For All Seasons: An Adirondack Sampler* (Lake George, NY: Adirondack Mountain Club, 1996), 99 & 100.

63. THE PINNACLE
Santa Clara Conservation Easement Tract

Type of Formation: Large Boulder
WOW Factor: 5–6
Location: Santa Clara (Franklin County)
Tenth Edition, NYS Atlas & Gazetteer: p. 21, C6; **Earlier Edition NYS Atlas & Gazetteer**: p. 101, CD5
Parking GPS Coordinates: 44º38.953'N 74º26.949'W
Boulder GPS Coordinates: Not determined
Summit GPS Coordinates: 44º39.181'N 74º27.119'W
Accessibility: 0.7-mile hike to summit
Degree of Difficulty: Moderate; 325-foot ascent to summit
Additional Information:
Map of the Santa Clara Conservation Easement Tract – dec.ny.gov/docs/lands_forests_pdf/mapsantaclara.pdf.

Description: One blog writer has stated that "interesting boulders" are to be found on the way up to the summit of The Pinnacle. In an article by Diane Chase, large boulders are mentioned.

Neal Burdick, in "Travels with Charlie," which appeared in the *Adirondack Explorer* writes, "We pass through gardens of glacial erratics, immense boulders deposited by glaciers more than ten thousand years ago."

BOULDERS BEYOND BELIEF

Unfortunately, on the day of my visit, a yellow barrier prevented me from driving to the trailhead, and I found myself unwilling to add on an additional 3.4 miles of monotonous hiking time to my day.

In hindsight, it would have been useful if I had brought along a mountain bike as back-up, just for this kind of occasion.

Pinnacle Road was closed on the day of my visit.

History: The Pinnacle (1,840′) is part of the 72,000-acre Santa Clara Conservation Easement Tract.

Directions: From southwest of Meacham Lake (junction of Routes 458 & 30), drive northwest on Route 458 for ~9.5 miles (or 0.5 mile before reaching the St. Regis River). Turn right at a brown ADK sign for The Pinnacle (44°38.028′N 74°26.329′W), and drive through an open yellow barrier (hopefully, it will be unlocked). Head north on Pinnacle Road (a dirt road) for 1.1 miles. At a fork, bear left at a second yellow gate, and proceed northwest for 0.7 mile. Park to your left in a small area, opposite the trailhead.

From here, follow a faint path opposite the parking area that leads to the summit of The Pinnacle in under 0.7 miles. Along the way, large boulders will be encountered.

Resources: adirondackhikes.blogspot.com/2012/09/the-pinnacle-santa-clara-ny.html – "interesting boulders" are mentioned.
visitadirondacks.com/hiking/the-pinnacle.
adirondackdailyenterprise.com/news/weekender-a-e/2017/08/easy-hikes-santa-claras-the-pinnacle-makes-the-grade – The article by Diane Chase appeared in the May, 08, 2018 issue of the *Adirondack Daily Enterprise*. Large boulders are mentioned along the hike.
Neal Burdick, "Travels with Charlie," *Adirondack Explorer* (May/June 2013), 12.

64. AZURE MOUNTAIN BALANCED ROCK

Type of Formation: Talus Block; Balanced Rock
WOW Factor: *Talus Blocks* – 4–5; *Balanced Rock* – 8
Location: Santa Clara (Franklin County)
Tenth Edition, NYS Atlas & Gazetteer: p. 21, D6; **Earlier Edition NYS Atlas & Gazetteer**: p. 101, D5
Parking GPS Coordinates: 44º32.272′N 74º29.134′W
Destination GPS Coordinates: *Talus Rocks* -- 44º32.480′N 74º29.739′W; *Perched Rock* -- 44º32.455′N 74º30.124′W
Accessibility: *Talus Blocks* – ~0.6 mile; *Balanced Rock* -- 1.0-mile hike; 950-foot ascent
Degree of Difficulty: Moderate

Description: *Balanced Rock* -- The Balanced Rock atop Azure Mountain is 8–9 feet high, and fairly round, much like a big ball of stone. At first glance, the boulder appears to be perched on top of the bedrock. However, if you take a closer look from the opposite side of the boulder, you will see that the rock is actually balanced on the edge of the underlying bedrock, overhanging it by 3 feet. This is truly a balanced rock! Furthermore, the boulder is but a scant 15 feet from the edge of a precipice, making its position seem all the more precarious.

In *A Century Wild (1885–1985): Essays Commemorating the Centennial of the Adirondack Forest Preserve*, Neal Burdick describes the rock in mythic terms

BOULDERS BEYOND BELIEF

when he calls it a "mysterious monolith perched there like a gargoyle high on a Gothic spire."

Azure Mountain Boulder.

Bruce Wadsworth, in *Day Hikes For All Seasons: An Adirondack Sampler*, philosophizes that "The huge boulder on the edge of the drop-off on the west side of the open rock is another of nature's mysteries. Why did the glaciers of the last ice age choose that spot to leave such a giant rock? Perhaps it is to remind us of the great powers of their forces."

In Martin Podskoch'a *Adirondack Fire Towers: Their History and Lore. The Northern District*, Albert LaGray (an old timer from the early 1900s) is quoted as saying "On top of the mountain, there was a very large egg-shaped stone and offers were made that anyone who could push it over with their bare hands would get $100." Thankfully, no one collected on this bet!

BOULDERS BEYOND BELIEF

Talus Rocks – According to a blog by Jeremy Evans, "... a small cliff and collection of boulders that looked like a lot of fun to explore" are found on the way up the mountain. In the March-April 2008 issue of *Adirondac*, Neal Burdick concurs, writing, "A little past the midway point, 'caves' on the right are fun to explore. These are not true caves, but the result of the jumbling of immense glacial erratics ("boulders,' to be less pedantic) transported here from several hundred miles north during the last Ice Age."

A number of blocks of talus lay at the bottom of this mid-level escarpment. The main block, closest to the trail, is 10 feet high. There is a passageway of sorts, and basically two levels to explore. It is a good spot for kids to stop and recharge.

Blocks of talus are fun to explore.

History: The balanced rock as well as the collection of talus rock are located on 2,518-foot-high Azure "Blue" Mountain. The peak was named Azure Mountain by Verplanck Colvin in 1883. Some locals, however, still call it "Blue."

The 35-foot-high fire tower was erected in 1918 and restored in 2002. From it, you can see as far north as Ontario, and as far south as the Great Range on a clear day.

The parking area occupies part of the former golf course for the Blue Mountain House—a rural hotel that vanished nearly a century ago. The mountain house was built in the 1870s by C. B. Merrill, and burned down in 1932.

Directions: From north of Paul Smiths (junction of Routes 458 & 30), drive northwest on Route 458 for ~13.0 miles (or 2.9 miles west past the St. Regis River), passing through Santa Clara in the process. Turn left onto Blue

BOULDERS BEYOND BELIEF

Mountain Road and head south for ~7.0 miles (the road starts paved and then becomes packed dirt). Turn right into a dirt road that leads in a few dozen yards to a small parking area.

For a more challenging drive from Paul Smith's, head west on Keese Mills Road for ~6.5 miles, and then bear right onto Blue Mountain Road and proceed north for ~10 miles. Along the way, you will pass by a DEC put-in site for Quebec Brook. Take note that a huge part of this section of Blue Mountain Road is seasonal, but drivable (I did it in a regular car). This route, however, may not be for everyone even though it is very scenic. You are heading through some very remote wilderness, and traveling at roughly 30 mph.

At ~16.5 miles, turn left into the parking area for Azure Mountain.

From the parking area, follow a 1.0-mile-long trail up to the summit of Azure Mountain. The first 0.3 mile of the hike is a gentle walk along an old road to the base of the mountain. From this point to the summit, the climb is steadily uphill.

Over halfway along the hike you will pass by a grouping of talus blocks to your right at the base of an escarpment. A short path leads up to the rocks.

Boulders along Blue Mountain Road.

When you reach the fire tower, turn left and head south, walking down a giant stairway to the brink of a towering cliff. Turn right here and follow the edge of the cliff west until you reach the balanced rock, roughly 0.1-mile from the fire tower.

Additional Site –

As you drive along Blue Mountain Road, you will pass by a grouping of boulders on the west side of the road, roughly 5.0 miles from Route 458, and 1.9 miles before you reach the parking area for Azure Mountain. The boulders are in the 10–15-foot range and are tightly packed along the side of a tiny hill. The GPS reading here is 44°33.834'N 74°28.902'W.

BOULDERS BEYOND BELIEF

Resources: cnyhiking.com/AzureMountain.htm.
azuremountain.org/towerrock.htm.
Neal S. Burdick (editor), *A Century Wild (1885–1985): Essays Commemorating the Centennial of the Adirondack Forest Preserve* (Saranac Lake, NY: The Chauncy Press, 1985).
azuremountain.org.
Bruce Wadsworth, *Day Hikes For All Seasons: An Adirondack Sampler* (Lake George, NY: Adirondack Mountain Club, 1996), 113 & 114.
saranaclake.com/blog/2017/10/azure-mountain-adventure – article submitted by Jeremy Evans, guest blogger.
John Freeman with Wesley H. Haynes, *Views from on High: Fire Tower Trails in the Adirondacks and Catskills* (Lake George, NY: Adirondack Mountain Club, Inc., 2001), 46.
Norm Landis & Bradly A. Pendergraft, *Adirondack Mountain Club Western Trails. First Edition* (Lake George, NY: Adirondack Mountain Club, Inc., 2016), 195. "A walk west along the top of the cliffs on the south side of the summit leads to an impressive glacial erratic perched on the verge of the precipice."
Neal Burdick, "Little Mountain with a Big View," *Adirondac* Vol. 82, no. 3 (March-April, 2018), 15.
Martin Podskoch, *Adirondack Fire Towers: Their History and Lore. The Northern District* (Fleischmanns, NY: Purple Mountain Press, 2005). Page 53 contains extensive history on the mountain.

65. JUMBO ROCK
Lake Ozonia

Type of Formation: Large Boulder
WOW Factor: Not determined
Location: Lake Ozonia (St. Lawrence County)
Tenth Edition, NYS Atlas & Gazetteer: p. 20, C4; **Earlier Edition NYS Atlas & Gazetteer**: p. 100, D4
Parking GPS Coordinates: 44º36.240'N 74º37.497'W
Destination GPS Coordinates: *Jumbo Rock #1* -- 44º35.760'N 74º36.588'W; *Jumbo Rock #2* -- 44º35.142'N 74º35.630'W
Accessibility: *Jumbo Rock #1* – 1.0-mile trek by water; *Jumbo Rock #2* -- 2.0-mile trek by water
Degree of Difficulty: Moderately easy
Additional Information: 10 horsepower restriction on outboard motor boats.
    dec.ny.gov/docs/fish_marine_pdf/lkozomap.pdf -- Map of Lake Ozonia.

BOULDERS BEYOND BELIEF

Description: In *Claims to Name: Toponyms of St. Lawrence County*, Kelsie B. Harder & Mary H. Smallman mention a Jumbo Rock at 405-acre Lake Ozonia, but give no details about it. I have decided upon two possible candidates for the rock, making the fragile assumption that Jumbo Rock is on or by the lake and can be seen using Google Earth. Needless to say, should this assumption prove wrong and Jumbo Rock is actually slightly inland from the lake, then all bets are off.

Jumbo Rock #1 looks like the better prospect of the two. Here, several sizeable boulders are grouped together, one of which looks like a split rock.

Jumbo Rock #2 is a stand-alone boulder lying in shallow water, its size difficult to determine using Google Earth.

A *Split Rock* is also located at the lake and may be what I identified as Jumbo Rock #1. In her article entitled "How Lake Ozonia suddenly acquired a 'Recluse': George Everett and his canoe paddles," Virginia Duffy McLaughlin writes "The deer plunged into the water and swam across to a sandy beach near Split Rock."

History: According to Kelsie Harder & Mary H. Smallman, in *Claims to Name: Toponyms of St. Lawrence County*, Ozonia—the name of the lake— means "...clear, invigorating air, commendatory for places where the air was thought to be good for breathing." This is substantiated by Edgar G. Blankman in *Geography of St. Lawrence County* when he writes that "A visit to this lovely spot, where one can breathe that intense form of oxygen known as ozone, which every countless leaf gives forth, will convince anyone why this lake is called Ozonia."

In the January 1974 issue of *The Quarterly*, published by The St. Lawrence County Historical Society, Mrs. Mollie McEwen writes in her memoirs, "There was a legend in connection with this gold mining which was that a group of Spiritualists gathered around Jumbo Rock and during the séance they were told to dig on the hill down at the right of the outlet and they would find gold." It must have been quite a sight watching the Spiritualists walk away from Jumbo Rock with their divining rods to prospect for gold.

Earlier, Lake Ozonia was known as Trout Lake.

Directions: From Hopkinton (junction of Routes 72 & 11B), drive southwest on Route 72 for 0.1 mile. Turn left onto Lake Ozonia Road and proceed

BOULDERS BEYOND BELIEF

southeast for ~7.8 miles. Then turn right onto Old Road and head south for ~0.1 mile to the DEC boat launch.

Jumbo Rock #1 -- From the boat launch, proceed southeast for ~1.0 mile. The grouping of rocks is located on a point of land jutting out from the mainland.

Jumbo Rock #2 – From the boat launch, proceed southeast for ~2.0 miles. Look for a rock located in the water near the shore along the west side of the lake.

Additional Site –

In the October 1974 issue of *The Quarterly*, an early 1900 photograph of a balanced rock near Lake Ozonia in Hopkinton is shown. I can find no current record of it and it may very well have been destroyed by lumbermen in the 1930s.

Resources: Kelsie B. Harder & Mary H. Smallman (editors), *Claims to Name: Toponyms of St. Lawrence County* (Utica, NY: North Country Books, Inc., 1992), 125 & 126.
Edgar G. Blankman, *Geography of St. Lawrence County* (Canton, NY: Plaindealer Presses, 1896), 120.
The Quarterly Vol. XIX, no. 1 (January 1974), 6.
Virginia Duffy McLoughlin, "How Lake Ozonia suddenly acquired a 'Recluse': George Everett and his canoe paddles," *The Quarterly* Vol. XXV, no. 3 (July 1980), 5. McLoughlin goes on to tell a story that seems unbelievable. Everett, upon seeing the deer, "leaped astride its back and managed to get hold of each of its front legs which he pulled up on both sides of the deer's body." Everett then wrestled the deer down while another man fetched his rifle and shot it. That all took place, allegedly, by Split Rock.

BOULDERS BEYOND BELIEF

66. CROGHAN ROCK

Type of Formation: Large Boulder
WOW Factor: 4
Location: Croghan (Lewis County)
Tenth Edition, NYS Atlas & Gazetteer: p. 34, B5; **Earlier Edition NYS Atlas & Gazetteer**: p. 85, AB4–5
Groghan Rock GPS Coordinates: 43º52.907'N 75º23.369'W
Accessibility: Roadside
Degree of Difficulty: Easy

Croghan Rock stands ready to greet incoming drivers.

Description: The Croghan Rock is a massive boulder accompanied by a large "CROGHAN" sign to announce that you are entering the village of Croghan.

History: The town and, by association, the rock, were named after George Croghan, a hero in the War of 1812.

Directions: From Croghan (junction of Route 812 & 126), drive south on Route 812 for ~0.7 mile. Look for the boulder, which will be on your left.

There is probably no reason to go out of your way to visit this rock, but if you are traveling on Route 812 anyhow, it is a must-see!

BOULDERS BEYOND BELIEF

67. NATURAL BRIDGE CAVERNS (Historic)

Type of Formation: Natural Bridge
WOW Factor: 6–7 (when the commercial attraction was in operation)
Location: Natural Bridge (Jefferson County)
Tenth Edition, NYS Atlas & Gazetteer: p. 26, E4; **Earlier Edition NYS Atlas & Gazetteer**: p. 92, D4
Natural Bridge Caverns GPS Coordinates: 44º04.224'N 75º29.602'W
Accessibility: On private property

Description: Natural Bridge is both the name of the hamlet as well as its former commercial attraction, Natural Bridge Caverns.

During the cavern's commercial days, tourists would climb into a small boat and be taken on a 1,200-foot-long trip, part of which was underground. According to John Mylrole in his article, "The Natural Bridge Cave System" that appeared in the *Northeastern Caver*, "Natural Bridge Cave is basically a wide, low oval tube with occasional enlargement and tube development along a fracture plane.... The passage averages 35 feet wide and 6 feet high for its 700 feet of main trend...The cave trends west from the entrance as a large passage 50 feet wide and 10 feet high."

Clay Perry, in *Underground Empire: Wonders and Tales of New York Caves*, writes that the cave "...forms a natural tunnel that provides an underground boat ride of about 600 feet. It is owned and promoted by a garage man whose place of business is nearby. You have to duck, for it is a 'low bridge' in places..."

Tourists taking the boat ride would frequently see debris clinging to the sidewalls all the way up to the ceiling. This was the result of spring freshets, when the cavern would flood up to the ceiling, with the excess flow then carried down the north channel of the Indian River. To be sure, no boat rides made it through during times when the cavern was flooded.

In "Joseph and the Hermits," the author of a website called *Finger Lynk* writes that the cavern tour "...takes people a hundred yards or so in a poled boat. You climb out at a sinkhole beach on the other side of the road."

The cave is formed out of Precambrian Grenville marble.

BOULDERS BEYOND BELIEF

History: Natural Bridge was created by the Indian River many millenniums ago and "discovered" in 1812 by a hunter named Aleasar Carr.

Boating through Natural Bridge Caverns. Postcard c. 1960.

Joseph Bonaparte, King of Spain, purchased land by the natural bridge in 1818, and is said to have built his frame mansion, which Joseph M. St. Amand in *Tales of Jayville New York and the North County* describes as "a pretentious summer camp," directly over or near the cavern so that he would have a means of escape should the occasion arise.

I have learned bits and pieces about the cave's ownership. Joseph (Moe) Morgan brought the cavern in 1963 from a developer named Walter Blanchard. Before Moe died, he turned the business over to his son, David. Then, after David died, the business was taken over by his sister, Cheri Murphy and her husband, Michael. I don't know when the business closed.

Directions: From Natural Bridge (junction of Routes 3 & 41), drive east on Route 3 for 0.3 mile and turn left onto Lime Street (the name of the street makes sense if you think of the permeability of limestone), and proceed north. In 0.1 mile, you will pass by the abandoned Natural Bridge Caverns tourist center, on your right. On your left is a sign that states "Entrance. The Natural Bridge Caverns are under you now."

If you continue down the road for another 0.1 mile, you will come to a bridge spanning the Indian River. Look upriver and you will see a part of the river diverted to the right into what appears to be a low-lying cave entrance. Obviously, this is not the opening to Natural Bridge, for it is too tiny to accommodate objects of anything size. The cave entranced used by the commercial attraction is most likely 0.1 mile farther upstream where the river does a reverse "S", directly behind the now-abandoned tourist center.

Abandoned Visitor Center.

Today, the property is privately owned and inaccessible to the public.

Looking at a Google Earth map, it seems likely that visitors entered the cave from behind the tourist center and exited southwest of the bridge from a diverted section of the river that cannot be seen from the bridge.

All of this is fun to ponder as you drive down Lime Street, viewing relics from the past, and then stopping at the Lime Street Bridge for scenic views of the Indian River.

Partially hidden sign.

Resources: John Mylrole, "The Natural Bridge Cave System," *The Northeastern Caver* Vol. XXIII, no. 3 (September, 1992), 89–94.
Franklin B. Hough, *History of Jefferson County in the State of New York* (Albany, NY: Joel Munsell, 1854), 304.
en.wikipedia.org/wiki/Natural_Bridge,_New_Yorkhttps://en.wikipedia.org/wiki/Natural_Bridge,_New_York.

adirondackscenicbyways.org/community/natural-bridge.html.
Northeastern Caver Vol. XLVIII, no. 2 (June 2017). An old photograph of tourists riding in a boat through Natural Bridge is shown on page 41.
Clay Perry, *Underground Empire: Wonders and Tales of New York Caves* (New York: Stephen Daye Press, 1948), 40.
fingerlynx.com/html/loonldgr/hist/kings5.html.

68. BONAPARTE'S CAVE
Bonaparte's Cave State Forest

Type of Formation: Shelter Cave
WOW Factor: 7–8
Location: Harrisville (Lewis County)
Tenth Edition, NYS Atlas & Gazetteer: p. 26, D5; **Earlier Edition NYS Atlas & Gazetteer**: p. 93, C4–5
Green Pond Parking GPS Coordinates: 44º09.179'N 75º21.768'W
Bonaparte's Cave Parking GPS Coordinates: 44º09.378'N 75º22.319'W
Bonaparte's Cave GPS Coordinates: 44º09.534'N 75º22.083'W
Accessibility: *Wooden Observation Platform at Green Lake* -- 0.5-mile walk; *Bonaparte Cave* – Two options: 1) A demanding 0.3-mile bushwhack from the wooden observation platform; or 2) A 0.4-mile hike from an alternate trailhead.
Degree of Difficulty: *Wooden Observation Platform* -- Moderately easy; *Bonaparte's Cave* – Difficult if you bushwhack from the lake platform; Moderate if you hike in from an alternate trailhead.
Additional Information: Trail map at dec.ny.gov/lands/41678.html – This is the traditional approach to the lake, but doesn't get you to Bonaparte's Cave.

Description: In *Underground Empire: Wonders and Tales of New York Caves*, Clay Perry writes, "It [the cave] is near the shore of a little green-water pond not far from the uninhabited northeast side of Bonaparte Lake. Here is a patch of seemingly isolated limestone, sandy and soft. In it is a small hole, which leads to a room large enough for a man to stand up in with bent head. The interior is a mass of fallen rocks through which passage can be made by crawling."

In the chapter "Escape from Alpina" in *Caves for Kids in Historic New York*, Patricia Edwards Clyne writes, "At first glance, the shallow cavity in the side of the rock face of the hill looked as if it were only an overhang. Further investigation, however, disclosed a low-roofed, narrow passageway at the left side of the shelter." She then goes on to describe the end of the passageway as a "large room maybe 20 feet long and 15 feet wide."

Bonaparte's Cave: Lateral view.

In my estimation, the cave looks like an enormous rock shelter, some 15 feet high, and 35–40 feet across, located not far from the edge of Green Pond itself. Small blocks of talus partially obscure the front of the cave.

BOULDERS BEYOND BELIEF

Like others before me, I noted the crawlspace leading off into the hillside from the rear of the cave, but didn't attempt to explore it. (I am still feeling the effects of a fractured left femur followed by recent surgery for a torn left meniscus – such is life if you do enough bushwhacking and exploring).

Bonaparte's Cave.

History: According to local lore, probably more fanciful than fact, after Joseph Napoleon and his family escaped from Europe and settled in the Adirondacks, they momentarily hid out at the cave overlooking Green Pond in order to escape assassins who they believed were in pursuit

The Bonaparte's Cave State Forest encompasses 1,435 acres of land.

Directions: From slightly north of Harrisville (junction of Routes 3 & 812), drive southwest on Route 3 for over 2.1 miles. Turn right onto North Shore Road and proceed north for 0.4 mile until you come to a "T". Then turn left, continuing northwest on North Shore Road.

Green Pond Trailhead Parking -- At 1.5 miles from the "T" junction, turn right into a parking area. Follow the Green Pond Trail (a grassy road) for 0.5 mile to reach a wooden observation platform that extends out onto Green Pond from the shoreline.

BOULDERS BEYOND BELIEF

To get to Bonaparte's Cave from here, there are two options to choose from: 1) The first option is to paddle northwest across the lake to Bonaparte's Cave, which is partially visible in the distance—a paddle of ~0.2 mile. This can be easily done if you thought to bring in a canoe or kayak on a carrier.

2) The second option is to bushwhack around the southwest perimeter of the lake (which I did and wouldn't recommend) for 0.3 mile. Much scrambling and climbing over blowdown is required, as well as dealing with drainage areas from the hill. It wasn't until I reached Bonaparte's Cave that I realized that an actual path led to it, only from a different direction, as I learned by following the path back out.

Boulder #1

Bonaparte's Trailhead Parking – At ~2.0 miles from the "T" junction, pull over to the side of the road. You should be roughly one hundred feet from a white-colored "40mph" sign as well as Reader Lane, which goes off to the left to Bonaparte Lake. At present, the trailhead is flagged by blue ribbons. These markings cannot be relied upon to still be there in the years to come, however. Look closely and you will see that an informal path heads into the woods. Upon closer examination, the path quickly becomes a faint, old road that can be followed, initially marked by red blazes; then, after 0.1 mile, by aqua-colored blazes.

The path ultimately leads down into the cove where Bonaparte's Cave is located.

BOULDERS BEYOND BELIEF

Additional Sites –
The people in Harrisville obviously take great pride in their rocks. There are two boulders worth noting as you drive through Harrisville from the junction of Routes 3 & 812, both next to houses:

Boulder #2

Boulder #1 – Drive southwest on Route 3 for ~1.5 miles and look to your left to see an enormous rock in front of a residential home [44°08.837'N 75°19.446'W]. What's impressive about the scene is that the homeowner has elected not to destroy the boulder, but to leave it there as part of the landscape. Brilliant!

Boulder #2 – As soon as you turn right onto North Shore Road from Route 3, look to your right to see a round, 6–7-foot-high glacial boulder next to a house. A stone wall perimeter has been constructed around its base, complete with manicured shrubs and a flagpole with an American flag in full display [44°08.688'N 75°20.236'W]. Once again, brilliant.

Resources: Patricia Edwards Clyne, *Caves for Kids in Historic New York* (Monroe, NY: Library Research Associations, 1980), 131–142. A photograph of cave can be seen on page 132.
dec.ny.gov/lands/8060.html.

BOULDERS BEYOND BELIEF

naturefind.com/places/bonapartes-cave-state-forest.
cnyartifactrecovery.wordpress.com/2013/11/24/bonapartes-cave.
Clay Perry, *Underground Empire: Wonders and Tales of New York Caves* (New York: Stephen Daye Press, 1948), 41.
Matthew J. Glavin, *Adirondack Treasure* (Utica, NY: Pyramid Publishing Company, 2012). Glavin's novel touches upon Bonaparte's Cave and a fictional story of the search for hidden monies that were taken from the Spanish treasury.

69. PULPIT ROCK

Type of Formation: Pothole
WOW Factor: 6
Location: Oxbow (Jefferson County)
Tenth Edition, NYS Atlas & Gazetteer: p. 26, B2; **Earlier Edition NYS Atlas & Gazetteer**: p. 92, BC2–3
Pulpit Rock GPS Coordinates: 44º16.843'N 75º37.626'W
Accessibility: Roadside
Degree of Difficulty: Easy

Description: Pulpit Rock is a huge pothole worn into a 45-foot-high cliff-face made of gneiss. It is described as being 70 feet high, with a cavity whose base measures 18 feet deep by 12 feet wide. The pothole rock lies in close proximity to two other potholes, one located 20 feet above, and one 40 feet to the left.

Geologists assume that the potholes were made by glacial meltwaters for there is no observable connection today with the present drainage system.

Franklin B. Hough, a nineteenth-century writer, describes Pulpit Rock as "...a singular precipice of gneiss rock, sixty or seventy feet high and quite perpendicular, upon the face of which is the section of a remarkable excavation, similar to the pot holes found in lime stone rocks, and worn by the rotation of pebbles in water."

In *Gazetteer of Jefferson County*, Hamilton Child writes, "By a fracture in the ledge by the roadside a huge pot hole is opened to view, which in its fancied resemblance to a pulpit has gained the name it bears, and it is said that a sermon was preached from it many years ago."

L. H. Everts, in *History of Jefferson County, New York*, states that "It is a high, perpendicular precipice of rock, in the face of which, at a considerable distance from the ground, is a niche or hole, or rather a section of such cavity, which has the appearance of having been worn by the long-continued rolling of stones in a pool of water." Everts goes on to dispute the claim that regular religious services were held at the rock, believing, rather, that it was used for a rural religious festival.

Pulpit Rock.

In his book, *Routes and Rocks of the North County, New York*, Bradford Van Diver cites C. Ervin Brown of the United States Geological Survey who mentioned that potholes of a similar kind can be found near Pierces Corners (north of Gouverneur) and Osborn Lake (also north of Gouverneur), both which are in the general area.

BOULDERS BEYOND BELIEF

The pothole not only faces the road, but is directly across from a pastoral setting of quiet farmlands.

History: According to a roadside historical marker, the Reverend Oliver Leavitt preached to a group of settlers at the site in 1820 — hence the name, Pulpit Rock. Undoubtedly Pulpit Pothole would have been a more accurate name.

The potholes are a creation of the last Ice Age, carved out by glacial meltwaters along a stream that is no longer discernable.

The hamlet of Oxbow got its name from a remarkable bend on the Oswegatchie River that, to early settlers, resembled the U-shaped collar of an ox yoke.

Directions: From Gouverneur (junction of Routes 11 & 58), take Route 11 (West Main Street) southwest across the Oswegatchie River, go 0.2 mile, and turn right onto Johnstown Street, which quickly becomes Route 12. Follow Route 12 southwest for ~8.5 miles, taking note that when you enter Jefferson County, Route 12 turns into Route 25. At the hamlet of Oxbow, turn left onto Pulpit Rock Road and drive south for 0.5 mile. Look for Pulpit Rock to your right by a roadside historical marker.

This natural formation is so well-known that it is listed on the Delorme NYS Atlas & Gazetteer as well as on Topo Software.

Additional Site –

At ~5.2 miles long the way to Pulpit Rock, turn right onto Kearney Road, and look to your immediate left for views of an impressive-looking escarpment [44°18.610'N 75°34.388'W] where large blocks of talus have collected at the bottom.

Kearney Road is as close as you can get to the escarpment, however. The land is posted and fenced in.

Resources: Bradford B. Van Diver, *Routes and Routes of the North Country, New York* (Geneva, NY: W. F. Humphrey Press, Inc., 1976), 57 & 58.
Franklin B. Hough, *History of Jefferson County in the State of New York, from the Earliest Period to the Present Time* (Watertown, NY: Sterling & Riddell, 1856), 92. A line drawing of the rock taken from Professor Emmons geological report on the 2nd District can be seen on the same page.

BOULDERS BEYOND BELIEF

Franklin B. Hough, *History of St. Lawrence and Franklin Counties, New York* (Albany, NY: Little & Co., 1853), 680. "The pot shaped cavity is about 18 feet deep and 10 feet wide, at the largest part."
geocaching.com/seek/cache_details.aspx?guid=afab7065-5f40-486c-baee-4ad918fc2216.
geocaching.com/geocache/GC1RBBT_pulpit-rock-pothole – This website contains a fair amount of geological information about Pulpit Rock.
The Quarterly Vol. 11, no. 3 (July 1966). On page 9 is a close-up photograph of Pulpit Rock.
Kelsie B. Harder & Mary H. Smallman (editors*)*, *Claims to Name: Toponyms of St. Lawrence County* (Utica, NY: North Country Books, Inc., 1992), 191.
lion-tales.blogspot.com/2012/07/northern-new-york-pulpit-rock.html.
Hamilton Child, *Gazetteer of Jefferson County, N.Y.: 1684–1890* (Syracuse, NY: The Syracuse Journal Company, 1890), 262.
L. H. Everts, *History of Jefferson County, New York* (Philadelphia: L. H. Everts & Co., 1878), 281.
Bradford B. Van Diver, *Upstate New York* (Dubuque, IO: Kendall/Hunt Publishing Company, 1980), 55 & 56.
Author not identified, *History of St. Lawrence County, New York* (Philadelphia: L. H. Everts, 1878), 13. "…and in the gneiss rock, near Ox Bow, in the edge of Jefferson County, is another example, which occurs on the face of a cliff some seventy feet in height, and is so remarkable a nature as to have attracted general curiosity….The pothole cavity is about 18 feet deep and 10 feet wide at its largest part."

70. AM'S ROCK (Historic)

Type of Formation: Historic Rock
WOW Factor: Unknown, but probably 1–2
Location: Unknown (St. Lawrence County)
Tenth Edition, NYS Atlas & Gazetteer: p. 20, E2–3; **Earlier Edition NYS Atlas & Gazetteer**: p. 94, A2–3.
Am's Rock GPS: Unknown
Accessibility: Unknown

Description: Am's Rock, aka Uncle Am's Rock, is not a big rock; probably no more than 3 feet high and 4–5 feet long—measurements based upon a photograph I saw of the boulder.

History: Am's Rock is named after Amaranth Felton, one of the first white settlers in the area. Felton set up a camp initially at the boulder and then, later, erected a log cabin next to it. He used the cleft in the rock as a fireplace both for heating and cooking.

Am's Rock.

At some point, Felton etched and then painted an inscription on the rock in large letters, most of which have faded away with the passage of time. The inscription reads:

In 1878 the 14th of July
I left Colton deserts
For Bog Mountain high
I cooked my pancakes, potatoes, and tea
By the hole in the rock you can plainly see
I chopped, built and hunted also
Until there fell 12 inches of snow
Then came Lonnie with horses and sled
Spotted cow, Boss Cook, and one feather bed.

Directions: According to one source, the rock is located in second growth between Carry Flow and the trail to Catamount Mountain. A second source states that the rock is on the right side of Catamount Mountain along an old highway, which was the original route to Hollywood and Tupper Lake.

I have not been able to track down any more specifics. To be sure, the rock is undoubtedly known to a handful of woodsmen in their wanderings, but no mention is made of it in the current literature.

Resources: Colton Historical Society, *Colton, New York: Story of a Town, II* (Baltimore, MD: Gateway Press, Inc., 1993), 158 & 159. A photograph of the rock can be seen on page 159.

71. COOPERS FALLS POTHOLE

Type of Formation: Pothole
WOW Factor: Unknown; probably 4–5
Location: De Kalb (St. Lawrence County)
Tenth Edition, NYS Atlas & Gazetteer: p. 18, D5; **Earlier Edition NYS Atlas & Gazetteer**: p. 99, D5
Launch site GPS Coordinates: 44º32.691'N 75º29.450'W
Coopers Falls GPS Coordinates: 44º31.163'N 75º20.484'W
Accessibility: The land by Coopers Falls is privately owned. Whether the pothole can be found and legally accessed by following the river upstream to the falls is unknown to me.

Description: In *Gazetteer and Business Directory of St. Lawrence County, N.Y., for 1873–4*, Hamilton Child writes "Near Coopers Falls, in this town [De Kalb] is a locality of considerable interest to geologists. Upon a high cliff of rock is a cavity of unknown depth worn in the sold rock, known locally as the *natural well*. The hole is about three feet in diameter, perfectly round and has a perpendicular descent. It is now nearly filled with debris; but previous to the recent war a few young men undertook to clean it out and succeeded in reaching a depth of thirty-seven feet."

Franklin B. Hough, in *History of St. Lawrence and Franklin Counties, New York*, states that "Near Coopers Falls, in DeKalb, is a cavity of several feet depth which has been worn in this way, but it is at a level far above the present river…"

BOULDERS BEYOND BELIEF

History: The pothole was formed by the Oswegatchie River, a large tributary to the St. Lawrence River.

A grist mill was established at the falls by 1803 by Judge Cooper, as well as a saw mill in 1804. Three brothers—Cyrus, Asahel, and Asa Jackson—worked the mills for Cooper. In 1854, DeKalb Works incorporated, becoming the Coopers Falls Iron Works, a major employer. The hamlet boomed and then went bust. By 1904, Coopers Falls had turned into a ghost-town.

The two islands that split the waterfall into separate entities are called Cat Rock.

In the past, the hamlet of Coopers Falls has also been called The Mills, The Falls, and Cooper's Mills.

In *The Quarterly*, a publication of the St. Lawrence Historical Association, Timothy M. Urnaitis mentions "...a large rock that remains as part of the falls. We have been told that one marking which says 'AP18, 1802' was put there at the high water line and is now 15 feet to 20 feet above the water level today"—another interesting piece of history associated with a rock.

Former old mills at Cooper's Falls.

Directions: From De Kalb (junction of Routes 812 & 17), drive north on Route 812 for 1.2 miles to Coopers Falls (the waterfall), which will be on your left, and not visible from the road without crossing private property.

Franklin B. Hough's observation that the pothole is found above the present level of the river suggests that it lies downstream from the falls.

Launch site -- From De Kalb (junction of Routes 812 & 17), drive north on Route 812 for ~3.2 mile. Turn right onto Route 16, and then immediately left into an area where you can park and then launch your watercraft. Go under the bridge and follow the Oswegatchie River south upstream for 1.8 miles to the base of the falls.

This gets you to the general area, but from here, you are on your own.

Resources: Hamilton Child, *Gazetteer and Business Directory of St. Lawrence County, N.Y., for 1873–4* (Syracuse, NY: Author, 1873), 106.
personalpages.tds.net/~hist1900/Coopersfalls1.htm.

BOULDERS BEYOND BELIEF

Franklin B. Hough, *History of St. Lawrence and Franklin Counties, New York* (Albany, NY: Little & Co., 1853), 670.
nnywaterfalls.com/oswegatchieriver/coopersfalls.
Author not identified, *History of St. Lawrence County, New York* (Philadelphia: L. H. Everts, 1878), 13. The author uses the same source contained in Hough's history book. On page 356, mention is made of Judge Cooper.
Kelsie B. Harder & Mary H. Smallman (editors*), Claims to Name: Toponyms of St. Lawrence County* (Utica, NY: North Country Books, Inc., 1992), 52.
The Quarterly Vol. 12, no. 3 (July 1967), 12 & 13.
Elsie H. Tyler (editor), "Early History of DeKalb" *The Quarterly* Vol. XXI, no. 1 (January 1976), 13.

72. INDIAN KETTLE (Historic)

Type of Formation: Pothole
WOW Factor: Unknown; probably 1–2
Location: Morristown (St. Lawrence County)
Tenth Edition, NYS Atlas & Gazetteer: p. 18, CD2; **Earlier Edition NYS Atlas & Gazetteer**: p. 98. D2
Parking GPS Coordinates: Unknown
Indian Kettle GPS Coordinates: Unknown
Accessibility: Unknown

Description: According to Lorraine B. Bogardus, in *River Reflections: A Short History of Morristown, New York*, "The kettle is a solid rock under a four foot ledge. The top is nearly round, 25 inches in diameter from side to side, 24 inches from front to back, and about 18 inches deep. It is smoothly cut or worn out of the floor of the rock."

History: Indian Kettle has been known about for centuries. The formation was created by glacial erosion, but researchers, after finding arrowheads and stone scrapers near the site, are convinced that the natural pot was used by Native Americans for grinding corn and cooking.

Morristown is named after Gouverneur Morris, one of the founding fathers of the United States, and a regional land baron.

The Indian Kettle that vanished! – Not all potholes fade into obscurity nor are destroyed by highway engineers. In the October 1967 issue of *The*

BOULDERS BEYOND BELIEF

Quarterly, a publication of the St. Lawrence Historical Association, Eugene Hatch writes about a glacial pothole in Russell (slightly southeast of Morristown) that is "...now at the Museum of Natural History in New York City." That's right. Highway engineers blasted out a block of bedrock encasing the pothole, and transported it to New York City. "The pothole was a circular, vertical cavity about two feet across in the slanting rock ledge of the Grenville series of limestone. The hole measured 3 feet deep on the front side of the rock, and 4 feet at the rear. This hole in the rock was known in my boyhood and usually referred to as an "Indian Kettle' as some persons assumed that the Indians used the aperture to grind their corn."

Directions: Morristown is located at the junction of Routes 37, 58, & 12.

A set of old directions I discovered probably no longer apply. To wit, "Take dirt road off 37 where two new houses are located. On top of a huge ledge which gradually descends westwards and to the right of two huge basswood trees, walk about 60 feet from the gravel road."

Additional clues are "The kettle is off of the Route 37 Bypass." The title of the chapter is "The Indian Kettle at Rock Cut," which suggests that the kettle is near a large rock cut in the road.

The chances of finding this natural rock formation on your own are pretty slim unless you run into a local who is familiar with the Indian Kettle.

Resources: Lorraine B. Bogardus, *River Reflections: A Short History of Morristown, New York* (Worcester, MA: Danbe Press, 1988), 156.
Kelsie B. Harder & Mary H. Smallman (editors*)*, *Claims to Name: Toponyms of St. Lawrence County* (Utica, NY: North Country Books, Inc., 1992), 118. The pothole is "...said to have been used as cooking place for Indians."
Eugene Hatch, "Russell's Scoughton Road," *The Quarterly* Vol. 12, no. 4 (October 1967), 3. On page 4 is a photograph of a work crew removing the historic pothole.

BOULDERS BEYOND BELIEF

73. DEVIL'S OVEN

Type of Formation: Sea Cave
WOW Factor: 5
Location: Devil's Oven Island (Jefferson County)
Tenth Edition, NYS Atlas & Gazetteer: p. 25, AB8; **Earlier Edition NYS Atlas & Gazetteer**: p. 91, B7
Parking GPS Coordinates: 44º19.402"N 75º56.057'W
Launch Site GPS Coordinates: 44º19.303'N 75º56.072'W
Devil's Oven GPS Coordinates: 44º19.770'N 75º55.879'W
Fee: Day-use fee for parking/launch site
Accessibility: ~0.5-mile trek by water
Degree of Difficulty: Moderately easy by boat or canoe/kayak
Additional Information: Keewaydin State Park, 45165 State Route 12, Alexandria Bay, NY 13607; (315) 482-2593

Boating to Devil's Oven Island.

Description: This sea cave, called the Devil's Oven, is located on Devil's Oven Island, aka Bill Johnson's Island, and visible from Alexandria Bay. The front of the cave is steeped in shallow water, but the back section is dry. All told, the cave is fairly narrow, dozens of feet long, and clearly inhospitable as a hideout.

In the chapter "Among the Thousand Islands, 1883" contained in *Tales of the Empire State*, Howard Pyle describes the island as "a cubical block of granite having almost the appearance of being carved by human hands, rejoicing in the not very savory name of The Devil's Oven, its summit giving sustenance to a few gaunt cedars, and its sides perforated by an almost circular opening which at a distance does bear some resemblance to a gigantic baker's oven."

According to Robert Carroll Jr. in the June 2010 issue of the *Northeastern Caver*, the Devil's Oven "...is a 50-foot gneiss/calcite/limonite solution cave—on an islet 160 feet wide, 210 feet long, and 30 feet high." Much like the cave, the island is itself comparatively small.

History: Folklore provides some interesting background about the Devil's Oven. Bill Johnson (one of the leading figures of the Patriot War and an "Admiral" of the Patriot Navy of the East) allegedly used the cave to hide out from capture in 1838 and 1839, kept supplied by his 19-year-old daughter, Kate Johnson, who would smuggle provisions over from across the shore at Alexandria Bay.

The story is undoubtedly apocryphal, for the cave entrance is clearly visible from Alexandria Bay (and therefore not much of a secret hideout), and Bill Johnson was a fairly large man who would have found the tiny alcove uncomfortable and claustrophobic.

Directions: From Alexandria Bay (junction of Routes 12 & 26), drive southwest on Route 12 for ~1.0 mile and turn right into Keewaydin State Park.

From the launch site at Keewaydin State Park, head upriver for ~0.5 mile, going northeast past Comfort Island, Stony Crest Island, Wauwinel Island, and Cuba Island.

When you come to Devil's Oven Island, paddle around to the right (east) side of the island to visit the cave.

Resources: Elise D. Chan, *Jefferson County: Images of America* (Charleston, SC: Arcadia Publishing, 2004), 53.
L. N. Fuller, *Northern New York in the Patriot War*, Watertown Daily Times, 1923.
Robert Carroll, Jr., "Other Ice Walks – Southern Lake Champlain and Elsewhere," *The Northeastern Caver* Vol. XXIV, no. 3 (September 1993), 106. The cave is described as a "linear Grenville gneiss/marble cave on rock islet southwest of Alexandria Bay."
thousandislandslife.com/BackIssues/Archive/tabid/393/articleType/ArticleView/articleId/499/Pirate-Bill.aspx.
"Image Gallery," *Northeastern Caver* Vol. XLI, no. 2 (June 2010), 64. On the same page is a photo of the island, a line drawing of the island, and a map created by Robert Carroll of the cave.
Susan Weston Smith, *The First Summer People: Thousand Islands* 1650–1910 (Erin, Ontario: Boston Mills Press, 1944), 76 & 77. A line drawing of the island can be seen on page 76.
Jno A. Haddock (editor), *A Souvenir of the Thousand Islands of the St. Lawrence River* (Alexandria Bay, NY: Jno A. Haddock, 1896), 63–64.

abay.com/alexandriabaynynews494.htm – The website shows a video exploration of the cave.

Frank Oppel (compiler), *Tales of the Empire State* (Secaucus, NJ: Castle, 1988). A line drawing of the Devil's Oven is shown on page 196.

Devil's Oven Island. Postcard c. 1920.

SECTION TWO: CENTRAL ADIRONDACKS

74. HOUGH'S CAVE

Type of Formation: Solutional Cave
WOW Factor: Unknown
Location: Martinsburg (Lewis County)
Tenth Edition, NYS Atlas & Gazetteer: p. 34, D4; **Earlier Edition NYS Atlas & Gazetteer**: p. 84, C4
Historical Marker GPS Coordinates: 43º43.305'N 75º28.035'W
Accessibility: Entrance on private property

Description: Hughes Cave was reputedly part of the Underground Railroad. The original entrance, set in the side of a hill, is 3–4 feet high and 15 feet wide. From it, a partially collapsed stream channel runs for several hundred feet, resurging on the other side of Route 26, which is probably where the historic marker was initially placed.

In *Underground Empire: Wonders and Tales of New York Caves*, Clay Perry writes about "…historical Hough's Cave—which appears to be one cave with two openings……Reputed to have a 'travelable' distance of 500 feet between the two entrances." It should be mentioned that Clay Perry never actually visited the cave, so his description of it is second hand at best.

Historians suspect that the cave, assuming it was ever used, served as a backup to Hough's barn.

History: The cave was named after Horatio G. Hough who participated in the Underground Railroad that was used to move runaway slaves to freedom. Hough's Cave was one of the stations.

A State Education Department historic marker was placed at the site in 1931.

In 2014, Benjamin D. Brown, chairman of the Niagara Frontier Grotto, the Western New York chapter of the National Speleological Society, and 8 cavers were the first to enter and explore the cave in over 50 years.

Directions: From Lowville (junction of Routes 26 & 12), take Route 26 southeast for ~4.2 miles. Look for a roadside historical marker on your right next to a cornfield, roughly 1.4 miles north of Route 29/West Road (which is where the Whetstone Gulf State Park is located).

I suspect this spot is not the original location for this historic marker, for according to accounts that I have read, Route 29 passed directly above the cave and may even have damaged the entrance, which would put the cave's entrance along Route 29/West Road, and not Route 26.

Resources: Marjorie G. Hough, "Hough's Cave," *North Country Life* Vol. 5, no. 4 (Fall 1951), 21–23.
watertowndailytimes.com/article/20140730/LJR01/140739884; as well as journalandrepublican.com/article/20140730/LJR01/140739884 – The same article by Steve Virkler appeared in the July 30th, 2014 issue of the *Watertown Daily Times* and the *Journal & Republican*.
lewiscountyhistory.org/horatioh.html -- This site provides a video of the history of the cave and the trial of Horatio Hough.
fultonhistory.com/Process%20small/Newspapers/Lowvile%20Ny%20Rebulican/1931/Newspaper%20Lowville%20NY%20Journal%20Republican%201931%20-%20(484).PDF – This newspaper account tells the story of the placement of the historic marker by the cave.
G. Byron Brown (editor), *History of Lewis County, New York: 1880–1965* (Lewis County, NY: Board of Legislators of Lewis County, 1970), 378.
Clay Perry, *Underground Empire: Wonders and Tales of New York Caves* (New York: Stephen Daye Press, 1948), 139.

75. DEERLICK ROCK

Type of Formation: Rock Mound
WOW Factor: 5–6
Location: Glenfield (Lewis County)
Tenth Edition, NYS Atlas & Gazetteer: p. 34, D5; **Earlier Edition NYS Atlas & Gazetteer**: p. 85, C4–5
Parking GPS Coordinates: Unknown
Deerlick Rock GPS Coordinates: 43º42.070′N 75º22.548′W
Accessibility: Unknown

Description: Deerlick Rock is big! In "Legends of Deerlick Rock" in *North Country Life*, Louis C. Mihalyi writes that "Its huge bulk, jutting up nearly one hundred feet and covering about five acres, is visible at considerable distances up and down the Black River Valley." The huge mound was named for a salt spring on its south side.

BOULDERS BEYOND BELIEF

Deerlick Rock is also described by Thomas C. O'Donnell in *The River Rolls On: A History of the Black River from Port Leyden to Carthage*. "The rock, above the low lands of the Black River from which it emerges, is around a hundred and fifty feet high. It covers less than an acre of ground and proceeds for the greater part with lifts that can make climbing to the top really difficult."

The rock, made of granite, has also gone by the Native American name *Ne-Na-To-Re*, meaning "Rock of the Pines."

A tiny creek runs past the south side of the giant rock and flows into the Black River, only 0.3 mile to the west.

History: Two legends are associated with Deerlick Rock. One states that during the French and Indian War in the mid-1700s, a column of French soldiers fleeing from British and Iroquois pursuers buried a payroll treasure next to Deerlick Rock. Needless to say, the money has never been recovered and today is referred to as the Deerlick Rock Cache. Apparently, there is sufficient lore to at least support the notion that something might still be underground at Deerlick Rock.

A second legend recounts the story of an Oneida princess forbidden by her father to marry a Tuscarora chief. The two lovers, running away together, are pursued to Deerlick Rock, which was considered sacred ground by the Oneidas. Confronted by sacred ground, the pursuing party was forced to camp out at the base of the rock to wait for the lovers to come down. Weakened by hunger and thirst, the two finally descended, but, upon reaching the bottom, jumped into quicksand at the edge of the swamp and died together rather than being captured and separated. Although this story resembles so many other Native American tales of unrequited or forbidden love and therefore, to me, sounds both improbable and implausible, there apparently is (or was) quicksand in the swampy area in front of the south side of the rock. So at least a part of the story may be true.

In 1930, Charles Mihalyi, of Glenfield, purchased Deerfield Rock with the intention of turning it into a park. He reforested the 60-acre parcel around the rock, but never followed through on his original plans, and the rock remains pretty much unchanged today.

BOULDERS BEYOND BELIEF

Directions: This is one of those instances where the exact location of a natural wonder, Deerlick Rock, is known (it shows up quite visibly on Google Earth) but where legal access to it is not known.

To get to the general area near Deerlick Rock, begin at Lyons Falls (junction of Routes 12 & 12D), and drive north on Route 12 for ~6.5 miles to Glenfield. Then turn right onto Main Street and proceed northeast for 0.5 mile. When you come to Greig Road (Route 40), turn right and drive southeast for 1.9 miles. At the intersection with Pine Grove Road (coming in on the left), you will now be due east of Deerlick Rock, only 0.4 mile away.

From here, it might be possible to bushwhack to the rock if the land isn't posted. There is a private road just before the intersection with Pine Cove Road that leads in 0.4 mile to a house only a short distance north of the rock, but this is not a likely way to approach the rock due to the land being privately owned.

It may also be possible to access Deerlick Rock from the Black River, which passes by 0.3 mile west of the rock, either by bushwhacking from the river across a meadow (a wet slog, no doubt), or following a tiny creek upstream (if possible) to the rock.

I recently scouted the area by car, and drew a blank.

Resources: Louis C. Mihalyi, "Legends of Deer Lick Rock," *North Country Life* (Vol. 14, no. 4, Fall 1960), 41–43. A photograph of the rock with tiny people standing on it can be seen on page 41.
Thomas C. O'Donnell, *The River Rolls On: A History of the Black River from Port Leyden to Carthage* (Prospect, NY: Prospect Press, 1959), 26–30. The section not only contains history, but a lengthy poem written in 1896 about Deer Lick Rock by Miss Lilian M. Holland. A photograph of the rock can be seen in an insert between pages 64 and 65.
rock-cache – This site describes the Deerlick Rock Cache, where some believe a huge payroll was buried near the rock.
cnyartifactrecovery.wordpress.com/tag/french-and-indian-wars.
cnyartifactrecovery.wordpress.com/tag/deerlick-rock-cache.
cnyartifactrecovery.wordpress.com/2013/09/23/new-yorks-deerlick-
G. Byron Brown (editor), *History of Lewis County, New York: 1880–1965* (Lewis County, NY: Board of Legislators of Lewis County, 1970), 212 & 213.

BOULDERS BEYOND BELIEF

76. SUGAR RIVER UNIQUE BEDROCK, POTHOLES, AND GLACIAL BOULDER

Type of Formation: Pothole; Large Boulder
WOW Factor: 6
Location: North of Boonville (Lewis County)
Tenth Edition, NYS Atlas & Gazetteer: p. 49, A5–6; **Earlier Edition NYS Atlas & Gazetteer**: p. 85, D5
Parking GPS Coordinates: 43º31.217'N 75º19.558'W
Destination GPS Coordinates: *North end* -- 43º31.241'N 75º19.383'W; *South End* -- 43º30.925'N 75º19.301'W
Accessibility: Unknown. Permission may be needed to access this area.
Degree of Difficulty: Moderate if access is permitted

Description: Franklin B. Hough, in *History of Lewis County*, writes, "The river [Sugar River] here tumbles down a hundred feet or more through a gorge worn in the limestone, which presents a succession of steps, having a general slope of about 45°. The banks on either side, above and below, are nearly vertical and from 100 to 200 feet in height….Several deep pot-holes, worn by pebbles occur above the falls."

Hough goes on to mention that 0.2 mile below the falls "…the whole of the river in the summer disappears in the fissure worn by the current, and about fifty rods [825 feet] below, again appears at the surface. The river road passes over this natural bridge thus formed."

A photograph of the fractured riverbed can be viewed in Bradford Van Diver's book, *Upstate New York*, along with the caption "Potholes and solution-widened joints in the Black River limestone with glacial erratic in background." The glacial erratic "… is 10 feet in diameter, rounded like a ball, made of pre-Cambrian granitic gneiss, and sits in the channel mid-way…"

According to Van Diver, this section of the Sugar River contains "…rock joints, limestone solution, potholes, a glacial erratic, and subterranean stream piracy." He also notes that the entirety of the river, under most conditions, flows into a cave opening, only to re-emerge later. In other words, the site has everything you could hope to see from a geological standpoint.

The Sugar River is a medium-sized stream that rises from the southwest corner of West Turin and flows into the Black River at Leyden.

Van Diver bemoans the fact that many classic geological sites are slowly becoming privatized—and he's right.

BOULDERS BEYOND BELIEF

History: The Sugar River is perhaps best known for producing 60-foot-high Talcottville Falls, aka Sugar River Falls, northwest of the hamlet of Talcottville.

Directions: From Boonville, drive north on Route 12 for ~2.5 miles.

Option #1 -- Park near the intersection of Kerwin Road and Route 12, not far from Pete's Storage, on the opposite side of Route 12. Cross Route 12 and walk southwest across a sloping hill down towards the river, a trek of only 0.1 mile. You will come to the rim of the gorge, from where the riverbed can be seen below. The problem is that there is no easy way to get down the steep sidewalls of the gorge to reach the riverbed. There's also the fact that although the land up to the gorge isn't posted, it is probably privately owned.

In the past, geologist Bradford Van Diver made arrangements to visit the site with Allied Chemical Company, Boonville Limestone Quarry. Present arrangements are unknown.

Option #2 – Paddle up the Black River to its confluence with the Sugar River. and then walk 0.3 mile up the Sugar River. It should be easy to do, since much of stream is underground along here, but then again, legal access could be an issue.

Option #3 – If the water level is sufficiently low, it might be possible to walk along the shoreline of the Sugar River from the Route 12 Bridge [43º31.522′N 75º19.489′W] to reach the area of geological interest. I regret now that I didn't explore this option when in the area to see if it was a possibility both physically and legally.

Resources: Franklin B. Hough, *History of Lewis County* (Albany, NY: Munsell & Rowland, 1860), 130.
Bradford B. Van Diver, *Upstate New York* (Dubuque, IO: Kendall/Hunt Publishing Company, 1980), 225.

BOULDERS BEYOND BELIEF

77. ELK LAKE ROAD BOULDER

Type of Formation: Large Boulder
WOW Factor: 3
Location: North Hudson (Essex County)
Tenth Edition, NYS Atlas & Gazetteer: p. 30, E3–4; **Earlier Edition NYS Atlas & Gazetteer**: p. 88, A3
Elk Lake Road Boulder GPS Coordinates: 44º00.913'N 73º49.657'W
Accessibility: 30-foot trek from road
Degree of Difficulty: Easy
Additional Information: Elk Lake Lodge, Inc., 1106 Elk Lake Road, North Hudson, NY 12855; (518) 532-7616; elklakelodge.com.

Elk Lake Lodge manager Mike Sheridan at Elk Lake Road Boulder.

Description: This fairly nondescript, 10-foot-high boulder lies along the west side of a road that leads to Elk Lake Lodge—a wilderness retreat rated as one of the ten best in North America by *Outside Magazine*.

A number of fairly small-to mid-sized glacial boulders are visible along the 5.0-mile-long Elk Lake Road, on the grounds of Elk Lake Lodge, as well as on Elk Lake's shoreline and islands. This particular stand-alone boulder, however, is by far the largest in the area.

Directions: From the Adirondack Northway (I-87), get off at Exit 29 for North Hudson and head west on Blue Ridge Road (Route 84) for over 4.0 miles. When you come to Elk Lake Road turn right and drive north for ~4.5 miles. Then turn left into a tiny pull-off along the road. A quick walk of 30 feet from the road takes you to the boulder, which is clearly visible from roadside.

BOULDERS BEYOND BELIEF

78. BALANCING ROCK: BLUE RIDGE ROAD

Type of Formation: Balanced Rock
WOW Factor: 6–7
Location: Boreas River (Essex County)
Tenth Edition, NYS Atlas & Gazetteer: p. 38, A2; **Earlier Edition NYS Atlas & Gazetteer:** p. 88, A2
Balancing Rock GPS Coordinates: 43º56.938′N 73º56.001′W
Accessibility: Near Roadside
Degree of Difficulty: Easy

Balancing Rock is a roadside wonder.

Description: According to William John Miller's 1919 *Geology of the Schroon Lake Quadrangle,* Balancing Rock is "…a rounded glacial boulder of Marcy anorthosite fully 14 feet in diameter resting in a remarkably balanced position upon another boulder of the same kind of rock..." Barney Fowler, in *Adirondack Album*, estimates the boulder to weigh over 25 tons.

In *Guide to Adirondack Trails: Central Region. Second Edition*, Bruce Wadsworth writes, "Balance Rock is a 12 ft.-diameter circular boulder perched on a second large slanting boulder. Why it doesn't roll off its sloping base is a curiosity."

History: The Balancing Rock has been visited frequently thanks to its proximity to Blue Ridge Road. Its immediacy and accessibility also serve to explain the vast swath of graffiti that has accumulated on the big rock.

The 17-mile-long Blue Ridge Road shares its namesake with Blue Ridge Falls, which lies along the south side of the highway, roughly 2.4 miles west of the Adirondack Northway. Here is your chance to see a waterfall and a unique, big rock on the same road.

Directions: From the Adirondack Northway (I-87), get off at Exit 29 for North Hudson. Head west on Blue Ridge Road (Route 84) for ~10.3 miles until you come to the pull-off for Balancing Rock, on your right, roughly 1.3 miles east of where Blue Ridge Road crosses the Boreas River.

Resources: Barbara McMartin, *Discover the Central Adirondacks* (Woodstock, VT: Backcountry Publications, Inc., 1986), 145. A photograph of the rock can be seen on page 154.
Barney Fowler, *Adirondack Album* (Schenectady, NY: Outdoor Associates, 1974), 180.
William John Miller, *Geology of the Schroon Lake Quadrangle* (Albany, NY: University of the State of New York, 1919).
historicnewspapers.guilpl.org/altamont-enterprise-1989-january-june/altamont-enterprise-1989-january-june%20-%200581.pdf.
dot.ny.gov/display/programs/scenic-byways/blue-ridge-road.
Bruce Wadsworth & Neal Burdick (series editor), *Guide to Adirondack Trails: Central Region. Second Edition* (Lake George, NY: Adirondack Mountain Club Inc., 1994), 193.

BOULDERS BEYOND BELIEF

79. RICH LAKE BOULDER

Type of Formation: Large Boulder
WOW Factor: 4–5
Location: Newcomb (Essex County)
Tenth Edition, NYS Atlas & Gazetteer: p. 37, A9; **Earlier Edition NYS Atlas & Gazetteer**: p. 87, A7
Parking GPS Coordinates: 43º58.470'N 74º11.234'W
Rich Lake Boulder GPS Coordinates: 43º58.576'N 74º11.504'W
Accessibility: 0.3-mile hike
Degree of Difficulty: Easy
Additional Information: Adirondack Interpretive Center, 5922 State Route 28N, Newcomb, NY 12852; (518) 582-2000; www.esf.edu/aic; aic@esf.edu;
   Open from January 1 – May 31st, Saturday-Sunday, 10 am – 4 pm; May 31st – October 31st, Wednesday – Sunday, 10 am – 5 pm.
   Closed November and December.
   Trail Map available at esf.edu/aic/documents/summermap.pdf

Description: This 15-foot-high, gum-drop-shaped boulder is one of the main attractions along the interpretive trails at the Adirondack Interpretive Center. A large, downward crack extends through the left side of the boulder, but has not widen sufficiently yet to split the rock into two pieces. When this happens, the Rich Lake Boulder will consist of one large piece and a smaller fragment.

   In her article in the *Adirondack Almanac* entitled "Adirondack Geology: Mysteries of Rocks and Minerals," Ellen Rathbone shares the same sentiment about the boulder's fate when she writes, "Here at the VIC in Newcomb we have a wonderful glacial erratic sitting next to the Rich Lake Trail. In almost ten years of passing this rock, I've noticed that the crack that runs down its face has widened. Water gets into this crack and alternately freezes and thaws,

The cracked boulder resembles, to a slight degree, the Liberty Bell in Philadelphia.

each year making the crack a little bit wider. Eventually, I suspect the slab will fall away from its parent rock, but probably not within my lifetime."

Elephant Island Caves – In Benson Lossing's book *The Hudson: From the Wilderness to the Sea*, the author writes, "Near the foot of the lake [downhill from Goodnow Mountain] is a wooded peninsula, whose low isthmus, being covered at high water, leaves it an island. It is called Elephant Island, because of the singular resemblance of some of the limestone formation that composes its bold shore to portions of that animal. The whole rock is perforated into singularly-formed caves."

I am not familiar with this formation, but would be intrigued enough to look for it by boat or kayak the next time I am up at Rich Lake.

ELEPHANT ISLAND.

History: The Adirondack Interpretive Center is part of the State University of New York (SUNY) College of Environmental Science & Forestry (ESF)'s Newcomb Campus.

The first Interpretive Center in the Adirondacks to open was at Paul Smiths in 1989. The Newcomb Interpretive Center followed in 1990. Both centers were subsequently sold by New York State to nearby colleges in 2011.

Rich Lake got its name from early prospectors who, upon seeing graphite flakes in the rocks, thought that they had encountered silver ore and were destined to become rich.

BOULDERS BEYOND BELIEF

Directions: From Long Lake (junction of Routes 28N & 30), drive east on Route 28N for ~12.5 miles and turn left at a sign for the Adirondack Interpretive Center.

From east of Newcomb (junction of Routes 28N and 84/Blue Ridge Road), head west on Route 28N for over 6.0 miles and turn right at the sign for the Adirondack Interpretive Center.

Drive northwest on a dirt road for 0.2 mile and turn into a parking area uphill from the Adirondack Interpretive Center.

From the parking area, walk downhill for a couple of hundred feet to the Adirondack Interpretive Center. Go to the left side of the building and follow the red-blazed Rich Lake Trail downhill, across a boardwalk, and then, a short distance later, across a small footbridge. At the end of the footbridge, you will reach a junction where the Rich Lake Trail loops around. Turn left and head west for 0.1 mile. At the junction with the Peninsula Trail, look for the boulder to your right.

Resources: Ellen Rathbone, "Adirondack Geology: Mysteries of Rocks and Minerals," *Adirondack Almanack* (Saturday, April 24th, 2010) adirondackalmanack.com/2010/04/adirondack-geology-mysteries-of-rocks-and-minerals.html.
adirondackalmanack.com/2010/04/ruminations-on-rock-tripe.html -- Ellen Rathbone offers some thoughts on the rock tripe covering part of the Rich Lake glacial boulder.
Benson Lossing, *The Hudson: From the Wilderness to the Sea* (Somersworth, NH: New Hampshire Publishing Company, 1972), 18 & 19. Originally published in 1866 by H. B. Nims & Co., Troy, NY.
John Hayes & Alex Wilson, *Quiet Water Canoe Guide: New York* (Boston: Appalachian Mountain Club, 1996), 287

80. ADIRONDACK HOTEL ROCK

Type of Formation: Medium-sized Boulder
WOW Factor: 3
Location: Long Lake (Hamilton County)
Tenth Edition, NYS Atlas & Gazetteer: p. 37, A6–7; **Earlier Edition NYS Atlas & Gazetteer**: p. 87, A5
Adirondack Hotel Rock GPS Coordinates: 43º58.437'N 74º25.341'W
Accessibility: Roadside

BOULDERS BEYOND BELIEF

Additional Information: Adirondack Hotel, 1245 Main Street, Route 30, Long Lake, NY 12847; (518) 624-4700

Description: The Adirondack Hotel Rock sits in the parking area directly in front of the Adirondack Hotel. The boulder is not a particularly large rock, but its location guarantees that it is frequently photographed by tourists. It also seems likely that the boulder has been struck more than once by inattentive drivers backing up out of the parking area.

History: The Adirondack Hotel, nicknamed "The Old Green Lady," dates back to the turn of the twentieth century. An earlier version of the hotel was built in 1879 by Cyrus and Christina Kellogg and was called the Lake House. It burned down in 1901 and was rebuilt in 1904. Patrick Moynehan, a lumberman and Raquette Falls businessman, became the new owner.

By good fortune, the hotel escaped the fire of 1908 that consumed most of the town, perhaps due to its location, downhill, at the west end of town, close to the water.

BOULDERS BEYOND BELIEF

Many celebrities have stayed at the hotel over the years, including scientist Albert Einstein, boxer Jack Dempsey, and Governor Alfred E. Smith.

Long Lake (the lake itself) is appropriately named, being 14 miles in length.

Directions: From Long Lake Village (junction of Routes 30 & 28N), drive northwest on Route 30 for less than 0.5 mile. The hotel and boulder are to your left, just before you cross over a bridge spanning a narrow section of Long Lake.

Resources: adirondackhotel.com.
Donald R. Williams, *The Adirondacks: 1931–1990* (Charleston, SC: Arcadia Publishing, 2003), 77.
Donald R. Williams, *Adirondack Hotels and Inns* (Charleston, SC: Arcadia Publishing, 2008), 41.
en.wikipedia.org/wiki/Adirondack_Hotel.
tripadvisor.com/ShowUserReviews-g48081-d2321528-r488525056-Adirondack_Hotel-Long_Lake_New_York.html.

81. BUTTERMILK FALLS BOULDER

Type of Formation: Medium-sized Boulder
WOW Factor: 3
Location: Deerland (Hamilton County)
Tenth Edition, NYS Atlas & Gazetteer: p. 37, AB6; **Earlier Edition NYS Atlas & Gazetteer**: p. 87, A4–5
Parking GPS Coordinates: 43º54.866′N 74º28.977′W
Buttermilk Falls Boulder GPS Coordinates: 43º54.900′N 74º29.044′W
Accessibility: 0.05-mile hike
Degree of Difficulty: Easy

Description: This large, 5-foot-high, 10-foot-long boulder, located on the east side of Buttermilk Falls, partially in the river, is part of the waterfall's allure. During times of high flow, the river literally bounces off the boulder and its smaller, 6-foot-high, 8-foot-long companion.

Fifty feet away uphill from the main boulder is an 8-foot-high boulder that, unfortunately, has attracted more than its share of pointless graffiti.

BOULDERS BEYOND BELIEF

Directions: From Deerland (junction of Routes 3 & 30/28N), drive southwest on Route 3 (North Point Road) for 2.0 miles. Pull over to your right at a designated, roadside parking area.

Follow a well-worn path 0.05 mile west to reach the waterfall. This is a chance to see a boulder associated with one of the most famous waterfalls in the Adirondacks.

Resources: Russell Dunn, *Adirondack Waterfall Guide* (Hensonville, NY: Black Dome Press Corp., 2004), 54–56.
Randi Minetor, *Hiking Waterfalls in New York* (Guilford, CT: Falcon Guide, 2014). A photograph of the base of Buttermilk Falls, showing the boulder, can be seen on page 200.
flickr.com/photos/30436878@N06/3641673009 shows a photograph of the boulder next to the waterfall taken by the "Waterfall Guy."
Nathan Farb, *Adirondack Wilderness* (New York: Rizzoli, 2009). A photograph of the waterfall and boulder can be seen on page 132.
Donald R. Williams, *Along the Adirondack Trail: Images of America* (Charleston, SC: Arcadia Publishing, 2004). A photograph of a man sitting on top of the boulder is shown.

BOULDERS BEYOND BELIEF

82. CASTLE ROCK

Type of Formation: Talus Block; Rock-Shelter
WOW Factor: 5–6
Location: Blue Mountain Lake (Hamilton County)
Tenth Edition, NYS Atlas & Gazetteer: p. 37, B6; **Earlier Edition NYS Atlas & Gazetteer**: p. 87, AB5
Parking GPS Coordinates: 43º52.383'N 74º27.023'W
Castle Rock GPS Coordinates: 43º52.560'N 74º28.078'W
Accessibility: *Talus blocks* -- 1.2-mile hike; *Castle Rock Overlook* -- 1.5-mile hike; 700' ascent
Degree of Difficulty: Moderate

Castle Rock's huge blocks of talus form passageways.

Description: Peter Kick provides a good description of the rocks in *Discover the Adirondacks*, "....where the ledge has fractured and huge talus blocks have created an intricate system of crevices and caverns. This system of natural buttresses, parapets, and rampartlike rock formations probably provided the Castle Rock's romanticized place-name."

In *Five-Star Trails in the Adirondacks: A Guide to the Most Beautiful Hikes*, Tim Starmer writes, "The base of the large granite outcrop towers above you on the right, with a narrow passage between it and some of the boulders that lie about...Paths that eventually lead back to the main trail weave through the maze of boulders, providing excellent opportunities for exploration."

It's an impressive area where an underlying section of a cliff face has collapse into rubble, leaving behind a huge overhang that produces a mammoth rock-shelter. There is even a tall, cave-like rock-shelter that can be entered for a tiny distance.

BOULDERS BEYOND BELIEF

Beyond are impressive boulders that also invite exploration.

When Barbara and I had hiked up to Castle Rock many years ago, it was the view of Blue Mountain Lake and its smorgasbord of islands that most impressed us; but, then again, this was before we were seeking out large boulders and rock formations.

History: Castle Rock, at the top of the cliff above the boulders, is a large, rocky, 2,480-foot-high promontory that overlooks Blue Mountain Lake, some 700 feet below.

Directions: From the hamlet of Blue Mountain Lake (junction of Routes 30/28N & 28), drive north on Route 30/28N for over 0.5 mile. Turn left onto Maple Lodge Road and proceed west for 1.5 miles until you reach the end of the road where parking is available by the Syracuse University's Minnowbrook Conference Center.

Follow the Sargent Pond Trail west for 0.2 mile. At a fork, bear right. At 0.3 mile, bear right again, following red-colored markers. At 0.4 mile, veer off onto the yellow-blazed Castle Rock Trail. You will come to an overhang and boulders at 1.2–1.3 miles.

The Castle Rock overlook can be reached in another 0.2–0.3 mile.

Resources: Barbara McMartin, *Discover the Central Adirondacks* (Woodstock, VT: Backcountry Publications, Inc., 1986). A winter photo of the boulders appears on page 110.
Tom Starmer, *Five-Star Trails in the Adirondacks* (Birmingham, AL: Menasha Press, 2010), 83.
Peter W. Kick, *Discover the Adirondacks* (Boston, MA: Appalachian Mountain Club Books, 2012), 196.
cnyhiking.com/CastleRock.htm.
Rose Rivezzi & David Trithart, *Kids on the Trails! Hiking with children in the Adirondacks* (Lake George, NY: Adirondack Mountain Club, 1997), 129–131.

83. LEVIATHAN ROCK
Cascade Pond Wilderness

Type of Formation: Large Boulder
WOW Factor: 7
Location: Blue Mountain Lake (Hamilton County)

BOULDERS BEYOND BELIEF

Tenth Edition, NYS Atlas & Gazetteer: p. 37, B6–7; **Earlier Edition NYS Atlas & Gazetteer**: p. 87, AB5
Leviathan Rock GPS Coordinates: 43º50.900'N 74º25.418'W
Accessibility: Roadside
Degree of Difficulty: Easy

Description: This large, stand-alone, glacial boulder, over 15 feet high and 25 feet long, is located next to the parking area used by hikers accessing the trail to Cascade Pond.

Leviathan Rock is well used by hikers and fishermen.

Barbara McMartin gives the rock a passing nod in *Fifty Hikes in the Adirondacks* when she writes, "The road goes to a picnic spot on the shore of Lake Durant, passing a big glacial erratic…" Big may not adequately describe this boulder. It is mammoth.

BOULDERS BEYOND BELIEF

At some point, someone added shark teeth to the front of the boulder but, quite honestly, it doesn't work as a piece of art, and makes the rock look unsightly and garish.

History: Close at hand is 289-acre Lake Durant and the considerably tinier, 0.5-mile-long Rock Pond which adjoins Lake Durant, separated by a floating footbridge.

Directions: From the hamlet of Blue Mountain Lake (junction of Routes 30 North/28 N & 28), drive southeast on Route 30/28 for 0.8 mile.

From the hamlet of Indian Lake (junction of Routes 30 South & 28), drive northwest on Route 30/28 for over 10.0 miles.

Coming from either direction, turn onto Durant Road (Route 19) and head west for 0.2 mile. Then bear left onto a dirt road (listed on MapQuest as Cascade Pond Trail) just before a cemetery. You will see a sign that says "Cascade Pond Wilderness. Blue Ridge Wilderness." Proceed south for 0.1 mile and bear left into a tiny parking area next to Leviathan Rock.

Resources: Barbara McMartin, *Fifty Hikes in the Adirondacks* (Woodstock, VT: Backcountry Publications, 1988), 173.
Robert J. Redington, *Guide to Trails of the West-Central Adirondacks* (Glens Falls, NY: Adirondack Mountain Club, Inc., 1984), 138. Mention is made of '…an informal campsite next to a large glacial boulder.'

84. SAWYER MOUNTAIN BOULDER

Type of Formation: Medium-sized Boulder
WOW Factor: 3
Location: Indian Lake (Hamilton County)
Tenth Edition, NYS Atlas & Gazetteer: p. 37, C8; **Earlier Edition NYS Atlas & Gazetteer**: p. 87, B6
Parking GPS Coordinates: 43º48.657'N 74º19.285'W
Sawyer Mountain Boulder GPS Coordinates: 43º48.374'N 74º19.912'W
Accessibility: 0.9-mile hike to boulder; 1.1-mile hike to summit; 630-foot ascent
Degree of Difficulty: Moderate

BOULDERS BEYOND BELIEF

Description: The 7-foot-high Sawyer Mountain Boulder is funky in its own way—slightly taller than an average human, somewhat cube-shaped, and trailside. Its appearance is both unexpected and surprising.

Sawyer Mountain trailside boulder.

History: Sawyer Mountain is 2,618 feet high and a popular hike for families with children. As it turns out, the view from Sawyer Mountain, which includes those of Wakely Mountain (3,744'), Snowy Mountain (3,904'), and Panther Mountain (3,720'), is not from the summit, but rather from a high rock outcrop 270 feet beyond the summit.

Directions: From the Village of Indian Lake (junction of Routes 30 & 28), head northwest of Route 28/30 for ~4.4 miles and turn left into the trailhead pull-off.

From Blue Mountain Lake Village (junction of Routes 28/30 & 28N), head southeast on Route 28/30 for ~6.8 miles and turn right into the pull-off.

BOULDERS BEYOND BELIEF

Follow the red-marked trail for 0.9 mile to reach a medium-sized boulder on your right. Sawyer Mountain's quasi-summit is reached at 1.1 miles.

Early on during the hike, a group of medium-sized rocks are passed to your left, but they are fairly nondescript in both size and shape, and will probably attract only minimal attention.

Resources: Rose Rivezzi & David Trithart, *Kids on the Trails! Hiking with children in the Adirondacks* (Lake George, NY: Adirondack Mountain Club, 1997), 140.
hikespeak.com/trails/sawyer-mountain-adirondacks.
Barbara McMartin & Lee M. Brenning, *Discover the West Central Adirondacks* (Woodstock, VT: Backcountry Publications, 1988), 166 & 167.
adirondackexperience.com/hiking/sawyer-mountain – The website mentions "an interesting rock feature" that is passed.

85. BALANCED ROCK: LITTLE SAWYER MOUNTAIN

Type of Formation: Balanced Rock
WOW Factor: 6
Location: Indian Lake (Hamilton County)
Tenth Edition, NYS Atlas & Gazetteer: p. 37, C7–8; **Earlier Edition NYS Atlas & Gazetteer**: p. 87, B6
Parking GPS Coordinates: 43º47.301'N 74º20.113'W
Estimated Balanced Rock GPS Coordinates: 43º47.721'N 74º19.207'W
Accessibility: 1.2-mile bushwhack; 575' ascent
Degree of Difficulty: Difficult due to bushwhack

Description: This medium-sized, unnamed, balanced rock stands 6 feet high and is poised near the edge of a ledge. Some have estimated the boulder to weigh as much as 8 tons. Only a small section of its underbelly is in contact with the bedrock, making it, in my estimation, a delicately balanced *perched* rock.

History: Little Sawyer Mountain rises to a height of over 2,340 feet. Nearby Sawyer Mountain, its big brother, is 2,618 feet in height.

At one time, a secondary trail from Sawyer Mountain led over to Little Sawyer Mountain, but that trail has since faded into obscurity.

BOULDERS BEYOND BELIEF

Directions: From Indian Lake (junction of Routes 30 & 28), drive west on Route 30/28 for 2.1 mile. Turn left onto Cedar River Road and proceed west for ~1.8 miles. Park in front of a dirt road that formerly led to an abandoned sandpit. It is now blocked by several weighty boulders.

From the sandpit, bushwhack northeast until you come to a small tributary to the Cedar River. Follow the brook upstream, continuing northeast for 0.8 mile. When you reach the swamp that the brook drains out from, turn right and, from there, bushwhack southeast for another 0.3 mile up to the summit of Little Sawyer Mountain. The boulder is just below the summit, perched on a ledge.

Little Sawyer Mountain Balanced Rock.

It is also possible to bushwhack up to Little Sawyer Mountain's summit from Route 30/28. Park approximately 0.5 mile east of the parking area for Sawyer Mountain, and bushwhack south into the woods for 1.0 mile. Potentially, this is a more difficult bushwhack for, unlike the first one that follows a stream part of the way up, this one has no distinctive land features to guide you. It is more suitable for hikers familiar with the use of compass or GPS unit, who have done bushwhacks before, and who are traveling with equally skilled companions.

Resources: James J. LaForest & Ann L. LaForest, *Along the Cedar River* (Authors, 2004), pages unnumbered.
adirondackexperience.com/blog/2015/11/little-sawyer-and-ledge-mountains -- Two photos of the balanced rock taken by regional author Spencer Morrissey can be seen.
adirondackexperience.com/recreation/little-sawyer-mountain – The website shows a photograph of the balanced rock as well as providing directions on how to bushwhack to the summit from Route 30/8.
mylonglake.com/what-2-do/hiking/sawyer-mountain.

BOULDERS BEYOND BELIEF

86. SPLIT ROCK: LEWEY LAKE
Lewey Lake Campground

Type of Formation: Split Rock
WOW Factor: 3
Location: Lewey Lake (Hamilton County)
Tenth Edition, NYS Atlas & Gazetteer: p. 37, E7; **Earlier Edition NYS Atlas & Gazetteer**: p. 87, CD5–6
Campground GPS Coordinates: 43º38.835'N 74º23.297'W
Split Rock GPS Coordinates: 43º38.563'N 74º23.550'W
Fee: Day-use fee charged
Accessibility: *By land* – Drive or walk 0.4 mile to campsite #119. A short path leads directly over to the lake and rock.
    By water -- 0.5-mile trek
Degree of Difficulty: Easy
Additional Information: Lewey Lake Campground, 4155 Route 30, Lake Pleasant, NY; (518) 648-5616.
    Campground map available at: dec.ny.gov/docs/permits_ej_operations_pdf/leweylake2016.pdf.

Split Rock at Lewey Lake. Postcard c. 1950.

Description: Split Rock is a 6-foot-high, 12–15-foot-long split rock that lies next to Lewey Lake's shoreline. It gained some notoriety after a postcard of it was published in the 1950s.

235

BOULDERS BEYOND BELIEF

History: Development of the Lewey Lake Campground began in 1920, was expanded in the 1930s through the Civilian Conservation Corps (CCC), and further developed after the creation of modern Route 30.

The campground and lake are named after Louis (Lewey) Seymour, a hermit who lived in a primitive camp at a spot then known as Lewey Bridge (the part of the campground north of the bridge).

The Lewey Lake Campground contains a total of 207 campsites.

Split Rock as it looks today.

Directions: From Speculator (junction of Routes 30 & 8 South), drive north on Route 30 for ~11.8 miles. Turn left into the Lewy Lake Campground and day-use area.

From Indian Lake (junction of Routes 30 & 28), drive south on Route 30 for ~11.8 miles. Turn right into the campground area.

By land -- Once inside the campground, follow a road around the east side of the lake to campsite #119, nearly at the end of the road. A 50-foot-long path from the campsite leads down to the rock. The last time I was there, a narrow, short board led from the shore over to the rock.

By water -- From the launch site, follow the east shoreline southwest for <0.5 mile. The boulder is just off-shore.

Resources: dec.ny.gov/outdoor/24475.html.
Russell Dunn, *Penultimate Paddles in the Piseco, Indian, & Canada Lake Region* (Albany, NY: John Haywood Photography, 2016), 47–49.

BOULDERS BEYOND BELIEF

87. SNOWY MOUNTAIN BOULDERS

Type of Formation: Large Boulder
WOW Factor: 8–9
Location: Sabael (Hamilton County)
Tenth Edition, NYS Atlas & Gazetteer: p. 37, D7–8; **Earlier Edition NYS Atlas & Gazetteer**: p. 87, C6
Parking GPS Coordinates: 43º41.597′N 74º20.507′W
Snowy Mountain Boulders GPS Coordinates: 43º41.754′N 74º21.055′W
Accessibility: 0.6-mile hike
Degree of Difficulty: Moderate

Description: A large number of enormous, weather-beaten boulders can be found along a path ultimately leading up to the Griffin Brook Slide (a gash on the side of Snowy Mountain that formed in the late 1990s). Of the rocks encountered along the way, Cave Rock has to be one of the most unique boulders in all of the Adirondacks. It is 10 feet high and 20 feet wide, with a 5-foot, claw-like overhang, pock-marked with tiny potholes, as though riddled by a shotgun blast.

In an article that appeared in the 2013 issue of *Adirondack Explorer* entitled "2 sides of Indian Lake," Bill Ingersoll writes, "Cave Rock, [is] the most impressive boulder I've seen anywhere in New York. One corner is missing, creating a chamber the size of a walk-in closet—the 'cave' that gives the boulder its name. The walls

Cave Rock.

237

BOULDERS BEYOND BELIEF

and ceiling are pocked with cavities, and cavities within cavities...They resemble potholes found in river bedrock, but these are tafoni, created by a process called 'cavernous weathering.'"

As strange and awesome as Cave Rock is, however, it is merely one of many strange, pockmarked boulders that you will see at this site.

History: This collection of unusual, large boulders is located on the east side of Snowy Mountain. It occupies the same drainage area as the Griffin Brook Slide.

Cave Rock was named for the shelter cave produced by its overhang.

Other boulders go by such colorful names as Deception Rising, Mass Disstruction, Nothing, Roost Beef, and Butter.

David "Buzz" Buzzelli (a New York State highway engineer) is credited for being the first to, if not discover then at least, bring this collection of boulders to the attention of the larger climbing community. More than 40 bouldering problems have been established here since 2006.

This particular kind of rock is known as *huecos*, which is Spanish for "large cavity." The pitted rock enables boulderers to climb quickly because of hand and foot holds provided by the cavities. The rock is also called *tafoni*, which refers to cave-like features sometimes found in granular rock. Many of the Snowy Mountain Boulders here are similarly honeycombed.

Geologists believe that the pockmarked boulders were not created by water pouring off of glaciers. Neither is there evidence to suggest that the boulders were once in a streambed where water could have modified them. The latest theory, expounded by Jim Lawyer & Jeremy Haas in *Adirondack Rock: A Climber's Guide*, is that the strange boulders formed when "...mineral clusters dissolved faster than the surrounding rocks."

Snowy Mountain (3,899'), from which the name of the rocks is derived, was earlier called Squaw Bonnet Mountain.

Directions: *Snowy Mountain Boulders* -- From Speculator (junction of Routes 30 & 8 South), drive north on Route 30 for ~16.0 miles.

BOULDERS BEYOND BELIEF

From Indian Lake Village (junction of Routes 30 & 28), drive south on Route 30 for ~7.6 miles.

The informal path begins along the west side of Route 30, ~0.6 mile south of the parking area for Snowy Mountain. The trailhead lies between yellow and green-colored highway markers, virtually next to a square-shaped, green-colored sign containing the numbers "30-2206-1425." Pay attention to these clues, because the trail is not so easily seen from the road otherwise.

Follow the path southwest for over 0.6 mile until you come to a field of boulders. A side path to the right leads to Cave Rock in 300 feet.

Should you continue following the trail uphill, you will eventually reach the base of the Griffin Brook Slide in 1.2 miles.

Squaw Brook Boulder.

Squaw Brook Boulder –

Squaw Brook Boulder is located not too far north of Snowy Mountain, and can be readily seen from roadside. The boulder lies at the terminus of Squaw Brook and stands 15 feet high, just downstream from a drainpipe that carries Squaw Brook under Route 30 [43°44.491'N 74°17.718'W] into a gorge, and then out into Indian Lake.

Readers should be cautioned that guardrails are present along both sides of Route 30 by Squaw Brook, making it virtually impossible to pull over. What is possible, however, is to pull off the road beyond the guardrails and walk back, but be mindful of fast-moving traffic if you do so.

The Squaw Brook Boulder is one rock that perhaps is be best viewed as a slowdown while traveling north (providing, of course, that no car is directly behind you)

Coming from Speculator (junction of Routes 30 & 8 South), drive north on Route 30 for ~20.2 miles.

BOULDERS BEYOND BELIEF

From Indian Lake (junction of Routes 30 & 28), drive south on Route 30 for ~3.5 miles.

The Squaw Brook Boulder is located in a tiny gorge on the east side of the road.

Resources: Justin Sanford, *New York Adirondack Park Bouldering* (Broadalbin, NY: Southern Adirondack Climber, LLC, 2015) 118–132.
Bill Ingersoll, "2 sides of Indian Lake," *Adirondack Explorer* (January/February, 2013), 14. The article includes a photograph of one of the unique boulders.
Bill Ingersoll, "Snowy Range Double Feature: Two hikes in the Southern Adirondacks," *Adirondack Sports & Fitness* (May, 2007).
en.wikipedia.org/wiki/Snowy_Mountain_(New_York).
adirondackexplorer.org/stories/ninecorners.php.
climbing.about.com/od/mountainandrockwords/a/HuecoDef.htm.
Evelyn Greene, "Holy boulders of the 'tafoni'" *Protect the Adirondacks* -- protectadks.org/2016/06/holy-boulders-of-the-tafoni-by-evelyn-greene.
communitywalk.com/adirondack_park/ny/boulders_in_the_adirondacks/map/299298.
Russell Dunn, *Adirondack Waterfall Guide* (Hensonville, NY: Black Dome Press, 2004), 50 & 51, regarding Squaw Brook.
Jim Lawyer & Jeremy Haas, *Adirondack Rock: A Climber's Guide* (Pompey, NY: Adirondack Rock Press, LLC, 2008), 530–532.
Bill Ingersoll, "2 sides of Indian Lake," *Adirondack Explorer* (January/February 2013), 14.

88. CHIMNEY FORMATION & CHIMNEY MOUNTAIN ICE CAVES
Siamese Pond Wilderness Area

Type of Formation: Chimney Formation; Tectonic Cave; Shelter Cave
WOW Factor: 8
Location: Wilderness Lodge (Hamilton County)
Tenth Edition, NYS Atlas & Gazetteer: p. 37, D9; **Earlier Edition NYS Atlas & Gazetteer**: p. 87, C7
Parking GPS Coordinates: 43º41.276'N 74º13.834'W
Chimney Mountain GPS Coordinates: 43º41.590'N 74º12.581'W
Fee: Small fee to park
Accessibility: ~1.2 mile-hike
Degree of Difficulty: Moderately difficult
Additional Information: Cabins can be rented at the base of Chimney Mountain at Kings Flow -- contact thecabinsatchimneymountain.com.

BOULDERS BEYOND BELIEF

Description: One of the most distinctive rock formations in the Adirondacks is the chimney-shaped spire near the summit of Chimney Mountain (2,700'). There is no mystery as to how this formation came to be named.

Chimney Mountain. Postcard c. 1930.

The Chimney rises up to a height of 35 feet, but actually extends considerably higher if you count the starting point as being from the bottom of the huge chasm that it overlooks. In *Fifty Hikes in the Adirondacks*, Barbara McMartin writes, "The Chimney itself rises 35 feet above the eastern rim, which falls beneath the Chimney, presenting a vertical drop of over 80 feet." Jerome Wyckoff, in *The Adirondack Landscape*, describes the pinnacle as being 60 feet high, undoubtedly starting his count from below the spire. The rock formation is truly massive. It would take a large party of hikers holding hands just to encircle the chimney portion, assuming that it was even possible to accomplish this feat.

The rift at the top of the mountain is equally as impressive. In some distant, cataclysmic moment eons ago, the top of the mountain was literally split into two, leaving behind a huge cleft over 600 feet long, 250 feet wide, and 200 feet deep. It's hard to imagine what kind of forces were being applied when this event occurred. The dimensions of the chasm were first presented in Medora Hooper Krieger's *The Geology of the Thirteenth Lake Quadrangle, New York: New York State Museum Bulletin* in May of 1937.

The Chimney is not the only point of interest on Chimney Mountain. Talus and tectonic caves have also formed where the mountaintop has cracked like an eggshell.

A word of advice If it is your intention to enter any of these caves, make sure that you are well equipped with a helmet, carry three sources of light, have warm clothing, bring rock climbing equipment (needed in some caves), and proceed ahead with several equally equipped companions. The reason for such caution is that a number of caves go down so deep that they contain ice chambers where the air temperature never rises above freezing. These are not places to visit in shorts and a T-shirt.

One interesting formation on the mountain is called the *Ship's Prow*. Here, you get to walk along a narrow peninsula (or spine) of rock. Just be aware that it slowly tapers, so that you may want to go only so far and not take a chance of losing your balance and tumbling off.

The Chimney.

Another interesting formation is the shelter cave on the side of the chimney, which is a great place to grab a bite in a rainstorm.

The Chimney formation itself holds its own kind of potential dangers. It beckons hikers to climb up to its heights, only to have those who made the climb suddenly realize that the hard part wasn't getting up, but rather coming back down.

BOULDERS BEYOND BELIEF

History: Chimney Mountain was formed eons ago by some almost unimaginable cataclysmic event, leaving behind a mountain top literally split in half as though by a giant cleaver.

Two boys explore the overhang shelter.

Directions: From the village of Indian Lake (junction of Routes 30 South & 28), drive south on Route 30 for 0.5 mile. Turn left onto Big Brook Road and proceed southeast for 3.4 miles. Along the way, when you come to a fork, bear right, heading southwest for nearly 0.7 mile. At a fork, bear left and go south for 1.0 mile. Turn right instead of going straight ahead on Moulton Road and drive southeast for 2.6 miles to reach the parking area for Chimney Mountain. Although street signs may be confusing, stay on Route 4 (Big Brook Road) for the entire distance.

From the parking area, follow the well-marked, well-worn trail up to the Chimney formation near the summit of Chimney Mountain, a hike of roughly 1.2 miles. From here, you can branch off in different directions to explore the rest of the mountain.

BOULDERS BEYOND BELIEF

Resources: Russell Dunn & Barbara Delaney, *Adirondack Trails with Tales: History Hikes through the Adirondack Park and the Lake George, Lake Champlain & Mohawk Valley Region* (Hensonville, NY: Black Dome Press, 2009), 197–205.
Medora Hooper Krieger's *The Geology of the Thirteenth Lake Quadrangle, New York: New York State Museum Bulletin #308*. (Albany, NY: The University of the State of New York, 1937).
Barbara McMartin, *Fifty Hikes in the Adirondacks* (Woodstock, VT: Backcountry Publications, 1988), 154–158.
Clay Perry, *Underground Empire: Wonders and Tales of New York Caves* (New York: Stephen Daye Press, 1948), 158–159. A rather unusual photograph of the Chimney is tucked away between pages 94 and 95.
Tom Starmer, *Five-Star Trails in the Adirondacks* (Birmingham, AL: Menasha Press, 2010), 87–93; 101–107.
Jerome Wyckoff, *The Adirondack Landscape* (Glens Falls, NY: Adirondack Mountain Club, 1967). Photograph of the rock formation is shown on page 21.
Barbara McMartin & Bill Ingersoll, *Discover the South Central Adirondacks. Third Edition* (Utica, NY: North Country Books, 2005), 126–131.
Bruce Wadsworth, *Day Hikes For All Seasons: An Adirondack Sampler* (Lake George, NY: Adirondack Mountain Club, 1996), 46 & 47.
Willard L. Reed, "Chimney Mountain Geological Wonder," *Adirondac* (Vol. XLVI, March 1982), 8 & 9.
Willard L. Reed, "The Beauty of the Caves," *Adirondac* (Vol. XLVI, March 1982), 10 & 11.
Dennis Aprill, *Paths Less Traveled* (Mt. Kisco, NY: Pinto Press, 1998), 125–129. A photo of the chimney is shown on page 127.
Barbara McMartin, *The Adirondack Park: A Wildlands Quilt* (Syracuse, NY: Syracuse University Press, 1999). A photo of the chimney includes people for scale.
Michael Sean Gormley with Ethan Gormley, "Chimney Kindles Kids' Curiosity," *Adirondack Explorer: 2005 Outings Guide*. The article, on page 9, talks about an adventure to locate some of the ice caves on Chimney Mountain. The article includes a photograph of the Chimney formation.
Arthur S. Knight (editor), *Adirondack Northway Guide* (Lake George, NY: Adirondack Resorts Press, Inc., 1964). A photograph inside one of the ice caves is shown on page 244.
Derek Burnett, "Adirondack Underground: Exploring Chimney Mountain," *Adirondac* (January/February, 2001), 18–21.
Donald R. Williams, *Adirondack Ventures: Images of America* (Charleston, SC: Arcadia Publishing, 2006). On page 107 is a photograph of the chimney.

BOULDERS BEYOND BELIEF

89. BLUE MOUNTAIN LAKE BOULDER

Type of Formation: Large Boulder
WOW Factor: 4–5
Location: Blue Mountain Lake (Hamilton County)
Tenth Edition, NYS Atlas & Gazetteer: p. 37, B6; **Earlier Edition NYS Atlas & Gazetteer**: p. 87, AB5
Blue Mountain Lake Boulder GPS Coordinates: 43º51.179'N 74º27.521'W
Accessibility: Roadside
Degree of Difficulty: Easy

Blue Mountain Lake Boulder, near roadside.

Description: The Blue Mountain Lake Boulder stands 15 feet high, and is 15 feet long. The rock is easily glimpsed from roadside. It is one of those unnamed, immense rocks that catches you by surprise with its sudden and unexpected appearance.

A narrow clearing behind the boulder affords limited views of Blue Mountain Lake.

BOULDERS BEYOND BELIEF

Directions: From the hamlet of Blue Mountain Lake (junction of Routes 28 & 30/28N), drive southwest on Route 28 for 1.5 miles. Pull over to the right side of the road. The boulder is quite visible, slightly downhill, less than 30 feet away. Undoubtedly, many drivers take a quick look at the boulder as they go by. In fact, while we were admiring the rock, a man on a motorcycle stopped, got off without saying a word, took a picture of the boulder, and then continued on his merry way.

90. HODGES ROCK

Hodges Rock (maybe) next to Loon Brook.

Type of Formation: Large Boulder
WOW Factor: *Hodges Rock* – 4; *Flume* -- 5
Location: Utowana Lake (Hamilton County)
Tenth Edition, NYS Atlas & Gazetteer: p. 37, BC5–6; **Earlier Edition NYS Atlas & Gazetteer**: p. 87, B4–5
Parking GPS Coordinates: 43º49.978'N 74º29.803'W

BOULDERS BEYOND BELIEF

Hodges Rock GPS Coordinates: 43º49.968'N 74º29.973'W
Accessibility: 0.05-mile walk
Degree of Difficulty: Easy

Description: In *A Deer Hunter's History*, Robert J. Elinskas writes that Hodges Rock "… is about 10 feet high and 14 feet in length…"

The boulder that I came upon is roughly 10 feet high and 15–20 feet long. Next to it is a 10-foot-high boulder, but considerably less massive. Possibly, the former is Hodges Rock.

The boulders are located just upstream from where Loon Brook, previously divided, rejoins before flowing into Utowana Lake.

Flume – The flume, which is crossed via a footbridge, is quite spectacular. Unlike most flumes, which possess near-vertical walls, this one is V-shaped, and roughly 100 feet in length. It literally looks like a water chute.

History: The rock as named after Fred Hodges, a local deer hunter.

Loon Brook, which rises from Blue Ridge, is a tributary to Utowana Lake.

Utowana Lake is notable for having once been owned by dime novelist Ned Buntline (remember the long-barreled Buntline special that Wyatt Earp is supposed to have used?). The land then passed on to Adirondack Great Camp developer William West Durant and, later, to mining magnate Berthold Hochschild (whose family still owns property at the north end of the lake).

Directions: The only directions I started with for locating Hodges Rock were from Robert J. Elinskas' book, *A Deer Hunter's History Book*, where the author explains that the boulder lies "…immediately south of the Big Bend on Loon Brook…" A quick glance at a regional topo map shows that the river bends significantly on both the north and south sides of Route 28. It seemed more likely to me that Hodges Rock, if I could find it, was on the north side of the road, closer to Otowana Lake. I did, in fact, find a large boulder which hopefully is Hodges Rock. Even if it isn't, it's still a big rock.

From Blue Mountain Lake (junction of Routes 28 & 30/28N), drive southwest on Route 28 for 3.9 miles and park to your right in a grassy area directly in front of the start of guardrails.

BOULDERS BEYOND BELIEF

Follow the faint outline of a road into the woods. It immediately turns into a footpath marked by red disks imprinted with the image of a hiker.

After walking downhill for a hundred feet, you will reach a junction. Should you continue straight ahead downhill, paralleling Loon Brook to your left, you will approach the lake, but there are no significant boulders to be seen along the way.

Instead, bear left at this junction, immediately crossing over a footbridge at the head of a narrow, deep flume. In another couple of hundred feet, a second footbridge is reached. This time, instead of crossing the bridge, bear right and proceed downstream for 20 feet, walking along a large area of exposed bedrock. Several boulders will be seen on your right. The larger one may be Hodges Rock.

I can't help but wonder if this trail may be a private footpath. Still, there are no posted signs or anything to indicate that public use of this path is restricted, so I remain uncertain as to the legality of this access.

Resources: Robert J. Elinskas, *A Deer Hunter's History Book* (Robert J. Elinskas, 2005), 74. On page 315 is a winter photograph of a man standing by the rock. en.wikipedia.org/wiki/Utowana_Lake.

91. UTOWANA LAKE BOULDER

Type of Formation: Large Boulder
WOW Factor: 7
Location: Utowana Lake (Hamilton County)
Tenth Edition, NYS Atlas & Gazetteer: p. 36, BC5; **Earlier Edition NYS Atlas & Gazetteer**: p. 87, B4–5
Parking GPS Coordinates: 43º50.106'N 74º32.146'W
Utowana Lake Boulder GPS Coordinates: 43º50.091'N 74º32.117'W
Accessibility: 100-foot-trek
Degree of Difficulty: Easy

Description: The Utowana Lake Boulder is a monster rock, some 20 feet high, 20 feet wide, and 30 feet long. Next to it is a 10-foot-high boulder also of respectable size. Between the two is a passageway wide enough to admit a hiker. A third, good-sized rock is directly behind the main boulder, next to the lake.

BOULDERS BEYOND BELIEF

History: Utowana Lake is connected to Raquette Lake to the west and Eagle Lake to the east. I'm not exactly sure what the name, Otowana, means, but there once was a USS Utowana—a fishing trawler built in 1891 that was acquired by the U.S. Navy during WWI and used as a mine-sweeper, so the name must mean something.

Utowana Rock and one of its rocky companions.

It is quite apparent that the rock receives a fair amount of traffic from boaters who must have to launch from Blue Mountain Lake and pass through Eagle Lake. The site is also used by paddlers as an entry point for their canoes and kayaks.

I am pleased to say that the boulder is in pristine condition, with no evidence of it having been mistreated or plastered with graffiti.

Directions: From Blue Mountain Lake (junction of Routes 28 & 30/28N), drive southwest on Route 28 for ~5.9 miles and turn right into a small dirt pull-off.

BOULDERS BEYOND BELIEF

From Raquette Lake where Route 28 crosses the South Bay Outlet, drive northeast for 4.7 miles and turn left into a small pull-off.

From the south end of the pull-off, walk over to the adjacent telephone pole. Follow a 100-foot-long path that leads down the embankment and over to the boulder, which is set back in the woods next to the lake.

Resources: adirondackexperience.com/fishing/utowana-lake – It was from this website that I first learned of the boulder's existence. The website includes a map showing the location of the site.
adksports.com/2016-05-paddling – The boulder is mentioned in an article by Rich Macha entitled "Marion River and the Art of the Carry."

92. ARNOLD'S ROCK

Type of Formation: Large Boulder
WOW Factor: 5
Location: Seventh Lake (Herkimer County)
Tenth Edition, NYS Atlas & Gazetteer: p. 36, CD3; **Earlier Edition NYS Atlas & Gazetteer**: p. 86, BC2–3
Estimated Eighth Lake Campground Parking GPS Coordinates: 43º45.932N 74º4'W
Arnold's Rock GPS Coordinates: 43º45.078'N 74º42.514'W
Accessibility: *By land* -- ~1.8-mile hike; B*y water* – 0.6-mile paddle
Degree of Difficulty: Moderate
Additional Information: cnyhiking.com/ArnoldsRockTrail.htm – for trail map to Arnold's Rock.

Description: In *Discover the West Central Adirondacks*, Barbara McMartin & Lee M. Brenning write that "A large rock known as Arnold's Rock, protrudes from the shore providing a good place to picnic, sunbathe, or enjoy the view of Seventh Lake Mountain across the way."

History: Arnold's Rock was named for Ed Arnold, who erected a frame camp on the shore of Seventh Lake at Arnold's Point in the late 1800s.

I suspect that there may also be a second rock along the shoreline that some have thought is Arnold's Rock.

BOULDERS BEYOND BELIEF

Directions: *Land Approach* -- The recommended approach to Arnold's Rock today starts from the Eighth Lake Campground. (An earlier approach began from a path off of Seventh Lake Road that was without parking options). From the southwest side of the campground, follow the red-blazed Uncas Trail west for 0.9 mile, and then turn left onto the green-blazed Arnold's Rock Trail, created in 2011. Follow the Arnold's Rock Trail south for 0.9 mile to Arnold's Rock where a connection with the Seventh Lake Trail is made.

Water Approach – From Inlet, drive east on Route 28 for ~4.0 miles to the Seventh Lake Boat Launch & Fishing Access, on your left, near the southeast end of Seventh Lake.

From the launch site, paddle north/slightly west for 0.6 to reach Arnold's Rock, which is only ~0.1 mile west of the line formed by a series of islands.

Arnold's Rock.

Resources: Barbara McMartin & Lee M. Brenning, *Discover the West Central Adirondacks* (Woodstock, VT: Backcountry Publications, 1988), 273.
cnyhiking.com/ArnoldsRockTrail.htm.
cnyhiking.com/SeventhLakeTrail.htm.
adirondackalmanack.com/2015/02/the-early-history-of-seventh-lake.html.

BOULDERS BEYOND BELIEF

David H. Beetle, *Up Old Forge Way* (Lakemont & Old Forge, NY: North Country Books, 1972), 138.
Arthur W. Haberl & series editor Neal Burdick, *Guide to Adirondack Trails: West-Central Region. Third Edition* (New York: Adirondack Mountain Club, Inc., 1994), 120.
Robert J. Redington, *Guide to Trails of the West-Central Adirondacks* (Glens Falls, NY: Adirondack Mountain Club, Inc., 1984), 84.

93. BATTLESHIP ROCK

Type of Formation: Large Boulder
WOW Factor: 3
Location: Seventh Lake (Herkimer County)
Tenth Edition, NYS Atlas & Gazetteer: p. 36, CD2; **Earlier Edition NYS Atlas & Gazetteer**: p. 86, BC2
Island Road Bridge GPS Coordinates: 43º44.821'N 74º45.764'W
Boat Launch Site GPS Coordinates: 43º44.665'N 74º43.504'W
Battleship Rock GPS Coordinates: 43º44.876'N 74º45.908'W
Degree of Difficulty: Moderate paddle

Description: Battleship Rock lies in very shallow waters next to the shoreline in a narrow area of islands between Sixth and Seventh Lake. The fact that the rock is surrounded by water is what led to its colorful appellation.

An old postcard shows the boulder jutting 4–5 feet above the surface of the water, its length considerable greater than its height. The rock has fractured horizontally along its length roughly halfway above the water line.

The rock visible today from the Island Road Bridge, ~0.1 mile due south of the bridge, looks somewhat like Battleship Rock, but there are discrepancies. The postcard illustration accompanying this chapter shows Battleship Rock located near the shoreline. The rock south of the bridge is at a significant distance from the shoreline. Still, it's possible that this discrepancy can be explained if the lake level has risen since the postcard was produced, causing the rock to move farther away from the shoreline as the lake increased in size.

Equally as possible is that Battleship Rock may lie slightly east of the bridge along the shoreline across from or next to Island Road. If this is so, then you will not be able to see the rock from the bridge, nor can it be viewed from Island Road due to the imposition of private homes.

When I asked one of the nearby residents about Battleship Rock, she knew nothing about it. It may be that this unique rock formation has fallen into obscurity, and that only a few know it by name.

The only sure way of seeing Battleship Rock, as far as I can determine, is to paddle or boat to it from the Seventh Lake Boat Launch & Fishing Access.

Battleship Rock. Postcard c. 1910.

History: Battleship Rock was featured in antique postcards of the Inlet area. The only reference I can find about the rock on the Internet states that it lies directly across the water from a house at #2 Island Road.

An earlier reference by David H. Beetle in *Up Old Forge Way* refers to "Battleship Rock being near Mingo Lodge." Since Mingo Lodge was located on Fourth Lake, this would place Battleship Rock in an entirely different location, assuming that Beetle is correct. I notice that there is a Mingo Road [43º45.733'N 74º50.780'W] that leads south from Route 28 to Fourth Lake, but I see no evidence, using Google Earth, of an off-shore boulder near the end of this road (although there is an oblong-shaped island 0.3 miles southeast of Mingo Road's terminus).

Other rocks of notoriety are located in the general area. Near Seventh Lake, according to David H. Beetle, is a flat boulder called Watcher's Rock, from which "…early hunters used to take pot-shots at swimming deer."

Directions: *Land view* -- From east of Inlet (junction of Routes 28 & 13/Seventh Lake Road), drive northeast on Route 13/Seventh Lake Road for 0.5 mile (or 0.2 mile past Island Avenue). When you come to a bridge, look to your left to see a long, rectangular boulder in the water, roughly 0.1 mile northwest of the bridge. This may be Battleship Rock. On the day I was there, a kayak was moored next to the rock, so it is obviously a popular destination.

Water view – From Inlet, drive east on Route 28 for ~4.0 miles (or 2.6 miles from Route 13/Seventh Lake Road) to the Seventh Lake Boat Launch & Fishing Access, on your left, near the southeast end of Seventh Lake.

Paddle west for a total of ~2.1 miles, rounding the north end of the islands (spanned by the Seventh Lake Bridge) and then south into the bay where the boulder lies.

You may want to bear left and explore the cove where more possible candidates for Battleship Rock can be found. A website for Waterfront Lodge Camp Mi-Wok at house #2 on Island Road mentions that "Battleship rock is just across the lake and has been the subject of vintage postcards. Just around the corner is the bridge on Seventh Lake."

Resources: Unnamed author, *Guide to Fulton Chain of Lakes* (Boonville, NY: Willard Press, undated). A photograph of the boulder is shown. The pages are unnumbered.
adkbyowner.com/listings/VR8019.html.
David H. Beetle, *Up Old Forge Way* (Lakemont & Old Forge, NY: North Country Books, 1972), 140.

94. NATURAL ROCK DAM
Moose River Recreation Area

Type of Formation: Natural Rock Dam
WOW Factor: 4
Location: Inlet (Hamilton County)

BOULDERS BEYOND BELIEF

Tenth Edition, NYS Atlas & Gazetteer: p. 36, DE2; **Earlier Edition NYS Atlas & Gazetteer**: p. 86, C2
Parking GPS Coordinates: 43º40.017'N 74º47.976'W
Natural Bridge GPS Coordinates: 43º39.196'N 74º47.784'W
Accessibility: 1.4-mile hike
Degree of Difficulty: Moderate
Additional Information: naturalatlas.com/trails/rock-dam-2193673 –
This map shows the road to where the trail begins.
Another map can be found at cnyhiking.com/MooseRiverPlainsCamping.htm.

Description: Natural Rock Dam, as its name suggests, is a natural, 250-foot-long rock formation at the confluence of the South Branch of the Moose River and Red River. Although it appears to be manmade, it isn't.

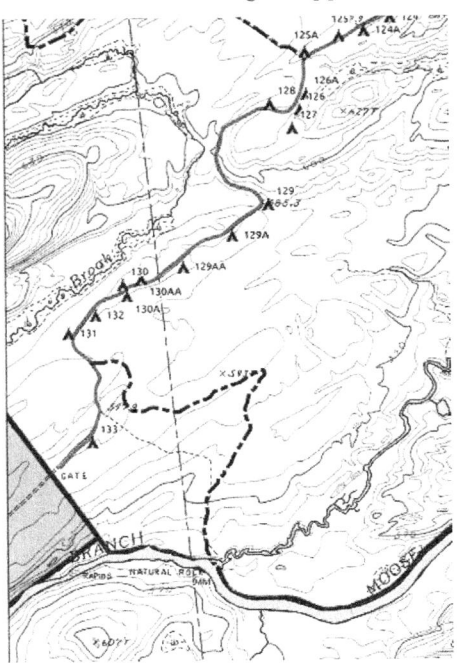

In *Guide to Adirondack Trails: West-Central Region. Third Edition*, the author writes, "In times of low flow, sturdy hikers wade out to the dam, which is a broad, smooth rock formation blocking the center of the river.... The Red River joins just above the dam."

History: The Natural Rock Dam is not the only one of its kind in the Adirondacks. There is also a 17-foot-high natural dam on the Oswegatchie River in the hamlet of Natural Dam [44º20.078'N 75º30.245'W], west of Gouverneur along Route 68. Gouverneur is named for Gouverneur Morris, who once had a summer home there. The area around the river is posted. For all I know, the natural dam may not even exist in its original state, possibly having been built upon to increase its height to better serve the industrialists.

In addition to the natural dam at Natural Dam, there is also a natural dam (of sorts) at Remsen Falls, which is described in the *Guide to*

BOULDERS BEYOND BELIEF

Adirondack Trails: West-Central Region. Third Edition as where "the falls, only a few feet high, are created by a natural rock barrier across the river." There are probably a number of such natural dams in New York State. Glenerie Falls in Saugerties is one that comes readily to mind.

Directions: From Inlet (junction of Route 28 & South Shore Road), drive west on Route 28 for ~0.7 mile, turn right onto Limekiln Road and head south. At 1.7 miles you will pass by the entrance to the Limekiln Lake Public Campground & Day Use Area on your right, which was purchased from the Gould Paper Company and turned into a campsite in 1963.

When you reach 1.8 miles, turn left onto an unpaved road at a sign that reads "Limekiln Lake Entrance: Moose River Plains Wild Forest." Some maps refer to the road as the Limekiln Lake-Cedar River Road. The presence of a yellow-colored, hinged barrier suggests the likelihood that the road is seasonal-only, and closed to vehicular traffic during the winter.

Drive south for ~4.6 miles. At a junction, proceed right (straight) onto Rock Dam Road, aka Indian Lake Road, and head southeast for ~ 3.8 miles.

Park at the trailhead on your left, just 0.4 mile before the barricaded end of Rock Dam Road. Follow the yellow-blazed Rock Dam Trail south for 1.4 miles to reach the confluence of the South Branch of the Moose River and the Red River, where the natural dam can be seen.

On the day prior to my visit, part of the road was being used for the 40-mile Black Fly Mountain Bike Challenge that took place between Inlet and Indian Lake.

Resources: naturalatlas.com/trails/rock-dam-2193673.
Robert J. Redington, *Guide to Trails of the West-Central Adirondacks* (Glens Falls, NY: Adirondack Mountain Club, Inc., 1984), 119.
Barbara McMartin & Lee M. Brenning, *Discover the West-Central Adirondacks* (Woodstock, VT: Backcountry Publications,
David H. Beetle, *Up Old Forge Way* (Lakemont & Old Forge, NY: North Country Books, 1972), 173. Beetle calls it "a natural river barrier."
Arthur W. Haberl & series editor Neal Burdick, *Guide to Adirondack Trails: West-Central Region. Third Edition* (New York: Adirondack Mountain Club, Inc., 1994), 221, 222, & 205.
Norm Landis & Bradly A. Pendergraft, *Adirondack Mountain Club Western Trails. First Edition* (Lake George, NY: Adirondack Mountain Club, Inc., 2016), 108 & 109.

BOULDERS BEYOND BELIEF

95. FERN PARK RECREATION AREA BOULDER
Fern Park Recreation Area

Type of Formation: Large Boulder
WOW Factor: 5
Location: Inlet (Hamilton County)
Tenth Edition, NYS Atlas & Gazetteer: p. 36, D2; **Earlier Edition NYS Atlas & Gazetteer**: p. 86, BC2
Parking GPS Coordinates: 43º44.859'N 74º47.846'W
Big Rock GPS Coordinates: Unknown
Accessibility: Unknown but probably <1.0 mile
Degree of Difficulty: Moderate
Additional Information: inletny.com/cross-country-skiing/fern-park-recreation-area – map of park;

Description: I have not actually been to this rock, but I know it's there. In their 1979 book, *25 Ski Tours in the Adirondacks,* Almy & Anne Coggeshall describe "a huge boulder" located on Trail #6 that appears to be over 20 feet high from a cropped photograph that they include in their book.

History: The Fern Park Recreation Area is a four-season recreational park that offers over 20 miles of trails. Much earlier, it was called the Inlet Ski Touring Center. The system of trails was established by Walter Schmid, a German champion cross-country ski racer, who leased the lands and, in the process, created one of the first ski touring centers in the Adirondacks.

Directions: From the center of Inlet (junction of Routes 28 & South Shore Road), drive southwest on South Shore Road for 0.2 mile. Turn left onto Loomis Road and drive south for 0.1 mile to the parking area by the kiosk.

Taking into consideration that there are over twenty miles of trails for cross-country skiing, snow-shoeing, and biking, readers can forgive me for not finding the giant rock during my visit. To be honest, I wasn't undertaking this quest without some prior knowledge. From the Coggeshall's book, I knew that "a large number of trails diverge from a common point." The authors suggest that you "take Trail #6 to the left. It will shortly pass just below a huge boulder."

Starting from the kiosk, I walked southeast along a road perpendicular to the one I had driven in on. Near the end of the field I followed this same road as it turned right. I could immediately see that the road lead uphill to a building. Rather than staying on this road, I continued straight ahead (southeast) past a 6-foot-high boulder to my left and then began walking along an abandoned, grassy road. Soon, I began to see blue and yellow disks on the trees. Within 0.3 mile, I had passed by a number of side path indicated by names and numbers. I actually did see a marking for Trail #6, but could make no sense out of it, for the trail quickly led nowhere, immediately turning into Trail # 5 or #7. After fumbling around at the junction for a while, and failing to decipher what the markings and color-coded names meant, I gave up.

Back at the parking area, the kiosk map displays all the trails color-coded and named, but makes no mention of the giant boulder. Quite frankly, I can't even tell for certain that the current Trail #6 is the same one mentioned by the Coggeshalls forty years ago.

Alas, I am forced to leave further exploration for others, but I'm all right with that. After all, this is an *explorer's* hiking guidebook.

Resources: Almy & Anne Coggeshall, *25 Ski Tours in the Adirondacks* (Somersworth, NH: New Hampshire Publishing Company, 1979). A map on page 116 shows the general location of the rock. A photograph of the rock appears on page 112.

96. NEODAK SPLIT ROCK (Historic)

Type of Formation: Split Rock
WOW Factor: 7
Location: Inlet (Hamilton/Herkimer County)
Tenth Edition, NYS Atlas & Gazetteer: p. 36, CD2; **Earlier Edition NYS Atlas & Gazetteer**: p. 86, BC2
Holls Inn GPS Coordinates: 43º45.015'N 74º48.171'W
Accessibility: On private property

Description: The Neodak Split Rock is a 20-foot-high boulder that is equally as long as it is tall. In *Memories of Inlet*, Letty Kirch Haynes writes, "Just a short hike through the woods across from the hotel [Neodak], it is a picturesque place where a huge rock shadows a small stream."

In its time, the Neodak Split Rock was a popular destination for tourists.

BOULDERS BEYOND BELIEF

History: The former Neodak Hotel was built by the Pratt family around 1900, and taken over by William Preston in 1905. The Neodak Split Rock proved to be a popular attraction for guests.

Neodak Split Rock. Postcard c. 1910.

In 1920, a much larger structure was erected by Roy and Emma Rogers that was capable of accommodating up to 60 guests. Unfortunately though, the unpredictable economy for tourism changed during World War II, and the hotel saw a major decline in business. After 1959, the Neodak Hotel, essentially in disuse, was burned to the ground and the land subsequently subdivided.

Directions: The Neodak Split Rock is off of South Shore Road, across from where the old Holls Inn used to be located. Unfortunately, the rock is now on privately owned property and not visible from roadside.

The only trace of Neodak today is a roadside sign that reads "Neodak Shores."

One cannot help but feel a sense of sadness and loss that the Town of Inlet failed to purchase the land surrounding the Neodak Split Rock to turn it into a park, much like they did with lakeside Arrowhead Park in the center of Inlet.

Resources: Letty Kirch Haynes, *Memories of Inlet* (Utica, NY: North Country Books, Inc., 2006), 6—11. A photo of Split Rock can be seen on page 9. On page 8 are photos of the former Neodak Hotel, located on the waterfront.
Author unnamed, *Guide to Fulton Chain of Lakes* (Boonville, NY: Willard Press, undated). A photo of Camp Neodak is shown; pages are unnumbered.
David H. Beetle, *Up Old Forge Way* (Lakemont & Old Forge, NY: North Country Books, 1972), 123. "…Holl's Inn private trail that slices through a boulder known as 'Split Rock'…"

97. ROOSEVELT ROCK & MARTIN ROAD BOULDERS

Type of Formation: Large Rock; Historic Rock
WOW Factor: 4–5
Location: Big Moose (Herkimer County)
Tenth Edition, NYS Atlas & Gazetteer: p. 36, BC1; **Earlier Edition NYS Atlas & Gazetteer**: p. 86, B2
Launch site Parking GPS Coordinates: 43º49.631'N 74º50.297'W
Destination GPS Coordinates: *Roosevelt Rock* -- 43º49.755'N 74º51.845'W; *Martin Road Boulders* -- 43º49.808'N 74º51.865'W
Accessibility: *Roosevelt Rock* – 1.5-mile trek by water; *Martin Road Boulders* -- Roadside
Degree of Difficulty: *Roosevelt Rock* – Moderate; *Martin Rock Boulders* -- Easy

Description: *Roosevelt Rock* is a medium-sized boulder of some historical significance. According to Jane A. Barlow in *Big Moose Lake in the Adirondacks,* "On the land side of an enormous glacial erratic that sits at the water's edge is carved the name "J. Roosevelt." The historical significance of this becomes apparent in a moment [see history section].

The rock is mostly immersed in the water and is roughly 8–10 feet in height. Its front is smooth and planned looking. Several large rocks sit behind the boulder on the upslope from the shoreline. If you are facing the boulder from the lake, the letters "J. Roosevelt" are visible on the right side of the rock. The years have taken their toll on the letter's legibility, but the name is still discernable.

BOULDERS BEYOND BELIEF

Uphill from Roosevelt Rock is "Vall-Kill by Roosevelt Rock," a private residence where no land access is permitted.

Back in the days when a plethora of hotels and resorts flourished around Big Moose Lake, a shoreline trail of sorts circumnavigated the lake, passing directly by Roosevelt Rock, where a teahouse could be found.

Martin Road Boulders – On the way to The Waldheim (43°49.866'N 74°51.533'W), which is located at the terminus of Martin Road, two sentinel rocks are passed. The one on the left side of the road is 10 feet high and 8 feet long; the one on the right side of the road, diagonally across, is 6 feet high with a tree growing on top of it.

Roosevelt Rock. The inscription, not visible, is on right side of the boulder.

History: Roosevelt Rock is named after John Ellis Roosevelt who was the cousin of and personal secretary to President Theodore Roosevelt. John Roosevelt began camping near the boulder, and then purchased four lots from the Ne-Ha-Sa-Ne Park Association in 1899. He constructed a primitive camp near the rock which he called Camp Roosevelt.

BOULDERS BEYOND BELIEF

One of the clues I used for locating this rock was from The Waldheim's website (thewaldheim.com/history) which read, "In 1901, when he was only twenty-nine, E. J. [E. J. Martin] was able to buy a large tract of land on the north side of the lake. This new purchase extended from the east line of the present Insley property (which then belonged to John Ellis Roosevelt, a cousin of President Theodore Roosevelt) to just east of the point where the present Waldheim beach is located."

Big Moose Lake got its name from its shape, which vaguely resembles a bull moose's head—not, as you might think, because a large moose was seen swimming across it. It was originally referred to as the "Third Lake on the North Branch of the Moose River" in the 1800s.

The lake achieved considerable notoriety during the twentieth-century trial of Chester Gillette, who murdered his pregnant girlfriend, Grace Brown, while rowing her across the lake. The tragic events were immortalized in Craig Branden's book *Murder in the Adirondacks: An American Tragedy Revisited*.

Roosevelt Boulder – At one time, a different boulder named Roosevelt Rock was located in Newcomb. Affixed to its surface was a plaque commemorating Theodore Roosevelt's mad dash through Newcomb to be sworn in as president of the United States after receiving word of President William McKinley's unexpected death. Although the boulder still exists, it has fallen into obscurity. The plaque that gave the boulder distinction was taken off when New York State established a new road, and affixed to a specially created stone monument.

Directions: From Eagle Bay (junction of Routes 1 & 28), take Route 1 (Big Moose Road) northwest for ~3.8 miles. Turn right onto Higby Road, and head northeast for 1.5 miles. At a fork, turn right onto the continuation of Higby Road. In another 0.1 mile (or a total of 1.6 miles from Route 1), you will come to the car-top boat launch. NOTE: This launch only accommodates kayaks and canoes.

From the launch site, paddle west across the lake for roughly 1.5 miles. A clue to the rock's location is that it is 0.2 mile southwest of The Waldheim.

Martin Road Boulders – From Eagle Bay (junction of Routes 1/Big Moose Road & 28), take Route 1 (Big Moose Road) northwest for 5.7 miles. When you come to Martin Road, turn right and proceed northeast for 1.3 miles. The two

BOULDERS BEYOND BELIEF

boulders are clearly visible next to the road, just like stone sentinels. To be sure, these are not huge boulders, so keep your expectations low.

The Waldheim is reached at 1.5 miles. While driving northeast along Martin Road, be sure to watch for two waterfalls that cascade down the cliff face on your left, their respective streams going under the road.

Resources: Jane A. Barlow (editor), *Big Moose Lake in the Adirondacks* (Syracuse, NY: The Big Moose Lake History Project, 2004). A photograph of the rock taken by Mark Barlow in 1999 can be seen on page 2. Information about the rock's history is found on page 179.

Lana Fennessy, *The History of Newcomb* (Newcomb, NY: 1996), 90. Mention is made of the fate of the Roosevelt Rock in Newcomb, including a picture of the rock.

98. BALANCED ROCK: BALD MOUNTAIN

Type of Formation: Perched Rock
WOW Factor: 7
Location: Old Forge (Herkimer County)
Tenth Edition, NYS Atlas & Gazetteer: p. 36, CD1; **Earlier Edition NYS Atlas & Gazetteer**: p. 86, BC1
Parking GPS Coordinates: 43°44.750′N 74°53.973′W
Balanced Rock GPS Coordinates: 43°44.268′N 74°54.863′W
Accessibility: 1.0-mile hike; 521-foot ascent
Degree of Difficulty: Moderate

Description: Balanced Rock is a 5-foot-high boulder that rests atop an inclined plane of bedrock. It is not so much balanced as perched, with the bedrock below it tilted just enough to make it easy to imagine the rock losing its purchase and tumbling into the valley below. Fortunately, such an event is not likely to happen soon, for the boulder is firmly planted and surprisingly stable, having undoubtedly been tested by groups of youngsters over the years.

The balanced rock is mentioned in an earlier version of the ADK *Guide to Trails of the West-Central Adirondacks*, where I first read it and saw it described as "…a balanced rock of sorts, a glacial boulder standing on a sloping ledge near the drop off."

BOULDERS BEYOND BELIEF

In *Up Old Forge Way*, David H. Beetle writes, 'The boulder—it's on the farther end as you go up the main trail—looks as though by eating the right kind of breakfast food you could easily push it off. Old Forge youths tried one Fourth of July with 16 sticks of dynamite, but the rock was unimpressed. Figuring out its weight has been a stock problem for Hamilton College geology students. They get an answer that's between 30 and 40 tons."

The Rondaxe Fire Tower, aka Bald Mountain Fire Tower, has stood on the summit of Bald Mountain since 1917. Closed in 1990, it was restored, beginning in 2002.

History: Bald Mountain (2,350') was originally called Pond Mountain, a name that arose from a small pond located at the base of its rocky, south face. Soon, the name changed to Bald Mountain to reflect its bare, rocky summit. Nevertheless, New York State decided to officially change the name to Rondaxe Mountain in order to eliminate any possible confusion with other peaks in the Adirondacks that were called Bald Mountain. The name Rondaxe came from the last two syllables in the word "Adi*rondack*s." The new name never really caught on, however, and almost everybody still calls the peak Bald Mountain.

Balanced Rock. Postcard c. 1910

Directions: From Old Forge, where Route 28 crosses over the Moose River, drive northeast on Route 28 for over 4.5 miles. Turn left onto Rondaxe Road (Route 93) opposite Fulton House Way and proceed northwest for 0.1 mile to a large parking area on your left. The trailhead to the summit of Bald Mountain begins here.

Part of the trail consists of walking along a hogback ridge that gradually turns into a narrow spine of rock. According to David H. Beetle, in *Up Old Forge Way*, the trail was clearly established by 1900.

When you reach the top of the mountain, continue past the fire tower, heading southwest along the rock crest, for ~450 feet. Balanced Rock will be to your left.

Roadside Rocks –

Between the villages of Old Forge and Inlet can be seen a series of large, roadside rocks along a cliff wall that, unfortunately, are on posted land. The rocks are located roughly 2.4 miles southwest of Rondaxe Road along the northwest side of Route 28 (43°43.554'N 74°56.095'W). A pull-off to your right, just before the rocks, provides a convenient place to park for those who wish to walk along the side of the road for a closer look.

Roadside Rocks.

Resources: *North Country Life* Vol. 11, no. 4 (Fall 1957). A photo of the enormous boulder is shown on page 3.
Joseph F. Crady, *The Adirondacks: Fulton Chain-Big Moose Region. The Story of a Wilderness* (Old Forge, NY: North Country Press, 1933), 59–61. How Bald Mountain came to be named is described in detail.
Barbara McMartin, *Discover the West Central Adirondacks* (Woodstock, VT: Backcountry Publications, 1988), 217 & 218.
Bruce Wadsworth, *Day Hikes For All Seasons: An Adirondack Sampler* (Lake George, NY: Adirondack Mountain Club, 1996), 53 & 54.
Dennis Aprill, *Paths Less Traveled* (Mt. Kisco, NY: Pinto Press, 1998), 69–72.
theadirondacker.com/2018/02/11/amazing-boulders-of-the-adirondacks.
Barbara McMartin, *The Adirondack Park: A Wildlands Quilt* (Syracuse, NY: Syracuse University Press, 1999). A photo of the balanced rock is shown on page 37.

BOULDERS BEYOND BELIEF

New York State Conservationist (December 1995). On the cover is a photograph of the boulder shot in the winter by Gary Randorf.
David H. Beetle, *Up Old Forge Way* (Lakemont & Old Forge, NY: North Country Books, 1972), 91 & 96.
John Freeman with Wesley H. Haynes, *Views from on High: Fire Tower Trails in the Adirondacks and Catskills* (Lake George, NY: Adirondack Mountain Club, Inc., 2001), 51. The trail "...reaches a balanced rock of sorts, a boulder standing on a sloping ledge near the drop-off."
Norm Landis & Bradly A. Pendergraft, *Adirondack Mountain Club Western Trails. First Edition* (Lake George, NY: Adirondack Mountain Club, Inc., 2016), 65.

Balanced Rock: Bald Mountain.

BOULDERS BEYOND BELIEF

99. CHAIN POND TRAIL BOULDERS
Pigeon Lake Wilderness

Type of Formation: Large Boulder; Talus Cave
WOW Factor: 5–6
Location: Eagle Bay (Herkimer County/Hamilton County)
Tenth Edition, NYS Atlas & Gazetteer: p. 36, C1; **Earlier Edition NYS Atlas & Gazetteer**: p. 86, B2
Parking GPS Coordinates: 43º48.233'N 74º50.914'W
Destination GPS Coordinates: *First Rock Site* -- 43º48.372'N 74º49.636'W; *Second Rock Site* -- 43º47.956'N 74º49.328'W to 43º48.528'N 74º49.013'W
Accessibility: ~2.4-mile hike
Degree of Difficulty: Moderately difficult

Rock-shelter: Site One.

Description: According to *Guide to Trails of the West-Central Adirondacks*, "…an interesting area of cliffs, crevasses, caves, and large boulders…" are encountered along the Chain Pond Trail.

As it turns out, two sets of interesting cliff walls are encountered. The first site consist of large blocks of talus that have fallen from a 45-foot-high cliff, both along the uphill climb, and then in a large, inclined area partially encased by rock walls, with huge 12–15-foot-high blocks, a split rock, and even a rock-shelter high up on the cliff wall.

The next site consist of one continuous, 30–35-foot-high rock wall that extends for over 0.2 mile, paralleled by the Cedar Pond Trail that follows close to the base of the wall.

BOULDERS BEYOND BELIEF

Dozens of 12–15-foot-high talus blocks can be seen along the way, as well as several small rock-shelters and talus caves.

Directions: From Eagle Bay (junction of Routes 1/Big Moose Road & 28), drive northwest on Route 1/Big Moose Road for 3.3 miles and turn right into the parking area for the Pigeon Lake Wilderness: Windfall Pond Trailhead.

Rock Wall: Site Two.

Follow the yellow-marked Queer Lake Trail east for 1.1 miles. At a junction next to Windfall Pond, bear right onto the blue-blazed Chain Pond Trail and proceed southeast. After 0.4–0.5 mile, you will ascend between large talus rocks under a 45-foot-high cliff, and come up into what I can only describe as a sweeping amphitheater of rock. Look up to see a high rock-shelter in the cliff wall. The trail immediately passes by a 10-foot-high split rock as it begins to descend.

In another 0.5-0.6 mile, the trail starts to follow along the base of a 30–35-foot-high rock wall to your left, and continues for another 0.3 mile. Along the way, you will repeatedly see large blocks of talus, small rock-shelters, and several talus caves. The rock wall essentially ends after you pass around a 5-foot-high boulder next to the trail. If you wish to continue farther, the rock wall is soon replaced by a deep gorge on your left containing no running water. At 1.6 miles, you will come to a junction where a trail sign indicates another 0.5 mile to Chain Pond.

Resources: Barbara McMartin & Lee M. Brenning, *Discover the West Central Adirondacks* (Woodstock, VT: Backcountry Publications, 1988), 235–237.
Arthur W. Haberl & series editor Neal Burdick, *Guide to Adirondack Trails: West-Central Region. Third Edition* (New York: Adirondack Mountain Club, Inc., 1994), 97.
Robert J. Redington, *Guide to Trails of the West-Central Adirondacks* (Glens Falls, NY: Adirondack Mountain Club, Inc., 1984), 101.
Norm Landis & Bradly A. Pendergraft, *Adirondack Mountain Club Western Trails. First Edition* (Lake George, NY: Adirondack Mountain Club, Inc., 2016), 57.

100. MIDDLE SETTLEMENT LAKE ROCKS
Ha-de-ron-dah Wilderness

Type of Formation: Large Rock; Rock-Shelter
WOW Factor: 7–8
Location: Thendara (Herkimer County)
Tenth Edition, NYS Atlas & Gazetteer: p. 35, D9: **Earlier Edition NYS Atlas & Gazetteer**: p. 85, C7
Parking GPS Coordinates: 43º40.545'N 75º03.161'W
Middle Settlement Lake Rocks GPS Coordinates: 43º41.298'N 75º05.559'W
Accessibility: Middle Settlement Lake -- 2.5-mile hike; Cedar Pond Rocks -- <1.0-mile hike from Middle Settlement Lake
Degree of Difficulty: Moderately difficult
Additional Information: cnyhiking.com/MiddleSettlementLake.htm – trail map

Middle Settlement Lake Rocks.

Description: Barbara McMartin writes in *Fifty Hikes in the Adirondacks* that "You know you are nearing Middle Settlement Lake when suddenly, in the midst of the unbroken forest, one of the Adirondack's great big boulders appears. It is part of the facing cliff that has split away." The cliff is reported as being 300 feet long and 30–35 feet high. Then, in *Adventures in Camping: An Introduction to Adirondack Backpacking*, McMartin goes on to say that you will

BOULDERS BEYOND BELIEF

find "...on a nearby lookout, even an area of giant boulders with a cave" and continues by saying that "At the base of some small cliffs, one large slab rests on other rocks forming a cave."

Cracked rock at Middle Settlement Lake.

Rhonda & George Ostertag, in *Hiking New York*, make reference to "...the gargantuan boulders at the end of the lake" but say nothing further about the rocks.

In *Guide to Adirondack Trails: West-Central Region. Third Edition*, mention is made of a "train of great boulders" just past where the trail from Cedar Pond enters from the right.

In *An Adirondack Sample II: Backpacking Trips* Bruce Wadsworth writes about approaching Middle Settlement Lake from Cedar Pond. Just before you reach the Middle Settlement Lake Access Trail, "An immense boulder is passed on the left....Just past it, on the right, is a smaller boulder, which has a small cave under it. Rocks have been used to fill in open spots around its entrance. At one time a wooden bed was inside, and winter campers have been known to sleep there."

The rock cave is fun to crawl into and explore. It formed when a slab of rock fell on top, creating a roof, and leaving a 2-foot-high gaping entrance.

Large rock with shelter. Middle Settlement Lake. Note figure in front.

History: Middle Settlement Lake is located in the 26,600-acre Ha-de-ron-dah Wilderness. The body of water came to be known as Middle Settlement Lake after one of John Brown's colonies, the Middle Settlement, took root nearby. According to nineteenth-century lawyer and historian, Charles E. Snyder, quoted in Henry A. L. Brown & Richard J. Walton's *John Brown's Tract: Lost Adirondack Empire*, "The Middle Settlement is now [by 1896] a mere tradition among a few old people. The remains of three houses are said to be still discernible in the woods...What was once a clearing has lapsed into a forest..."—and that was written over a century ago!

Thendara, for those who enjoy etymology, means "rim of the forest."

BOULDERS BEYOND BELIEF

Directions: From where Route 28 crosses over the Middle Branch of the Moose River in Old Forge, drive southwest on Route 28 for nearly 4.0 miles and turn left into a large rest area.

Rock Cave at Middle Settlement Lake.

From where Route 28 crosses the Moose River in McKeever, drive northeast on Route 28 for ~5.7 miles and turn right into a large rest area.

Park at the north end of the rest area.

To begin the hike, cross over Route 28 and walk north along Route 28 for 150 feet to the trailhead. Follow the red-blazed Scusa Access Trail northwest for 0.7 mile. At a junction, turn left and take the yellow-marked Brown's Tract Trail west for 0.9 mile, passing by the north shoulder of Bare Mountain (2,026') along the way. Then bear right onto the blue-marked Middle Settlement Lake Access Trail and proceed northwest for ~1.0 mile to reach the northeast end of Middle Settlement Lake. The huge rocks are located next to a marshy cove, virtually at the junction of the Middle Settlement Lake Access Trail and the Cedar Pond Trail.

The rocks are impressive indeed. Some are free-standing, but most are in a jumble, forming interesting nooks and crannies.

BOULDERS BEYOND BELIEF

One particularly big rock is located at the beginning of the Cedar Pond Trail where the path goes by the large boulder, on your right, and a tiny, but intriguing, rock cave, on your left.

Cedar Pond Trail Boulders -- From the Middle Settlement Lake Access Trail junction with Cedar Pond Trail, head east on the yellow-marked Cedar Pond Trail. As already mentioned, you will immediately pass by a large boulder and, opposite it, a low-lying, rock shelter.

Boulder along Cedar Pond Trail.

The path passes by the marshy area to your right and then enters the woods. Sometime later on, you will cross over the outlet stream from Cedar Pond. Soon after, you will see two 15–20-foot-high boulders partially embedded in the woods to your left.

In another 0.1 mile, a 12-foot-high, 8-foot-wide boulder behind several smaller ones off in the woods comes into view on your left, just before the west end of Cedar Pond/marshlands is reached.

BOULDERS BEYOND BELIEF

Resources: Barbara McMartin, *Fifty Hikes in the Adirondacks* (Woodstock, VT: Backcountry Publications, 1988), 86.
cnyhiking.com/MiddleSettlementLake.htm.
Rhonda & George Ostertag, *Hiking New York* (Guilford, CT: The Globe Pequot Press, 2002), 93—97. The authors describe the loop trail hike. A map is included on page 95.
cnyhiking.com/MiddleSettlementLake.htm. Basic information on the hike is provided.
Bruce Wadsworth, *An Adirondack Sample II: Backpacking Trips* (Glens Falls, NY: Adirondack Mountain Club, 1986), 74.
Barbara McMartin, *Adventures in Camping: An Introduction to Adirondack Backpacking* (Utica, NY: North Country Books, Inc., 1996), 76 & 77.
Arthur W. Haberl & series editor Neal Burdick, *Guide to Adirondack Trails: West-Central Region. Third Edition* (New York: Adirondack Mountain Club, Inc., 1994), 196 & 197.
Barbara McMartin & Lee M. Brenning, *Discover the West Central Adirondacks* (Woodstock, VT: Backcountry Publications, 1988), 195 & 196. "In front of you lies a jumble of boulders, some quite large, that have broken away from the steep rock wall behind them. One large slab resting on some smaller boulders forms a cave of sorts and over the years, people have filled in gaps with other stones to create a cozy shelter."
Norm Landis & Bradly A. Pendergraft, *Adirondack Mountain Club Western Trails. First Edition* (Lake George, NY: Adirondack Mountain Club, Inc., 2016), 92 & 93.
Lisa Densmore Ballard, *Hiking the Adirondacks. Second Edition* (Guilford, CT: Falcon Guides, 2017), 327. A striking photograph by the author shows a hikers standing next to a 25-30-foot-high boulder.
Henry A. L. Brown & Richard J. Walton. *John Brown's Tract: Lost Adirondack Empire* (Canaan, NH: Phoenix Publishing, 1988), 129.
Norm Landis, "4 favorite hikes," *Adirondack Explorer* Vol. 9, no. 2 (March/April 2007), 49. "I figured that I was nearing my destination when I spotted the roof of the lean-to on the northwest shore. However, the 'roof' turned out to be a large rock, one of many on the east end of the lake."
Bill Ingersoll, "Five hikes for four seasons," *Adirondack Explorer*: *2006 Outings Guide*. Ingersoll writes about "...a massive rock face where cabin-size boulders have split away and fallen below."
Jeff Mitchell, *Backpacking New York: 37 Great Hikes* (Mechanicsburg, PA: Stackpole Books, 2016), 175. "Here the trail winds through massive, jumbled boulders."
Jim Lawyer & Jeremy Haas, *Adirondack Rock: A Climber's Guide* (Pompey, NY: Adirondack Rock Press, LLC, 2008), 573–575. House size boulders are reported.

BOULDERS BEYOND BELIEF

101. FLATROCK BOULDERS
Flatrock Mountain Demonstration Forest

Type of Formation: Large Boulder
WOW Factor: 5
Location: Thendara (Herkimer County)
Tenth Edition, NYS Atlas & Gazetteer: p. 35, D9; **Earlier Edition NYS Atlas & Gazetteer**: p. 85, C7
Parking GPS Coordinates: 43º40.104'N 75º03.948'W
Split Rock GPS Coordinates: 43º40.084'N 75º04.035'W
Accessibility: 0.05–0.4-mile bushwhack
Degree of Difficulty: Moderate

One of many boulders to be found by Flatrock Mountain.

Description: Boulderers divide the Flatrock Boulders into three zones—A, B, and C. Each section contains several boulders and all zones are in close proximity to one another.

BOULDERS BEYOND BELIEF

The first boulder encountered (in zone A) is Split Rock, a 20-foot-high rock that has cracked but has yet to break into two pieces.

Less than 30 feet away from Split Rock is an 8-foot-high boulder.

With a little bit of bushwhacking, you will encounter a number of other boulders with such colorful names as Subterranean, Swamp Thing, and Creature.

Directly across Route 28 are several smaller boulders that lie uphill from the side of the road, presumably on private land. It only takes a minute to realize that this is an area rich in glacial erratics.

History: The Flatrock Boulders are named for their association with Flatrock Mountain (2,055'), part of the 500-acre Flatrock Mountain Demonstration Forest, purposed for sustainable forest management.

Directions: From where Route 28 crosses over the Middle Branch of the Moose River in Old Forge, drive southwest on Route 28 for ~4.7 miles and turn left onto an old, short loop road.

From where Route 28 crosses over the Moose River in McKeever, drive northeast for ~4.6 miles and turn right onto an old abandoned road that loops back to Route 28, >0.1 mile after passing by the upper end of Scusa Road.

Park at the southwest end of the loop road. Proceeding on foot, walk south along the edge of the woods for ~100 feet. When you come to a tiny notch/gully on your left, follow it up an embankment into the woods for 20 feet. Split Rock is visible to your left, only 10 feet from the edge of the woods.

A phone line runs parallel to the road where several of the boulders can be found, starting with Split Rock.

Be prepared to do short bursts of bushwhacking on this trek. Take note that the terrain is very uneven.

Resources: Justin Sanford, *New York Adirondack Park Bouldering* (Broadalbin, NY: Southern Adirondack Climber, LLC, 2015) 282–293.
mountainproject.com/v/flatrock-boulders-/108324278.
northernlogger.com/association/flatrock-mountain-demonstration-forest.

BOULDERS BEYOND BELIEF

102. PUTT'S MONUMENT

Type of Formation: Large Rock; Rock-Shelter
WOW Factor: 7
Location: White Lake - Woodgate (Oneida County)
Tenth Edition, NYS Atlas & Gazetteer: p. 49, A8; **Earlier Edition NYS Atlas & Gazetteer**: p. 85, D6–7
Parking GPS Coordinates: 43°32.864'N 75°08.739'W
Putt's Monument GPS Coordinates: 43°32.899'N 75°08.753'W
Accessibility: 0.1-mile bushwhack

Description: According to David H. Beele in "We Get Around: Putt's Monument and Sugar River," Putt's Monument is "…a natural stone pinnacle perhaps 60 feet high up White Lake Way. It's about the size of a small barn at the bottom; tapers almost to a small point on top…..The pinnacle itself is right smack in a hardwood forest and is only a few yards from the face of a shelving cliff."

The caption next to an old photograph of the rock mentions a cave, the creation of two rocks, with one leaning against the other.

Putt's Monument is huge, and obviously was once part of the escarpment wall until it broke away, creating an identity all of its own

View of Putt's Monument from top of escarpment.

History: Reputedly, the name of the rock formation comes from a fellow named Putnam, shortened to "Putt," who ran a local tavern in the 1850s.

Directions: From where Route 28 crosses over White Lake's outlet stream, drive north for ~0.2 mile and park to your left in an unoccupied area between two camps. To figure this out, I used the directions David Beetle had given in his article. To wit: "As you head north, it's just beyond the White Lake outlet, and perhaps a quarter of a mile to the right of Route 28. A twisting footpath leads to it from a point near a green garage." Amazingly, the green garage is still on the right side of the road, just as it was nearly seventy years ago! However, I parked south of the garage, not wishing to trespass on someone's property and also noting that no path was visible from behind the garage.

View of Putt's Monument from base of escarpment. Postcard C. 1910

To reach Putt's Monument, bushwhacked straight into the woods for several hundred feet, climbing up a small hill. Pause when you reach a point where an escarpment begins rising up to your left. From here, you have two choices:

Option #1 --Stay at ground level and follow around and along the base of the escarpment as it quickly increases in height. You will immediately pass by large talus blocks and a talus cave. Beyond this point, the way ahead becomes challenging, for you not only have blocks of talus to deal with, but much thick brush and blowdown. In less than 0.1 mile you will come to the base of Putt's Monument.

Option #2 – Begin climbing uphill, following along the escarpment edge, but keeping back a safe distance. In less than 0.1 mile, you will come to a clearing with views, looking east, from the top of an 80–90-foot-high cliff. You will also see the top of Putt's Monument, to the right of the clearing.

Note: When I returned home later and plugged my GPS coordinates into Google Earth, nothing really made a lot of sense, so be advised. I wouldn't put a lot of stock into the GPS coordinates I have given, although the directions are spot on.

Putt's (talus) Cave. Old Photograph.

Be sure to take note that the land south of where I entered is posted. Although I never saw any posted signs during my trek, I am certain that the land must belong to someone. Should the property become posted in the future, it needs to be given wide berth.

Resources: David H. Beetle, "We Get Around: Putt's Monument and Sugar River," *Woodgate History*, Sunday, October 22, 1950.

BOULDERS BEYOND BELIEF

103. MONUMENT PARK BOULDERS

Type of Formation: Large Boulder
WOW Factor: 6
Location: Atwell (Herkimer County)
Tenth Edition, NYS Atlas & Gazetteer: p. 49, A10; **Earlier Edition NYS Atlas & Gazetteer**: p. 86, D1
Parking GPS Coordinates: 43º31.338'N 74º56.520'W
Gravel Pit GPS Coordinates: 43º31.135'N 74º56.491'W
Boulder GPS Coordinates: 43º31.174'N 74º56.372'W
Accessibility: 0.4-mile walk (or 0.1-mile walk if you drive in to the gravel pit)
Degree of Difficulty: Moderately easy

Description: In *Discover the Southwestern Adirondacks*, Lee M. Brenning, etc., write that "...you will see two large erratics off to your left. Turning south and going downhill, you will see more off to the right. Area residents who frequented the site noticed the individuality of each rock and bestowed such names on them as 'Haystack' (the largest one), the 'Cabins,' and the 'Steps.'"

Without much effort, I came across two boulders—one 12 feet high and one 15 feet high, but probably never reached the main bouldering area.

History: The Monument Park Area was developed as a bouldering site in 2008 by Neal Knitel.

North Lake is the lake source of the 125-mile-long Black River.

Directions: From Forestport (junction of Routes 72/North Lake Road & 28), drive northeast on Route 72/North Lake Road for ~16.0 miles to reach Atwell at the south end of North Lake. Take note that Route 72 changes to Route 214 along the way.

At the southwest end of North Lake, you will cross over a spillway. Continue 0.4 mile farther. Then turn right onto a tiny dirt road between a

BOULDERS BEYOND BELIEF

camp and a 4-foot-high boulder, and drive south for 0.1 mile until you come to a fork. I parked in a pull-off at this point. If you wish, you can drive up to the gravel pit (0.3 mile away), but I elected to turn the trek into a little walk.

At the fork, bear left and proceed southwest along an old road. You will soon come to a beaver-created pond, and then continue around its west end, as the road now heads east; then south. In roughly 0.3 mile from where you parked, you will come to a gravel pit, located to your left. Walk into the gravel pit and then up its opposite side, now proceeding east into the woods. Within 0.1 mile, you will begin encountering boulders as the land begins rising up in front of you.

One of the Monument Park Boulders.

If circumstances had been different on the day of my visit, I would have walked south along the base of the hill to reach other boulders. As it was, I had foolishly left my backpack in the car, thinking I was just going to reconnoiter the area, staying on the grassy road, and nothing more. In the excitement, however, I entered the woods from the gravel pit, thinking I would just walk in for a short distance, and that since the sun was against my back, all I had to do was to turn around and head back towards the sun to reach the gravel pit. Although I had ventured in only 0.1 mile from the gravel pit, upon turning around, nothing looked familiar, nor did the way back seem suddenly so clear. The sky also seemed to have clouded over. It was then that I realized my stupidity. No one on Earth knew where I was 16 miles from civilization in a very desolate area of the Adirondacks. If, by chance, I could not retrace my way back to the gravel pit; if I somehow missed it or went desperately off in a wrong direction, I could be in a world of hurt, for I had no food, no water, no layers, no compass—Nothing. You would think that, at age

71, I would know better than to put myself in this kind of predicament, but apparently I had forgotten what hard-learned lessons I had benefited from earlier in life.

Anyhow, I found the gravel pit (although I arrive 100 feet east of where I had started) and made it back without incident. Obviously, nothing happened—but could have. That was the end of the day for me.

Although no posted signs were evident, a house was under construction near where I parked. It may be that in the near future, access to boulders in this area will become more difficult or impossible due to the imposition of private homes and camps.

Resources: Lee M. Brenning, William P. Ehling, & Barbara McMartin, *Discover the Southwestern Adirondacks* (Woodstock, VT: Backcountry Publications, 1987), 96 & 97.
mountainproject.com/area/113685864/ice-cave-mountain.
communitywalk.com/map/list/299298 – This website contains a section on the Atwell Boulders. "There are 2 boulders on your left as you are walking in. Farther along the trail you will notice the Haystack boulder on the right which in my opinion is the most prominent [rock]."
adkbouldering.blogspot.com/2008/10/atwell-boulders.html.

104. PEAKED MOUNTAIN BOULDERS

Type of Formation: Large Boulder
WOW Factor: 7–8
Location: North River (Warren County)
Tenth Edition, NYS Atlas & Gazetteer: p. 37, D10; **Earlier Edition NYS Atlas & Gazetteer**: p. 88, C1
Parking GPS Coordinates: 43º43.084'W 74º07.104'N
Peaked Mountain Boulder GPS Coordinates in general: ~43º43. 236'N 74º08.784'W
Accessibility: 1.4–2.0-mile hike to boulders; 3.5-mile hike to summit; 1,270' ascent
Degree of Difficulty: B*oulders* – Moderate; *Summit* -- Difficult

Description: A grouping of large boulders can be found along the trail up to Peaked Mountain Lake, the tallest rock being over 30 feet high.

In "A peek at Peaked Mt." in the *Adirondack Explorer 2013 Outings Guide*, Susan Bibeau writes, "Michelle [Hannon] spots an enormous erratic—a large boulder deposited by a glacier. This one is more than thirty feet high…..As we continue up the trail we see six or seven equally big boulders. Michelle describes them as 'glacier art'."

Rich Elton at a Peaked Mountain Boulder. Photograph by Kurt Wisell.

History: Peaked Mountain (2,919') overlooks Thirteenth Lake and is, itself, blessed with a high mountain pond that is overlooked by its own mountain peak.

Directions: From North Creek (junction of Routes 28 & 28N), drive northwest on Route 28 for ~5.2 miles. At North River, turn left onto Thirteenth Lake Road and head southwest for over 3.3 miles. Bear right at a fork and drive south for another 0.6 mile. Pull into the parking area for Thirteenth Lake.

Follow the Peaked Mountain Trail southwest for 0.8 mile as it leads along the west side of the lake. Turn right, just before Peaked Mountain

Brook, and head west, proceeding steadily uphill. During the next 0.6–1.2 miles, you will see multiple boulders as well as cascades along Peaked Mountain Brook.

If you wish, you can travel the initial part of the trek by water. From the boat launch, paddle 0.7 mile southwest, pulling into a landing for the water-access trailhead; then follow the foot-trail next to Peaked Mountain Brook.

Resources: Barbara McMartin, *Fifty Hikes in the Adirondacks* (Woodstock, VT: Backcountry Publications, 1988), 69—73.
Rhonda & George Ostertag, *Hiking New York* (Guilford, CT: The Globe Pequot Press, 2002), 97—100. On page 98, the authors mention that "massive boulders loom trailside…"
Tom Starmer, *Five-Star Trails in the Adirondacks* (Birmingham, AL: Menasha Press, 2010), 101—107.
Susan Bibeau, "A peek at Peaked Mt." *Adirondack Explorer 2013 Outings Guide*, 55.
Barbara McMartin, *Discover the Adirondacks, 1* (Somersworth, NH: New Hampshire Publishing Company, 1979). On page 73 McMartin writes, "The last glacial cataclysm sprinkled cabin-sized boulders along the narrow valley."
Susan Bibeau, "A peek at Peaked Mt.," *Adirondack Explorer: 2013 Outings Guide*. A photograph of Michelle Hannon overshadowed by a large glacial erratic can be seen on page 55.
Barbara McMartin & Bill Ingersoll, *Discover the South Central Adirondacks. Third Edition* (Utica, NY: North Country Books, 2005), 151.

105. SEVERANCE HILL BOULDER

Type of Formation: Medium-sized Boulder
WOW Factor: 2–3
Location: Severance (Essex County)
Tenth Edition, NYS Atlas & Gazetteer: p. 38, B4; **Earlier Edition NYS Atlas & Gazetteer:** p. 88, AB3–4
Parking GPS Coordinates: 43º51.744'N 73º45.338'W
Destination GPS Coordinates: *Boulder* -- 43º51.908'N 73º46.127'W; *Summit* -- 43º52.069'N 73º46.031'W
Accessibility: 0.9-mile hike to boulder; 1.2-mile hike to summit; 800-foot ascent
Degree of Difficulty: Moderate

BOULDERS BEYOND BELIEF

Description: Having recently read that a large boulder can be seen on the hike up Severance Hill, I decided to check it out firsthand. The large boulder turned out to be more medium-sized, roughly 6 feet high, 8–10 feet wide, and 12 feet long. It is located directly next to the trail and provides a convenient spot for hikers wishing to take a breather before the final hurrah.

Severance Hill Boulder—a convenient rest-stop on the way to the summit.

History: The summit of Severance Hill (1,638'), aka Mount Severance, provides view of Schroon Lake and the Pharaoh Lake Wilderness Area. Its proximity to the Adirondack Northway ensures that it will get its fair share of visitors.

Directions: From the Adirondack Northway (I-87), get off at Exit 28, turn right at the end of the exit ramp, and drive east for a hundred feet to a blinking traffic light on Route 9. Turn right, and drive south on Route 9 for nearly 0.6 mile. Then bear right into a large parking area.

From the parking area, walk west through two long culverts that go under the north and south-bound lanes of the Northway, and then follow the yellow-blazed trail (an old road) north for 0.9 mile to reach the boulder, which is to your left, just before the beginning of a major ascent.

Continuing up the mountain for another 0.3 mile, you will come to spectacular views of Schroon Lake from a rocky overlook.

Resources: David Thomas Train (editor), *Adirondack Mountain Club: Eastern Trails*. 4th Edition (Lake George, NY: Adirondack Mountain Club, Inc., 2012), 139. "…a large boulder [is passed] on the L at 0.9 mi…"

Barbara McMartin, *Fifty Hikes in the Adirondacks* (Woodstock VT: Backcountry Publications, 1988), 142–144.

106. HOFFMAN NOTCH BOULDERS
Hoffman Notch Wilderness

Type of Formation: Large Boulder
WOW Factor: 5–6
Location: Schroon Lake (Essex County)
Tenth Edition, NYS Atlas & Gazetteer: p. 38, B3; **Earlier Edition NYS Atlas & Gazetteer**: p. 88, B3
Parking GPS Coordinates: 43º52.083'N 73º53.340'W
Estimated Hoffman Notch Boulders GPS Coordinates: None taken on earlier visit
Accessibility: 1.6–2.0+ -mile hike
Degree of Difficulty: Moderate
Additional Information: Trail map at: dec.ny.gov/docs/lands_forests_pdf/recmaphnwa.pdf

Description: A variety of 15–20-foot-high boulders can be seen near trailside along the North Branch of Trout Brook (and later, Hoffman Notch Brook).

History: The boulders are located in the 38,500-acre Hoffman Notch Wilderness Area that falls within the towns of Minerva, Schroon, and North Hudson. The area is dominated by 3,693-foot-high Hoffman Mountain and penetrated by a 7.4-mile-long trail that, along the way, extends through a high mountain pass, finally coming out onto Blue Ridge Road.

According to Barbara McMartin in her book, *Fifty Hikes in the Adirondacks*, "Erratics and boulders fill the valley…." She particularly describes "… a giant rounded boulder shaped like the back of a sleeping dinosaur…."

BOULDERS BEYOND BELIEF

One of the larger boulders is passed at around 2.0 miles into the hike.

In *Adirondack Cross Country Skiing: A Guide to Seventy Trails* Dennis Conroy writes, "Numerous boulders fractured off Washburn Ridge dot this side of the valley…"

Hoffman Notch Boulder. Photograph by B. Delaney,

Directions: From the Adirondack Northway (I-87), get off at Exit 27 for South Schroon and drive north on Route 9 for ~4.0 miles. Turn left onto Hoffman Road (Route 24) and head west for ~5.4 miles. When you come to Potash Hill Road, turn right and drive 1.1 miles. Then turn right onto Lock Mueller Road and follow it northwest for 1.2 miles. Finally, bear right onto a secondary road that leads quickly to a grassy parking area.

Follow the Hoffman Notch path north for >1.6 miles to begin encountering a number of glacial erratics in Hoffman Notch.

Bailey Hill Boulder –

According to Spencer Morrissey, regional author, in a blog note (schroonlakeregion.com/blog/2016/09/glacial-litter-or-unforeseen-beauty), nearby Bailey Hill (3,050′) is blessed with a 12-foot-high, moss-covered, rounded boulder on its summit. Getting to it is the trick, however, for a rather extensive bushwhack is required.

Resources: Barbara McMartin, *Fifty Hikes in the Adirondacks* (Woodstock, VT: Backcountry Publications, 1988), 220–226.
schroonlakeregion.com/blog/2016/09/glacial-litter-or-unforeseen-beauty.

BOULDERS BEYOND BELIEF

Tim Starmer, *Five-Star Trails in the Adirondacks: A Guide to the Most Beautiful Hikes* (Birmingham, AL: Menasha Ridge Press, 2010), 96 & 97.
Dennis Conroy with Shirley Matzke, *Adirondack Cross Country Skiing: A Guide to Seventy Trails* (Woodstock, VT: Backcountry Publications, 1992), 125. On page 124 is a winter photograph of one of the boulders.
offonadventure.com/2015/01/bailey-hill-3054-hoffman-notch_11.html — This website shows a picture of one of the boulders in heavy snow.
schroonlakeregion.com/blog/2016/09/glacial-litter-or-unforeseen-beauty.
Bruce Wadsworth & Neal Burdick (series editor), *Guide to Adirondack Trails: Central Region. Second Edition* (Lake George, NY: Adirondack Mountain Club Inc., 1994), 194–198. "The first of many large glacial erratics is seen at 1.6 mi. in a lush fern meadow."

107. GULL POND BOULDERS
Pharaoh Lake Wilderness Area

Type of Formation: Large Talus Block
WOW Factor: 6–7
Location: Gull Pond (Essex County)
Tenth Edition, NYS Atlas & Gazetteer: p. 38, BC5; **Earlier Edition NYS Atlas & Gazetteer**: p. 88, B4
Parking GPS Coordinates: 43º50.067'N 73º43.028'W
Talus slope GPS Coordinates: 43º49.951'N 73º42.365'W

BOULDERS BEYOND BELIEF

Accessibility: 0.5-mile hike + 0.4-mile bushwhack (totaling 0.9 mile)
Degree of Difficulty: Moderate

Description: A series of huge blocks of talus have broken off from a towering cliff face above the east shore of Gull Pond and now lie along a downhill slope below the base of the cliff extending to the waterline. Some of these blocks are truly massive in size, equaling the dimensions of garages and small houses. Tiny talus caves and rock-shelters abound in the talus field which extends for 200 feet, paralleling the pond.

A number of large rocks, 10–12-foot-high or greater, have also formed along the sloping east hillside of Gull Pond.

Gull Pond Boulders. Photograph by Christy Butler.

History: Gull Pond is a 0.2-mile-wide body of water located in the 46,283-acre Pharaoh Lake Wilderness. The rocky bluffs on the west side of Gull Pond provide a perfect spot to picnic and to enjoy the cliff views across the pond.

Directions: From the Adirondack Northway, get off at Exit 28 for North Schroon Lake, and turn right at the end of the exit ramp. At a blinking traffic light, cross over Route 9 and proceed east on Route 74 for ~1.4 miles. When you come to Severance Road, turn right and drive south for 0.9 mile. Then turn left onto Alder Meadow Road and head east for 0.9 mile. Upon reaching Adirondack Road at a fork, bear right and head south for ~1.6 miles, turning left into the trailhead parking area for Gull Pond.

Follow the yellow-marked trail east for 0.5 mile to arrive at the west side of Gull Pond. From low-lying bluffs, you will be afforded unparalleled views of the stupendous cliffs overlooking a wide talus field. The cliffs are your destination.

Leaving the trail behind, bushwhack along the south side of the pond for ~0.4 mile, keeping to higher ground in order to avoid any unnecessary scrambling. At the southeast end of the pond, you will ascend a small hillock where a 12-foot-high rock is encountered. Descending, you will quickly start up the next slope, which is Gull Pond Hill, and pass by a 20-foot-high rock with a 6-foot-deep rock-shelter on its downslope side.

From here, gradually make your way diagonally down toward the lake and talus field. You will quickly reach the beginning of the 200-foot-long talus slope filled with impossibly large rocks. It is a fun area worthy of exploration.

Gull Pond Rock.

If you choose to climb up to the summit, you will be rewarded with awesome views to your west. Stay back a safe distance from the sheer ledges.

Resources: communitywalk.com/map/list/299298.
Barbara McMartin with Edythe Robbins & Chuck Bennett, *Discover the Eastern Adirondacks* (Canada Lake, NY: Lake View Press, 1998), 143.
cnyhiking.com/GullPondTrail.htm.
schroonlakeregion.com/what-to-do/attractions/gull-pond.
schroonlakeregion.com/what-to-do/hiking/gull-pond-and-gull-pond-hill.

BOULDERS BEYOND BELIEF

108. CROWN POINT POTHOLE (Historic)
Crown Point State Historic Site

Type of Formation: Pothole
WOW Factor: 6 before the hole was filled in
Location: Crown Point (Essex County)
Tenth Edition, NYS Atlas & Gazetteer: p. 31, E8–9; **Earlier Edition NYS Atlas & Gazetteer**: p. 97, D6
Parking GPS Coordinates: 44º01.818′N 73º25.690′W
His Majesty's Fort of Crown Point GPS Coordinates: 44º01.728′N 73º25.770′W
Accessibility: 0.1 mile walk to fort's entrance
Degree of Difficulty: Easy
Additional Information: Crown Point State Historic Site, 21 Grandview Drive, Crown Point, NY 12928; (518) 597-4666
Map at avenzamaps.com/maps/355253

His Majesty's Fort at Crown Point.

Description: In *Glacial Pot-Holes at Crown Point*, Eugene Barker states that the pothole "… extends to a depth of 14 feet 7 inches into the topmost strata of the Chazy limestone formation. The aperture at the surface is an irregular oblong measuring 6 feet 4 inches by 9 feet 7 inches."

According to authorities that I spoke with, the pothole is located inside the British fort. But you will never find it if you look. When the fort became a tourist attraction, the pothole was at first fenced off to prevent visitors from accidentally tumbling in. During this period of time, the pothole could still be viewed from the perimeter. That ended when authorities filled in the pothole with gravel and earth, totally obliterating its presence, perhaps in response to liability concerns.

The glacial pothole is still there technically, only buried under a fill of gravel and dirt.

History: The Crown Point Reservation is listed as a National Historic Landmark in the National Register of Historic Places designated by the United States Secretary of the Interior.

Crown Point is notable for being the site of two major fortifications— Fort St. Frederic, built by the French in 1734–1737 and used as a base for staging raids on British settlements in New York and New England; then later, His Majesty's Fort of Crown Point, which was built by the British after 1759, and which became a site of contention between the British and Colonials when the American Revolutionary War broke out. The fort enclosed seven acres of land and truly was one of the largest fortifications built by the British in North America.

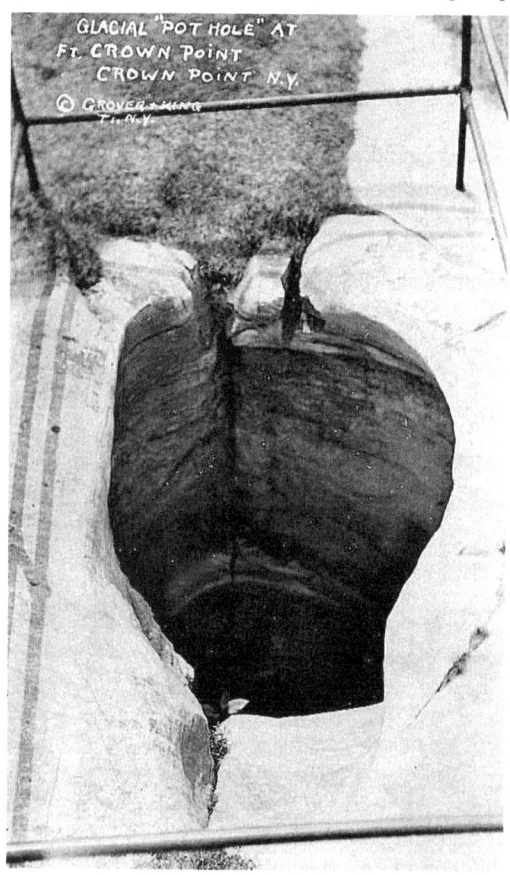

Crown Point Pothole. Old photograph.

The ruins of both forts and surrounding land were acquired by New York State in 1910.

Archbald Pothole -- In case you're curious, the world's largest pothole— or at least the largest in the United States— is the Archbald Pothole located at the Archbald Pothole State Park in Eynon, Pennsylvania. It measure 42 feet in diameter and drops to a depth of 38 feet.

Directions: From Crown Point (junction of Routes 22/9N & 50), proceed northwest on Route 22/9N for 2.5 miles. Turn right onto Route 17 and head east, then north, for ~3.7 miles to the Crown Point Reservation, on your left, where parking is available.

Resources: journals.uchicago.edu/doi/abs/10.1086/622089?journalCode=jg.
E. Eugene Barker, "Glacial Pot-Holes at Crown Point, New York," *The Journal of Geology* 21, no. 5 (Jul. - Aug., 1913), 459.
journals.uchicago.edu/doi/10.1086/622089.
en.wikipedia.org/wiki/Archbald_Pothole_State_Park.

109. NATURAL STONE BRIDGE & CAVES

Type of Formation: Natural Bridge; Boulder; Pothole; Cave
WOW Factor: 9–10
Location: Pottersville (Warren County)
Tenth Edition, NYS Atlas & Gazetteer: p. 38, CD3; **Earlier Edition NYS Atlas & Gazetteer**: p. 88, BC3
Parking GPS Coordinates: 43º44.848'N 73º51.116'W
Fee: Admission charged
Hours: Daily, May 19th–September 3rd, 9 am–6 pm; September 3rd–October 14th, 10 am–5 pm
Accessibility: Very short scrambles from one site to the next
Degree of Difficulty: Moderately easy

Description: Natural Stone Bridge & Caves is a unique, natural wonder that was carved out of rock by Trout Brook at the end of the last Ice Age. In the 1940s, it became a commercial attraction, and has been family-run ever since.

Natural Stone Bridge -- The Natural Stone Bridge is 62 feet high and 180 feet across. It was originally called *Ponte de Dios* (meaning "Bridge of God") by early explorers. In 1956, an estimated nine hundred ton block of rock dropped from the roof of the amphitheater, and now lies below in the streambed, making the bridge even higher than ever. According to the National Speleological Society (NSS), the Stone Bridge may be the largest natural marble cave entrance in the Eastern United States.

BOULDERS BEYOND BELIEF

Boulders – The area contains several large boulders of varying sizes.

Potholes – Large potholes can be seen in the bedrock at multiple spots, particularly near Echo Cave. In an article in *North Country Life* entitled "Cave Woman of 1950," the anonymous author writes, "Many of the gaping potholes which pit the boulder-strewn floor of the canyon beside the brook still hold the smoothly worn rocks that were whirled and ground into the soft limestone by ancient torrents."

Natural Stone Bridge.

One of the potholes was called the *Wishing Well*, probably because visitors threw coins into its depths.

Caves – Natural Stone Bridge (a super-large cave entrance) is not the only cave. Several others can be seen, including Noisy Cave, Geyser Cave, Echo Cave, Garnet Cave, and Lost Pool Cave.

In *Underground Empire: Wonders and Tales of New York Caves*, Clay Perry writes, "The caves have been named for their principal characteristics, such as Echo Cave, which extends some 60 feet into the rock and which can be visited only by swimming in or taking a boat ride. Geyser Cave spouts a veritable

BOULDERS BEYOND BELIEF

geyser against its own ceiling, in high water, and normally the water is 12 feet deep and flows underground some 25 feet in the cave before it vanishes."

"Noisy Cave is the largest and most spectacular one...This cavern opens into Peter Pan's Pothole, an inverted kettle extending 40 feet above and with a lofty balcony where the venturesome can lean over the edge and look down into Noisy Cave..."

Noisy Cave.

History: The waterfall on Trout Brook at Natural Stone Bridge & Caves was originally the site of Jacob Van Benthuysen's saw mill, which he erected in the late 1700s after receiving a land grant for his services during the Revolutionary War.

In the late 1800s and early 1900s, the site was popular for tourists vacationing in the Adirondacks, who would stop by informally for a picnic or a swim. In 1944, things changed dramatically when a young woman named Lydia Neubuck and her mother brought the 300-acre property. Together, they developed a system of trails and walkways, including the main infrastructure that still exists today. In time, they also created a brochure that visitors could use to take self-guided trips through the gorge.

In 1970, Lydia's youngest sister, Jenny Beckler, and her husband, Ed, took over the operation. Thirty-three years later, they turned the business over to their son and daughter-in-law, Greg and Dee Beckler, who currently operate the tourist attraction.

Pottersville was named after Joel E. Potter, who opened the first store in the village in 1839.

BOULDERS BEYOND BELIEF

Trout Brook is a medium-sized stream that rises in North Hudson, descends through Hoffman Notch, and then flows into the south end of Schroon Lake.

Glacial potholes are part of the amazing landscape.

Directions: Heading north on the scenic Adirondack Northway (I-87), get off at Interchange 26 and proceed west on a connecting road for 0.4 mile. Turn right onto Route 9 and head north for 0.8 mile. Then turn left onto Natural Stone Bridge Road and head northwest for 2.4 miles to the end of the road at Natural Stone Bridge & Caves.

Heading south on the Adirondack Northway (I-87), get off at Exit 27. Turn right onto Natural Stone Bridge Road and proceed northwest for ~2.0 miles to reach the parking area.

Hudson River Natural Bridge –

The Natural Stone Bridge in Pottersville is not the only natural bridge in the Adirondacks. In the November 1969 issue of the *Northeastern Caver*, Ernst Kastning writes, "The Hudson River Natural Bridge is a solutional tunnel (in marble) 62 feet long....It averages 30 feet wide and eight feet high inside" It is formed on a tributary to the Hudson River and is visible from Route 9 by looking across the Hudson River at its north bank, roughly 3.5 miles northwest of the village of North Creek. A stream comes out of the cave creating an actual cascade.

BOULDERS BEYOND BELIEF

There is also a natural bridge in the hamlet of Natural Bridge [see chapter on Natural Bridge].

Resources: Edward B. Beckler (compiler) & Dr. Brian B. Turner, *Natural Stone Bridge & Caves* (booklet) (Burlington, VT: George Little Press printers, 1973).
Clay Perry, *Underground Empire: Wonders and Tales of New York Caves* (New York: Stephen Daye Press, 1948), 36–40.
Anonymous, "Cave Woman of 1950," *North Country Life* (Summer 1950), 10–13. The article includes photographs of Noisy Cave, Garnet Cave, and the Natural Stone Bridge.
Russell Dunn & John Haywood, *Natural Stone Bridge & Caves in 3D* (Albany, NY: John Haywood Photography, 2016).
H. P. Smith, *History of Warren County* (Syracuse, NY: D. Mason & Co., 1885), 537.
Bradford B. Van Diver, *Routes and Routes of the North Country, New York* (Geneva, NY: W. F. Humphrey Press, Inc., 1976), 135.
Russell Dunn, *Adirondack Waterfall Guide* (Hensonville, NY: Black Dome Press Corp, 2003), 180–182.
Mike Storey, *Why the Adirondacks Look the way they do* (Desk Top Publishing by Sue Bibeau, 2006). A photograph of the potholes can be seen on page 15.
Scherelene L. Schatz, *The Adirondacks: Postcard History Series* (Charleston, SC: Arcadia Press, 2008). Two postcard photos of Natural Stone Bridge & Caves can be seen on page 19.
Northeastern Caver Vol. XLVIII, no. 2. Photographs of the natural stone bridge in winter, taken by owner Greg Beckler, are shown on page 36. On the cover of this issue is Noisy Cave.
Arthur S. Knight (editor), *Adirondack Northway Guide* (Lake George, NY: Adirondack Resorts Press, Inc., 1964), 221 & 225.
Carl Heilman II, *The Adirondacks* (NY: Rizzoli, n. d.). A photograph of the natural stone bridge is shown.
Ernst Kastning, "Notes on some Warren County caves," *Northeastern Caver* Vol. 1, no. 11 (November 1969), 134.
Donald R. Williams, *Adirondack Ventures: Images of America* (Charleston, SC: Arcadia Publishing, 2006). On page 111 is a photograph of the Natural Stone Bridge.

LAKE GEORGE AREA: CHAPTERS 108–113

110. ELEPHANT ROCK

Type of Formation: Painted Rock
WOW Factor: 5
Location: Graphite (Warren County)
Tenth Edition, NYS Atlas & Gazetteer: p. 39, CD7; **Earlier Edition NYS Atlas & Gazetteer**: p. 89, BC5
Elephant Rock GPS Coordinates: 43º45.119'N 73º34.197'W
Accessibility: Roadside

Elephant Rock waits patiently at roadside to surprise unsuspecting drivers.

Description: Elephant Rock is a section of roadside bedrock that has been artfully painted to resemble the head and upper body of a mammoth elephant. To accomplish this feat, the artist applied a series of white lines to the rock to create tusks and eyes, enhancing the shape of the rock by accentuating features that were already present. Unlike most graffiti, this bit of artwork was tastefully done and, best of all, without the use of a chisel and hammer. It's hard not to be secretly impressed by an imaginative undertaking of this magnitude, although, quite frankly, such praise should not be used as an excuse for the creation of new graffiti.

History: Elephant Rock has been a local attraction for decades. Although the rock is now an accepted part of the scenery, it doesn't hurt to realize that real-life elephants never actually roamed the landscape in New York State—that is, unless you are counting wooly mammoths.

According to one web-site I consulted, the image was created in the 1980s by Hague resident Michael Coffin. It was sometime later that the Department of Transportation planned to blast the rock apart in order to straighten out the road. They were met with opposition by Beatrice McCoy Frazier who organized a petition to save the elephant. It worked, for the elephant remains on Route 8 today, surprising drivers with the suddenness of its appearance.

To be sure, like Elephant Rock, not all rocks in the Lake George area are boulders. Reids Rock, Artist Rock, and Joshua Rock are just a few Lake George examples of overlooks and rock outcroppings that sound like they might be boulders, but aren't!

Directions: From Hague (junction of Routes 8 & 9N), drive west on Route 8 for over 4.3 miles. Look for Elephant Rock on your left, next to the road.

From the Adirondack Northway (I-87), get off at Exit 25 for Chestertown and Hague and drive northeast on Route 8 for ~13.5 miles. The rock profile is on your right.

Although it is possible to park off the side of the road to take a picture, extreme care must be exercised, for there is no official pull-off, and the road is well-traveled.

Resources: Chris Gethard, *Weird New York: Your Travel Guide to New York's Local Legends and Best Kept Secrets* (New York: Sterling Publishing Co., Inc., 2005), 160.
theadirondacker.com/2018/02/11/amazing-boulders-of-the-adirondacks.
roadtrippers.com/us/hague-ny/attractions/elephant-rock-in-adirondacks-hague and at roadsideamerica.com/tip/7272 – This website shows a photo of Elephant Rock.
timbitsblog.wordpress.com/2015/04/03/wonder-6-elephant-rock -- Tim Schaffer's "Tmbits." A winter shot of Elephant Rock is shown.

BOULDERS BEYOND BELIEF

111. SPLIT ROCK: HAGUE (Historic)

Type of Formation: Split Rock
WOW Factor: 7–8
Location: Hague (Warren County)
Tenth Edition, NYS Atlas & Gazetteer: p. 39, D7; **Earlier Edition Delorme NYS Atlas & Gazetteer**: 89, BC5
Split Rock GPS Coordinates: ~43º43.453'N 73º30.686'W
Accessibility: Visible from roadside when trees are bare of leaves. Located on private property.

Split Rock. Postcard c. 1910.

Description: Split Rock is an 18-foot-high, 40-foot-wide boulder that weighs ~500 tons according to one estimate. It is truly a massive rock cleaved nearly exactly in half. For years, it served as a major landmark in the hamlet of Hague, and was visited by thousands of tourists. The gap between the two halves is so wide that a normal-sized person can easily traverse the passageway.

Early postcards show the boulder resting in an open field, which was par for the course in the late 1800s and early 1900s when loggers virtually denuded the landscape. Over the years, the boulder was reclaimed by the forest only to be made more visible again recently due to the woods being partially cleared.

In *Guide to the Geology of the Lake George Region*, David Newland and Henry Vaughan state that "The rock is a stray, carried by the ice and dropped in its present place. It is syenite gneiss carrying numerous garnets, very similar to much of the syenite on Rogers rock from which vicinity it may well have come from, as that locality lies in the direction of glacial movement." They suggest that the boulder was cracked not by lightning, as told in the well-known legend of Split Rock, but rather by "...frost action along a plane of weakness or incipient joint in the rock."

History: Folklore recounts the story of the Great Spirit of the Adirondacks sending down a bolt of lightning to kill an evil sorcerer who lived in a den under the boulder. Having struck the den, the lightning bolt split the boulder in half in the process, which is how Split Rock, if mythology is to be believed, came to be formed.

Directions: From Hague (junction of Routes 9N & 8), head south on Route 9N for 1.3 miles. Turn right onto Split Rock Road and drive uphill, heading west, for over 0.6 miles. Look for the enormous boulder to your left, 100 feet across a fairly open field, just before you reach Pine Land (also on your left).

The split in Split Rock.

The boulder can be appreciated from roadside.

Resources: D. H. Newland & Henry Vaughan, *Guide to the Geology of the Lake George Region* (Albany, NY: The University of the State of New York, 1942), 213. A photograph of Split Rock can be seen on page 215.
Thomas Reeves Lord, *Stories of Lake George Fact and Fiction* (Pemberton, NJ: Pinelands Press, 1987), 145.

BOULDERS BEYOND BELIEF

Thomas Reeves Lord, *More Stories of Lake George Fact and Fiction* (Pemberton, NJ: Pinelands Press, 1994), 164 & 165.
Thomas Reeves Lord, *Still More Stories of Lake George Fact and Fiction* (Pemberton, NJ: Pinelands Press, 1999), 178. In this photo, the rock is heavily obscured by a forest that has regrown around it.
Erica Henkel-Karras, *Postcard History Series: Lake George 1900–1925* (Charleston, NC: Arcadia Publishing, 2005), 93.
theadirondacker.com/2018/02/11/amazing-boulders-of-the-adirondacks.
David H. Newland & Henry Vaughan, *Guide to the Geology of the Lake George Region* (Albany, NY: The University of the State of New York, 1942), 213. A photograph of the rock can be seen on page 215.
timbitsblog.wordpress.com/2015/03/19/wonder-4-split-rock – This website tells the folklore story of how Split Rock came to be.

112. INDIAN KETTLES (Historic)

Type of Formation: Pothole
WOW Factor: 4
Location: Hague (Warren County)
Tenth Edition, NYS Atlas & Gazetteer: p. 39, C8; **Earlier Edition NYS Atlas & Gazetteer**: p. 89, B6
Indian Kettle GPS Coordinates: 43º46.358'N 73º29.261'W
Accessibility: Private property

Description: Indian Kettles consist of a grouping of glacial potholes worn into gneiss bedrock along the shore of Lake George. The largest pothole is 4 feet in diameter and 6–7-feet deep. Some folks call it the Cauldron.

Betty Ahearn Buckell, in *Stuff: the absolute true adventures of men, women and critters*, states that "They [the Indian Kettles] are usually a foot or more in diameter with a perfectly smooth interior, and as carefully made as though a stone cutter had worked them out of the solid bedrock."

According to Chas H. Possons, the potholes are "...round holes in solid rock, close to the water's edge, varying in size from a pail to double that of a barrel."

Timothy Dwight's 1802 account is written up in a footnote in *Chronicles of Lake George: Journeys in War and Peace*. "On a rock opposite Anthony's Nose, our guide, who had seen them, informed us, that there were about a dozen mortars, wrought in the solid stone by the Indians, for the purpose of

BOULDERS BEYOND BELIEF

pounding their corn; some of them are capable of containing half a barrel, and others of inferior capabilities down to half a peck. They are very smooth, and exactly circular."

This was written at a time when it was thought that the potholes might have been artificial, chiseled out by Native Americans. Even though Seneca Ray Stoddard believed they were naturally formed, he couldn't help but write, in his book *Lake George and Lake Champlain*, that "...you wonder whence the grinding power that should create them...by the side of quiet waters." Most potholes, you see, were found in moving streams, where the source of power—moving water—was evident.

Indian Kettles & The View Restaurant from Lake George.

In *Guide to the Geology of the Lake George Region*, D. H. Newland & Henry Vaughan write that "One may ponder a bit on the time it must have taken to abrade a hole five or six feet deep in hard tough rock with no more efficient tool than rock pebbles and sand rotating in a water current." Truly, if given sufficient time, Nature can accomplish some pretty amazing things.

History: The Indian Kettles have been known about for centuries due to their proximity to the shoreline of Lake George. They are not the only potholes in the immediate area. According to S. R. Stoddard in *Lake George: A Book of To-*

BOULDERS BEYOND BELIEF

Day. Seventeenth Edition, "There is also [an Indian Kettle] on an island in the Narrows, and several near Rogers' Slide."

Early on, the Indian Kettles Hotel, owned by W. R. Slack of Stamford, Connecticut, operated at the Indian Kettles until fire destroyed the business in November of 1929.

In 1946, the Reynolds family established The View Restaurant at the site, and operated it for 54 years. The restaurant was then sold to Brad Wisher in 2001 who operated it until his death. The establishment closed for good in 2007.

In 2011, the property was purchased by Troy developer David Bryce and his wife, Astri, and converted into a private residence.

As of 2018, the property is again up-for-sale.

Directions: Access by land is no longer possible due to a private residence now occupying what was once a commercial property.

However, it is possible to partially view the kettles from the lake. To do so, set off from the public boat launch next to the public beach in Hague [43°44.672′N 73°29.931′W] and paddle north for ~2.5 water miles.

By car, the site of the former "The View" Restaurant is passed on your left at 7.3 miles driving south on Route 9N from Ticonderoga (junction of Routes 9N & 74), and at 2.3 miles on your right, heading north on Route 9N from Hague (junction of Routes 9N & 8).

Resources: Russell P. Bellico, *Chronicles of Lake George: Journeys in War and Peace* (Fleischmanns, NY: Purple Mountain Press, 1995), 222.
Russell Dunn, *A Kayaker's Guide to Lake George, the Saratoga Region, and Great Sacandaga Lake* (Hensonville, NY: Black Dome Press, 2012), 40.
Thomas Reeves Lord, *Stories of Lake George Fact and Fiction* (Pemberton, NJ: Pinelands Press, 1987), 159.
Betty Ahearn Buckell, *Stuff: the absolute true adventures of men, women and critters* (Lake George, NY: Buckle Press, 1942), 158. A turn-of-the-century photograph shows a number of Victorian strollers standing upright in the potholes.
S. R. Stoddard in *Lake George: A Book of To-Day. Seventeenth Edition* (Glens Falls, NY: Author, 1887), 113.
Wallace E. Lamb, *Lake George Fact and Anecdote* (Bolton Landing, NY: Author, 1936). A photograph of the Indian Kettles can be seen on page 51.
D. H. Newland & Henry Vaughan, *Guide to the Geology of the Lake George Region* (Albany, NY: The University of the State of New York, 1942), 112 & 204. A photo of the kettles is shown on page 110.

Chas. H. Possons, *Possons' Guide to Lake George, Lake Champlain, and Adirondacks* (Glens Falls, NY: Chas. H. Possons, 1892), 87. Possons describes the kettles as "...round holes in the solid rock, close to the water's edge, varying in size from a pail to double that of a barrel."

S. R. Stoddard, *Lake George and Lake Champlain* (Glens Falls, NY: Author, 1890), 67.

blog.timesunion.com/tablehopping/362/view-restaurant-at-indian-kettles-closes, timbitsblog.wordpress.com/2015/03/15/wonder-3-the-indian-kettles.

"Indian Kettles Inn Razed by Fire Last Friday." *Ticonderoga Sentinel* 07 Nov. 1929: 2. *NYS Historic Newspapers*. Web. 24 Feb. 2015.

113. ROGERS ROCK BOULDERS

Type of Formation: Large Boulder
WOW Factor: 5–6
Location: Hague (Warren County)
Tenth Edition, NYS Atlas & Gazetteer: p. 39, C8; **Earlier Edition NYS Atlas & Gazetteer**: p. 89, B6
Parking GPS Coordinates: 43º47.722'N 73º28.424'W
Destination GPS Coordinates: *Cove Boulders* -- 43º47.747'N 73º28.378'W; *Campground Boulders* -- ~43º47.149'N 73º29.160'W; *Rogers Rock & Underwater Boulders* -- 43º47.798'N 73º28.012'W
Fee: Day-use charge
Accessibility: *Cave Boulders and Campground Boulders* -- 0.05 mile walk; *Rogers Rock & Underwater Boulders* – 0.8-mile paddle
Degree of Difficulty: *Cave Boulders and Campground Boulders* – Easy; *Rogers Rock & Underwater Boulders* – Moderately easy
Additional Information: Rogers Rock Campground map available at dec.ny.gov/docs/permits_ej_operations_pdf/rogersrock2015.pdf.

Rogers Rock Campground, 9894 Lake Shore Drive, Hague, NY 12836; (518) 585-6746.

Description: *Cove Boulders* – These medium-to large-sized boulders are located below a cliff called Campground Wall. Grouped together, they are named for their close proximity to a nearby sheltered cove.

Campground Boulders – These series of large boulders can be found below Campsite #126 at the far south end of the campground.

BOULDERS BEYOND BELIEF

Rogers Rock & Underwater Boulders -- Interestingly, the *USA Today* website mentions huge boulders at the base of Roger's Rock that skin divers and snorkelers like to maneuver around and explore.

View from Roger's Rock.

History: The boulders have served as a playground for campers for many years. It probably wasn't until the 1990s, however, that they began to be used for more serious pursuits by boulderers.

The land encompassing the Rogers Rock Campground was purchased in 1936. The Civilian Conservation Corps (CCC) began working to develop the site into a campground. Later, additional work was done by New York State. The campground finally opened up to the public in 1947.

The campground is named after Robert Rogers, an eighteenth-century ranger and frontiersman, who, during the French and Indian War, supposedly escaped from a party of pursuing Indians by jumping/sliding down the great rock that today is called Roger's Rock/Roger's Slide. A similar story, only with a different protagonist, is told at Sam's Point in the Shawangunks.

Directions: From Hague (junction of Routes 9N & 8), drive north on Route 9N for 3.8 miles and turn right into the entrance for the Rogers Rock Campground (43°47.618N 73°29.193′W).

From Ticonderoga (junction of Routes 9N & 74), drive south on Route 9N for 5.8 miles and turn left into the campground entrance.

Cove Boulders -- From the entrance station, turn left and follow the road east to the large boat launch parking area. From there, continue further on to a smaller parking area before a metal orange gate and bathroom facilities.

Now on foot, walk past the metal gate and head downhill. The first, and largest, boulder encountered is the Captain Boulder. From here, the boulders continue north with such nautical names as Pirate, Black Sails, and Mutiny.

Campground Boulders – From the entrance, drive or walk south for as far as you can until the road begins to circle back north. This is where campsite # 126 is located. The boulders are just beyond this point.

Rogers Rock & Underwater Boulders – From the launch site, paddle east for 0.5 mile to Juniper Island, which is just west of Rogers Rock. Go past the island and continue northeast for another 0.3 mile to reach the main section of Rogers Rock/Slide.

Resources: Justin Sanford, *New York Adirondack Park Bouldering* (Broadalbin, NY: Southern Adirondack Climber, LLC, 2015), 192−201.
Russell Dunn & Barbara Delaney, *Adirondack Trails with Tales: History Hikes through the Adirondack Park and the Lake George, Lake Champlain & Mohawk Valley Region* (Hensonville, NY: Black Dome Press, 2009), 73–78. The story behind Rogers Rock is told in detail.
communitywalk.com/adirondack_park/ny/boulders_in_the_adirondacks/map/299298.
mountainproject.com/v/cove-boulders/111950561.
traveltips.usatoday.com/camping-rogers-rock-new-york-57305.html – USA Travel website
Phil Brown, "Grand-scale adventure," *Adirondack Explorer 2018 Annual Outings Guide*, 80–81. This article talks about paddling over to Rogers Rock and climbing it.

BOULDERS BEYOND BELIEF

114. NORTH BOLTON BOULDERS

Type of Formation: Large Boulder
WOW Factor: *Freight Train -- 5–6; Gunite & Highwall -- 7–8*
Location: North Bolton (Warren County)
Tenth Edition, NYS Atlas & Gazetteer: p. 39, E6; **Earlier Edition NYS Atlas & Gazetteer**: p. 89, CD5
Parking GPS Coordinates: 43º39.256'N 73º35.825W
Destination GPS Coordinates: *Freight Train & Coal Cart* -- 43º39.222'N 73º35.824'W; *Gunite & Highwall* -- 43º39.205'N 73º35.783'W
Accessibility: *Freight Train & Coal Cart*—200-foot hike; *Gunite & Highwall* -- <0.1-mile bushwhack
Degree of Difficulty: *Site #1* -- Moderately easy; *site #2* -- Moderate

Freight Train. Photograph by Christy Butler.

Description: There are two sites containing large rocks that are in close proximity to one another. The first site (the one closest to Route 9N) contains one respectable-sized rock, Freight Train, and one of modest size, Coal Cart. Freight Train is massive, some 10–12 feet high, equally as wide, and 25–30 feet long. Adjacent to it is 10-foot-high Coal Cart, dwarfed by the size of its partner.

Christy Butler lends scale to the size of these rocks.

The second (upper) site contains huge blocks of talus that have broken off from a high cliff and have come to rest on the downslope from its base. Two of the massive, 20–25-foot-high blocks—Gunite and Highwall—have fallen together in such a way as to create a rock-shelter and, on the west side, a short talus cave that you can walk through.

Timber rattlesnakes have been reported in the nearby Tongue Mountain Range, so it is probably wise to stay alert while exploring these rocks, particularly flat surfaces where snakes might be sunning themselves.

History: The area became of interest to boulderers in 2012 when Scott Meyer "discovered" the site while exploring the Tongue Mountain Range.

BOULDERS BEYOND BELIEF

One of the rocks, Gunite, was named for a kind of shotcrete, or "sprayed concrete," that is projected through a hose at high velocity for use in construction sites. How this term applies I don't know.

In Justin Sanford's *New York Adirondack Park Bouldering*, the North Bolton Boulders are referred to as the Tongue Mountain Range Boulders, aka Wild Pines.

Directions: From the Adirondack Northway (I-87), get off at Exit 24 for Bolton's Landing and proceed southeast on Route 11 (Riverbank Road), for 4.7 miles. When you come to Route 9N, turn left and head northeast for ~6.4 miles (or nearly 0.8 mile from where Padanarum Road, an unmarked dirt road, enters on your left). Along the last 0.8 mile, you will pass by marshlands on both sides of the road and then begin an uphill climb. As soon as you drive through the second rock-cut on your right, look to your left for a grassy area between guardrails where three cars can park perpendicular to the road.

From here, walk back down the road for 100 feet. At the end of the rock-cut, look for a tiny, informal path that leads uphill into the woods. Once you crest the top of the embankment, proceed left, heading uphill and slightly east to reach the first grouping of rocks (Freight Train and Coal Cart). From this point, head away from the road, proceeding up a steep hill for several hundred feet to reach the next gathering of rocks, which include massive Gunite and Highwall.

Resources: Justin Sanford, *New York Adirondack Park Bouldering* (Broadalbin, NY: Southern Adirondack Climber, LLC, 2015), 182–191.

115. BUCK MOUNTAIN BOULDER

Type of Formation: Large Boulder
WOW Factor: 5
Location: Pilot Knob (Washington County)
Tenth Edition, NYS Atlas & Gazetteer: p. 53, A6; **Earlier Edition NYS Atlas & Gazetteer**: p. 89, D5
Parking GPS Coordinates: 43º30.552'N 73º37.830'W
Buck Mountain Boulder GPS Coordinates: Not taken
Accessibility: ~0.8 mile
Degree of Difficulty: Moderate

BOULDERS BEYOND BELIEF

Description: Lisa Densmore Ballard, in *Hiking the Adirondacks*, describes the 12-foot-high, 20-foot-long rock as a "...cube-shaped glacial erratic beside the trail."

History: There's always a danger when one makes an assumption, but it seems relatively safe in this case to assume that Buck Mountain was named for its abundance of male deer.

Directions: From near Katskill Bay (junction of Routes 9L & 32/Pilot Knob Road), head north on Route 32/Pilot Knob Road for 3.3 miles to reach the trailhead, which is on your right.

Hike southeast, following the yellow-marked trail as it parallels Butternut Brook, for ~0.8 mile to reach the boulder. It is a hike of 3.3 miles if you wish to continue up to the summit of Buck Mountain.

Additional Site –

Buck Mountain can also be approached via a 2.5-mile-long trail from Hogtown Road. This trailhead [43º31.886'N 73º33.940'W] is off Shelving Rock Road, 0.7 mile north of the junction of Sly Pond Road and Hog Town Road. In *Adirondack Mountain Club: Eastern Trails. 4th Edition*, David Thomas Train writes that "three huge boulders" are passed at 1.7 miles, followed by the trail going between "two walls of boulders" at 2.1 miles.

Resources: Lisa Densmore Ballard, *Hiking the Adirondacks. Second Edition* (Guilford, CT: Falcon Guides, 2017), 229. A photograph of a large, square-shaped boulder is shown.
Barbara McMartin with Edythe Robbins & Chuck Bennett, *Discover the Eastern Adirondacks* (Canada Lake, NY: Lake View Press, 1998), 24–26.
David Thomas Train (editor), *Adirondack Mountain Club: Eastern Trails. 4th Edition* (Lake George, NY: Adirondack Mountain Club, Inc., 2012), 96 & 97.
lakegeorge.com/hiking/buck-mountain.

SECTION THREE: SOUTHERN ADIRONDACKS

116. HIGH ROCK (Historic)

Type of Formation: Historic Rock
WOW Factor: 3–4
Location: Northville – Great Sacandaga Lake (Fulton County)
Tenth Edition, NYS Atlas & Gazetteer: p. 51, E9; **Earlier Edition Delorme NY State Atlas & Gazetteer**: p. 79, C7
General GPS Coordinates: 43º13.040'N 74º11.450'W
Accessibility: On private property

Description: High Rock is an 10-foot-high glacial boulder that lies partially embedded in the side of a hill overlooking the Great Sacandaga Lake.

High Rock. Postcard c. 1900

History: What's interesting about High Rock is that it rose into prominence in the late 1800s when Sacandaga Park—a large amusement park with hotels, theaters, rides, as well as a sports island—was created along the Sacandaga

BOULDERS BEYOND BELIEF

River, just south of present-day Northville. Up until then, High Rock was just an obscure boulder on a nameless hill overlooking the Sacandaga Valley.

Undoubtedly, High Rock would have remained obscure and unnoticed were it not for two events that happened fairly close together time-wise. First, the influx of tourists coming to Sacandaga Park created a demand for lodging facilities. Three hotels were built in the park—the Adirondack Inn, Old Orchard Inn, and The Pines. The fourth, High Rock Lodge, was erected in 1901 outside of the park next to the boulder and, by turning the boulder into something that it really wasn't, utilized the rock's unique position above the valley to draw attention to the hotel.

Secondly, the hotels at Sacandaga Park afforded wonderful views of the Sacandaga River and were close to all of the action, but otherwise were fairly limited. Farther uphill at High Rock, however, you could see the big picture—the Sacandaga River extending into the distance north and south, and the interior of the valley. High Rock Lodge provided the perfect opportunity for tourists to leave the claustrophobic confines of the valley for soaring views.

High Rock's days of fame were to be short lived, however. With the creation of the Sacandaga Reservoir (later re-named the Great Sacandaga Lake) in 1930, much of Sacandaga Park was flooded, including many of its hotels and 120 cottages. Tourism sharply waned. Despite the fact that the High Rock Lodge was located above the area flooded, the effect on it was just as devastating. Symbiotically tied to Sacandaga Park, High Rock Lodge soon folded, and became just a restaurant. Even then, the volume of business continued to be fairly low. When the building burned to the ground in 1951, no attempt was made to rebuild it.

Over time, the forest grew back over the hillside, enclosing High Rock again. The boulder is now on private property and inaccessible. It remains only as an interesting footnote in the lake's history, a memory perhaps kept alive by the name of nearby High Rock Road.

Today, if you were to come across High Rock, you might not even recognize it for what it once was. Its days of glory depended upon a clear view of the valley and its close association with the High Rock Lodge, both of which are now gone. The forest has essentially reclaimed the boulder.

Saratoga Spring's High Rock – There was also a High Rock in Saratoga Springs (as well as in Warrensburg as mentioned in an earlier chapter), its claim to fame being that an ailing Sir William Johnson, who served as

Superintendent of Indian Affairs during the French & Indian War, was taken there in 1771 to be cured by its magical waters—and was! It is said that General George Washington, upon hearing of the spring's rejuvenate powers, visited the spring at High Rock and tried to buy it, but was unsuccessful in his attempt.

Directions: None given to High Rock at the Great Sacandaga Lake due to the boulder's inaccessibility.

Resources: Russell Dunn, "The Saga of High Rock," *Adventures Around the Great Sacandaga Lake. Revised and Illustrated* (Troy, NY: Troy Bookmakers, 2011), 147–153.
K. B. Shaw, *Northampton Then and Now* (Broadalbin, NY: 1975).
Eleanor Early, *Adirondack Tales* (Boston: Little, Brown & Company, 1939), 19. The story of Saratoga Spring's High Rock is recounted.

117. TORY ROCK (Historic)

Type of Formation: Large Boulder; Historic Rock
WOW Factor: 6–7
Location: Brooks Bay -- Great Sacandaga Lake (Saratoga County)
Tenth Edition, NYS Atlas & Gazetteer: p. 52, D2; **Earlier Edition Delorme NY State Atlas & Gazetteer**: p. 80, BC2
General GPS Coordinates: 43º15.978'N 73º57.316'W
Accessibility: On private, posted land

Description: Tory Rock is an enormous, 18-foot-high, egg-shaped, glacial erratic located near the confluence of Daly Creek and Black Pond Creek, less than 1.3 miles south of the Great Sacandaga Lake.

History: Tory Rock has stood the test of time and, most assuredly, will continue to endure for millenniums to come. Native Americans made use of the rock as a natural landmark to help guide them through a landscape that was mostly featureless and over-run by endless forest.

Tory Rock became well-known to Europeans trappers who passed through the area in search of game, and then, later, to settlers as they began to take up permanent residence. It is believed that Tories used the rock as a meeting place during the Revolutionary War, which is how the boulder came to be named.

Tory Rock lies close to Daly Creek.

During the late 1800s, a local resident named Ira Gray became forever associated with Tory Rock. Ira Gray was to the Sacandaga Valley what Old Mountain Phelps was to the Adirondacks—a guide, hunter, woodsman, storyteller, and author. Popularly known as Adirondack Ike, he wrote two books—*Follow My Moccasins Tracks* and *Adirondack Ike: Memories from 1 to 91*—that contain information about Tory Rock. Gray was able to accomplish this task easily, for his camp on Daly Creek, called Hi 'n Dry, was only a half mile distant from the boulder.

As a point of interest, *Tory Cave* near Indian Ladder at John Boyd Thacher Park is another rock formation with a Tory preface. It is mentioned in my first book of New York State rocks, *Rambles to Remarkable Rocks*.

Today, Tory Rock is on private land, although it does seem like the rock is used as a geocaching site.

Directions: Not given

BOULDERS BEYOND BELIEF

Resources: Ira Gray, *Follow My Moccasin's Tracks* (Queensbury, NY: Sunset Enterprises, 1967), 64.
Russell Dunn, "Tory Rock," *Adventures Around the Great Sacandaga Lake. Revised and Illustrated* (Troy, NY: Troy Bookmakers, 2011), 158–160.
geocaching.com/geocache/GC1BPV4_tory-rock-glacial-erratic.

118. MANVILLE ROCK

Type of Formation: Large Boulder
WOW Factor: 5
Location: Lake Desolation (Saratoga County)
Tenth Edition, NYS Atlas & Gazetteer: p. 66, A2; **Earlier Edition NYS Atlas & Gazetteer**: p. 80, CD2
Parking GPS Coordinates: 43º09.287'N 73º58.004'W
Estimated Manville Rock GPS Coordinates: Not determined
Accessibility: Road/trail-side
Degree of Difficulty: Moderate

Description: The Manville Rock is 12 feet high, 20 feet long, and 15 feet across.

History: The rock's name goes back to the early 1800s when a family named Manvill (for unknown reasons, an "e" was added on when the boulder was named) owned a small, primitive structure next to or possibly joined to the large boulder. This was during the period of time when an old highway called Plank Road connected Porters Corner with Fox Hill Road. Supposedly, Lucinda, Manvill's daughter, died of a broken heart here.

At least that's the legend. According to Sandra Arnold, who has done a PowerPoint presentation on Lucinda Manvill for the Town for Greenfield Historical Society, there is strong evidence that Lucinda Manvill never lived by the Manville Rock, but rather farther downhill, possibly near Bucket Pond. It was her father, Adrian Manvill, who lived by the rock in some kind of crate dwelling during his later years. He was a peddler of "Dr. Manvil's Mandrake Pills."

The general area near Archer Vly is historically known as Mount Pleasant and in the 1800s was host to a bottle factory (whose ruins can be seen on the opposite side of the road from the Archer Vly Access sign).

BOULDERS BEYOND BELIEF

Archer Vly is part of a 2,000-acre tract of land that runs along Lake Desolation Road.

Manville Rock. Old photograph from the Saratoga County Historian's office.

Directions: Near the east end of the Batchellerville Bridge at the Great Sacandaga Lake, turn east from South Lake Shore (Route 7), and head southeast on Fox Hill Road for ~7.8 miles (or 1.0 mile north of the northwest end of Lake Desolation). You will see a sign for "Conservation Easement Lands. Lake Desolation Road Tract. Archer Vly Access" [43°09.194'N 73°58.130'W] on your left. Turn left onto the old Plank Road, drive east for 0.1 mile, and then left into a parking area next to Archer Vly, a 22-acre pond accessible to hand-launch boats. From here, walk back out to Plank Road, and then head east on Plank Road.

This is where the problem begins. We visited Manville Rock twelve years ago, but approached it via a snowmobile trail from Lake Desolation since, at that time, threatening signs were posted at the entrance to Plank

Road, and we were afraid to hike in least someone take a shot at us (I'm not kidding).

Times have changed over the last decade. The threatening signs are gone, and an easement along Plank Road has been obtained. Barbara and I have hiked along Plank Road twice now and have yet to locate the boulder, even though it is still there. In our explorations, we took the first right road leading off from the main road, but that led downhill in less than 0.2 mile to a barrier and, beyond that, old private camps.

We then continued on the main road to where the road divides, and have followed both roads for another half mile or so without seeing the rock.

It's there! Maybe you'll have better luck than we had. According to our recollection, the Manville Rock is on the right side of the road, maybe 10–20 feet into the woods. It should be visible even when trees are leaf-bearing.

Resources: Ron Fuelner, *Lucinda or The Mountain Mourner; An Old Story Retold by Ron Fuelner. Third Edition* (Middle Grove. NY: Morning Sun Enterprises, 1998)).
Russell Dunn, "The Manville Rock" *Adventures Around the Great Sacandaga Lake. Revised and Illustrated* (Troy, NY: Troy Bookmakers, 2011), 165 & 166.
timesunion.com/tuplus-sports/article/Archery-Vly-a-hidden-treasure-nearby-7235238.php.
Clayton H. Brown (preparer), *Greenfield Glimpses* (Greenfield, NY: Greenfield Town Board, 1976), 185 & 186.

119. IRVING POND ROCKS
Shaker Mountain Wild Forest

Type of Formation: Large Boulder
WOW Factor: 3–4
Location: Wheelerville (Fulton County)
Tenth Edition, NYS Atlas & Gazetteer: p. 65, A6; **Earlier Edition NYS Atlas & Gazetteer**: p. 79, C5
Parking GPS Coordinates: 43º09.782'N 74º28.640'W
Destination GPS Coordinates: *Water Rock* -- 43º09.829'N 74º28.583'W; *#475 Boulders* -- 43º10.011'N 74º28.540'W
Accessibility: *Water Rock* – 0.05-mile trek or paddle; *#475 Boulders* – 0.2-mile paddle/0.4 mile trek
Degree of Difficulty: Easy

BOULDERS BEYOND BELIEF

Additional Information: cnyhiking.com/IrvingPond-BellowsLake.htm — Website contains a topo map of the area.

Description: The *Water Rock* is 10 feet or more in height if you count the part that's underwater.

The *#475 Boulders* offer a curious feature, for the number 475, in large letters, has been chiseled into the side of the left-most boulder.

Readers should take into consideration that the accompanying photograph makes the Water Rock look larger than it really is. The rock is big—but not that big!

Irving Pond Water Rock.

History: Irving Pond is named after James Irving who created the 134-acre pond in 1855 by erecting a 23-foot-high dam on the pond's outlet stream. At that time, the body of water was called Mill Pond, acknowledging the fact that water from the dam was used to power a sawmill. At some point, Irving built a large, two-story house on a knoll overlooking the pond.

The mill ceased operations in the early 1900s and was torn down between 1910 and 1912. All traces of both the home and sawmill are gone today, and have been for many years.

BOULDERS BEYOND BELIEF

The previous dam was removed in 1996, resulting in the lake level dropping precipitously. Fortunately, beavers went on to dam up the outlet stream, raising the height of the lake up to its present level.

Directions: From Caroga Lake (junction of Routes 29A & 10 South), head northwest on Route 29A/10 for 1.7 miles. Opposite the Nick Stoner Lodge, turn right onto Irving Pond Road and proceed northeast for 0.2 mile. Bear left at a fork and continue on Irving Pond Road for another 0.5 mile as it parallels Irving Pond's outlet stream, to your left. Park in a small area that overlooks Irving Pond.

The Water Rock can be reached either by paddling 0.05 mile to it, or by walking northeast near the shoreline, a trek also of 0.05 mile.

The #475 Boulders are located on the shoreline virtually 0.2 mile due north from the Water Rock. It is possible to hike to the boulders by crossing over the outlet stream and then bushwhacking 0.3 mile around the west side of the lake. However, it is far easier just to bring along a canoe or kayak and paddle over to them.

Resources: Russell Dunn, *Penultimate Paddles* (Albany, NY: John Haywood Photography, 2016), 81–83.
Bill Ingersoll, *Discover the Southern Adirondacks* (Barneveld, NY: Wild River Press. 2014), 105 & 106.
Barbara McMartin, *Discover the Adirondacks 2: Walks, Waterways and Winter Treks in the Southern Adirondacks* (Somersworth, NH: New Hampshire Publishing Company, 1980), 71 & 72.
Barbara McMartin, *Caroga: The Town Recalls its Past* (Caroga Lake, NT: Town of Caroga, 1976), 111–115.

120. LILY LAKE ROCKS

Type of Formation: Large Boulder
WOW Factor: 3
Location: Canada Lake (Fulton County)
Tenth Edition, NYS Atlas & Gazetteer: p. 65, A6; **Earlier Edition NYS Atlas & Gazetteer**: p. 79, C4–5
Parking GPS Coordinates: 43º10.536'N 74º31.863'W
Destination GPS Coordinates: *Grouping #1* -- 43º09.332'N 74º32.979'W; *Grouping #2* -- 43º09.382'N 74º33.033'W

BOULDERS BEYOND BELIEF

Accessibility: ~2.5-mile paddle
Degree of Difficulty: Moderate

Description: Two sets of large boulders can be seen near the southwest end of Lily Lake. Both make for interesting destinations, but it is the paddle itself that is the main attraction.

History: Lily Lake was created when Sprite Creek was dammed up at Stewart Landing. Until then, these boulders were in fields or marshlands.

Lily Lake Boulders.

Directions: From Caroga Lake (junction of Routes 29A & 10 South), drive northwest on Route 29A/10 for ~4.3 miles. Turn left onto West Lake Road. After 100 feet, bear right at a fork, continuing on West Lake Road for 0.2 mile to the parking area.

Proceeding by kayak, canoe, or boat, head southwest down the inlet stream for 0.4 mile to reach West Lake. Turn left and bear southwest for 0.3 mile. As soon as you pass by the tip of Dolgeville Point (on your right), you are on Canada Lake. Turn right here and proceed southeast for 0.5 mile. Very soon, the lake narrows and becomes channel-like. Look for a large, dome-shaped boulder on your right—a great spot for taking a break or to picnic. After 0.2 mile, the channel opens up into a 0.6-mile-long body of water called Lily Lake, named for its proliferation of lilies. The two grouping of boulders, essentially on opposite sides of the lake, are located near the southwest end of Lily Lake.

BOULDERS BEYOND BELIEF

Resources: Phil Brown, "Two Sides of Sprite Creek," *Adirondack Explorer* Vol. 8, No. 5 (September/October, 2006). On page 6 is a photograph of Phil Brown standing atop a large boulder surrounded by water.
Russell Dunn, *Penultimate Paddles* (Albany, NY: John Haywood Photography, 2016), 87–90.

121. PINNACLE BOULDERS

Pinnacle Boulder.

Type of Formation: Large Boulder
WOW Factor: 6
Location: Wheelerville (Fulton County)
Tenth Edition, NYS Atlas & Gazetteer: p. 64, A6; **Earlier Edition NYS Atlas & Gazetteer**: p. 79, C4–5
Parking GPS Coordinates: 43º10.033'N 74º30.054'W

BOULDERS BEYOND BELIEF

Pinnacle Boulders GPS Coordinates: 43º10.1030'N 74º30.071'W
Degree of Difficulty: Moderate easy
Accessibility: 0.05-mile trek

Description: A series of boulders and blocks of talus can be found in several sections along the bottom of a ridge line above Canada Lake.

History: The Pinnacle Boulders, aka Canada Lake Boulders and Pinnacle Pullout Boulders, got their name from the nearby, former Pinnacle Restaurant & Motel.

The rock's potential for bouldering has been known about since 2004, but really only exploited since 2005.

The boulders are located on an 18.5-acre tract consisting of New York State DEC lands—property donated by Ellen Wood, a private landowner who recognized the need for the establishment of a bouldering park. The park was made possible by Access Fund.

Directions: From Caroga Lake (junction of Routes 29A and 10 South), drive northwest on Route 29A/10 for ~2.7 miles and park in a large pull-off on your left. Cross over the road, walk northwest for a couple of hundred feet to a gully on your right, and then follow a herd path into the woods, heading uphill through the gully for 100 feet to reach the first grouping of boulders.

The boulders are found in two fields, or zones, paralleling Route 29A. The big rocks have acquired such names as Kissing Couple, Sloppy, Overlook, Little Buster, and Warm-up Wall.

Interestingly, a number of sizeable boulders can be seen along the road leading up to the former Pinnacle Restaurant & Motel but, as might be expected, are located on private property.

Resources: Justin Sanford, *New York Adirondack Park Bouldering* (Broadalbin, NY: Southern Adirondack Climber, LLC, 2015) 24–35.
accessfund.org/news-and-events/news/preserve-the-pinnacle-boulders.
outdoorindustry.org/press-release/adirondack-bouldering-area-preserved-further-support-needed.
accessfund.org.
adirondackrock.com/SouthernMountains_2010.pdf.
Jim Lawyer & Jeremy Haas, *Adirondack Rock: A Climber's Guide* (Pompey, NY: Adirondack Rock Press, LLC, 2008), 597.
mountainproject.com/area/106501197/pinnacle-pullout-boulders.

BOULDERS BEYOND BELIEF

122. GREEN LAKE BOULDERS

Type of Formation: Large Boulder
WOW Factor: 7
Location: Green Lake (Fulton County)
Tenth Edition, NYS Atlas & Gazetteer: p. 50, E5; **Earlier Edition NYS Atlas & Gazetteer**: p. 79, C4–5
Parking GPS Coordinates: 43º10.807'N 74º30.275'W
Green Lake Boulders GPS Coordinates: 43º10.778'N 74º30.384'W
Accessibility: 0.1-mile hike
Degree of Difficulty: Easy

Andrew Canavan stands atop Green Lake Boulder.

Description: Two mammoth boulders lie in close proximity to one another. The first one encountered, called *Rookie* by boulderers, is 20 feet high by 30 feet long. The second boulder, called *All-Star*, is 25 feet high, and 30 feet long. A narrow slice from this boulder broke off at some time earlier and lies next to the big rock, forming a kind of platform.

BOULDERS BEYOND BELIEF

Although the trail leading to the boulders is somewhat faint, once you reach the boulders, the earth and grass around them is well-worn, revealing that this site gets a fair amount of use.

History: The boulders are notable for being in close proximity to the trail to Kane Mountain's summit (2,180′). The summit contains a fire tower from where there are great overlooks of the Canada Lake region.

The boulders were "discovered" in 2000 by Joshua Bingham, Paul Denisulk, Shawn Martin, and Leslie Schul.

Directions: From Caroga Lake (junction of Routes 29A & 10 South), drive northwest on Route 29A/10 for 3.4 miles. Turn right onto Green Lake Road and head northeast for 0.5 mile. Along the way you will pass by White Rock Boulder. A camp was built in 1909 next to it and, not surprisingly, was called White Rock Camp.

Bear left at a fork onto a dirt road that leads in several hundred feet to the parking area for Kane Mountain.

After parking, walk back along the road for 70 feet. Look for a faint herd path on your right and follow it uphill for 0.1 mile to reach the boulders.

Green Lake Shelter Cave –

A shelter cave first written up by Barbara McMartin in *Discover the Adirondacks 2: Walks, Waterways and Winter Treks in the Southern Adirondacks* can be found below cliffs above the southeast shore of Green Lake. McMartin writes, "… a natural overhang creates a small cave-like area that shelters deer in the winter. Luminous moss has been found in the cave."

Many years ago, I located the cave, which is formed by a 20-foot overhang, and wrote it up for the March 1995 issue of the *Northeastern Caver*. It can be reached by bushwhacking >0.2-mile from Route 29A/10 at the southeast side of the lake, following a ridge line that leads up to the top of the hill. Look for the shelter cave at the base of the cliff.

Resources: Justin Sanford, *New York Adirondack Park Bouldering* (Broadalbin, NY: Southern Adirondack Climber, LLC, 2015), 36–42.
Barbara McMartin, *Discover the Adirondacks 2: Walks, Waterways and Winter Treks in the Southern Adirondacks* (Somersworth, NH: New Hampshire Publishing Company, 1980), 66 & 67.

Russell Dunn, "Shelter Cave on Green Mountain," *Northeastern Caver* Vol. XXVI, no. 1 (March 1995), 12 & 13.
southernadirondackclimber.blogspot.com/2013/08/summer-ascents-at-green-lake-boulders.html.
bing.com/videos/search?q=green+lake+boulders+ny&qpvt=+green+lake+boulders+ny&FORM=VDRE – This site contains a number of videos of climbers bouldering at Green Lake and at several other sites.
mountainproject.com/area/112827144/green-lake-boulders.

123. GREEN LAKE ROCKWALL

Type of Formation: Rockwall
WOW Factor: 6
Location: Green Lake (Fulton County)
Tenth Edition, NYS Atlas & Gazetteer: p. 50, E5; **Earlier Edition NYS Atlas & Gazetteer**: p. 79, C4–5

BOULDERS BEYOND BELIEF

Parking GPS Coordinates: 43º10.811'N 74º30.273'W
Green Lake Rockwall GPS Coordinates: 43º10.577'N 74º29.932'W
Accessibility: <0.2 mile-hike
Degree of Difficulty: Moderately easy

Description: Although not technically a boulder, this unexpected rock wall has to be seen to be believed, and it is for this reason that I have included it in the book. The cliff wall is 50–60 feet high, totally vertical, and seemingly emerges full-blown from the side of a hill.

Although there are a couple of 5–6-foot-high boulders in the woods to the left of the rock wall, they are insignificant compared to the wall, and are likely destined to remain in relative obscurity.

Directions: From Caroga Lake (junction of Routes 29A & 10 South), drive northwest on Route 29A/10 for 3.4 miles. Turn right onto Green Lake Road and head northeast for 0.5 mile. Bear left at a fork onto a dirt road that leads in several hundred feet to the parking area for Kane Mountain.

From the parking area, walk back down the road to Green Lake Road, turn left, and follow the road around the north end of the lake for ~0.3 mile. When you come to camp #270 (the Beekman residence), look for a small stream on your left. The GPS reading here is 43º10.616'N 74º30.076W. Then look for a faint path to the left of the stream and follow it into the woods. The path immediately becomes easier to follow and appears to be used by mountain bikers. Although the path zigs and zags, follow it uphill, staying close to the stream, which will remain on your right.

Eventually you will come out to an impossibly high rock face that clearly is used by rock climbers, for pitons are permanently affixed to the cliff face.

Resources: youtube.com/watch?v=LwjnTeXPM90.
communitywalk.com/adirondack_park/ny/boulders_in_the_adirondacks/map/299298 – This website shows the rockwall's location.
dpmclimbing.com/climbing-videos/watch/adirondack-bouldering-green-lake-boulders.
southernadirondackclimber.blogspot.com/2013/08/summer-ascents-at-green-lake-boulders.html – This site contains a photograph of the rock wall as well as one with the rock climbing routes.

BOULDERS BEYOND BELIEF

124. PRISON BOULDER

Type of Formation: Large Boulder
WOW Factor: 7–8
Location: Green Lake (Fulton County)
Tenth Edition, NYS Atlas & Gazetteer: p. 50, E5; **Earlier Edition NYS Atlas & Gazetteer**: p. 79, C4–5
Parking GPS Coordinates: 43º10.447′N 74º30.852′W
Prison Boulder GPS Coordinates: 43º10.487′N 74º30.879′W
Accessibility: 250–foot hike
Degree of Difficulty: Moderately easy

Description: Prison Boulder is a large, 25-foot-high boulder located on the side of a hill near the bottom of Kane Mountain. A huge part of the boulder has fallen away to the left and, by doing so, has become a rock of formidable size as well.

I have no idea why this rock is called Prison Boulder.

Directions: From Caroga Lake (junction of Routes 29A & 10 South), drive northwest on Route 29A/10 for 3.5 miles (or 0.1 mile past Green Lake Road). As soon as you drive by Old State Road on your left, turn into a pull-off on the left side of the road. The Canada Lake Store and Marine will be directly to your left.

Walk across Route 29A to the north shoulder of the road and proceed west along Route 29A for 100 feet, passing by a huge rock-cut on your right. When you come to a ravine on your right at the end of the rock-cut, follow the gully uphill for 100 feet and then bear right, heading up the side of a hill. After 100–150 feet, look for the boulder to your left.

Take note of a posted sign just uphill from the boulder and go no further. Should the land by the boulder become posted in the future, then the boulder will no longer be accessible.

Resources: communitywalk.com/map/list/299298 – Prison Boulder site is mentioned on this website.

BOULDERS BEYOND BELIEF

Prison Boulder. Look for Andrew Canavan standing on left side of rock.

BOULDERS BEYOND BELIEF

125. PINE LAKE BOULDERS

Type of Formation: Large Boulder
WOW Factor: 8
Location: Pine Lake (Fulton County)
Tenth Edition, NYS Atlas & Gazetteer: p. 50, E5; **Earlier Edition NYS Atlas & Gazetteer**: p. 79, C4–5
Parking GPS Coordinates: 43º11.881'N 74º30.882'W
Pine Lake Boulders GPS Coordinates: *Megalodon & Creekside* -- 43º12.156'N 74º30.828'W
Accessibility: 0.4-mile hike + 0.1-mile bushwhack
Degree of Difficulty: Moderately easy hike + moderate bushwhack
Additional Information: *Camping & RV Park* -- Pine Lake Park. 136 Timberline Lane. Caroga Lake, NY 12023

Megalodan.

Description: *Megalodon* is the largest by far of the glacial erratics in this collective. It is over 30 feet high and just as long, if not longer—a truly massive, hulking boulder. The word Megalodon means "big tooth," and refers to a 50-foot-long prehistoric shark that lived 2.6 to 23 million years ago. It had 7-inch-long teeth and possessed the most powerful bite of any animal on Earth. It is now featured in a 2018 movie called Megalodon.

BOULDERS BEYOND BELIEF

Creek Side is a 15-foot-high boulder that stands virtually next to Megalodan and, as the name suggest, lies right next to the streambed.

Dinosaur Egg is the last significant boulder in this collective.

History: The boulders were "discovered" by Fred Abbuhl in the late 1990s. At the time, he called Megalodon the "Monster Boulder."

Directions: From Pine Lake (junction of Routes 29A West & 10 North), drive south on Route 29A/10 for 100 feet and turn left on Pine Lake Road

From Caroga (junction of Routes 29A & 10 South), head northwest on Route 29A/10 for ~5.3 miles and turn right onto Pine Lake Road just before the intersection of Routes 29A & 10 North.

Drive northeast on Pine Lake Road, proceeding along the west side of Pine Lake for 0.7 mile. Park in a small area at the end of the road. From here, follow a well-worn path along the west side of Pine Lake for over 0.4 mile. When you come to a second, tiny stream crossing, look for a cairn and a faint path leading left uphill. Take note that in the summer both stream crossings will be essentially dry. The GPS reading for the start of this bushwhack is 43°12.115'N 74°30.731'W.

Follow the streambed uphill for 0.1 mile to reach the boulders, which will be on the left side of the creek.

Note: It is also possible to paddle up Pine Lake from the parking area to where the bushwhack begins. Going 0.4 mile by water, you will come to a natural landing, complete with a flat rock in the water, and a 50-foot path that leads up to the main trail.

Second note: Virtually at the start of the hike, you will pass by two 8-foot-high boulders in the woods to your left. Neither rock looks all that inviting and, I suspect, are basically ignored by hikers and boulderers.

Resources: Justin Sanford, *New York Adirondack Park Bouldering* (Broadalbin, NY: Southern Adirondack Climber, LLC, 2015), 44–49.
Barbara McMartin, *Discover the Adirondacks 2: Walks, Waterways and Winter Treks in the Southern Adirondacks* (Somersworth, NH: New Hampshire Publishing Company, 1980), On page 84 McMartin writes, "This path [the one following along the shoreline] also gives access to the two low hills just to the west that are lined with huge boulders and short cliffs."
rockclimbing.com/routes/North_America/United_States/New_York/Central/Nine_Corner_Boulders.

BOULDERS BEYOND BELIEF

126. NINE CORNER LAKE BOULDERS

Type of Formation: Large Boulder
WOW Factor: 6–7
Location: Northwest of Caroga Lake (Fulton County)
Tenth Edition, NYS Atlas & Gazetteer: p. 50, E5; **Earlier Edition Delorme NYS Atlas & Gazetteer**: p. 79, C4–5
Parking GPS Coordinates: 43º11.634′N 74º31.488′W
Nine Corner Lake Boulders GPS Coordinates: 43º11.663′N 74º32.540′W
Accessibility: 1.0-mile hike
Degree of Difficulty: Moderate
Additional Information: A map of the boulder field, showing four different sites that are in fairly close proximity to one another, can be found at scribd.com/document/59491653/Dr-topo-9-Corner.

Boulders at Nine Corner Lake.

Description: A variety of large boulders, ranging in size from very small to over 25 feet in height, can be found near the northeast corner of Nine Corner Lake. In "Problem Solving: Nine Corner Lake Boulders" that appeared in *Adirondack Explorer: 2012 Outings Guide*, Alan Wechsler writes, "…the place is a labyrinth of giant erratics—boulders left behind when the last glacier melted thousands of years ago." He particularly mentions *Tower of Power*, a

BOULDERS BEYOND BELIEF

25-foot-high boulder located in a section of the boulder field called Middle Earth ("...a maze of house-size rocks"). Wechsler refers to this particular boulder as a "highball"—a boulderer's term for a boulder that is sufficiently high that if you were to fall off from near the top, you could sustain serious injuries.

Boulderers have grouped the boulder site into six zones, listed A–F. The majority are straight ahead, to the left, after you cross over the rip-rap dam.

Such colorful names as Lost Dog, Fortress, Nick Stoner (after the famous local frontiersman), Suitcase, Castle, and so on, have been given to the boulders.

Not surprisingly, a number of good-sized boulders are also encountered at different spots around the shoreline of the lake; even near the middle of the bay at Nine Corner Lake's northwest side.

History: Nine Corner Lake has been attracting boulderers since the early 2002 when its potential was first identified by Josh Karns, a well-known Pennsylvania rock climber, and several of his friends. It is considered by many to be the largest developed bouldering area in the Adirondack State Park.

Nine Corner Lake was named for its amoeba-like appearance and multitude of corners. Even before the advent of bouldering, the lake was heavily utilized for camping and recreation.

In *Discover the Southern Adirondacks*, Bill Ingersoll writes, "This is indeed quite the assemblage of jumbled rocks, as though a glacier collided with the un-named hill to the north and sprayed this debris field along the southern slope. It is a natural jungle gym that will bring out the child even in non-climbers."

The riprap dam that you cross over to get to the boulder field serves as more a berm than a dam, for there is no spillway associated with it.

Directions: From Pine Lake (junction of Routes 29A West & 10 North), drive west on Route 29A for over 0.1 mile. Pull over to your right at the trailhead parking for Nine Corner Lake. (On the opposite side of the road is the trailhead parking for West Lake).

Proceeding on foot, follow the Nine Corner Lake Trail (an old road) west. At 0.9 mile you will come to a fork. Bear right, following the main trail that leads to a riprap dam in 0.1 mile. Cross over the dam and head straight into the woods. You will immediately encounter the beginning of the large rocks [43º11.584'N; 74º32.570'W].

Resources: Justin Sanford, *New York Adirondack Park Bouldering* (Broadalbin, NY: Southern Adirondack Climber, LLC, 2015) 50–88.
Alan Wechsler, "Problem Solving: Nine Corner Lake Boulders," *Adirondack Explorer: 2012 Outings Guide*, 40 & 41.
Barbara McMartin, *Discover the Adirondacks 2* (Somersworth, New Hampshire: New Hampshire Publishing Company, 1980), 93–95.
Bill Ingersoll, *Discover the Southern Adirondacks* (Barneveld, NY: Wild River Press. 2014), 85–88.
rockclimbing.com/routes/North_America/United_States/New_York/Central/Nine_Corner_Boulders.
mountainproject.com/area/106229917/nine-corners-lake.
timetoclimb.com/bouldering/boulderingintheadirondacks - The website contains a number of photographs of the rocks.
Jim Lawyer & Jeremy Haas, *Adirondack Rock: A Climber's Guide* (Pompey, NY: Adirondack Rock Press, LLC, 2008), 548–554.
Linda Laing & series editor Neal Burdick, *Guide to Adirondack Trails: Southern Region. Second Edition* (New York: Adirondack Mountain Club, Inc., 1994), 187. "The south end is strewn with large boulders that lead down into the water and create excellent access steps for the swimmer."

127. WEST LAKE TRAIL BOULDERS

Type of Formation: Large Boulder
WOW Factor: 3–4
Location: Canada Lake (Fulton County)
Tenth Edition, NYS Atlas & Gazetteer: p. 65, A5–6; **Earlier Edition NYS Atlas & Gazetteer**: p. 79, C4–5
Parking GPS Coordinates: 43º11.458'N 74º31.652'W
Destination GPS Coordinates: *Boulder #1* -- 43º11.318'N 74º31.683'W; *Cue-Ball* -- 43º11.206'N 74º31.814'W
Accessibility: *Boulder #1* – 0.2-mile hike; *Cue-Ball* – 0.4 mile hike
Degree of Difficulty: Moderately easy

Description: In Barbara McMartin's *Caroga: An Adirondack Town Recalls its Past*, a photograph of a 15–20-foot high boulder called Strobeck Rock is shown.

BOULDERS BEYOND BELIEF

My wife, Barbara Delaney, and I decided to see if we could find McMartin's historic rock despite the lack of any specific details. We choose to hike along a trail that started from Route 29A near Pine Lake and that ended at West Lake. Although the odds were slim, we hoped that because the trail led through a mile of woods, we might inadvertently come across the historic boulder. Needless to say, we failed to find Strobeck Rock; however, we did encounter a couple of medium-to large-sized boulders worth mentioning --

Boulder #1 is 8 feet high and 15 feet long, resting on top of a tiny hillock next to the trail.

Cue-Ball is an impressive 10-foot-high boulder whose roundness suggested to me the shape of an enormous billiard ball, so I called it Cue-Ball. You're welcome to call it whatever you like.

Cue-Ball.

History: In the 1870s, Strobeck Rock was a favorite camping site near West Lake. In her book, *Caroga: An Adirondack Town Recalls its Past*, McMartin writes, "One family group located at Strobeck Rock on West Lake and another called their camp Saint's Retreat." Later, McMartin also calls the camp Saint's Rest.

Directions: From Pine Lake (junction of Routes 29A West & 10 North), drive west on Route 29A for over 0.1 mile. Pull over to your left at the trailhead parking for the 1.1-mile-long trail to the West Lake Boat Launch (This trail is opposite the trailhead for Nine Corner Lake).

Follow the red-marked snowmobile trail for >0.2 mile to the first large boulder, which is on your right, 20 feet from the trail on a tiny hillock,

335

opposite a marshland created by the outlet streams from Nine Corner Lake and Pine Lake.

The second large boulder is reached before 0.4 mile, to you your right, less than 100 feet up a slight incline in the woods.

At the very beginning of the hike, you will cross over the outlet stream from Nine Corner Lake.

Resources: Barbara McMartin, *Caroga: An Adirondack Town Recalls its Past* (Caroga Lake, NY: Town of Caroga, 1998), 58, 61, & 82.

128. EAST STONER LAKE OUTLET STREAM ROCK & ROCK-SHELTER

Stoner Lake Outlet Rock-Shelter.

Type of Formation: Large Boulder; Rock-Shelter
WOW Factor: *Outlet Stream Rock* -- 4–5; *Rock-Shelter* -- 3–4
Location: East Stoner Lake (Fulton County)
Tenth Edition, NYS Atlas & Gazetteer: p. 50, E5; **Earlier Edition NYS Atlas & Gazetteer**: p. 79, BC4–5
Parking GPS Coordinates: 43º13.387'N 74º31.486'W
Outlet Stream Rock GPS Coordinates: 43º13.342'N 74º31.512'W
Accessibility: 0.05-mile hike
Degree of Difficulty: *Outlet Stream Rock* – Moderately easy; *Rock Shelter* – Moderate; stream crossing required

BOULDERS BEYOND BELIEF

Description: Even if there were no big rocks to be seen, this would be a very pretty, short hike as you follow a cascading stream through a steeply cut ravine along its east bank, taking you past a series of gentle cascades and slabs of bedrock.

Outlet Stream Rock. Photograph by Barbara Delaney.

Outlet Stream Rock is massive—25 feet high, 15–20 feet long, and 15 feet wide. It lies tilted at a 60°angle on the east bank of the gorge, with its front end partially submerged in a pool of water at the bottom of a small cascade.

BOULDERS BEYOND BELIEF

Rock-shelter is located at the base of a small cliff. The enclosure measure 5 feet high by 8 feet deep, and clearly has been used in the past. Unfortunately, some miscreant has elected to paint his name on the rock.

History: The Stoner Lake system consists of 64-acre West Stoner Lake, 77-acre East Stoner Lake, and Little Stoner Lake. The outlet stream drains East Stoner Lake.

The Stoner Lakes are named after Nick Stoner, a regional trapper who rose to the rank of major in the War of 1812. Like Timothy Murphy of Schoharie Valley fame, Stoner became a legend and namesake around Canada Lake posthumously.

Originally the lakes were called Stink Lakes, a name that demanded revision and, by good fortune, got it. The original name arose after hundreds of fish were caught behind a beaver dam as the lake receded, producing a terrible stench as they died and rotted.

The lakes have also gone by such other names as Vrooman Lake, Deline Lake, and Beaver Lake.

Directions: From northwest of Canada Lake (junction of Routes 29A West & 10 North), drive north on Route 10 for ~2.5 miles and turn right onto East Stoner Road. Park immediately in a small space to your right, just before crossing over the outlet stream.

Outlet Stream Rock -- Walk back up East Stoner Road for 20 feet (almost to Route 10), and then turn left onto a path that quickly leads along the outlet stream's west bank. You will come to Outlet Stream Rock on the east bank in 0.05 mile.

Rock-Shelter -- The rock-shelter lies on the opposite side of the creek, just upstream from the Outlet Stream Rock, but on the opposite side of the creek. To see it close up, you must cross over the stream, and then bushwhack over to it—a distance of 75 feet from the east bank of the creek.

Resources: stonerlake.com/the%20lakes/the%20lakes.htm.
Barbara McMartin & Bill Ingersoll, *Discover the Adirondacks 2* (Somersworth, New Hampshire: New Hampshire Publishing Company, 1980), 112–114.
Barbara McMartin, *Discover the Southern Adirondacks* (Canada Lake, NY: Lake View Press, 2005), 89 & 90.
stonerlake.com/the%20lakes/the%20lakes.htm – This website, in one of its two photographs, actually shows the lower part of the Outlet Stream Rock.

BOULDERS BEYOND BELIEF

129. SHERMAN MOUNTAIN BALANCED ROCK & BOULDERS

Type of Formation: Balanced Rock; Large Boulder
WOW Factor: 6–7
Location: Arietta (Hamilton County)
Tenth Edition, NYS Atlas & Gazetteer: p. 50, D5; **Earlier Edition NYS Atlas & Gazetteer**: p. 79, B4
Parking GPS Coordinates: 43º15.325'N 74º31.850'W
Destination GPS Coordinates: *Balanced Rock Boulder* --43º16.037'N; *Lost Hunter's Cliff Boulders* -- 74º31.081'W
Lost Hunter's Cliff GPS Coordinates: 43º16.256'N 74º31.078'W
Accessibility: ~1.2-mile hike along informal trail; partial bushwhack
Degree of Difficulty: Difficult if informal trail is not easy to follow

Description: *Balanced Rock Boulder* -- In his book, *Discover the Southern Adirondacks*, Bill Ingersoll writes about an interesting balanced rock by Sherman Mountain. "From the upstream side it looks as though a glacier dropped a massive block precariously on top of a pyramidal base rock; from other angles the formation is revealed to be one impressive boulder that was chiseled by natural forces into its unusual shape, not two separate ones placed improbably together." It is reminiscent of something that you might see out in Colorado's Canyons of the Gods.

Lost Hunter's Cliff Boulders – As it turns out, the Balanced Rock Boulder reported by Ingersoll is just one of a number of large glacial boulders that are described in Justin Sanford's *New York Adirondack Park Bouldering*. These boulders can be found along the Lost Hunter's Cliff next to a small stream flowing south down the mountain.

The boulders are also reported in Jim Lawyer & Jeremy Haas' *Adirondack Rock: A Climber's Guide*. Particularly mentioned are "large boulders—including two stacked car-sized boulders…"

Directions: From Pine Lake (junction of Routes 10 North & 29A west), drive north on Route 10 for ~5.5 miles. Turn right into a pull-off >0.2 mile before the second bridge spanning the West Branch of the Sacandaga River.

From the parking area, walk back (south) along Route 8 for several hundred feet. Then turn left onto an informal fisherman's path and follow it as it heads northeast, contouring around the southeast side of Chub Lake. Although not visible, Chub Lake Mountain (~2,150') is off to your right.

BOULDERS BEYOND BELIEF

Continue on the path as it now turns slightly left and heads north. In ~0.8 mile, you will come to the west end of a Beaver-created meadow and swamp. Cross the outlet stream here and follow the path as it leads east above the beaver swamp-land and then veers northeast away from the swamp. In less than another 0.4 mile, you will arrive at the beginning of the boulder field, along a drainage field that continues north for another 0.2–0.3 mile.

Resources: Bill Ingersoll, *Discover the Southern Adirondacks. Fifth Edition* (Barneveld, NY: Wild River Press, 2014), 145. A photograph of the rock can be seen on page 146.
Justin Sanford, *New York Adirondack Park Bouldering* (Broadalbin, NY: Southern Adirondack Climber, LLC, 2015), 90–95. A photograph of the unusual rock described by Ingersoll can be seen on page 92, where it is listed as Boulder D.
Lawrence King, "Sherman Mountain: A Bushwhack on Snowshoes to its Unusual Erratics and Upper Cliffs," *Adirondac* (February/March 1984), 8–10. The article includes a hand-drawn map.
Jim Lawyer & Jeremy Haas, *Adirondack Rock: A Climber's Guide* (Pompey, NY: Adirondack Rock Press, LLC, 2008), 555–558. The boulders are listed under the section for Lost Hunter's Cliffs.

130. GOOD LUCK CLIFFS BOULDERS & TALUS CAVES

Type of Formation: Talus Rock; Shelter Cave
WOW Factor: 8
Location: Arietta (Hamilton County)
Tenth Edition, NYS Atlas & Gazetteer: p. 50, D5; **Earlier Edition NYS Atlas & Gazetteer**: p. 79, BC4–5
Parking GPS Coordinates: 43º15.357′N 74º32.299′W
Good Luck Cliff Boulders GPS Coordinates: 43º14.940′N 74º33.420′W
Accessibility: 1.8-mile hike
Degree of Difficulty: Moderately difficult
Additional Information: A map of the hike can be found at: cnyhiking.com/GoodLuckMountainCliffs.htm

Description: A fabulous collection of enormous boulders, talus, and rock slabs have come to rest at the base of the massive, nearly 500-foot-high cliff on Good Luck Mountain. A few of them are the size of garages and houses.
   The boulders have created a series of talus caves, including an impossible-to-miss shelter cave at the beginning of the boulder-choked gorge.

BOULDERS BEYOND BELIEF

Barbara McMartin, in *Discover the Adirondacks 2*, writes, "Here a huge rock slab shelters a small cave, and the rock top gives views of the valley below and the cliffs above. That rock is, in turn, guarded by a giant rock spire that looms like the jaw of a prehistoric animal."

Reports made by cavers in the 1980s indicate that the Good Luck Cliffs area contains a 1,650-foot-long talus cave system. That number may have since increased over the last 35 years.

Good Luck Cliffs talus cave. Note figure near cave entrance.

History: The mountain and cliffs are named after nearby Good Luck Lake. According to Jeptha Root Simms in his 1850 book *Trappers of New York*, the lake's name arose from an incident when the rifle of deputy surveyor John Vrooman's son-in-law burst into a shower of fragments as he tried to shoot a loon. Fortunately, no one was hurt by any of the discharged fragments. Now, that's what you would call good luck.

Jim Vermeulen and Bill Morris are the first reported hikers/climbers to begin climbing in the Good Luck Gorge, starting in 1986.

BOULDERS BEYOND BELIEF

Directions: From northwest of Canada Lake (junction of Routes 10 North & 29A), drive north on Route 10 for ~6.0 miles (<0.2 mile north of a second bridge spanning the West Branch of the Sacandaga River).

Head west on the trail for over 0.5 mile. At a junction, turn left and proceed south, then west, for another 0.7 mile, following sign for Good Luck Lake and Spectacle Lake. Just before you come to a large snowmobile bridge, turn right by the snowmobile sign and follow an unmarked, but well-worn, trail northwest for 0.6 mile to reach the cliffs on Good Luck Mountain. Along the way, you will pass by numerous large rocks.

Resources: Russell Dunn, "The caves at Good Luck Cliffs," *Northeastern Caver* Vol. XXIV, no. 3 (September, 1993), 98 & 99.
Barbara McMartin, *Discover the Adirondacks 2* (Somersworth, New Hampshire: New Hampshire Publishing Company, 1980), 146—148 and 152—155.
Barbara McMartin, *Fifty Hikes in the Adirondacks* (Woodstock, VT: Backcountry Publications, 1988), 53—56.
Tim Starmer, *Five-Star Trails in the Adirondacks* (Birmingham, AL: Menasha Ridge Press, 2010), 167. "The huge boulders provide an excellent opportunity for exploration, including many small caves that are formed in the mass of rock."
Winnie Yu, "Good Luck doesn't fail," *Adirondack Explorer* Vol. II, No. 5 (September/October, 2009). On page 19 can be seen a photograph of Yu's daughter, Annie, looking at an enormous shelter cave created by fallen rocks.
The Good Luck Caves are mentioned in a number of issues of the *Northeastern Caver*—Vol. XXV, no. 1 (March, 1994), 4; Vol. XXVII, no. 1 (March, 1996), 11; and Vol. XXVIII, no. 3 (September, 1997), 93.
Jeptha Root Simms, *Trappers of New York* (Albany, NY: J. Munsell, 1850), 169.
cnyhiking.com/GoodLuckMountainCliffs.htm.
Linda Laing & series editor Neal Burdick, *Guide to Adirondack Trails: Southern Region*. Second Edition (New York: Adirondack Mountain Club, Inc., 1994), 207. "Here, next to the path, several enormous boulders are jumbled together to create tiny caves, which are most interesting to explore."
Rose Rivezzi & David Trithart, *Kids on the Trails! Hiking with children in the Adirondacks* (Lake George, NY: Adirondack Mountain Club, 1997), 143. "The way heads up a ravine filled with many large boulders....At about 1.9 mi. (3.0 km) the path winds past boulders tumbled together and forming many small caves."
Jim Lawyer & Jeremy Haas, *Adirondack Rock: A Climber's Guide* (Pompey, NY: Adirondack Rock Press, LLC, 2008), 559–565. The Good Luck Boulders are mentioned on page 564.
Linda Laing & series editor Neal Burdick, *Guide to Adirondack Trails: Southern Region*. Second Edition (New York: Adirondack Mountain Club, Inc., 1994), 205–207. On page 207 Laing writes that "...several enormous boulders are jumbled together to create tiny caves..."

BOULDERS BEYOND BELIEF

131. STALLION BOULDER
Ferris Lake Wild Forest

Type of Formation: Large Boulder
WOW Factor: 6
Location: Averys Place (Hamilton County)
Tenth Edition, NYS Atlas & Gazetteer: p. 50, D5; **Earlier Edition NYS Atlas & Gazetteer**: p. 78, B4.
Parking GPS Coordinates: 43º18.053'N 74'33.914'W
Stallion Boulder GPS Coordinates: 43º18.075'N 74º33.946'W
Accessibility: 300-foot trek; partial bushwhack
Degree of Difficulty: Moderately easy

Description: This large, 15-foot-high boulder, surrounded by a retinue of smaller rocks, some as high as 6 feet in height, is called Stallion Boulder, a name given to it by boulderers.

History: The boulder was "discovered" by Justin Sanford in 2010.

The word "Stallion" refers to an uncastrated, adult, male horse. You will need to draw your own conclusions as to how this rock was named.

The Stallion Boulder is located in the 147,454-acre Ferris Lake Wild Forest.

The hike up to Jockeybush Lake is 1.1 miles in length should you wish to add some physical activity to your outing. Herd paths continue around both sides of the lake. The lake's name is somewhat of a mystery, dating back as far as 1874 according to Stephen Williams in "A Winter Ramble: Snowshoers enjoy a wild jaunt to Jockeybush Lake."

Stallion Boulder. Photograph by Barbara Delaney

Directions: From northwest of Caroga Lake (junction of Routes 10 North & 29A West), drive north on Route 10 for ~9.6 miles.

From Piseco Lake (junction of Routes 10 & 8 West), drive south on Route 10 for ~7.7 miles.

Coming from either direction, park in a marked pull-off for Jockeybush Lake on the west side of the road.

From the parking area, follow the blue-blazed Jockeybush Lake Trail uphill for less than 100 feet to the trailhead register. From here, continue uphill for another 50 feet until you come to an intersecting snowmobile trail. Turn right, following the faint snowmobile trail uphill for 150 feet. At this point, the boulder can be clearly seen to your right, less than 50 feet away.

Resources: Barbara McMartin, *Discover the Adirondacks 2* (Somersworth, New Hampshire: New Hampshire Publishing Company, 1980), 157 & 158.
Justin Sanford, *New York Adirondack Park Bouldering* (Broadalbin, NY: Southern Adirondack Climber, LLC, 2015), 100–105.
Stephen Williams, "A Winter Ramble: Snowshoers enjoy a wild jaunt to Jockeybush Lake," *Adirondack Explorer 2018 Annual Outings Guide*, 71.

132. NORTHVILLE-PLACID TRAIL GLACIAL ERRATIC

Type of Formation: Large Boulder
WOW Factor: 6
Location: Piseco (Hamilton County)
Tenth Edition, NYS Atlas & Gazetteer: p. 50, B5; **Earlier Edition NYS Atlas & Gazetteer**: p. 79, A4–5
Parking GPS Coordinates: 43º27.517'N 74º31.321'W
Estimated Destination GPS Coordinates: Not taken
Accessibility: ~2.5-mile hike
Degree of Difficulty: Moderately difficult

Description: Barbara McMartin & Lee M. Brenning, in *Discover the West Central Adirondacks*, write, "There is a huge glacial erratic on the lip of the escarpment" as you hike along the Piseco Lake section of the Northville-Placid Trail.

BOULDERS BEYOND BELIEF

Directions: From east of Piseco Lake (junction of Route 24/Old Piseco Road & 8), drive northwest on Route 24/Old Piseco Road for 2.2 miles. Turn right onto Haskells Road and proceed north for 0.7 mile. Park in an area on your right just before crossing over the Cold Stream Bridge.

Proceeding on foot, walk across the bridge and head north for another 0.1 mile to reach the trailhead register. From here, continue north, then abruptly northwest for ~2.5 miles (a guesstimate) until you come to the glacial erratic. Part of this hike is made exciting by the fact that you will be following along the edge of an escarpment, with the valley floor more than 70 feet below you.

Resources: Barbara McMartin & Lee M. Brenning, *Discover the West Central Adirondacks* (Woodstock, VT: Backcountry Publications, 1988), 39.
Jeffrey and Donna Case (editors) & Neal Burdick (series editor), *Adirondack Trails: Northville-Placid Trail. Fourth Edition* (Lake George, NY: Adirondack Mountain Club, Inc., 2007), 59–62.

133. COUCH ROCK & SQUARE ROCK

Type of Formation: Medium-sized Boulder
Location: Piseco Lake (Hamilton County)
Tenth Edition, NYS Atlas & Gazetteer: p. 50, BC5; **Earlier Edition NYS Atlas & Gazetteer**: p. 78, A4
Parking GPS Coordinates: 43º24.669'N 74º33.432'W
Destination GPS Coordinates: *Square Rock* -- 43º24.954'N 74º33.964'W; *Couch Rock* -- 43º24.914'N 74º33.996'W
Accessibility: *Square Rock & Couch Rock* -- 0.5-mile hike; *Echo Cliffs* -- 0.7-mile hike; 715-foot elevation change
Degree of Difficulty: Moderate

Description: In *Kids on the Trails! Hiking with children in the Adirondacks*, Rose Rivezzi & David Trithart write, "At 0.6 mi. (1.0 km) a large boulder appears on the left, looking from below like a gigantic cube. Just beyond is a lounge-chair-shaped rock that must be tested for comfort."

Square Rock is a substantial sized, 8-foot-high trailside boulder. Lisa Densmore Ballard, in *Best Easy Day Hikes. Adirondacks*, describes the rock as a

BOULDERS BEYOND BELIEF

"...square, flat-topped boulder..." Its pull on kids, who love to climb up it, is simply irresistible.

Couch Rock, aka Chair Rock, is a 3-foot-high, 6-foot-long boulder that resembles a post-modern, mid-1950s chair. In *Guide to Adirondack Trails: Southern Region. Second Edition*, Linda Laing writes, "The trail soon reaches a chair-shaped boulder on the left that makes a great resting spot for hikers in need of some time to recover."

On my last visit, Couch Rock looked more and more like an automobile carved out of a block of wood than a lounging chair. Hikers have placed two round rocks exactly where wheels on a car would be.

Square Rock.

Both rocks lie along the trail leading up to Echo Cliffs—a 2,420-foot-high overlook that provide great views of Piseco Lake.

Directions: From the southeast shore of Piseco Lake (junction of Routes 8 North & 10), go west on Route 8 for 2.8 miles. Turn right onto West Shore Road and drive northeast for 3.6 miles to the Echo Cliffs trailhead, 0.5 mile south of the entrance to Little Sand Point Campground.

Couch Rock.

From Speculator (junction of Routes 8 & 30 North), drive southwest on Route 8 for 8.8 miles. Turn right onto Route 24 and proceed west, then south, around the northwest corner of Piseco Lake. At 5.3 miles, you will see the trailhead sign for Panther Mountain and the Echo Cliffs. Turn into a long pull-off on your left.

BOULDERS BEYOND BELIEF

Follow the blue-blazed path northwest up the shoulder of Panther Mountain. After 0.4 mile, huge bluffs below the Echo Cliffs overlook can be seen uphill to your right. At 0.5 mile you will come to Square Rock and then, 100 feet beyond, Couch Rock. Both rocks are on the left side of the trail.

The Echo Cliffs are less than 0.2 mile farther.

Resources: Tim Starmer, *Five-Star Trails in the Adirondacks: A Guide to the Most Beautiful Hikes* (Birmingham, AL: Menasha Ridge Press, 2010), 64 & 65. Starmer mentions Square Boulder and includes a photograph of the rock on page 67.
Peter Klein, *Adirondack Hikes in Hamilton County* (Blue Mountain Lake, NY: Ravenwolf Publishing, 2006), 96.
Barbara McMartin, *Fifty Hikes in the Adirondacks* (Woodstock, VT: Backcountry Publications, 1988), 61–63.
Barbara McMartin, *Discover the West Central Adirondacks* (Woodstock, VT: Backcountry Publications, 1988), 31 & 34.
Dennis Aprill, *Paths Less Traveled* (Mt. Kisco, NY: Pinto Press, 1998), 65–68.
cnyhiking.com/EchoCliffs.htm.
Bruce Wadsworth, *Day Hikes For All Seasons: An Adirondack Sampler* (Lake George, NY: Adirondack Mountain Club, 1996), 44–46.
Lisa Densmore Ballard, *Best Easy Day Hikes. Adirondacks. Second Edition* (Guilford, CT: Falcon Guides, 2017), 81.
Linda Laing & series editor Neal Burdick, *Guide to Adirondack Trails: Southern Region. Second Edition* (New York: Adirondack Mountain Club, Inc., 1994), 158.
Rose Rivezzi & David Trithart, *Kids on the Trails! Hiking with children in the Adirondacks* (Lake George, NY: Adirondack Mountain Club, 1997), 139.

134. WEST BRANCH BOULDERS

Type of Formation: Large Boulder
WOW Factor: 5–6
Location: Whitehouse (Hamilton County)
Tenth Edition, NYS Atlas & Gazetteer: p. 51, C6; **Earlier Edition NYS Atlas & Gazetteer**: p. 79, AB5
Parking GPS Coordinates: 43º22.353'N 74º25.910'W
Estimated West Branch Boulder GPS Coordinates: 43º22.592'N 74º28.403'W
Accessibility: 2.5-mile hike
Degree of Difficulty: Difficult

BOULDERS BEYOND BELIEF

Description: A huge number of massive, stacked boulders can be both seen and climbed up and through along the north side of the first waterfall on the West Branch of the Sacandaga River.

West Branch Boulders.

History: Whitehouse is the site of a former lumber camp, hunting & fishing lodge, and boy's camp. Today, it serves as the trailhead campsite for the upper West Branch area, including a fishing site called Big Eddy.

Farther downstream, the West Branch of the Sacandaga River, rising from several sources west of Whitehouse, joins with the main trunk of the Sacandaga River south of Wells near the Sacandaga Campground.

Directions: Starting from the southeast end of Algonquin Lake at Wells, head southwest on Algonquin Drive for 0.7 mile. Then turn left onto West River Road and drive west, paralleling the West Branch of the Sacandaga River for >7.0 miles to reach the Whitehouse campsite and parking area. At this point, you are only 0.2 linear mile from where the Northville-Placid Trail suspension bridge crosses over the West Branch of the Sacandaga River.

From the west end of the parking area, follow a connecting spur path west for 0.1 mile to reach the Northville-Placid Trail. Turn right onto the Northville-Placid Trail and proceed northwest for 0.5 mile. At a fork, bear left onto an abandoned logging road, leaving the Northville-Placid Trail behind, and follow it west for 0.7 mile to the outlet stream from Hamilton Lake. This stream can be difficult to ford in high water, so you might want to do the hike during the dryer months of summer. As soon as you cross over the stream, the path quickly leads to the West Branch of the Sacandaga River. Follow it upstream for 0.8 mile and then cross over Cold Brook, a tributary, where an upstream cascade can be seen. This creek is easier to ford than the outlet stream from Hamilton Lake. From here, it is another 0.5 mile until you come to the first fall on the West Branch with its massive boulders.

Once again, it is best to undertake this hike in the summer when less water is flowing, for you will want to follow the West Branch upstream by staying inside the gorge when you come to it. If too much water is flowing through the West Branch Gorge, then it would be best to abandon the hike here, and view the boulders from the top of the gorge, if possible.

Resources: Barbara McMartin, *Discover the Adirondacks 2: Walks, Waterways and Winter Treks in the Southern Adirondacks* (Somersworth, NH: New Hampshire Publishing Company, 1980). A photograph of the boulders can be seen on page 206.
Barbara McMartin, *Fifty Hikes in the Adirondacks* (Woodstock, VT: Backcountry Publications, 1988). A photograph of the large boulders can be seen on page 50.
visitadirondacks.com/hiking/falls-the-west-branch-of-the-sacandaga-river-and-cold-brook-falls.
Bill Ingersoll, *Discover the Southern Adirondacks* (Barneveld, NY: Wild River Press, 2014), 290–293.
adirondack.net/business/falls-on-west-branch-of-sacandaga-river-and-cold-brook-falls-22985.

135. BIDWELL'S HOTEL ROCK

Type of Formation: Perched Rock; Split Rock
WOW Factor: 7
Location: Gilmantown (Hamilton County)
Tenth Edition, NYS Atlas & Gazetteer: p. 51, B8; **Earlier Edition NYS Atlas & Gazetteer**: p. 79, A6
Bidwell's Hotel Rock GPS Coordinates: 43º29.419'N 74º20.116'W
Accessibility: Roadside
Degree of Difficulty: Easy

Description: Bidwell's Hotel Rock is a massive split rock with a large, 5-foot-high boulder balanced on top of the 15-foot-long, larger half of the rock formation. The split is 3 feet wide and spacious enough to accommodate an average size person.

Bidwell's Hotel Rock.

History: According to what sounds like a true story, Charles Bidwell, a mail deliveryman, was driving his horse and sleigh along the old Gilmantown Road in the 1870s when a fierce snowstorm erupted, forcing him to seek shelter. He drove his horse and sled into a wide split in the rock, and was able to weather out the storm. This incident led to the rock becoming known as Bidwell's Hotel Rock, a humorous nod to the fact that Bidwell spent the night there.

Directions: From the northwest end of the Route 30 bridge in Wells, drive north on Route 30 for less than 0.3 mile. Then turn left onto Gilmantown Road and drive north for 7.1 miles. Look for a historic marker on your left.

From Speculator (junction of Routes 30 & 8), drive southeast on Route 30 for 0.8 mile. Turn right onto Downey Avenue and head southeast for 0.1

mile. Bear right onto South Shore Drive and proceed southeast for 0.2 mile. When you come to Gilmantown Road, turn left and head east for 0.5 mile. Look for the historic marker on your right. The rock is located behind the sign, several feet into the woods.

The best approach is to walk southeast on Gilmantown Road for 50 feet from the historic marker; then turn right onto a secondary, dirt road and head back 50 feet to see the boulder, now on your right.

Resources: Ted Aber & Stella King, *Tales from an Adirondack County* (Prospect, NY: Prospect Books, 1961), 61–61. A photo of the rock can be seen in an insert between pages 80 and 81.
Ted Aber & Stella King, *The History of Hamilton County* (Lake Pleasant, NY: Great Wilderness Books, 1965), 653 & 654.
historylakespec.wordpress.com/bidwells-hotel.
Barney Fowler, *Adirondack Album #2* (Schenectady, NY: Outdoor Associates, 1980), 86. The article includes a photograph of the rock with a dog about to enter the split in the rock.
historylakespec.wordpress.com/bidwells-hotel.

136. INDIAN FACE & ROADSIDE BOULDERS

Type of Formation: Painted Rock; Rock Profile
WOW Factor: 2–3
Location: Speculator (Hamilton County)
Tenth Edition, NYS Atlas & Gazetteer: p. 51, B8; **Earlier Edition NYS Atlas & Gazetteer**: p. 79, A6–7
Destination GPS Coordinates: *Indian Face* -- 43º30.026'N 74º16.816'W; *Roadside Boulders* -- 43º26.062'N 74º15.822'W
Accessibility: *Indian Face* – Roadside; *Roadside Boulders* – near roadside
Degree of Difficulty: Easy-Moderately easy

Description: *Indian Face* is a deftly painted profile of an Indian face, taking advantage of a jagged section of the cliff face.

Roadside Boulders consist of a long stretch of medium-sized boulders along Route 30 between Wells and Speculator.

History: *Indian Face* – I believe that this painted rock is of relatively recent origin, for my wife and I do not recall seeing it previously in our many

BOULDERS BEYOND BELIEF

excursions along Route 30. In its present form, the image may not last long for the paint already seems to be fading rapidly.

At one time there was also a similar painted Indian face that stood out prominently from a rock wall on the drive to Tenant Creek Falls near the vanished hamlet of Hope Falls.

Directions: *Indian Face* -- From north of Wells (junction of Routes 30 & 8 North), drive north on Route 30 for 4.3 miles. The rock formation is on the left side of the road and can only be seen driving south, so you will need to turn around after 4.3 miles and start back to view it.

From Speculator (the junction of Routes 30 & 8 South), drive south on Route 30 for ~5.3 miles. The rock profile is on the right side of the road.

Indian Face Rock along Route 30.

Roadside Boulders -- From north of Wells (junction of Routes 30 & 8), drive south on Route 30 for 1.0 mile and turn into a large pull-off on your left. From here, walk across Route 30 and head south along the shoulder of the road, being mindful of traffic. Over the next 0.2 mile, you will see numerous medium-sized boulders near roadside in the woods that invite exploration. Best of all, the rocks are entirely on state land. Have fun!

Resources: A photograph of Indian Face can be seen at adirondack/experience.com/blog/2016/09/rock.

BOULDERS BEYOND BELIEF

137. CAMP-OF-THE-WOODS BOULDERS
Camp-of-the-Woods

Type of Formation: Large Boulder
WOW Factor: 3
Location: Speculator (Hamilton County)
Tenth Edition, NYS Atlas & Gazetteer: p. 51, B7; **Earlier Edition NYS Atlas & Gazetteer**: p. 79, A6
Parking GPS Coordinates: *Boat Launch site* -- 43º29.754'N 74º21.526'W; *Camp-of-the-Woods* -- 43º29.460'N 74º21.186'W
Destination GPS Coordinates: *Camp-of-the-Woods Boulder* -- 43º29.363'N 74º21.209'W; *Beach Boulder* -- 43º29.637'N 74º21.441'W
Accessibility: *By water* – 0.3 mile paddle to the Beach Boulder; 0.6-mile paddle to Camp-of-the-Woods Boulder
 By foot – 0.1-mile walk to Camp-of-the-Woods Boulder
Degree of Difficulty: Easy

Camp-of-the-Woods Boulder (at far right). Postcard c. 1950.

Description: *Camp-of-the-Woods Boulder* -- This 9-foot-high boulder is located at the south end of the Camp-of-the-Woods beach. The rock is about 10 feet wide at the base, narrowing as its top is reached.

BOULDERS BEYOND BELIEF

Beach Boulder is a massive rock that lies on a sandy beach (43°29.363'N 74°21.209'W) 0.4 mile northwest of the Camp-of-the-Woods Boulder. The boulder is visible from the lake, but is on private property.

Camp-of-the-Woods Boulder today.

History: Camp-of-the-Woods, located on the shore of Lake Pleasant, is a 90-acre Christian resort and conference center for individuals and families desiring spiritual growth, relaxation, and recreation. It was founded in 1900 by George "Pop" Tibbitts.

Directions: *By wa*ter -- From Speculator (junction of Routes 30 & 8 South), drive southeast on Route 30 for 0.5 mile. Turn left onto a dirt road just before crossing over Lake Pleasant's outlet stream, proceed northeast for 60 feet, and then turn right. The launch site and parking area are only 150 feet away, heading south.

Once in the water, paddle upstream on the Sacandaga River for 0.1 mile and then turn left onto the lake. You will pass by the Beach Boulder to your left in < 0.2 mile, and then come to the Camp-of-the-Woods Boulder at 0.5 mile.

BOULDERS BEYOND BELIEF

By land – From Speculator (junction of Routes 30 & 8), drive southeast on Route 30 for 0.8 mile. Turn right onto Downey Avenue and, within 0.1 mile, bear right into Camp-of-the-Woods. Take note that this is a private resort, but open to the public as long as you are a registered guest.

Resources: Donald R. Williams, *Adirondack Ventures: Images of America* (Charleston, SC: Arcadia Publishing, 2006). On page 19 is a photograph of the beach, including the boulder to the far right.

138. KUNJAMUK CAVE
Speculator Tree Farm Tract

Type of Formation: Cave
WOW Factor: 6
Location: Speculator (Hamilton County)
Tenth Edition, NYS Atlas & Gazetteer: p. 51, A7–8; **Earlier Edition NYS Atlas & Gazetteer**: p. 87, D6
Parking at paved end of Elm Lake Road GPS Coordinates: 43º31.182′N 74º20.883′W
Kunjamuk Cave GPS Coordinates: 43º31.149′N 74º19.723′W
Accessibility: 1.5-mile walk, bike, ski, or drive from the paved end of Elm Lake Road
Degree of Difficulty: Moderate

Description: Kunjamuk Cave is a 20-foot-long, 8-foot-high, smoothly contoured cave that goes straight into the interior of Cave Hill for 25 feet. Curiously, it has a 2-foot diameter skylight that forms a ventilation shaft.

In *Adirondack Trails: Central Region*, Laurence T. Cagle offers a fairly detailed description of the cave. "The 4 ft by 4.5 ft cave entrance cuts directly into the face of Cliff Hill. A ceiling hole has been cut for sunlight. The ceiling increases from the opening to a height of 15 ft at the back of the 20 ft cave. Its walls are smooth."

History: No one knows for sure how the cave came about. There are some who believe that the cave formed naturally. Barbara McMartin, for one, in her early writings, was of that opinion when she wrote that the "…the smooth face of its back and roof suggest that a geological explanation for its existence may be more logical. The entire Kunjamuk valley was a glacial lake; layers of very fine sand cover it today. Perhaps the cave was formed as a pothole worn in the rock of the side hill by glacial melt waters churning grindstones."

The majority opinion today, however, is that the cave was chiseled out by prospectors looking for precious minerals.

It is presumed that the skylight was created by hunters who needed ventilation in order to build fires inside the cave.

The famous regional hermit, French Louie (Louis Seymour), is alleged to have stayed here to sleep off hangovers.

Until the mid-1800s, Kunjamuk was spelled *Cungemunk* on early maps.

The cave is contained in the Speculator Tree Farm Tract.

Kunjamuk Cave: Inside looking out.

Directions: From Speculator (junction of Routes 30 & 8 South & Elm Lake Road), drive northeast on Elm Lake Road for nearly 1.5 miles and park at the end of the paved road (optional). From here, proceed ahead either on foot, bike, or skies for an enjoyable jaunt.

It is also possible to drive to the cave via rough roads if you so desire. Continuing straight ahead from the paved end of Elm Lake Road, turn right at 0.2 mile where a sign indicates "Cave Hill Road," and head east. At 0.5 mile, continue straight ahead (east) where a secondary road goes off to your right.

Now heading northeast, you will come to the junction with the Perkins Clearing Road at 0.9 mile. Bear right, staying on the main road as you now head southeast. In 1.3 miles from the start, you will cross over the Kunjamuk River via a snowmobile bridge. Continue east for another 0.2 mile (or a total of 1.5 miles from the start), and you will come to a sign to your left directing you to Kunjamuk Cave, which is only 100 feet away from the road. If you are driving a vehicle, pull into a space on your right that can accommodate 1–2 cars. The short path to the cave starts on the left side of the road. Be prepared to descend 8 feet via rock steps to reach the start of the 100-foot-long path.

Resources: Russell Dunn, "In Search of Kunjamuk Cave," *Adventures Around the Great Sacandaga Lake. Revised and Illustrated* (Troy, NY: Troy Bookmakers, 2011), 189—192.
Clay Perry, *Underground Empire: Wonders and Tales of New York Caves* (New York: Stephen Daye Press, 1948), 133. Perry mentions a book by George F. Tibbitts called *The Mystery of Kun-Ja-Muck Cave*.
Russell Dunn & Barbara Delaney, *Adirondack Trails with Tales: History Hikes through the Adirondack Park and the Lake George, Lake Champlain & Mohawk Valley Region* (Hensonville, NY: Black Dome Press, 2009), 206–210.
Russell Dunn, "Kunjamuk Cave," *Northeastern Caver* Vol. XXV, no. 3 (September 1994), 83 & 84.
Barbara McMartin & Bill Ingersoll, *Discover the South Central Adirondacks. Third Edition* (Utica, NY: North Country Books, 2005), 79.
historylakespec.wordpress.com/kunjamuk-cave.
adirondackexperience.com/recreation/kunjamuk-cave.
timesunion.com/adirondacks/the-mysterious-kunjamuk-cave/295.
onlyinyourstate.com/new-york/kunjamuk-cave-ny.
Barbara McMartin, *Discover the Adirondacks, 1* (Somersworth, NH: New Hampshire Publishing Company, 1979), 83.
Mark Bowie, "Unwind on the Kunjamuk," *Adirondack Explorer* (May/June, 2012). On page 11 is a photo of Mike Prescott (the dam historian) looking out from the interior of the cave.
Laurence T. Cagle (editor) & Neal Burdick (series editor), *Adirondack Trails: Central Region* (Lake George, NY: Adirondack Mountain Club, Inc., 2004), 103.
Bruce Wadsworth & Neal Burdick (series editor), *Guide to Adirondack Trails: Central Region. Second Edition* (Lake George, NY: Adirondack Mountain Club Inc., 1994), 121–122.
Mark Bowie, "Unwind on the Kunjamuk," *Adirondack Explorer 2018 Annual Outings Guide*, 29. "This egg-shaped cavity was dug maybe thirty feet straight into exposed bedrock."

BOULDERS BEYOND BELIEF

139. PIG ROCK

Type of Formation: Painted Rock
WOW Factor: 5–6
Location: Speculator (Hamilton County)
Tenth Edition, NYS Atlas & Gazetteer: p. 51, A7; **Earlier Edition NYS Atlas & Gazetteer**: p, 87, D5–6
Pig Rock GPS Coordinates: 43º33.886'N; 74º23.791'W
Accessibility: Roadside
Degree of Difficulty: Easy

The unforgettable Pig Rock.

Description: Pig Rock is a 5-foot-high, 6-foot-long, roadside boulder that protrudes from the hillside. The rock bears a striking resemblance to the head and snout of a gargantuan pig. Some, including my wife, Barbara, see a wolf's visage instead.

History: Pig Rock is arguably the most recognizable, painted rock in the Adirondacks—perhaps even in all of New York State. Every year since sometime in the 1960s, the boulder has been repainted to prevent the image from fading into obscurity, initially by camp residents of Deerfoot Lodge (a boy's Christian summer camp); then later by local High School students. According to my sources, the rock was first painted by the daughters of a Whitaker Lake resident. That Pig Rock exists at all was due to the New York State Department of Transpiration's road construction in 1955.

To be sure, not everyone has been delighted with Pig Rock. Barney Fowler, in his first *Adirondack Album* in 1974, decried the proliferation of massive amounts of graffiti in the Adirondacks, calling such desecration the Pig Syndrome. Fowler point was validly made, but Pig Rock has become such a well-known, local landmark that folks would undoubtedly be very displeased were it to be removed today.

In the 1990s, the Department of Transportation wanted to demolish the rock to further widen the road's shoulder. They were met by resistance from protestors determined to "Support Pig Rock," and indeed, the supporters prevailed.

Philosophically speaking, there is some justification for allowing painted rocks of historic significance (now virtually landmarks) to be grandfathered in, providing they don't become the model for future imitations.

Directions: From Speculator (junction of Routes 30 & 8 South), head north on Route 30 for 5.0 miles. Look for the rock formation to your right, just before reaching Deerfoot Lodge Road—a dirt road leading east to Deerfoot Lodge, a wilderness camp that has been in operation since 1930.

Keep in mind that Pig Rock is only recognizable when driving north on Route 30. If you are driving south, the rock will pass by you virtually unnoticed.

Resources: Barney Fowler, *Adirondack Album* (Schenectady, NY: Outdoor Associates 1974), 127.
adirondackexperience.com/blog/2015/03/7-weird-adirondack-things.
adirondackscenicbyways.org/resource/pig-rock.html.
Barbara McMartin, *Discover the Adirondacks, 1* (Somersworth, NH: New Hampshire Publishing Company, 1979), 100. "The jeep road to Whitaker Lake, 5 and ½ miles north of Speculator on Route 30, is marked by a huge boulder whose resemblance to a pig's snout has been emphasized by a fresh coat of paint. The desecration will probably continue for years." In her last sentence pronouncement, McMartin was absolutely correct. Forty years later, Pig Rock is still going strong.
theadirondacker.com/2018/02/11/amazing-boulders-of-the-adirondacks.

BOULDERS BEYOND BELIEF

140. HADLEY MOUNTAIN BOULDERS

Type of Formation: Large Boulder
WOW Factor: 3–4
Location: Hadley (Saratoga County)
Tenth Edition, NYS Atlas & Gazetteer: p. 52, C2; **Earlier Edition NYS Atlas & Gazetteer**: p. 80, AB2
Parking GPS Coordinates: 43º22.359'N 73º57.048'W
Destination GPS Coordinates: *Boulder #1* -- 43º22.378'N 73º57.314'W; *Boulder #2* -- 43º22.364'N 73º57.420'W; *Boulder #3* --43º22.304'N 73º57.652'W; *Boulder #4* -- 43º22.294'N 73º57.787'W
Accessibility: *Boulder #1* – 0.2-mile hike; *Boulder #2* -- >0.2-mile hike; *Boulder #3* – 0.5-mile hike; *Boulder #4* – 0.8-mile hike; *Summit* -- 1.6-mile hike
Degree of Difficulty: Moderate

Hadley Mountain Boulders.

Description: *Boulder #1* is a 6-foot–high, 10-foot-wide fractured rock. With a little imagination, you can easily visualize how the three pieces could be fitted together, much like pieces in a jig-saw puzzle.

BOULDERS BEYOND BELIEF

Boulder #2 is the tallest boulder I saw, well over 10 feet in height, and over 10 feet in width. Despite having a wide vertical split and being located on a pronounced slope, the two sections of the rock still remain enjoined.

Boulder #3 is interesting in that the rock lies propped up against a 15–20-foot-high cliff. Several chunky rocks lay about in the ravine.

Boulder #4 is fairly ordinary looking, roughly 6 feet high, but I mention it because it is trailside and looks like a large baseball.

Hadley Mountain boulder.

Linda Laing, in *Guide to Adirondack Trails: Southern Region. Second Edition*, writes, "At 0.6 mi. rock formations can be seen on the right. These are 10 to 15 ft. high; while attractive in summer, they are noted in winter for their colorful blue-green ice formations."

In *Five-Star Trails in the Adirondacks: A Guide to the Most Beautiful Hikes*, Tim Starmer writes, "Over this first section, large rocks and cobbles are strewn across many portions..."

Lisa Nesmore Ballard, in *Hiking the Adirondacks*, states that "...a large boulder with a tree growing on its top" is passed at ~1.1 miles.

BOULDERS BEYOND BELIEF

History: Hadley Mountain is notable for being not only the second highest mountain in Saratoga County, but for having its own fire tower, which was erected by the Conservation Commission in 1917. Hadley Mountain is the tallest of the three peaks in the West Mountain Range.

Directions: From Hadley (junction of Route 1/Stony Creek Road & Route 4/North Shore Road), drive northwest on Route 1/Stony Creek Road for 3.0 miles. Turn left onto Hadley Hill Road and proceed west for 4.3 miles. When you come to Tower Road (a dirt road), turn right and head north for 1.4 miles. Finally, turn left into the parking area for Hadley Mountain.

Follow the red-blazed trail uphill, always climbing steadily. Boulder #1 is encountered along the left side of the trail after 0.2 mile. You will see a sign with number 3 on it. Boulder #2, located on the right side of the trail, 40 feet into the woods, is reached after another 0.05 mile.

Boulder #3, to the right, is encountered after hiking uphill another 0.2 mile. Linda Laing, in *Guide to Adirondack Trails: Southern Region. Second Edition*, writes that at 0.5 mile, "an attractive, large boulder makes a good resting place."

Boulder #4, directly next to the trail, is reached at 0.8 mile.

If you continue on the trail which, in some places, almost looks paved because of the exposed bedrock, you will pass by other rocks, reach a point where the trails levels off momentarily at 0.9 mile, only to ascend to the summit after a total of 1.6 miles.

Resources: Bill Ingersoll, *Discover the Southern Adirondacks. Fifth Edition* (Barneveld, NY: Wild River Press, 2014), 389–393.
en.wikipedia.org/wiki/Hadley_Mountain.
Barbara McMartin, *Fifty Hikes in the Adirondacks* (Woodstock, VT: Backcountry Publications, 1980), 33–36.
Tim Starmer, *Five-Star Trails in the Adirondacks: A Guide to the Most Beautiful Hikes* (Birmingham, AL: Menasha Ridge Press, 2010), 176.
Bruce Wadsworth, *Day Hikes For All Seasons: An Adirondack Sampler* (Lake George, NY: Adirondack Mountain Club, 1996), 38.
Linda Laing & series editor Neal Burdick, *Guide to Adirondack Trails: Southern Region. Second Edition* (New York: Adirondack Mountain Club, Inc., 1994), 34.
David Thomas Train (editor), *Adirondack Mountain Club: Eastern Trails. 4th Edition* (Lake George, NY: Adirondack Mountain Club, Inc., 2012), 144 & 145.
Lisa Densmore Ballard, *Hiking the Adirondacks. Second Edition* (Guilford, CT: Falcon Guides, 2017), 271.

BOULDERS BEYOND BELIEF

Rose Rivezzi & David Trithart, *Kids on the Trails! Hiking with children in the Adirondacks* (Lake George, NY: Adirondack Mountain Club, 1997), 154. "A small stream is crossed at 0.5 mi. (0.8 km). At 0.6 mi. (1.0 km) some interesting rocks appear on the right."

141. GRIFFIN & AUGER FALLS BOULDERS

Type of Formation: Large Boulder; Pothole
WOW Factor: 3–4
Location: Griffin (Hamilton County)
Tenth Edition, NYS Atlas & Gazetteer: p. 51, B8; **Earlier Edition NYS Atlas & Gazetteer**: p. 79, A6–7
Parking GPS Coordinates: 43º28.413'N 74º13.422'W
Destination GPS Coordinates: *Griffin Boulder* -- 43º28.358'N 74º13.409'W; *Auger Falls Boulder* -- 43º28.080'N 74º14.752'W
Accessibility: *Griffin Boulder* – 100-foot downhill scramble; *Auger Falls Boulder* -- 1.3-mile trek
Degree of Difficulty: *Griffin Boulder* – Moderately easy; *Auger Falls Boulder* -- Moderate

Description: The boulders described in this chapter at Griffin and Auger Falls are representative of large boulders that lie in and about Adirondack streambeds. The number of such boulders are too vast to count. Unlike boulders lost in the woods, or half-buried in the earth, boulders in rivers and streams tend to be fully exposed due to the surrounding earth being swept away by the current.

Griffin Boulder.

What makes these two boulders particularly appealing is that, in order to see both, you will need to walk from Griffin Falls to Auger Falls, and back—and what could be a more enjoyable outing than visiting two Adirondack waterfalls while looking for big rocks.

BOULDERS BEYOND BELIEF

Griffin Boulder – This potato-shaped boulder is ~10 feet high and ~15 feet long. There are other boulders scattered about in the Griffin Gorge, but this one is particularly noteworthy.

Take note that over 0.1 mile downstream from the iron bridge is Griffin Falls, a pretty, 6–8-foot-high waterfall that cannot be glimpsed from the bridge due to the architecture of the gorge, but that can be readily accessed via a short trail from the northwest side of the river.

Auger Falls Boulder. Photograph by Barbara Delaney.

Auger Falls Boulder – This large boulder has a very broad, inclined surface that can be easily walked up onto. Just downriver from the boulder is Auger Falls, which Barbara McMartin, in *Discover the Adirondacks, 1*, describes as "… a series of short cascades that drop over 100 feet, tracing an 8 through the sharp curve of the gorge."

Auger Falls Potholes – According to Barbara McMartin & Bill Ingersoll, in *Discover the South Central Adirondacks. Third Edition*, "The rock slides beside the falls are gouged with potholes; one that is visible in late summer and fall is four feet deep. Some have rocks in them that continue to churn and grind them deeper."

Auger Falls Shelter Cave -- On the opposite (west) side of Augers Falls is a tiny shelter cave created by a configuration of rocks. This tiny cave is best accessed from the main parking area for Auger Falls (43°28.177'N

BOULDERS BEYOND BELIEF

74º15.112'W) along Route 30, 1.7 miles north of the junction of Routes 30 & 8 North, and involves a short hike of 0.4 mile.

Directions: From north of Wells (junction of Routes 8 North & 30), drive northeast on Route 8 North for 2.5 miles. Turn left onto a dirt road and follow it for 0.2 mile downhill and across a recently renovated bridge spanning the East Branch of the Sacandaga River. Park in an area at the end of the bridge.

Griffin Boulder – This large boulder can be easily glimpsed from the iron bridge as you look upstream. It lies along the northwest shoreline, less than 100 feet from the bridge. You can also scamper down a faint path near the northeast end of the bridge, and then scramble upstream for less than 100 feet to reach the boulder.

Auger Falls Boulder – From the Griffin iron bridge, follow an old road west for 1.2 miles, initially paralleling the East Branch of the Sacandaga River. At the point when you start to hear the distant roar of Auger Falls, turn left by a sign urging caution. The spur path leads quickly to the falls and gorge, which are located on the main trunk of the Sacandaga River. The large boulder is upstream from the top of the falls.

Resources: Barbara McMartin, *Discover the Adirondacks, 1* (Somersworth, NH: New Hampshire Publishing Company, 1979), 29.
Russell Dunn, *Adirondack Waterfall Guide* (Hensonville, NY: Black Dome Press, 2003), 41–43.
Barbara McMartin & Bill Ingersoll, *Discover the South Central Adirondacks. Third Edition* (Utica, NY: North Country Books, 2005), 70.

142. DEAN MOUNTAIN ROAD ROCK

Type of Formation: Large Rock
WOW Factor: 5
Location: Hadley/Lake Luzerne (Saratoga County)
Tenth Edition, NYS Atlas & Gazetteer: p. 52, D3; **Earlier Edition NYS Atlas & Gazetteer**: p. 80, B2–3
Dean Mountain Road Rock GPS Coordinates: 43º18.332'N 73º51.686'W
Accessibility: Roadside
Degree of Difficulty: Easy

BOULDERS BEYOND BELIEF

Description: Dean Mountain Road Rock is a monster rock, some 15 feet high, 10 feet wide, and nearly 20 feet long.

Kids will enjoying scampering about on this behemoth, for it can be easily scaled from its left side.

Dean Mountain Road Rock. Photograph by Barbara Delaney.

History: The *Dean Mountain Road White Water Park*, which provides excellent views of the Sacandaga River from a wooden deck overlook, is another attraction along Dean Mountain Road.

Directions: From the southeast end of the Stewart Pond Bridge (junction of Mt. Anthony Road & Route 7), head east on Mt. Anthony Road for 0.5 mile. Then bear left onto Dean Mt. Road and proceed northeast for 0.9 mile, turning left into a pull-off next to the rock.

143. POTASH MOUNTAIN BOULDER #1

Potash Mountain Boulder #1. Photograph by Barbara Delaney.

Type of Formation: Large Boulder
WOW Factor: 5
Location: Fourth Lake (Warren County)
Tenth Edition, NYS Atlas & Gazetteer: p. 52, C3–4; **Earlier Edition NYS Atlas & Gazetteer**: p. 80, AB3
Parking GPS Coordinates: 43º22.514'N 73º49.967'W
Potash Mountain Boulder #1 GPS Coordinates: 43º22.643'N 73º49.975'W
Accessibility: 0.2-mile uphill trek following a power line corridor

BOULDERS BEYOND BELIEF

Degree of Difficulty: Moderately easy

Description: This large boulder, split horizontally in front, is ~7 feet high and 15 feet long. The rock would remain hidden in the woods were it not for the cleared powerline corridor that runs over the shoulder of Potash Mountain.

History: Potash Mountain (1,752'), aka The Potash, is described as a "...hemisphere fifteen hundred feet high, rocky and bold" in *Peep at Luzerne*. The mountain is unusual in that its summit consists of state land that lies entirely surrounded by private lands. Fortunately, the recent establishment of the Harris Preserve at the junction of Dunkley Road and Potash Road has created a legal way for hikers to access Potash Mountain's summit. The initial 107 acres of land were donated by Alice Harris, followed by a crucial 6.6-acre donation by Richard and Joanne Sehlmeyer that connected the Harris Preserve to State land.

Directions: From Lake Luzerne village (junction of Routes 9N & 16), drive north on Route 9N for ~3.6 miles. Turn left onto Potash Road and head northwest for ~1.1 miles. Park off to the right side of the road by the power lines. Follow the powerline corridor uphill, heading north, for 0.2 mile.

Resources: Russell Dunn, "Potash Mountain: Gatekeeper to the Adirondacks," *Adventures Around the Great Sacandaga Lake. Revised and Illustrated* (Troy, NY: Troy Bookmakers, 2011), 122–125.
Unknown author, *Peep at Luzerne* (Albany, NY: Weed, Parsons & Company, printers, 1877).
walkingman247.blogspot.com/2017/09/potash-mountainsouthern-adirondacks.html
glensfallschronicle.com/alice-harris-gift-of-107-acres-a-boon-to-hiking-up-potash-mtn.

144. POTASH MOUNTAIN BOULDER #2

Type of Formation: Large Boulder
WOW Factor: 5
Location: Fourth Lake (Warren County)
Tenth Edition, NYS Atlas & Gazetteer: p. 52, C3–4; **Earlier Edition NYS Atlas & Gazetteer**: p. 80, AB3
Parking GPS Coordinates: 43º21.926'N 73º48.675'W

BOULDERS BEYOND BELIEF

Potash Mountain Boulder #2 GPS Coordinates: 43º21.943'N 73º48.707'W
Accessibility: 150-foot bushwhack
Degree of Difficulty: Easy

Description: Potash Mountain Boulder #2 is a bulky, 12-foot-high rock that stands alone at the bottom of a sloping hill with no additional rocks in sight.

History: The Potash Mountain Boulder was "discovered" in 2003 by Jeremy Haas, coauthor of *Adirondack Rock* (2008).

Potash Mountain Boulder #2.

Directions: From Hadley (junction of Route 9N & Mill Road, opposite the Luzerne Heights Public Beach) drive north on Route 9N for 3.7 miles (or 0.9 mile past the NYSDEC campground for Fourth Lake; or 0.1 mile past Dunkley Road). Pull over to the side of the road.

Walk across the road and look for a green-colored marker that reads "9N 1702 1050." From here, follow a faint, mostly dry drainage bed north for ~150 feet to reach the boulder, which rests at the bottom of a sloping hill.

Resources: Justin Sanford, *New York Adirondack Park Bouldering* (Broadalbin, NY: Southern Adirondack Climber, LLC, 2015), 160–165.
communitywalk.com/adirondack_park/ny/boulders_in_the_adirondacks/map/299298.
offonadventure.com/2017/04/potash-mountain-lake-luzerne-ny-4817.html.
walkingman247.blogspot.com/2017/09/potash-mountainsouthern-adirondacks.html.

BOULDERS BEYOND BELIEF

145. BOULDERWOODS & NATURAL BRIDGE
Crane Mountain

Type of Formation: Large Boulder; Natural Bridge
WOW Factor: *Boulderwoods* -- 7–8; *Natural Bridge* -- 4
Location: Garnet Lake (Warren County)
Tenth Edition, NYS Atlas & Gazetteer: p. 52, A2; **Earlier Edition NYS Atlas & Gazetteer**: p. 88, D2
Parking GPS Coordinates: 43º32.259'N 73º58.075'W
Destination GPS Coordinates: *Boulderwoods* -- 43º32.253'N 73º57.935'W; *Natural Bridge* -- 43º32.708'N 73º58.732'W
Accessibility: *Boulderwoods* -- 0.1-mile hike; *Natural Bridge* – 1.1-mile hike; *Boulders along trail beyond Natural Bridge* – 1.3-mile hike
Degree of Difficulty: *Boulderwoods* – Easy; *Natural Bridge and Boulders along trail to Crane Mountain Pond* -- Moderate

Rocks at Boulderwoods.

Description: *Boulderwoods* (a term given to the rock field by the rock-climbing/bouldering community), aka the Crane Mountain Boulders, consist of a grouping of six boulder fields, labelled A–F, which are in relatively close

BOULDERS BEYOND BELIEF

proximity to one another except for Zone F, which is farther northwest. Each zone contains a significant number of impressive boulders.

The trail from the parking area leads quickly to the entrance to boulder zone A, where you pass between several large boulders, the largest being a 20-foot-high rock on your left called *Sentry Rock*. Two boulders, uphill to the right, 50 feet away, are called *Splitting Headache*. Each is 15 feet high

About 300 feet farther along the trail, over 50 feet to the left, are two house-sized rocks. One is called the *Whale*; the other the *King*.

Splitting Headache Rock.

You can spend hours exploring this area with its multiple boulder fields and impressively large boulders. I have only scratched the surface, talking just about Zone A.

Natural Bridge – The Natural Bridge is a section of trail, 20 feet wide or more, which crosses over a tiny stream where it goes underground.

In *Fifty Hikes in the Adirondacks*, Barbara McMartin writes, "…the trail crosses a stream on a natural stone bridge. The tiny stream disappears into a cave of Precambrian marble, and re-emerges about 500 feet away, only to disappear permanently in a still larger cave."

BOULDERS BEYOND BELIEF

In David Thomas Train's *Adirondack Mountain Club: Eastern Trails. 4th Edition*, mention is made of "...a natural rock bridge over a rushing brook....the brook has carved a tunnel-like cavern through the rock."

It was at Natural Bridge that I had one of my most harrowing experiences. I had gone to the edge of the sinkhole to take some pictures when all at once I felt a bite in the center of my back. "Damn horsefly!" I exclaimed, only to quickly abandon that thought when I was all at once engulfed by a swarm of angry bees who had emerged with lightning speed from a ground nest next to where I was standing. Panicked and flailing helplessly with my arms, I ran as fast as I could back up to the trail to get away.

Finally, realizing that I had outdistanced the bees and no longer was being pursued, I stopped to take a breather. Despite my feeble attempts to fend off the attackers, I had received at least 10–12 stings on my face, arms, and back; even the knuckle of my hand. As if that wasn't bad enough, I also noticed that both my stereo camera and notepad were no longer in the carry-bag, having bounced out during my less than dignified, hasty retreat. It took all the courage I could muster to slink back to the sinkhole, grab my equipment, and then run again like hell up to the main trail. Fortunately, the bees gave no chase, most likely having returned to their hideaway.

Back on the trail I began to think more seriously about my overall situation. I had taken quite a few stings. What about anaphylactic shock? I had never been allergic to bee stings before, but would it hold true now—especially given the number of times I had been stung. My plan to hike further uphill to photograph some of the large rocks along the trail to Crane Mountain Pond was immediately abandoned. If I started to swell up from the bee stings, I could be in a real predicament, for I was all alone and facing at least a mile hike back to my car. I hastened back to the parking area as quickly as I could.

By virtue that I am writing this account, nothing serious happened to me (Thank goodness!). But I hadn't seen the last of Mister Bee. As I was driving down the dirt road from the parking area, I suddenly felt a sharp pain in my right arm. I glanced over and saw that a half dead bee was clinging to my shirt sleeve. I had never noticed him on the hike back. I got stung at least 3 more times before I finished him off.

The moral to the story is, "Bee alert."

BOULDERS BEYOND BELIEF

Boulders – In addition to the large boulders near the parking area, there are also sizeable boulders along the hike up to Crane Mountain Pond. In *Adirondack Mountain Club: Eastern Trails. 4th Edition*, David Thomas Train writes, "At 1.2 mi [from the trail register] the trail begins to be very steep, with numerous large boulders for the hiker to negotiate. The next 0.7 mile of trail is very steep and zig-zags over and across numerous ledges and large boulders."

There is also a pretty shelter cave on Crane Mountain, a photograph of which appears in Paul Schaefer's *Adirondack Cabin Country*. I have probably passed by it earlier in my life, but have no recollection of it.

Demolition of the Crane Mountain Fire Tower in 1987.

History: Jay Harrison, a rock climbing guide and local route developer, is credited for being the first person to map out the boulder field near the parking area and to give many of the rocks their names.

You will find such colorful boulder names as Splitting Headache, Trauma, Sentry, Hive, Safari Hobbit, Empire, and many, many more.

BOULDERS BEYOND BELIEF

Directions: From Weaverton (junction of Routes 8 & 28), drive west on Route 8 for 1.6 miles to Johnsburg. Turn left onto South Johnsburg Road (Route 57) and proceed south towards Thurman for 6.8 miles. When you come to Garnet Lake Road South (Route 72), turn right and head southwest for 1.2 miles. Then turn right onto Ski Hi Road (where a sign indicates the way to Crane Mountain), and proceed uphill for 1.9 miles. Along the way, the road narrows at 1.4 miles. At 1.5 miles, you will pass by a large roadside boulder (the shape of things to come) and then pass by marshlands both to the right and left where a large boulder can be seen. The trailhead parking is reached at ~1.9 miles.

Boulderwoods – From the parking area, follow a well-trodden, yellow-marked path across a drainage area as it heads east and up onto a low ridge. After less than 0.1 mile, you will reach the first pair of boulders, which is fittingly called Splitting Headache. From here, continue to follow the trail as it takes you from one site to the next.

Natural Bridge – Starting at the trail register, turn left onto a 0.2 mile connector trail to the old Putnam Farm Road (now a trail). Bear right, and head northwest on the Putnam Farm Road Trail for 0.8 mile. Along the way, you will pass by a 15-foot-high seasonal cascade on your right coming off the top of an escarpment.

Bear right when you come to a barrier across the road (the land beyond is privately owned) and proceed uphill following the blue-blazed Crane Mountain trail for less than 0.1 mile. You will know that you have reached the natural bridge, for drop-offs will be visible on both sides of the wide trail. To your right is where the stream insurges, going underground. To your left is a very large sinkhole that can be easily reached by a short spur path. From the edge of the sinkhole, it is possible to scramble down into its interior, but no one should try to enter the cave unless they are an experienced caver with a group of similarly prepared and outfitted companions.

By the way, keep an eye out for nesting bees in the ground.

Boulders along trail to Crane Mountain Pond – From the Natural Bridge, continue up the blue-blazed trail north for another 0.2 mile to reach a succession of large boulders.

Resources: Barbara McMartin, *Fifty Hikes in the Adirondacks* (Woodstock, VT: Backcountry Publications, 1988), 145–149.

BOULDERS BEYOND BELIEF

Justin Sanford, *New York Adirondack Park Bouldering* (Broadalbin, NY: Southern Adirondack Climber, LLC, 2015), 134–159.
David Thomas Train (editor), *Adirondack Mountain Club: Eastern Trails. 4th Edition* (Lake George, NY: Adirondack Mountain Club, Inc., 2012), 148 & 150.
boulderproblems.com/areas/crane-mountain-boulderwoods.
Barbara McMartin, *Discover the Southeastern Adirondacks* (Woodstock, VT: Backcountry Publications, 1986). On page 89, McMartin mentions that "Upstream the brook disappears into the ground, emerging just downstream from the bridge from a small cave leached from the soft marble layer at the base of the mountain."
Michael Nardacci (editor-in-chief), *Guide to Caves and Karst of the Northeast: 50th Anniversary NSS Convention* (Huntsville, AL: National Speleological Society, 1991). A map of the cave is shown on page 6; on page 5 is a photo taken inside the cave by Arthur N. Palmer. The cave involves short crawls, waterfall drops, a 32-foot-high dome, and a junction where five other passageways intersect with the entrance passage.
Paul Schaefer, *Adirondack Cabin Country* (York State Books, 1993). A photograph of a shelter cave taken by Dan Ling appears on page 166.
Linda Laing & series editor Neal Burdick, *Guide to Adirondack Trails: Southern Region. Second Edition* (New York: Adirondack Mountain Club, Inc., 1994). 38–41, & 43.
Lisa Densmore Ballard, *Hiking the Adirondacks. Second Edition* (Guilford, CT: Falcon Guides, 2017), 2. A photograph is shown of a 12-foot-high glacial erratic on the Crane Mountain loop.
Jim Lawyer & Jeremy Haas, *Adirondack Rock: A Climber's Guide* (Pompey, NY: Adirondack Rock Press, LLC, 2008), 488.

146. PAINT MINE BOULDERS

Type of Formation: Large Boulder
WOW Factor: 8
Location: Garnet Lake (Warren County)
Tenth Edition, NYS Atlas & Gazetteer: p. 52, A2; **Earlier Edition NYS Atlas & Gazetteer**: p. 88, D2
Crane Mountain Trailhead GPS Coordinates: 43º32.259′N 73º58.075′W
Estimated Paint Mine Boulders GPS Coordinates: 43º34.082′N 73º58.518′W
Accessibility: >3.5-mile hike
Degree of Difficulty: Difficult due to quasi-bushwhack
Additional Information: adirondackrock.com/vol2_pages214-215.pdf.

BOULDERS BEYOND BELIEF

This map shows a hiking route that follows a stream downhill into the valley from the west side of the northern knob on Crane Mountain Pond into the valley; and then northwest, ultimately paralleling Paint Bed stream.

Paint Mine Boulders.

Description: In her 1986 book, *Discover the Southeastern Adirondacks*, Barbara McMartin mentions reaching a spot along Paint Mine Brook "...near a complex of boulders with a protected cavelike opening among the enormous rocks...Someone has devised a new route that will take you beneath these gigantic boulders, some as tall as three or four stories." In *Discover the Southern Adirondacks*, Bill Ingersoll writes that "...an area at the foot of

BOULDERS BEYOND BELIEF

Huckleberry [is] riddled with housesized boulders. (One boulder, dubbed "caveman rock," features an overhang broad enough that you can camp underneath it)."

It just so happens that my wife, Barbara Delaney, and I visited this spot many years ago and observed the immense boulders first-hand, but that was when you could readily access the area from Hudson Street. That access is no longer allowed, and has been off limits for many years.

History: The area is rich in vanished history. The Glen Mining Company's paint works once operated in this area from 1894 to 1902. The dark, red paint that was produced was used to color barns and other structures. Pits and foundations are still visible today.

The Paint Mine Boulders are surrounded by woods.

Directions: Fifteen years ago, when Barbara and I hiked in from Hudson Street, it was a relatively simple trek. Things have changed since then, however, and access across a landowner's private property is no longer an option.

Today, in order to reach the Paint Mine area, you must first hike up to Crane Mountain Pond [see previous chapter for directions to the Crane Mountain trailhead], and then head down the mountain's northern slope following a faint path, or a streambed (either one will work), to reach an old tote road in the valley that heads in a northwest direction.

There is more to it than this, however. I would highly recommend purchasing Bill Ingersoll's *Discover the Southern Adirondacks* for precise directions. I have not personally taken this route from Crane Mountain Pond, and therefore feel inadequate to describe it any detail. The map under "Additional Information" will give you a pretty clear picture of what is involved in undertaking this hike, part of which is a semi-bushwhack.

BOULDERS BEYOND BELIEF

Resources: Barbara McMartin, *Discover the Southeastern Adirondacks* (Woodstock, VT: Backcountry Publications, 1986), 92 & 93. A somewhat indistinct photograph of a couple of the boulders can be seen on page 92.

Bill Ingersoll, *Discover the Southern Adirondacks* (Barneveld, NY: Wild River Press. 2014), 361 & 362.

Linda Laing & series editor Neal Burdick, *Guide to Adirondack Trails: Southern Region. Second Edition* (New York: Adirondack Mountain Club, Inc., 1994), 37. "Several enormous rocks will be seen...Some of these are as large as a two- to three-story building. They make very interesting subjects to explore."

Jim Lawyer & Jeremy Haas, *Adirondack Rock: A Climber's Guide* (Pompey, NY: Adirondack Rock Press, LLC, 2008), 492–504. Descriptions of the rocks are provided in the chapter on Huckleberry Mountain. The directions given, however, are outdated and no longer apply.

147. SCHAEFER TRAIL BOULDERS

Type of Formation: Large Boulder
WOW Factor: 5
Location: North Creek (Warren County)
Tenth Edition, NYS Atlas & Gazetteer: p. 38, D1; **Earlier Edition NYS Atlas & Gazetteer**: p. 88, C1–2
Parking GPS Coordinates: 43º41.589′N 73º59.452′W
Large Rock GPS Coordinates: 43º41.351N 74º00.469′W
Accessibility: *Karate Rock* – 1.7-mile hike; *Chanol's Rock* – 2.2-mile hike; *Lean-to Rock* – 2.3-mile hike;
Degree of Difficulty: Moderately difficult
Additional Information: Ski Bowl Trail Map can be seen at -- upperhudsontrails.org/wp-content/uploads/2015/07/SkiBowlMap.jpg

Rocks along the Schaefer Trail.

Description: *Karate Rock* – In *Adirondack Trails: Central Region* Laurence T. Cagle talks about "...an interesting split boulder (Karate Rock) on the right of the trail at 1.7 miles." It seems clear from this description how the split rock came to be named.

Chanol's Rock – Cagle describes the rock as a "...pile of rock slabs stacked domino-style against one another."

Lean-to Rocks consist of two boulders leaning, one against the other.

Moby Dick Boulder – located by the Twister Glade Ski Trail.

Rocks along Schaefer Trail.

History: The trail was named after Paul Schaefer and his brothers, Vincent and Carl.

Directions: From North Creek (junction of Routes 28 & 28N), drive south on Route 28 for 0.2 mile. Turn right onto Ski Bowl Road and proceed northwest, continuing straight ahead on the main road, for less than 0.2 mile. Park near the trailhead for the blue-marked Schaefer Trail, which begins on your right leading you through an opening in the chain-linked fence.

At its lower elevation, the Schaefer Trail takes you across a wide ski trail and intersects twice with a bike trail. Eventually you will come to a "T." Turn right (left will take you downhill to Becks Tavern on Peaceful Valley Road). Quickly, the trail begins paralleling a deep gorge soon leads you past one waterfall after another over a distance of 0.2 mile or more. The waterfalls continue past the first ski-road bridge as well as the second ski-road bridge. This is a very dynamic area in terms of sound and scenery, and is well worth the hike even if you don't see any awesome boulders.

I followed the trail all the way up past an abandoned, once-dammed pond to a junction, a distance of 2.2 miles. Quite honestly, although I saw many rocks and boulders, I saw nothing exceptionally large nor distinctive, and certainly nothing that looked like a Karate Rock, which I assumed was a split boulder.

As a result, on the way back down, I tried to reconsider what Karate Rock might look like. The only thing I could come up with were two mammoth 15 by 20-foot rocks in the streambed downstream from the first ski-road crossing, with the stream gushing between the two. I don't believe, however, that I located Karate Rock, because the rocks I saw were on the left side of the trail, and not the right.

It may be I was off my game here. On the drive up to Gore Mountain off Route 8, I collided with two deer on Peaceful Valley Road. After being contacted, an officer arrived on the scene and it was necessary to put down one of the deer, who obvious had broken legs. I felt terrible. It was quite traumatic.

The front end of the car was pretty smashed up as well, but the car (miraculously) was still drivable, so I continued on to the Schaefer Head Trailhead, only half a mile away, and did the hike, all the time brooding about what had happened.

Once done with the hike, I abandoned all thoughts of doing any more exploring. The car hadn't leaked fluids, so I felt optimistic that I could make it back to Albany—and did. As I write this, the Subaru is in the body shop with an estimated $9,000 worth of damage.

I read that Karate Rock is reportedly encountered at 1.7 miles, while probably is in the vicinity of the second bridge; and Chanol's Rock, at ~2.2 miles (I didn't see that one either).

There obviously is more to explore—the Moby Dick Boulder sounds interesting, for instance—and I probably will be back again in the future. If you're a waterfall lover, you won't be disappointed with this trek.

Resources: Barbara McMartin & Bill Ingersoll, *Discover the South Central Adirondacks. Third Edition* (Utica, NY: North Country Books, 2005), 159.

BOULDERS BEYOND BELIEF

Laurence T. Cagle (editor) & Neal Burdick (series editor), *Adirondack Trails: Central Region* (Lake George, NY: Adirondack Mountain Club, Inc., 2004), 49. adirondack.net/business/schaeffer-trail-north-creek-reservoir-11821.
Laurence I. Cagle, "In the heart of the park," *Adirondack Explorer* Vol. 6, no. 5 (September/October 2004), 24. Cagle mentions a split rock named Karate Rock, a rock amphitheater named Dave's Cirque and, at 2.0 miles, a "curious pile of rocks that look like dominoes stacked together."
Jim Lawyer & Jeremy Haas, *Adirondack Rock: A Climber's Guide* (Pompey, NY: Adirondack Rock Press, LLC, 2008), 505 & 506.

148. PAUL SCHAEFER BOULDER

Type of Formation: Large Boulder
WOW Factor: 6
Location: Bakers Mills (Warren County)
Tenth Edition, NYS Atlas & Gazetteer: p. 38, E1; **Earlier Edition NYS Atlas & Gazetteer**: p. 88, CD1
GPS Coordinates: Unknown
Accessibility: Unknown; possibly on private property

Photograph from Adirondack Cabin Country.

Description: In Paul Schaefer's *Adirondack Cabin County*, a photograph of a large glacial erratic with a man standing on top is shown. Judging from the size of the man, the boulder must be ~25 feet high and 35 feet or more in length. As glacial erratics go, it is very impressive. According to Schaefer, the boulder "...lies in an overgrown field near the cabin" [which, in turn, is next to the Second Pond Flow trail in the general Thirteenth Lake area—all which are near Bakers Mills].

History: This boulder is historically significant due to its close association with, and proximity to, Paul Schaefer and his former cabin—a man who helped to co-found several organizations for the preservation of the Adirondack, as well as playing a significant role in the creation of the Adirondack State Park. It is a boulder that deserves recognition.

Directions: The exact location of this massive boulder is unknown to me, and may very well be on private land and ultimately inaccessible

Resources: Paul Schaefer, *Adirondack Cabin County* (York State Books, 1993). 112. adirondackwild.org/who-we-are/paulschaefer.html.

149. BLIND ROCK

Type of Formation: Historic Rock
WOW Factor: 2–3
Location: North Glens Falls/Queensbury (Warren County)
Tenth Edition, NYS Atlas & Gazetteer: p. 53, C6; **Earlier Edition NYS Atlas & Gazetteer**: p. 81, B4–5
Blind Rock GPS Coordinates: 43º20.122'N 73º40.589'W
Accessibility: Near roadside
Degree of Difficulty: Easy

Description: Blind Rock is a 4-foot-high, 11-foot-long, 7-foot-wide rock made of granite located in a 1.0-acre preserve. The rock's unusual name comes from a blind man having been allegedly tortured on the boulder by Indians. Another version contends that his eyes were gouged out by his tormentors and then thrown into burning embers on the rock.

Blind Rock has also been called Torture Rock, Indian Rock, Indian Bounds, and Split Rock according to the Warren County Historical Society.

A large cleft/crevice in the center of the rock is believed to have been caused by fires built repeatedly on the rock.

In his account of the "Legend of Blind Rock," Dr. A. W. Holden describers the rock as being "…deeply embedded beneath the drift and soil, the slow accumulation of untold ages…" and that it is "…so filled up in the inequalities of the surface that but a very small portion of the crown of the rock is visible." This would suggest, then, that the rock is much larger than its surface appearance would suggest.

BOULDERS BEYOND BELIEF

History: The Mohawks called the rock *Kenakwadione*, meaning "a place to kill."

Rich Elton kneels to inspect Blind Rock more closely.

Blind Rock is associated with historical accounts of captives being tortured on the rock by Indians during the 1700s. The rock may also have served as a boundary marker between the Hudson River and Lake George, as well as a dividing line between French forces, to the north, and British forces, to the south.

Early on, the land was owned by the Miller family. Later, the property was acquired by the Kapoor family. It lies directly behind the Sleep Inn and Uno's Chicago Grill, both which are presently owned by the Kapoor family.

At some point in the past, there was discussion about moving the rock to a more permanent location, but ultimately no action was taken since what made the rock so special was both its history and location.

In 2013, Blind Rock's future was secured when a small parcel of land around the rock was obtained. The town highway department established roadside parking for the preserve, a boy scout's troop and community advocates put down a wood chip path to the rock, and Mary Lee Gosline donated a wrought-iron fence to mark off the rock's location.

BOULDERS BEYOND BELIEF

Directions: From the Adirondack Northway, get off at Exit 19 and head east on Aviation Road (Route 254) for 0.6 mile. Turn left onto Route 9 and proceed northwest for over 0.4 mile. Look for the roadside historic sign by the junction of Route 9 & Montray Road. Then, turn right onto Montray Road and proceed east for 0.1 mile. The tiny park is on your left.

Resources: Thomas Reeves Lord, *More Stories of Lake George Fact and Fiction* (Pemberton, NJ: Pinelands Press, 1994), 35. The brief article also includes a photograph of the rock.
poststar.com/news/local/queensbury-set-to-take-over-historic-blind-rock-property/article_1df11a06-7617-11e2-b30d-001a4bcf887a.html.
Robert L. Eddy, *Queensbury's Heritage* (Queensbury, NY: Author, 1991). Chapter on "Legend of the 'Blind Rock'" by Dr. A. W. Holden, 155 & 156.
warrencountyhistoricalsociety.org/publications/rewind-october-15-2017-abraham-lincoln-and-upstate-new-york/rewind-back-issues-2013/rewind-october-15-2013-queensburys-blind-rock – This website contains a great deal of information about Blind Rock and its lore.

150. HIGH ROCK (Historic)

Type of Formation: Large Rock; Balancing Rock
WOW Factor: The rock no longer exists, but probably was a 7
Location: Warrensburg (Warren County)
Tenth Edition, NYS Atlas & Gazetteer: p. 52, B4; **Earlier Edition NYS Atlas & Gazetteer**: p. 80, A3–4
Accessibility: Inaccessible. The rock was physically destroyed in the 1900s.

Description: High Rock is a large rock that, at one time, was registered in Washington, D.C. as one of America's notable balanced rocks. The rock's distinguishing feature was that it partially overhung the highway, much like the Sword of Damocles, ready to drop on those passing by below.

History: During the late 1800s or early 1900s, Albert Alden was hired by Henry Griffin to build a stone wall in front of High Rock to keep the boulder from sliding or tumbling onto the highway.
  Apparently, this solution ultimately proved unsatisfactory, for in May of 1931, High Rock was blasted into pieces by the New York State Department of Transportation (DOT) as they widened the road. Up until

then, the rock had been a favorite landmark for tourists passing through Warrensburg.

According to legend, High Rock served as a place for Native American council meetings. The rock was significant enough to be mentioned in one of James Fenimore Cooper's tales.

Directions: The boulder was previously located across from Judd Bridge (aka the Plank Road Bridge, and Iron Bridge), where route 9 crosses over the Schroon River

High Rock-Warrensburgh, N.Y. "In the Adirondacks".

High Rock. Postcard from the Gary Bernhardt collection.

Resources: Marie H. Fisher, *North from the Plank Road Bridge: Sketchbook of Warrensburgh* (1974). On page 5 is a sketch of High Rock.
warrencountyhistoricalsociety.org/publications/back-story/rewind-back-issues-2012/rewind-back-issues-2014/rewind-may-15-2014-high-rock-warrensburg-new-york.
warrensburgheritagetrail.org/high-rock.html.
warrencountyhistoricalsociety.org/publications/back-story/rewind-back-issues-2014/rewind-may-15-2014-high-rock-warrensburg-new-york.
Donald R. Williams, *Adirondack Ventures: Images of America* (Charleston, SC: Arcadia Publishing, 2006). On page 99 is a photograph of High Rock.

BOULDERS BEYOND BELIEF

151. PACK FOREST ROCKS
Pack Demonstration Forest

Type of Formation: Medium-sized Boulder
WOW Factor: *Charles Lathrop Rock* – 2; *Split Rock* -- 3
Location: Warrensburg (Warren County)
Tenth Edition, NYS Atlas & Gazetteer: p. 52, A4; **Earlier Edition NYS Atlas & Gazetteer**: p. 88, D3
Parking GPS Coordinates: 43º32.921'N 73º48.187'W
Destination GPS Coordinates: *Charles Lathrop Pack Rock* -- 43º33.070'N 73º48.574'W; *Split Rock* -- 43º32.991'N 73º48.748'W
Accessibility: 0.2-mile walk
Degree of Difficulty: Easy
Additional Information: Pack Forest, 276 Pack Forest Road, Warrensburg, NY 12885
    townofwarrensburg.org/forms/maps/Pack%20Forest%20Nature%20Trail.pdf
– This site contains a map of the Pack Forest Nature Trail.

Commemorative Rock.

Description: The *Charles Lathrop Pack Commemorative Rock*, at the end of a short trail, is 4 feet high and 6 feet long.

Split Rock is a 20-foot high, 8-foot wide section of rock that has split off from a small escarpment.

According to Mark Bertozzi, there is a large glacial erratic near the swampy section of the lake, but I have not been to it. Google Earth suggests that something big might be at 43º33.897'N 73º49.134'W, which places it directly west of the north end of Pack Lake, over halfway between the lake and the swamp

History: In 1926, Charles Lathrop Pack, the son of a lumber baron, purchased 2,200 acres of land northwest of Warrensburg and, a year later, passed on the property's title and management responsibilities to the New York State College of Forestry at Syracuse University.

BOULDERS BEYOND BELIEF

The camp at Pack Forest opened in 1998. The centerpiece of the forest is its 85-acre lake.

Directions: From northwest of Warrensburg (junction of Routes 9 & 28), head north on Route 9 for 0.6 mile. Turn left at a large sign that reads "Pack Demonstration Forest" and proceed northwest. When you come to a Y at 0.3 mile, bear left. After another 0.1 mile, turn right into a parking area for visitors.

From the parking area, continue following the loop road on foot as it leads back down to the main road. Go past the white-colored house on your left, and then through a gate, following the road north for less than 0.2 mile.

Pack Rock -- Turn right onto a short path that leads to the Charles Lathrop Pack Rock in 150 feet.

Split Rock -- Return to the main road and proceed north for 0.05 mile to the southwest corner of Pack Lake. Look for a barricaded, old road/path to your left and follow it uphill for 150 feet to reach a ridge on your left where a section of rock has split off.

Additional Site –

The Rock [43°33.399'N 73°46.687'W], aka Gull Rock, is not part of Pack Forest, but lies close by in the middle of Kelm Lake, some 1.5 miles distant. In *Kelm Lake and its People*, Lise Kure-Jensen mentions the rock, saying that parts of it are variably exposed in accordance with lake level fluctuations. In earlier days, when the lake was considerably higher, very little of the rock showed.

This rock is mentioned for the sake of historical record. As far as I know, there is no public access to the lake.

Resources: Dennis Aprill, *Short Treks in the Adirondacks and Beyond* (Utica, NY: Nicholas K. Burns, 2005), 68–73. Basic information about Pack Forest is provided.
Robert F. Hall, *Pages from Adirondack History* (Fleischmanns, NY: Purple Mountain Press, 1992), 6–12. The chapter contains information about Pack Forest and forest conservation in general.
dec.ny.gov/education/1875.html.

BOULDERS BEYOND BELIEF

152. WILKIE RESERVOIR SPLIT ROCK

Type of Formation: Split Rock
WOW Factor: 5–6
Location: Glens Falls (Warren County)
Tenth Edition, NYS Atlas & Gazetteer: p. 52, C4–5; **Earlier Edition NYS Atlas & Gazetteer**: p. 80, B3–4
Wilkie Reservoir GPS Coordinates: 43º21.258'N 73º45.434'W
Accessibility: Located on Glens Falls Reservoir Property. No public access at this time.

Wilkie Reservoir Split Rock.

Description: This 12-foot-high, 25-foot-long split rock is located near the summit of a small hill overlooking the Wilkie Reservoir.

The rock is covered with a massive amount of a lichen known as rock tripe which, although leathery in appearance, is perfectly edible. In fact, early explorers have historically used rock tripe as famine food when other food sources were unavailable.

History: The 22-acre Wilkie Reservoir, completed in 1914, is owned by the City of Glens Falls and used as one of five sources of drinking water.

Surprisingly, even though the reservoir is seemingly outside the Adirondack Park due to its proximity to Glens Falls, it actually falls within the Blue Line of the Adirondacks. One can only hope that the land will become accessible to the public at some time in the future.

Directions: The reservoir, located at the end of Travers Road, is posted and off-limits to the public

Resources:
poststar.com/wilkie-reservoir/image_38835b8c-b618-5fd3-b567-5f2b5b50fe34.html.

153. COOPER'S CAVE

Type of Formation: Cave
WOW Factor: 3
Location: South Glens Falls (Warren County)
Tenth Edition, NYS Atlas & Gazetteer: p. 53, D6; **Earlier Edition NYS Atlas & Gazetteer**: p. 81, B4–5
Parking GPS Coordinates: 43º18.203'N 73º38.466'W
Cooper's Cave GPS Coordinates: 43º18.284'N 73º38.382'W
Accessibility: <0.1-mile walk
Degree of Difficulty: Easy

Description: According to Gwen Palmer, Bob Bayle, and Stan Malecki in *Glens Falls: Images of America*, Cooper's Cave is an "…eroded passageway in the limestone rock"—not a true cave. As Clay Perry writes in *Underground Empire*, the cave is "…a shallow alcove which has resulted from stream erosion of the bedrock."

Louis Fiske Hyde, in *History of Glens Falls, New York, and its Settlements*, quotes from an article that appeared in the *Troy* in 1871: "The cave is more properly a natural bridge, lying transversely to the direction of the river, its floor somewhat above low-water mark, and its arched roof of rock considerably below the level of high water."

Cooper's Cave. Postcard c. 1920.

The cave is described by geologists D. H. Newland & Henry Vaughan in *Guide to the Geology of the Lake George Region* as "…a rock tunnel open at both ends that has been cut by the river itself in former times when the falls were probably situated in the vicinity. The tunnel is 40 or 50 feet long by 10–12 feet high and lies transverse to the stream channel. It was excavated by crosscurrents that were directed by the jointing of the rock along a north-south course, across the main stream flow."

Although the real-life Cooper's Cave is spectacular in its own way, it is nothing like the cave that is portrayed in the 1992 movie, *The Last of the Mohicans*.

History: Cooper's Cave came into notoriety when it was featured in James Fennimore Cooper's novel, *The Last of the Mohicans*. Cooper had been inspired to write the novel after returning from the Adirondacks in 1825. Until then, little, if any, attention had been paid to the cave.

BOULDERS BEYOND BELIEF

In *History of Glens Falls, New York, and its Settlements*, Louis Fiske Hyde writes that "It was near here, probably, that Father Jacques crossed the river [the Hudson]—the first white man to see the cataract [Glens Falls]—on his mission of salvation to the Indians." If so, then he was also probably the first white man to see Cooper's Cave.

In the early years, the cave was easily accessed via a descending, spiral stairway constructed in 1915 that led down from a bridge spanning the Hudson River between Glens Falls and South Glens Falls. This lasted until 1961, when the stairway was closed off and the bridge ultimately replaced. In 2003, an even newer bridge was constructed, called the Cooper's Cave Bridge, and in 2006 an observation platform was established under the southwest end of the bridge, from where Cooper's Cave can be partially glimpsed.

To be sure, South Glens Falls is not strictly in the Adirondack Park; however, Cooper's Cave is strongly associated with the Adirondacks as a result of James Fenimore Cooper's tale, and thus is included for its historical significance.

Directions: From Glens Falls, drive south on Route 9. As soon as you cross over the Cooper's Cave Bridge spanning the Hudson River, turn right onto River Street. You will immediately see a sign for Cooper's Cave, and then a right-hand turn onto Coopers Cave Drive that leads down to the cave (and parking for disabled drivers). Instead of turning here, continue straight ahead on River Street for another 100 feet and then left into a paved parking area.

From the parking area, walk back down River Street, and follow Coopers Cave Drive to a platform overlooking the falls and Cooper's Cave, both which lie partially beneath Cooper's Cave Bridge.

Resources: Thomas Reeves Lord, *Still More Stories of Lake George Fact and Fiction* (Pemberton, NJ: Pinelands Press, 1999), 32.
Gwen Palmer, Bob Bayle, and Stan Malecki, *Images of America: Glens Falls* (Charleston, SC: Arcadia Publishing, 2004). A photograph, circa 1870, of the cave is shown on page 15. On page 14 is a photograph, circa 1890, of the view looking out from the cave's entrance.
Max Reid, *Lake George and Lake Champlain* (New York: F. P. Putnam's Sons, 1910). Photos taken from inside Cooper's Cave can be seen between pages 98 and 99.
Russell Dunn & Barbara Delaney, *Adirondack Trails with Tales: History Hikes through the Adirondack Park and the Lake George, Lake Champlain & Mohawk Valley Region* (Hensonville, NY: Black Dome Press, 2009), 104–118.

BOULDERS BEYOND BELIEF

Russell Dunn, Cooper's Cave, *Northeastern Caver* Vol. XXIII. No. 3 (September 1992), 95—97.
Barney Fowler, *Adirondack Album. Volume Two* (Schenectady, NY: Outdoor Associates, 1974). A photograph of the interior of Cooper's Cave is shown on page 157.
Clay Perry, *Underground Empire: Wonders and Tales of New York Caves* (New York: Stephen Daye Press, 1948), 190.
Russell Dunn, "Cooper's Cave: Fact & Fiction," *Glens Falls Magazine* Vol. 5, no. 5 (Spring 2004), 25—30.
sgfny.com/Coopers-Cave.htm.
Louis Fiske Hyde, *History of Glens Falls, New York, and its Settlements* (Fort Edward, NY: 1936), 45.
Wayne Wright (compiler), *"Listening In": Memories of Glens Falls 1755–1931*. On page 272 are two photographs of Cooper's Cave taken by William W. Kennedy.
lakegeorgemirrormagazine.com/2017/02/28/cooper's-cave-america's-first-roadside-attraction.
D. H. Newland & Henry Vaughan, *Guide to the Geology of the Lake George Region* (Albany, NY: The University of the State of New York, 1942), 168.

Ned Buntline's Home. Eagle Lake. Postcard c. 1910.

BOULDERS BEYOND BELIEF

154. ADDITIONAL BOULDER & ROCK FORMATION REFERENCES

North Elba -- Robert Morton (editor), *Early Days in the Adirondacks: The Photographs of Seneca Ray Stoddard* (New York: Harry N. Abrams, 1997). *Tenth Edition, NYS Atlas & Gazetteer*: p. 30, C2; *Earlier Edition NYS Atlas & Gazetteer*: p. 96, BC2. On page 108/109 is a photograph of two large boulders pressed against two trees, surrounded by other rocks, entitled "South from Ames, North Elba."

On an insert between pages 52 and 53 is an iconic photograph of hikers climbing steeply uphill through boulders in Avalanche Pass—another section of the Adirondacks where boulders and rocks can be found in great numbers.

Ha-de-ron-day Wilderness -- Lee Decoster, "Hiker resting in fractured rock. Ha-de-ron-day Wilderness Area," *Adirondack Life: Annual Guide to the Adirondacks. 1993* (Vol. XXIV. No. 4). A photograph of a large, 15-foot-high split rock can be seen on page 42/43.

Wells -- Donald R. Williams, *Adirondack People & Places: Images of America* (Charleston, SC: Arcadia Publishing, 2012). *Tenth Edition, NYS Atlas & Gazetteer*: p. 51, C8; *Earlier Edition NYS Atlas & Gazetteer*: p. 79, AB6. On page 106 is an old photograph of an unidentified, large, square-shaped rock with a wooden ladder propped up against its side. People are standing on top. The caption suggests that the rock is located in or near Wells.

Indian Lake -- Linda Laing & series editor Neal Burdick, *Guide to Adirondack Trails: Southern Region. Second Edition* (New York: Adirondack Mountain Club, Inc., 1994), 182. *Tenth Edition, NYS Atlas & Gazetteer*: p. 51, E6; *Earlier Edition NYS Atlas & Gazetteer*: p. 79, C5. On Indian Lake (not the big Indian Lake), "A path to the left along the shore leads another 0.2 mi. to a huge rock that juts out into the lake. This enormous and attractive rock contains small pockets of garnet interspersed with feldspar, an interesting and attractive combination. The rock is a fine observation and/or picnic spot..."

Bald Mountain -- Bill Ingersoll, *Discover the Southern Adirondacks* (Barneveld, NY: Wild River Press. 2014). *Tenth Edition, NYS Atlas & Gazetteer*: p. 52, B2; *Earlier Edition NYS Atlas & Gazetteer*: p. 80, A2. On page 401, Ingersoll mentions "an intriguing egg-shaped rock" on Bald Mountain (which is accessible via a bushwhack from Tucker Road in the Stony Creek area). This is likely the same rock that Barbara McMartin refers to as "a balanced rock" on page 107 in *Discover the Southeastern Adirondacks* (Woodstock, VT: Backcountry Publications, 1986), a picture of which appears on page 106.

475 Rock at Irving Pond. Photograph by Barbara Delaney.

Split Rock Bay -- Six sources depict boulders, including a mammoth split rock, at Pharaoh Lake. *Tenth Edition, NYS Atlas & Gazetteer*: p. 39, C6; *Earlier Edition NYS Atlas & Gazetteer*: p. 89, B4–5:

1) Barbara McMartin, *Fifty Hikes in the Adirondacks* (Woodstock, VT: Backcountry Publications, 1988), 135. "The east side of the ridge overlooks Split Rock Bay [at the north end of Pharaoh Lake], which serves as a reflecting pool for a group of nature's more handsome sculptures, boulders worn smooth by the last glacier."

2) Barbara McMartin, *The Adirondack Park: A Wildlands Quilt* (Syracuse, NY: Syracuse University Press, 1999). On page 3 is a photo taken by Chuck Bennett of three large blocks in shallow water at the head of Pharaoh Lake.

3) Tim Starmer, *Five-Star Trails in the Adirondacks* (Birmingham, AL: Menasha Ridge Press, Inc., 2017). At the beginning of the book is a photograph of several boulders contained in Split Rock Bay.

On page 134, the author writes that "…the trail, now marked in yellow, winds along another bay with large boulders sticking up in the middle. This is Split Rock Bay. From the opposing shore, the split rocks appear to be a pair of obelisks with an eerie and unnatural quality."

4) Barbara McMartin with Edythe Robbins & Chuck Bennett, *Discover the Eastern Adirondacks* (Canada Lake, NY: Lake View Press, 1998), 131. "A huge split rock looms up in the bay, surrounded by smaller boulders artistically placed by the glacier. The small bay provides a reflecting pool for the sculptural mass."

5) Rhonda & George Ostertag, *Hiking New York* (Guilford, CT: The Globe Pequot Press, 2002), 84. "...Split Rock Bay, named for a distinctive offshore feature." A map of the hike from Crane Pond Road can be seen on page 81.

6) Jeff Mitchell, *Backpacking New York: 37 Great Hikes* (Mechanicsburg, PA: Stackpole Books, 2016), 157. "There are big rocks at the edge of the peninsula with awesome views of almost the entire lake…"

A substantial hike is involved to reach these rocks.

Dexter Lake -- Linda Laing & series editor Neal Burdick, *Guide to Adirondack Trails: Southern Region. Second Edition* (New York: Adirondack Mountain Club, Inc., 1994). *Tenth Edition, NYS Atlas & Gazetteer*: p. 50, DE4; *Earlier Edition NYS Atlas & Gazetteer*: p. 78, BC4. Laing mentions "…two or three huge boulders jutting into the water…" near a camping area on Dexter Lake.

Puffer Pond Basin -- Barbara McMartin & Bill Ingersoll, *Discover the South Central Adirondacks. Third Edition* (Utica, NY: North Country Books, 2005), 166. *Tenth Edition, NYS Atlas & Gazetteer*: p. 37, D9–10; *Earlier Edition NYS Atlas & Gazetteer*: p. 87, C7. Mention is made of a "large erratic" and "a larger split erratic" in the Puffer Pond Basin, presumably along the faint Puffer Pond Trail.

Cascade Mountain -- Barbara McMartin & Lee M. Brenning, *Discover the West Central Adirondacks* (Woodstock, VT: Backcountry Publications, 1988), 229. *Tenth Edition, NYS Atlas & Gazetteer*: p. 36, C2; *Earlier Edition NYS Atlas & Gazetteer*: p. 86, B2. The authors mention that "two large balancing rocks" are encountered on "an extensive bald crest on the ridge." It is important to note that this hike involves a bushwhack, and that the Cascade Mountain discussed is not the one near Lake Placid, but rather the mountain near Old Forge and Cascade Lake.

BOULDERS BEYOND BELIEF

Cascade Pass: Lost Arrow – Grace L. Hudowalski (editor), *The Adirondack High Peaks and the Forty-Sixers* (Albany, NY: The Peters Print, 1970). *Tenth Edition, NYS Atlas & Gazetteer*: p. 30, C3; *Earlier Edition NYS Atlas & Gazetteer*: p. 96, BC2–3. On page 139 is a photograph of Dave Bernays standing on top of the Lost Arrow. The upright rock spire appears to be at least 25 feet high.

Don Mellor, *Climbing in the Adirondacks: A Guide to Rock and Ice Routes in the Adirondack Park* (Lake George, NY: Adirondack Mountain Club, 1989). On page 130, Mellor writes, "This is the amazing rock that stands like a tractor trailer on end…"

Picture Rock once overlooked Canada Lake until it was blasted to bits decades ago. If memory serves me correctly, the rock outcrop was located where the parking area for the Pinnacle Boulders presently is.

Gleasmans Falls -- Lee M. Brenning, William P. Ehling, & Barbara McMartin, *Discover the Southwestern Adirondacks* (Woodstock, VT: Backcountry Publications, 1987), 194. *Tenth Edition, NYS Atlas & Gazetteer*: p. 35, C6; *Earlier Edition NYS Atlas & Gazetteer*: p. 85, B5. Mention is made of "two huge boulders" that are passed by on the trail to Gleasmans Falls, as well as "the wall of a story-high boulder" at the waterfall.

BOULDERS BEYOND BELIEF

Lisa Densmore Ballard, *Hiking the Adirondacks. Second Edition* (Guilford, CT: Falcon Guides, 2017), 323. At 2.5 miles "The trail passes a large boulder" and then descends to the river.

Jayville -- Joseph M. St. Amand, *Tales of Jayville New York and the North Country* (2008). *Tenth Edition, NYS Atlas & Gazetteer*: p. 27, D7; *Earlier Edition NYS Atlas & Gazetteer*: p. 93, C6. The author talks about a visit to *Huckelberry {sic} Rock* near Twin Pond, but no specific directions are given.

Split Rock Road -- Kelsie B. Harder & Mary H. Smallman (editors*), Claims to Name: Toponyms of St. Lawrence County* (Utica, NY: North Country Books, Inc., 1992), *Tenth Edition, NYS Atlas & Gazetteer*: p. 26, A1; *Earlier Edition NYS Atlas & Gazetteer*: p. 92, AB2. The authors cite Split Rock Road, off of Route 3, whose name suggests that there must be a split rock somewhere on or near this road.

Huntingtonville -- Edgar C. Emerson, *Jefferson County, New York* (Watertown, NY: 1898), 64. *Tenth Edition, NYS Atlas & Gazetteer*: p. 33, A9; *Earlier Edition NYS Atlas & Gazetteer*: p. 84, A1. "At Huntingtonville, just east of, and up the river from the city of Watertown, is a wide area of denuded rock along the river shore of Huntington Island.....just above the dam, and now partly covered with water by the pond, are a very interesting group of pot holes, sharply and deeply cut, and in many instances, having the original pieces of hard stone in them." A photo of the river bed can be seen on an insert between pages 64 and 65.

Cobble Hill -- Barbara McMartin, *Discover the Central Adirondacks* (Woodstock, VT: Backcountry Publications, Inc., 1986), 33–34. *Tenth Edition, NYS Atlas & Gazetteer*: p. 38, B3; *Earlier Edition NYS Atlas & Gazetteer*: p. 88, B3. McMartin describes a bushwhack to a split glacial erratic near the base of Cobble Hill that measures "33 feet long, 27 feet wide, and 25 feet high." Thirty years have gone by since McMartin visited the boulder. Whether it is still possible to locate the boulder based upon her directions is something I leave for others to determine.

Tongue Mountain Range -- David Thomas Train (editor), *Adirondack Mountain Club: Eastern Trails. 4th Edition* (Lake George, NY: Adirondack

BOULDERS BEYOND BELIEF

Mountain Club, Inc., 2012), 74. *Tenth Edition, NYS Atlas & Gazetteer*: p. 39, E7; *Earlier Edition NYS Atlas & Gazetteer*: p. 89, CD5. Before reaching 4.4 miles, the Tongue Mountain Range Trail passes by a "couple of interesting boulder." Make of this what you will.

West Pond Rocks near Moose Lake.

Ice Cave Mountain -- Arthur W. Haberl & series editor Neal Burdick, *Guide to Adirondack Trails: West-Central Region. Third Edition* (New York: Adirondack Mountain Club, Inc., 1994), 272–275. *Tenth Edition, NYS Atlas & Gazetteer*: p. 36, E1; *Earlier Edition NYS Atlas & Gazetteer*: p. 86, D2. "The Ice Cave is actually a 96-ft.-deep trench located on the SW end of the mountain which collects winter snows and remains icy into the summer months….The summit is mostly a jumble of boulders covered by a thin quilt of soil which doesn't quite fill the gaps. There are many boulders standing along the ridge where they have broken away and begun to slide off. One gigantic boulder stands precariously on the very steep W slope about 0.4 mi. NE of the cave."

Reaching Ice Cave Mountain involves driving on back roads and then taking a fairly lengthy hike, ultimately followed by a bushwhack up to the summit of the mountain. References can also be found at: trails.com/trail-ice-cave-mountain-herkimer-953572.html. peakbagger.com/peak.aspx?pid=6122.

Diamond -- Orrinda Moreton, *History of the Town of Worth: 1795–1976* (no info provided), 34. *Tenth Edition, NYS Atlas & Gazetteer*: p. 33, D9; *Earlier Edition NYS Atlas & Gazetteer:* p. 83, C7. A photograph is shown of a boy standing by "Big Rock," which looks to be about 8 feet high and 15 feet long. Big Rock is

BOULDERS BEYOND BELIEF

located in Diamond, aka South Woods, which is at the southwest part of the Town of Worth.

Star Lake – Shawn R. Bauerschmidt, *Star Lake: Images of America* (Charleston, SC: Arcadia Publishing, 2006). *Tenth Edition, NYS Atlas & Gazetteer*: p. 27, D9; *Earlier Edition NYS Atlas & Gazetteer:* p. 93, C7. On page 96 is a photograph taken in 1910 of the lake and Zimmerman's Rock, which looks fairly small.

St. Regis Falls – Paula LaVoy Trim, *Water Over the Fall: St. Regis Falls History* (1984). *Tenth Edition, NYS Atlas & Gazetteer*: p. 20, B5; *Earlier Edition NYS Atlas & Gazetteer:* p. 101, C4–5. On page 37 is a photograph of an odd-looking rock shaped like a sliced loaf of bread. The caption reads "Where is this great boulder? Can you see anything unusual about it?" – not much to go on.

Treadway Mountain Rocks.

BOULDERS BEYOND BELIEF

BOOKS & WEBSITES ON ADIRONDACK BOULDERING & ROCK CLIMBING (Note: This list is by no means comprehensive)

Books

Tim Kemple, *New England Bouldering* (New Castle, CO: Wolverine Publishing, 2004).

Jim Lawyer & Jeremy Haas, *Adirondack Rock: A Rock Climbers Guide* (Pompey, NY: Adirondack Rock Press, LLC, 2014).

Don Mellor, *Climbing in the Adirondacks: A Guide to Rock and Ice Routes in the Adirondack Park* (Lake George, NY: Adirondack Mountain Club, 1996).

Justin Sanford, *Adirondack Park Bouldering* (Broadalbin, NY: Southern Adirondack Climber, LLC, 2015).

Websites

visitadirondacks.com/recreation/rock-climbing.
rockclimbing.com/routes/North_America/United_States/New_York/Adirondack_park.
communitywalk.com/boulders_in_the_adirondacks/map/299298 – This site contains a map of bouldering sites.
lakeplacid.com/do/outdoors/summerfall/rock-climbing.
mountainproject.com/area/105910378/adirondacks.
adkbouldering.blogspot.com.
saranaclake.com/blog/2017/07/mckenzie-road-bouldering.
rockclimbing.com/routes/North_America/United_States/New_York/Adirondack_park.
adirondackexperience.com/blog/2016/09/rock – This website contains photographs of some of the Adirondack's fantastic rocks.
tupperlake.com/blog/2016/09/rocky-tales-overlooked-landmarks – This text is by Michelle Clement.
southernadirondackclimber.blogspot.com/2013/08/summer-ascents-at-green-lake-boulders.html.

BOULDERS BEYOND BELIEF

ARTICLES ON BOULDERING

Nicole Banta, "Erratic Activities: The Growing Sport of Bouldering," *Local adk Adirondack Mountains* Vol. 4, Issue 2 (Fall, 2016), 43–6.
Phil Brown, "Bouldering comes of age," *Adirondack Explorer* (September/October 2016), 64 & 65. Brown discusses bouldering in general, and specifically reviews Justin Sanford's book, *Adirondack Park Bouldering* published in 2016 by Southern Adirondack Climber.
Josh Potter, "Adirondack Bouldering on the Rise," *Adirondack Sports & Fitness* (June, 2012).
Alan Wechsler, "Hey, you got a problem? Bouldering buffs can help you solve it," *Adirondack Explorer* Vol. 7, No. 5 (September/October, 2005), 7 & 51.

Oliva Zook at McKenzie Pond Boulders.

BOULDERS BEYOND BELIEF

ACKNOWLEDGMENTS

I am indebted to the following individuals for their contributions: Rich Elton, for photographs and information on chapters related to the Wilkie Reservoir Boulder, Blind Rock, Peaked Mountain Boulders, and the Lindsay Brook Boulder; Jane Bouder, for photographs of the massive Lindsay Brook glacial erratic, and her consultation on the feasibility of directing hikers to this rock; Chuck Porter, for his photograph of the Bald Peak boulder; Mike Prescott, for information on honeycombed rocks and the location of the Underwood Bridge regarding Captain Peter's Rock; Gary Bernhardt, for his postcard contributions; Sandra Arnold for her valuable input on the history of Manville Rock, photo contribution, and assistance in sending postcard images to me; Bill O'Connor, Director of Security at the Ausable Mountain Reserve for three decades, for information on the Boulder Cottage; Neal Burdick, author and editor of *Adirondac Magazine,* for his help on the Natural Bridge in Natural Bridge and the Azure Mountain boulder; Reggie Chambers, for information provided on Neodak Rock; Bobbie Sweeting, unfailing researcher and waterfall expert, and creator Bobbies Waterfall website for checking out two sites for me; Mark Bertozzi for information concerning a large glacial boulder in the Pack Demonstration Forest; Nancy M. Pratt, Waldheim, for information provided on Roosevelt Rock; Andrew Coulter, intern at the Adirondack Interpretive Center, who perked my curiosity regarding St. Regis Mountain's glacial erratics; Michael G. Roets, site manager at the Crown Point State Historic Site, for background information on the Crown Point pothole, and photographic help; Rebecca Terry, Director of Camp Pack Forest, for her help in locating a large boulder on their property; Olivia Zook, Chris Minichello and Andrew Glose for entertaining us with their feats of bouldering; and last, but not least, my good friends Christy Butler, who hiked with me to several boulders, contributed several stunning photographs, and designed the book cover; and John Haywood, for his many photographic contributions and for handling the publishing aspect of this book.

I would be remiss if I didn't give special mention to my wife and adventure companion, Barbara Delaney, whose presence is felt throughout the entire book, and whose photographs, both as photographer and subject, have made *Boulders Beyond Belief* even more wonderful. She also took on the prodigious job of proofreading the text.

BOULDERS BEYOND BELIEF

OTHER BOOKS BY RUSSELL DUNN

Waterfall Guidebooks

Adirondack Waterfall Guide: New York's Cool Cascades (Black Dome Press, 2003).

Catskill Region Waterfall Guide: Cool Cascades of the Catskills & Shawangunks (Black Dome Press, 2004).

Hudson Valley Waterfall Guide: From Saratoga and the Capital Region to the Highlands and Palisades (Black Dome Press, 2005).

Mohawk Region Waterfall Guide: From the Capital District to Cooperstown & Syracuse (Black Dome Press, 2007).

Berkshire Waterfall Guide: Cool Cascades of the Berkshire & Taconic Mountains (Black Dome Press, 2008).

Vermont Waterfalls: A Guide (Countryman Press, 2015).

Keene Valley Region Waterfall Guide: The Search for Cool Cascades in the Heart of the Adirondacks (Black Dome Press, 2017).

Coauthored with Christy Butler

Connecticut Waterfalls: A Guide (Countryman Press, 2013).

Paddling Guidebooks

A Kayaker's Guide to New York's Capital Region: Albany, Schenectady & Troy (Black Dome Press, 2010).

A Kayaker's Guide to Lake George, the Saratoga Region, and Great Sacandaga Lake (Black Dome Press, 2012).

Paddling the Quiet Waters of Mid-Eastern New York (Troy Book Makers, 2014).

Penultimate Paddles of the Piseco, Indian, and Canada Lakes Region (John Haywood Photography, 2016).

Hiking Guidebooks

Rambles to Remarkable Rocks: An Explorer's Hiking Guide to Amazing Boulders & Rock Formations of the Capital Region, Catskills, & Shawangunks (John Haywood Photography, 2018).

Coauthored with Barbara Delaney

Trails with Tales: History Hikes through the Capital Region, Saratoga, Berkshires, Catskills, and Hudson Valley (Black Dome Press, 2006).

BOULDERS BEYOND BELIEF

Adirondack Trails with Tales: History Hikes through the Adirondack Park and the Lake George, Lake Champlain & Mohawk Valley Regions (Black Dome Press, 2009).

<u>Coauthored with Christy Butler</u>

Rockachusetts: An Explorer's Guide to Amazing Boulders of Massachusetts (Butler & Dunn, 2016).

3-D Books

Waterfalls of New York in 3D. Vol. 1 (John Haywood Photography, 2016).
Waterfalls of New York in 3D. Vol. 2 (John Haywood Photography, 2016).
Ogunquit in 3D (John Haywood Photography, 2016).
Adirondacks in 3D. Volume One (John Haywood Photography, 2016).
Helderbergs in 3D (John Haywood Photography, 2016).
Great Sacandaga Lake in 3D (John Haywood Photography, 2016).
Albany in 3D (John Haywood Photography, 2016).
Catskills & Shawangunks in 3D (John Haywood Photography, 2017).
Berkshires in 3D (John Haywood Photography, 2017).
Rome in 3D (John Haywood Photography, 2017).
Florence & Scenes of Italy in 3D (John Haywood Photography, 2017).
Adirondacks in 3D. Volume Two (John Haywood Photography, 2017).

<u>Coauthored with Barbara Delaney</u>

3-D Guide to the Empire State Plaza and its large works of art (Troy Book Makers, 2012).

<u>Coauthored with John Haywood</u>

Ausable Chasm in 3D (John Haywood Photography, 2015).
Natural Stone Bridge & Caves in 3D (John Haywood Photography, 2016).

Miscellaneous

Adventures around the Great Sacandaga Lake (Nicholas K. Burns, 2002).
Adventures around the Great Sacandaga Lake. Revised & Illustrated (Troy Book Makers, 2011).

<u>Coauthored with John Haywood & Sean Reines</u>

Ausable Chasm: In Pictures and Story (John Haywood Photography, 2015).

Russell Dunn can be reached at rdunnwaterfalls@yahoo.com.

BOULDERS BEYOND BELIEF

INDEX

A

Abbuhl, Fred, 331
Abenaki, 162
abolition, 127
abri, 27
Access Fund, 323
Adirondac, 31, 140, 187
Adirondac Almanac, 222
Adirondack Album, 221, 359
Adirondack Cabin Country, 373, 381
Adirondack Cross-Country Skiing, 287
Adirondack Explorer, 102, 118, 138, 183, 237
Adirondack Explorer 2012 Outings Guide, 332
Adiondack Explorer 2013 Outings Guide, 282
Adirondack Fire Towers: Their History and Lore. The Northern District, 186
"Adirondack Geology: Mysteries of Rocks and Minerals", 222
Adirondack High: Images of America's First Wilderness, 139
Adirondack High Peaks and the Forty-Sixers, The, 396
Adirondack Hotel, 225
Adirondack Hotel Rock, 224–226, 225 (photo)
Adirondack Ike, 315
Adirondack Ike: Memories from 1 to 91, 315
Adirondack Inn, 313
Adirondack Interpretive Center, 222–224
Adirondack Landscape, The, 50, 142, 241
Adirondack Lean-to, 86
Adirondack Life Annual Guide to the Adirondacks: 1999, 393
Adirondack Life 2011 Annual Guide to the Great Outdoors, 173
Adirondack Life 2018 Guide to the Great Outdoors, 99
Adirondack Loj, 104
Adirondack Mountain Club, 151
Adirondack Mountain Club: Eastern Trails, 311, 372, 373, 398
Adirondack Mountains, 38
Adirondack Northway, 42, 114, 221, 285
Adirondack Park: A Wilderness Quilt, 394
Adirondack Park Bouldering, 339
Adirondack Pass, 111
Adirondack People and Places, 393
Adirondack Rock: A Climber's Guide, 238, 339
Adirondack Sample II, An, 270
Adirondacks Illustrated, The, 45
Adirondacks: Wild Island of Hope, The, 104, 137, 138
Adirondack Trails: Central Region, 355, 378
Adirondack Trails: High Peaks Region, 52, 65, 80, 82, 85, 92, 101, 125, 137, 138, 142, 143, 221
Adirondack Town Recalls its Past, An, 334, 335
Adirondack Wilderness, 140
Adrenaline Falls, 167
Adventures in Camping, 269
Albany, 380
Alden, Albert, 384
Alexander Bay, 210, 211
Algonquin, 42
Algonquin Lake, 348
Algonquin Peak, 137, 138, 145
Algonquin Peak Boulders (photo), 29
"Allen's Bear Fight Up In Keene," 92
Allied Chemical Company, 218
All-Star (boulder), 324
Altamont, 163
"Amazing Grace", 138
Ampersand Creek, 153
Ampersand Mountain, 152, 153 (photo)
Ampersand Mountain Rocks, 152–155
Amphitheater, 176, 268, 293
Ams Rock, 204–206, 205 (photo)
anorthosite, 21, 39, 97, 98, 121, 125, 147, 220
anorthosite boulder, 121
Anthony's Nose, 302
Appalachians, 39
Arab Mountain, 164
Archbald Pothole, 292
Archbald Pothole State Park, 293
Archer Vly, 316, 317
Arietta, 340
Arizona, 23
Arnold, Ed, 250
Arnold, Sandra, 316
Arnold's Point, 250
Arnold's Rock, 250–252, 251 (photo)

Arnold's Rock Trail, 251
Arrowhead Park, 260
Arthur, Andy, 48
Arctic circle, 31
Artist Rock, 299
artists, 76
"Art of Nathan Farb, The", 140
Atwell, 280
Auger Falls, 363, 365
Auger Falls Boulder, 363–365, 364 (photo)
Auger Falls Potholes, 364
Auger Falls Shelter Cave, 364, 365
Ausable Chasm, 28, 44–47
Ausable Chasm Bridge, 46
Ausable Chasm in Pictures and Story, 46
Ausable Club, 72, 73
Ausable Forks, 121
Ausable Lake Dam, Lower, 74
Ausable Lake, Lower, 144
Ausable River, 44, 45
Ausable River, East Branch, 72, 74, 77, 78, 95, 96, 142
Ausable River, West Branch, 119, 121–123
Australia, 24
Avalanche Pass, 138, 393
Averys Place, 343
Ayres Jr., Douglas, 110
Azure Mountain, 185, 187, 188
Azure Mountain Balanced Rock, 185–189, 186 (photo)

B

Backpacking New York: 37 Great Hikes, 395
Bakers Mills, 381
balanced rocks, 23, 349
Balanced Rock: Bald Mountain, 263–266, 264 (postcard), 266 (photo)
Balancing Rock: Blue Ridge Road, 220, 220 (photo), 221
Balanced Rock: Little Sawyer Mountain, 233, 234
Balanced Rock: Pitchoff Mountain, 100–103, 101 (photo)
Balancing Rock: Gothics, 76, 77
Balderdash (rock), 65
Bald Mountain, 23, 264, 265, 393

Bald Mountain Fire Tower, 264
Bald Peak, 49, 50
Bald Peak Boulder, 49, 49 (photo), 50
Ballard, Lisa Densmore, 20, 42, 48, 76, 79, 145, 311, 345, 361, 397
Ballerina Rock, 23
Bark Easter Inn, 92
Barker, Eugene, 291
Barlow, Jane A., 260
Barn Boulder, 127, 127 (photo)
Bare Mountain, 272
Basford Falls, 166
Basin Mountain, 87
Batchellerville Bridge, 317
Battleship Rock, 252–254, 253 (postcard)
Battleship (rock), 65
Bauerschmidt, Shawn R., 399
Bayle, Bob, 389
Beach Boulder, 354
Bear Mountain, 109
Bear Mountain Boulder, 174, 174 (photo), 175
Beaver Lake, 338
Beaver Meadow Brook, 142
Beaver Meadow Falls, 77, 142
Beckler, Dee, 295
Beckler, Ed, 295
Beckler, Greg, 295
Beckler, Jenny, 295
Beck's Tavern, 379
Beede Brook, 64
Bees, 372
Beetle, David H., 253, 254, 264, 265, 277
Believe it or Not, 182
Bennett, Chuck, 394
Bernays, Dave, 396
Bernhardt, Gary, 385
Bertozzi, Mark, 386
Best Easy Day Hikes: Adirondacks, 79, 345
Bibeau, Susan, 138, 282
Bidwell, Charles, 350
Bidwell's Hotel Rock, 349–351, 350 (photo)
Big Balanced Rock, 23
Big Bend, 247
"Big Blowdown of 1950", 117
Big Crow Mountain, 89
Big Eddy, 348

BOULDERS BEYOND BELIEF

Big Moose Lake, 261, 261
Big Moose Lake in the Adirondacks, 260
Big Rock, 183, 399
Big Rock Rock-shelter, 27
Big Slide Trail, 83
Bill Johnson's Island, 210
Bingham, Joshua, 325
Black Fly Mountain Bike Challenge, 256
Black Pond Creek, 314
Black River, 215–217
Black River Valley, 214
Black Sails (boulder), 307
Blanchard, David, 194
Blanchard, Walter, 194
Blankman, Edgar G., 190
Blind Rock, 382–384, 383 (photo)
Bloomingdale, 152
Blueberry Mountain, 88
Blueberry Mountain Boulder, 87, 88
Blue Mountain, 229
"Blue" (mountain), 187
Blue Mountain House, 187
Blue Mountain Lake, 229, 245, 249
Blue Mountain Lake Boulder, 245–247, 245 (photo)
Blue Ridge, 221, 247
Blue Ridge Falls, 221
Bluff Island, 158, 159
Bluff Mountain, 144
Bogardus, Lorraine B., 208
Bonaparte, Joseph, 194, 198
Bonaparte Lake, 196
Bonaparte's Cave, 196–201, 197 (photo), 198 (photo)
Bonaparte's Cave State Forest, 198
Boonville, 217
Boonville Limestone Quarry, 218
Boquet River, 72
Boquet River, North Fork, 56–59, 61
Boquet River, South Fork, 62
Boreas River, 221
Bouder, Jayne, 27
Boulder Bend (photo), 142
Boulder Cottage, 71, 72
Boulders across road from Chapel Pond Parking Area, 67–69

Boulderwoods, 370–375, 370 (photo), 371 (photo)
Brandt, Joel, 157
Brenning, Lee M., 250, 280, 344, 395, 396
"Bridge of God", 293
British, 215, 292, 383
Broken Needle, 46
Brothers, The, 82, 84
Brown, Benjamin D., 213
Brown, C. Ervin, 202
Brown, Henry A. L., 271
Brown Farm State Historic Site, John, 125
Brown, Grace, 262
Brown, Henry A. L., 271
Brown, John (North Elba), 92, 126, 127
Brown, John (Old Forge), 271
Brown, Louis, 98
Brown Memorial Statue, John, 128
Brown, Phil, 79, 82, 88, 118, 139
Brown's Boulders, John, 125–128, 126 (photo), 127 (photo)
Brown, Scott, 72
Brown's Tract: Lost Adirondack Empire, John, 271
Browns Tract Trail, 272
Bryce, Astri, 304
Bryce, David, 304
Buckell, Betty Ahearn, 302
Bucket Pond, 316
Buck Island, 171
Buck Mountain, 311
Buck Mountain Boulder, 310, 311
Bulkhead Falls, 166–168
Bulkhead Falls Boulder, 166–168, 168 (photo)
bullersten, 22
Buntline, Ned, 247, 392 (postcard)
Burdick, Neal, 143, 173, 183, 185, 187, 393, 395, 398
Burger, Billy, 86
Burnside, James R., 49, 82, 136
Butler, Christy, 30, 33, 34, 58, 59, 289, 308
Butter (boulder), 238
Buttermilk Falls, 226, 227
Buttermilk Falls Boulder, 226, 227, 227 (photo)
Butternut Brook, 311
Buzzelli, David "Buzz", 238
By Foot in the Adirondacks, 100

C

Cabins (boulder), The, 280
Cagle, Laurence T., 355, 378
Cairo, Egypt, 152
Campground Boulders, 305, 307
Campground Wall, 305
Camp-of-the-Woods, 354, 355
Camp-of-the-Woods Boulder, 353–355, 353 (postcard), 354 (photo)
Canada Lake, 173, 321, 325, 338
Canada Lake Boulders, 328
Canada Lake Store & Marina, 328
Canadian Shield, 38
Canavan, Aidan, 9, 66, 66 (photo)
Canavan, Andrew, 9 (photo), 66, 66 (photo), 324 (photo), 326 (photo), 329 (photo)
Cannon Beach, Oregon, 179
Canyons of the Gods, 339
Captain Boulder, 307
Captain Peter, 162
Captain Peter's Rock, 162, 163
Carey's Rock, 143
Carnes Granite Co., Inc., 98
Carnes, Wilfred, 98
Caroga Lake, 320, 321, 323
Carr, Alexander, 194
Carroll Jr., Robert, 110, 210
Carry Flow, 205
Cascade Lakes, 97, 99, 101, 104, 138 (postcard)
Cascade Mountain Boulders, 103–105, 102 (photo)
Cascade Mountain (North Elba), 97, 98, 102, 104
Cascade Mountain (Old Forge), 395
Cascade Mountain/Porter Mountain Trail, 104, 106
Cascade Pass, 97, 396
Cascade Pass Road, 92
Cascade Pond, 230, 231
Cascade Pond Wilderness, 231
Castle (Boulder), 333
Castle Rock, 229
Castle Rock (boulder), 228, 228 (photo), 229
Castle, The, 125
Catamount Mountain, 143, 205, 206
Cathedral Rock, 176, 176 (postcard), 177
Cat Rock, 207
Catskills, 34, 38
Cattaraugus County, 132
Cauldron, The, 302
Cave Hill, 355
Caveman Rock, 377
"cavernous weathering", 238
Cave Rock, 237 (photo)
Caves for Kids in Historic Hudson New York, 172, 196
Cedar Pond, 270, 273
Cedar Pond Trail, 267, 272, 273, 273 (photo)
Cedar River, 234
Century Wild (1885–1985): Essays Commemorating the Centennial of the Adirondack Forest Preserve, An, 185
Chain Pond, 269
Chain Pond Trail, 267, 268
Chain Pond Trail Boulders, 267
Chair Rock, 346
Chair Rock Creek, 171
Chair Rock Island, 171
Champagne, Linda M., 136
Champlain Area Trails (CATS), 54
Chanol's Rock, 379, 380
Chapel Pond, 62, 74, 67–69
Chapel Pond Parking Area, Boulders Across From, 67–69
Charlotte, N. C., 27
Chase, Diane, 183
Chasm Cascade, 56, 57
Cheney, John, 54
Cheney Mountain, 54, 55
Cheney Mountain Boulders, 54–56, 54 (photo)
Child, Hamilton, 201, 206
Chimney Mountain, 240–244, 241 (postcard), 242 (photo), 243 (photo)
Chimney Mountain Chimney, 241
China, 28
Chiricahua National Monument Park, 23
Chronicles of Lake George: Journeys in War and Peace, 302
Chub Lake, 339
Cirques, 39
Civilian Conservation Corps (CCC), 175, 236,

306
Civil War, 127
Claims to Names: Toponyms of St. Lawrence County, 190, 397
Clare, 168, 169
Clement, Michelle, 400
Cliff Wall, 158
Climbing in the Adirondacks: A Guide to Rock and Ice Routes in the Adirondack Park, 396
Clyne, Patricia Edwards, 172, 196
CNY Hikers, 54
Coal Cart, 308–310
Cobble Hill, 397
Coffin, Michael, 229
Coggeshall, Almy, 257
Coggeshall, Anne, 257
Cold Brook, 349
Colden Boulder, Mount, 34 (photo), 143
Cold Pond, 179
Cold River, 139 (postcard)
Cole, Glyndon, 141
College of Environmental Science & Forestry, SUNYA, 223
College Rock, 178
Collier, Patricia, 141
Colossus Rock, 72–74, 73 (photo)
Colton, 179
Colton Historical Society, 179
Colton, New York: Story of a Town II, 179
Colvin, Verplanck, 42, 187
Comet 67P/Churyumov-Gerasimenko, 23
Comfort Island, 211
Connery Pond, 117
Conroy, Dennis, 50, 70, 140, 141, 144, 287
Conservation Commission, NYS, 149, 362
Cooper, James Fenimore, 385
Cooper, Judge, 207
Cooper's Cave, 389–392, 390 (postcard)
Coopers Falls, 206
Coopers Falls Pothole, 206–208
Coopers Falls Iron Works, 207
Cooper's Mills, 207
Copper Rock Falls, 166
Cottage Boulder, 71–73, 72 (photo)
Couch Rock, 345–347, 346 (photo)
Cove Boulders, 305

Cranberry Lake, 144, 166, 170, 175
Cranberry Lake Biological Station, 170, 171
Cranberry Lake hydro-dam, 171
Cranberry Pond, 166
Crane Mountain, 373, 374, 377
Crane Mountain Boulders, 370
Crane Mountain Natural Bridge, 371
Crane Mountain Pond, 373, 377
Crane Mountain Trail, 374, 377
Crawford, Eli Montgomery, 81
Creature (boulder), 276
Creek Side (boulder), 331
crepuscular cave, 27
Cribbage (rock), 65
Croghan, 192
Croghan, George, 192
Croghan Rock, 192, 192 (photo)
Crown Point, 55
Crown Point Pothole, 291–293, 292 (photo)
Crown Point Reservation, 292
Crown Point State Historic Site, 291
Crows, The, 89
Cuba Island, 211
Cue-Ball (boulder), 335, 335 (photo)
Cungemunk, 356
Curtis Pond, 173

D

Daly Creek, 314, 315
Dave's Cirque, 381
Dawson, James C., 140, 141, 144
Day Hikes for all Seasons: An Adirondack Sampler, 89, 100, 129, 186
Dean Mountain Road Rock, 365, 366, 366 (photo)
Dean Mountain Road White Water Park, 366
Deception Rising (boulder), 238
DeCosse, Bessie, 143
Decoster, Lee, 393
Deer Brook, 85
Deer Brook Falls, 78
Deer Brook Gorge, 78
Deer Brook Shelter Cave, 77–79, 78 (photo)
Deerfoot Lodge, 358, 359
Deerhead, 41
Deer Hunter's History, 247

Deerland, 226, 227
Deerlick Rock, 214–216
Deerlick Rock Cache, 215
Degrasse, 166
DeKalb, 206, 207
Dekalb Iron Works, 207
Delaney, Barbara, 21, 39, 42, 112, 114, 144, 154, 160, 164, 287, 335, 337, 343, 350, 364, 366, 367, 377,
    394, 398, 402
Delaney, Bill, 23
Delaney, Tom, 23
Deline Lake, 338
Dempsey, Jack, 226
Devil's Marbles, 24
Devil's Oven (Ausable Chasm), 45
Devil's Oven (Devil's Oven Island), 210–212
Devil's Oven Island, 210, 210 (postcard), 212 (postcard)
Devil's Pulpit (Ausable Chasm), 46
Dexter Lake, 395
Diamond, 398, 399
Dinosaur Egg (boulder), 331
Discover the Adirondacks, 153, 228
Discover the Adirondacks, 1, 364
Discover the Adirondacks, 2, 325, 340
Discover the Adirondack High Peaks, 88, 105, 139
Discover the Northeastern Adirondacks, 70, 140, 141, 144
Discover the Northern Adirondacks, 91, 94, 141, 144, 145, 153
Discover the Northwestern Adirondacks, 50, 171, 176
Discover the South Central Adirondacks, 364, 395
Discover the Southeastern Adirondacks, 376, 394
Discover the Southern Adirondacks, 333, 339, 376, 377, 393
Discover the Southwestern Adirondacks, 280, 396
Discover the West Central Adirondacks, 250, 344, 397
Dix Mountain, 23, 59, 61
Dog Hikes in the Adirondacks, 139
Dolgeville Point, 321
Donaldson, Alfred L., 111
Douglas, Mabel Smith, 135
Durant, Lake, 231

Durant, William West, 247
Dwight, Timothy, 302

E

Eagle Bay, 263, 268
Eagle Lake, 249
East Dix Mountain, 138
East Inlet, 173
East River Trail, 74
East River Trail Boulders, 71–74
Echo Cave, 294
Echo Cliffs, 346, 347
Echoes from Whiteface Mountain: A Brief History of Wilmington, 121
Ehling, William P., 31, 396
Eighth Lake Campground, 251
Einstein, Albert, 226
Elephant Head, 44, 44 (postcard)
Elephant Island, 223 (old illustration)
Elephant Island Caves, 223
Elephant Rock, 298, 298 (photo), 299
Elinskas, Robert J., 247
Elizabethtown, 72, 92
Elk Lake, 219
Elk Lake Lodge, 219
Elk Lake Road Boulder, 219, 219 (photo)
Elm Lake, 355, 356
Elton, Rich, 283, 383
Emerson, Edgar C., 397
Emmons, Professor Ebenezer, 113
Erratic Wandering, 34
Essex County Highway Department, 132
Evans, Jeremy, 187
Everett, George, 190
Everts, L. H., 202
Exploring the Adirondacks 46 High Peaks, 49, 82
Eynon, P. A., 293

F

Face on Mars, 26
Fadden, Ray, 140, 141
Fairy Bridge, 28
Falls, The, 207
Far East (boulder), 132
Farb, Nathan, 137, 140
Fedorick, Peter, 101

Felton, Amaranth, 204, 205
Fennessy, Lana, 107
Fernow, Bernard E., 160, 161
Fernow Experimental Forest, 160
Fernow Forest Boulder, 160, 160 (photo), 161
Fern Park Recreation Area, 257
Fern Park Recreation Area Boulder, 257, 258
Ferris Lake Wild Forest, 343
Fifty Hikes in the Adirondacks, 269, 286, 371, 394
Finger Lynk, 93
Fiore, Luciano, 66 (photo)
fire towers, 149, 164, 177, 187, 188, 264, 265, 325, 362, 373 (photo),
First Brother, 82, 83
First Brother Rock-Shelter, 82, 83
First Pond, 157, 159
Fish, Pete, 107
Fissure caves, 27
Five-Star Trails in the Adirondacks, 148, 228, 361, 394
Flatrock Boulders, 275, 275 (photo), 276
Flatrock Mountain, 276
Flatrock Mountain Demonstration Forest, 276
Flume, 247, 248
Flume Brook, 80
Flume Falls, 56
Footbridge Boulder, 71, 74
Forever Wild, 121
Fortress Boulder, 333
Fort St. Frederic, 292
475 Boulder, 319, 320
Fourth Lake, 253, 369
Fowler, Barney, 221, 359
France, 215
Frazier, Beatrice McCoy, 299
Freight Train, 30 (photo), 308–310, 308 (photo)
French & Indian War, 215, 306
French Louie, 356
Front (boulder), The, 133
Fulton House Way, 264

G
Gallos, Phil, 100, 141
Garden, The, 81–84, 86
Garnet Cave, 294
Garnet Lake, 370, 375

Garrison, Timothy, 55
Gateway Boulder, 62
"gateway to the Adirondacks", 42
Gazetteer and Business Directory of St. Lawrence County, N.Y., for 1873–4, 206
Gazetteer of Jefferson County, 201
Geography of St. Lawrence County, 190
Geology of the Adirondack High Peaks, 39, 97
Geology of the Schroon Lake Quadrangle, 220
Geology of the Thirteenth Lake Quadrangle, New York, 242
Geyser Cave, 294
Giant Mountain, 39, 50, 62, 64, 66, 69, 70, 79, 141, 142
Giant Mountain Boulders, 65–67
Giant Mountain Wilderness, 66
"Giant of the Valley", 66
Giant of the Valley Rocks, 62–65, 64 (photo), 66
Giant Rock, 24
Giants Nubble Trail, 66
Gill Brook, 76
Gill Brook Boulders, 75
Gill Brook Rock-Shelter, 75, 75 (photo), 76
Gill Brook Trail, 75, 76
Gillette, Chester, 262
glacial erratics, 19
glacial erratics (definition), 25
"Glacial Pothole at Crown Point", 291
glaciers, 20–22, 40
Gleasmans Falls, 396
Glenerie Falls, 256
Glen Falls, 389, 391
Glen Falls: Images of America, 389
Glenfield, 215, 216
Glen Mining Company, 377
gneiss, 39, 217
Goliath Rock, 62–64, 63 (photo), 64 (photo)
Good Luck Cliffs, 25, 341
Good Luck Cliffs Boulders, 340–342, 341 (photo)
Good Luck Gorge, 341
Good Luck Lake, 341, 342
Good Luck Mountain, 340
Goodnow Mountain, 20
Goodwin, Tony, 52, 65, 80, 85, 92, 125, 137,

138, 142, 147
Google Earth, 151, 190, 195. 216, 253, 279, 386
Gore Mountain, 380
Gostline, Mary Lee, 383
Gothics, 142
Gothics-Armstrong Trail, 77
Gould Paper Company, 256
Gouverneur, 202, 255
Grace Peak, 61, 138
"Grand Canyon of the East", 45
Grandfather Rock, 85
Grand Flume, 46
granite, 21, 41, 98, 125, 210, 215, 382
granite gneiss, 41
Grant Cottage State Historical Site, 107
Grant Rock, 106–108
Grant, Ulysses. S., 107
Grass River, South Branch, 166, 168
Gravesite Rock, 126, 126 (photo)
Gray, Ira, 315
"Great Adirondack Pass, The", 113
Great Camp, Adirondack, 247
Great Flood, 31
Great Range, 70, 187
Great Rock, 113
Great Sacandaga Lake, 312–314
"Great South Woods", 181
Great Spirit, 301
Great Wall of China, 30
Greenfield Historical Society, 316
Green Lake, 325
Green Lake Boulders, 324–326, 324 (photo)
Green Lake Rockwall, 326, 326 (photo), 327
Green Lake Shelter Cave, 325
Green Pond, 197, 198
Griffin, 363–365
Griffin Boulder, 363–365, 363 (photo)
Griffin Brook Slide, 237–239
Griffin Falls, 364
Griffin Gorge, 364
Griffin, Henry, 384
Guardrail Boulder, 67 (photo)
Guide to Adirondack Trails: Central Region. Second Edition, 221, 288
Guide to Adirondack Trails: Southern Region. Second Edition, 346, 361, 362, 393, 395
Guide to Adirondack Trails: West-Central Region. Third Edition, 255, 256, 263, 267, 270, 398
Guide to the Geology of the Lake George Region, 24, 301, 303, 390
Gull Pond, 289
Gull Pond Boulders, 288–290, 289 (photo), 290 (photo)
Gull Pond Hill, 290
Gull Rock, 158, 158 (photo), 159
Gull Rock (Kelm Lake), 387
Gull Rock & Bluff Island Wall, 158, 158 (photo), 159
Gumdrop Boulder, 168–170, 169 (photo)
Gunite, 309, 310

H
Haas, Jeremy, 238, 339, 369
Haberl, Arthur W., 398
Ha-de-ron-dah Wilderness, 271, 393
Hadley, 362
Hadley Mountain, 362
Hadley Mountain Boulders, 360–363, 360 (photo), 361 (photo)
Hague, 300, 304
Hamilton College, 264
Hamilton Lake, 348
Hanging-Garden, 46
Hannon, Michelle, 282, 283
Harder, Kelsie, 146, 162, 190, 397
Harper's Ferry, 92, 127
Harrietstown, 145
Harris, Alice, 368
Harrison, Jay, 373
Harris Preserve, 368
Harrisville, 200
Haynes, Letty Kirch, 258
Haystack (Atwell), 280
Haystack Rock, 177–179, 178 (photo)
Haystacks, 137
Haystacks, Mount, 87
Haywood, John, 64, 123
Heart Lake, 104, 109
Heaven Up-h'isted-ness, 100
Hedgehog Mountain Trail, 80
Henderson, David, 113
He-no-do-as-da, 113

BOULDERS BEYOND BELIEF

Henodowanda Megalith Cave System, 110
Hidden Heritage, 162
Hi 'n Dry, 315
Highball (boulder), 333
High Falls Gorge, 28, 119, 121
High Falls Gorge Potholes, 119–122, 120 (postcard)
High Peaks, 38–40, 66, 77, 81, 124, 136
High Peaks Information Center, 107, 113
High Rock Lodge, 313
High Rock (Sacandaga Park), 312–314, 312 (postcard)
High Rock (Saratoga Springs), 313, 314
High Rock (Warrensburg), 384, 385, 385 (postcard)
Highwall, 309, 310
Hiking New York, 270, 395
Hiking the Adirondacks. Second Edition, 42, 48, 76, 311, 361, 397
His Majesty's Fort of Crown Point, 291, 292
Historical Sketches of Franklin County and its Several Towns, 162
History of Clinton and Franklin Counties, New York, 44, 46
History of Glens Falls, New York, and its Settlements, 389
History of Jefferson County, New York, 201
History of Lewis County, 217
History of Newcomb, 107
History of the Adirondacks, A, 111
History of the Town of Worth: 1795–1976, 398
History of St. Lawrence and Franklin Counties, New York, 206
Hive (boulder), 373
Hochschild, Berthold, 247
Hodges, Fred, 247
Hodges Rock, 246–248, 246 (photo)
Hoffman Mountain, 286
Hoffman Notch, 287, 296
Hoffman Notch Boulders, 286–288, 287 (photo)
Hoffman Notch Brook, 286
Hoffman Notch Wilderness Area, 286
Hogtown, 311
Holden, A. W., 382
Holls Inn, 259

Hollywood, 206
Homer, Winslow, 113
Hope Falls, 352
Hopkinton, 191
Hough, Franklin B., 201, 206, 217
Hough, Horatio G., 213
Hough's Cave, 213, 214
Huckelberry Rock, 397
Huckleberry Mountain, 377
Hudowalski, Grace L., 396
Hudson from the Wilderness to the Sea, The, 223
Hudson River, 111, 296, 383
Hudson River Natural Bridge, 296
huecos, 238
Hughes, John (Photo), 29.
Huntington Island, 397
Huntingtonville, 397
Huntley Pond, 24
Huntley Pond Boulder, 24 (photo)
Hurd, Duane Hamilton, 44, 45
Hurricane Mountain, 139
Hyde, Louis Fiske, 389
Hydes Cave, 44, 45
hyperthermia, 36
hypothermia, 36

I

Iberian Peninsula, 61
Ice Age, 40, 45, 173, 203, 293
Ice Cave Mountain, 398
ice caves, 298
Idaho, 27
Idol Rock, 23
igneous rock, 21
Images of America's First Wilderness, 137
Indian Face, 351, 352, 352 (photo)
Indian Head Trail, 76
Indian Kettle (Morristown), 208, 209
Indian Kettles Hotel, 304
Indian Kettles (Lake George), 302–305
Indian Ladder, 315
Indian Lake, 393
Indian Pass, 101
Indian Pass, 101, 109
Indian Pass Boulders, 109–116, 111 (photo), 112 (photo), 114 (photo)

413

Indian Pass Brook, 111
Indian River, 193–195
Indian Rock, 382
Ingersoll, Bill, 171, 176, 237, 333, 339, 364, 376, 377, 393, 395
Ingham, Charles, 111
Inlet, 259
Inlet Ski Touring Center, 257
Inner Sanctum Trail, 44
Interior Outpost Ranger Station, 83, 142
Iron Bridge, 364, 365, 385
Iroquois, 215
Iroquois Peak, 145
Irving, James, 319
Irving Pond, 319, 320
Irving Pond Rocks, 318–320, 319 (photo), 394 (photo)
Island Road Bridge, 252

J

Jackrabbit Trail, 92, 93
Jackrabbit Trail Boulders: Alstead Hill Approach, 90–93
Jackrabbit Trail Boulders: Mountain Road Approach, 93–95, 94 (photo)
Jackson, Asa, 207
Jackson, Asahel, 207
Jackson, Cyrus, 207
Jacob's Ladder, 46
Jacob's Well, 44, 45 (photo)
Jamieson, Paul, 163
Jacques, Father, 391
Jaques, Adeline F., 121
Jay, 95
Jay Boulder, 95, 96, 96 (photo)
Jay Covered Bridge, 95, 96
Jay, John, 96
Jayville, 397
Jefferson County, New York, 397
Jesse, Elizabeth, 39, 40, 97
Jesse, Howard, 39, 40, 97
Jockeybush Lake, 343, 344
Joe Indian Island, 171, 172
Johannsen, Herman, 92
Johns Brook, 81
Johns Brook Lodge, 87

Johns Brook Trail, 84
Johnson, Bill, 211
Johnson, Kate, 211
Johnson Pond Boulders, 53, 53 (photo)
Johnson, Sir William, 313,
Johnson's Island, Bill, 210
Joshua Rock, 299
Judd Bridge, 385
Jumbo Rock, 189–191
Juniper Island, 307

K

Kane Mountain, 325, 327, 328
Kapoor family, 383
Karate Rock, 378–380
Kastning, Ernst, 296
Keene Valley, 80, 81, 83
Keene Valley Region Waterfall Guide, 76
Keeseville, 28
Keewaydin State Park, 211
Kellogg, Christina, 225
Kellogg, Cyrus, 225
Kelm Lake and its People, 387
Kelm Lake/Pond, 387
Kenakwadione, 383
Kick, Peter, 153, 228
Kids on the Trail: Hiking with Children in the Adirondacks, 175, 347
King (boulder), 371
Kissing Couple (boulder), 323
Knitel, Neal, 280
Krieger, Medora Hooper, 242
Krishna's Butter Ball, 24
Kunjamuk Cave, 355–357, 356 (photo)
Kunjamuk River, 356
Kunjamuk Valley, 355
Kure-Jensen, Lisa, 387

L

Lady in the Lake, A, 135
LaGray, Albert, 186
Laing, Linda, 346, 361, 362, 393, 395
Lake Champlain, 91
Lake Colden, 143
Lake Desolation, 317
Lake Durant, 230, 231

Lake George, 294, 302, 303, 383
Lake George: A Book of Today, 303, 304
Lake George and Lake Champlain, 303
Lake House, 225
Lake Luzerne, 368
Lake Ontario, 92, 191
Lake Ozonia, 190
Lake Placid, 99, 102, 107, 113, 116, 118, 121, 123, 128, 133, 135, 396
Lake Pleasant, 354
Lake Road Trail, 73, 76
Lampson Falls, 169
Lampson Falls Boulder, 169
Landers, California, 24
Last of the Mohicans, 390
Latham Trail, 176
Laundry Brook, 72, 74
Laurentian Shield, 38
Laurentide Glaciation, 38, 40
Lawyer, Jim, 238, 339
Leaning Potato, 54, 55 (photo)
Lean-to Rocks, 379
Leavitt, Reverend Oliver, 203
Ledge Boulder, 66
Leviathan Rock, 229–231
Lewey Bridge, 236
Lewey Lake, 235
Lewey Lake Campground, 236
Leyden, 217
Liberty Bell, 222 (photo)
"life on the slide", 118
Lily Lake, 321
Lily Lake Rocks, 320–322, 321 (photo)
Limekiln Lake Public Campground, 256
limestone, 21, 217, 291
Lindsay Brook Glacial Erratic, 27
Little Buster (boulder), 323
Little Crow Boulders, 88–90
Little Crow Mountain, 89, 89 (photo)
Little Marcy, 139
Little Meadows, 105
Little Porter Mountain, 139
Little Sand Point Campground, 346
Little Sawyer Mountain, 233, 234
Little Sawyer Mountain Balanced Rock, 233, 234, 234 (photo)

Long Lake, 226
Loon Brook, 246–248,
Lord, Thomas Reeves, 223
Lost Arrow, 396
Lost Dog (boulder), 333
Lost Hunter's Cliffs, 339
Lost Hunter's Cliffs Boulder, 339
Lost Pool Cave, 294
Lower Saranac Lake, 159
Lowrie, Dr. Walter, 86
Luzerne Heights Public Beach, 369
lyme disease, 37
Lyon Mountain, 48
Lyon Mountain Boulder, 47, 48
Lyon, Nathaniel, 48

M

Mahabalipuram, India, 24
Mojave Desert, 24
Makaia (boulder), 132
Malecki, Stan, 389
Mammoth Cave, 141
Manvill, 316
Manvill, Adrian, 316
Manville Rock, 316–318, 317 (photo)
Manvill, Lucinda, 316
marble, 21, 193, 293 , 296, 371
Marcy Airport, 88
Marcy Massif, 39
Marcy, Mount, 9, 20, 40, 86, 107, 108, 143 (postcard)
Martin, E. J., 262
Martin Road Boulders, 261–263
Martin, Shawn, 325
Mass Disstruction (boulder), 238
Matterhorn, 40
McEwen, Mollie, 190
McIntyre Range, 110
McKay, Paul John, 129
McKeever, 272
McKenzie Pond Boulders, 131–133, 131 (photo), 133 (photo), 144 (photo)
McKinley, President William, 262
McMartin, Barbara, 88, 91, 94, 105, 139, 140, 141, 145, 147, 153, 171, 176, 230, 241, 250,269, 286, 325, 334, 335, 340, 344, 355, 364, 376, 394,

395, 396, 397
McMartin, Duncan, 113
Meacham Lake, 184
Meadow Boulder, 91, 93
Meadowcroft Rock Shelter, 27
Megalith, 110
Megalodon, 330, 330 (photo), 331
Mellor, Don, 396
Memories of Inlet, 256
metamorphic rocks, 21
Middle Earth (boulder field), 333
Middle Saranac Lake, 159
Middle Settlement, 271
Middle Settlement Access Trail, 270, 272, 273
Middle Settlement Lake, 269–271
Middle Settlement Lake Rocks, 269–274, 269 (photo), 270 (photo), 271 (photo), 272 (photo)
Mihalyi, Charles, 215
Mihalyi, Louis C., 214
Military and Civil History of the County of Essex, New York, The, 113
Mill Brook, West, 140
Miller family, 383
Miller, William John, 220
Mill Pond, 319
Mills, The, 207
Minerva, 286
Mineville, 55
Mingo Lodge, 253
Mini-Falls, 121
Mitchell, Jeff, 395
Moby Dick Boulder, 379, 380
Mohawks, 383
Monster Rock, 157, 157 (photo)
Monument Park Boulders, 280–282
Moon, 39
Moon-rock, 39
Moose River, 262
Moose River, Middle Branch, 272
Moose River Plains Wild Forest, 256
Moosie, 42
Moravia, 24
Moreton, Orrinda, 398
Morgan, Joseph "Moe", 194
Moriah Center, 55
Moriah, Town of, 54

Morrill, C. B., 187
Morris, Bill, 391
Morris, Gouverneur, 208, 255
Morristown, 208, 209
Morton, Robert, 393
Mosley, Heidi, 64, 109
Mount Arab, 164
Mount Arab Rock, 163–165, 164 (photo), 165 (photo)
Mount Arab Trail, 164
Mount Colden Boulder, 34 (photo), 143
Mount Colvin, 140
Mount Gilligan, 52
Mount Gilligan Rocks, 51, 51 (photo), 52
Mount Haystacks, 87
Mount Jo, 109
Mount Jo Trail, 109
Mount Jo Trailhead Boulders, 198, 109 (boulder)
Mount Lane Trail, 94
Mount Marcy, 9, 20, 40, 86, 107, 108, 143 (postcard)
Mount Marcy: The High Peak of New York, 86
Mount McGregor, 107
Mount McMartin, 113
Mount Pleasant, 316
Mousetrap (rock), 65
Moynehan, Patrick, 225
Murder in the Adirondacks: An American Tragedy Revisited, 262
Murphy, Cheri, 194
Murphy, Michael, 194
Murphy, Tim, 336
Museum of Natural History, New York City, 209
Mutiny (boulder), 307
Mylrole, John, 193
"Mystery of the Lost Cave, The", 141
Mystic Gorge, 46

N
Narrows, The, 304
National Historic Landmark, 292
National Register of Historic Places, 181, 292
National Speleological Society (NSS), 213, 293
Native Americans, 179, 208, 215, 302, 303, 314,

382, 383, 385
Natural Bridge, 28, 193, 194, 297
Natural Bridge Caverns, 193–196, 194 (photo)
Natural Bridge (Crane Mountain), 317, 372
Natural Bridge, Hudson River, 296
natural bridges, 28, 217
Natural Bridges National Monument, 28
Natural Dam, 28, 255
natural dams, 28
Natural Rock Dam, 254–256
Natural Stone Bridge, 293, 294 (photo)
Natural Stone Bridge & Caves, 22, 28, 293–297
Natural Well, 206
Nature Conservancy, 102
Nature Trail Boulder, 122
Naughton, Joe, 171
Navy, U. S., 249
Near Keene Valley, 79
Ne-ha-sa-ne Park Association, 261
Ne-na-ta-re, 215
Neodak Hotel, 259
Neodak Split Rock, 258–260, 259 (photo)
Neubuck, Lydia, 295
Newcomb, 113, 222, 262
New Hampshire, 26
Newland, David H., 24, 301, 303, 390
New Russia, 50, 142
New York Adirondack Park Bouldering, 65, 310
New York City, 209
New York Tradition, 141
Nez Perde National Historic Park, 27
Niagara Frontier Grotto, 213
Nichols Brook, 93
Nick Stoner (boulder), 333
Nine Corner Lake, 332, 333, 335
Nine Corner Lake Boulders, 332–334, 332 (photo)
Nine Corner Lake Trail, 333
Nippletop Mountain, 136
Noah, 31
Noisy Cave, 294, 295, 295 (photo)
Noonmark Mountain, 72, 140
North Bolton Boulders, 308–310
North Country Life, 214, 294
North Country School, 100
North Creek, 296

Northeastern Caver, 193, 210, 296, 325

Northeastern New York and the Adirondack Wilderness, 126
North Elba, 92, 127, 393
Northern Research Station, U. S. Forest Services, 161
North Fork Boulder & Potholes, 56, 57, 57 (photo)
North Glens Falls, 382
North Hudson, 114, 286, 296
North Lake, 280
North River, 283
North Schroon Lake, 289
Northside Trail, 84
Northville, 313
Northville-Placid Trail, 344, 348
Northville-Placid Trail Glacial Erratic, 344, 345
Norton Mountain, 141
Norway, 23, 92
"Not so Erratic History of Erratics, The", 31

O

O'Donnell, Thomas C., 215
Office of Parks, Recreation and Historic Preservation, NYS, 128
Ogdensburg, 171
Old Forge, 264, 272, 396
Old-Man-of-the-Mountain, 26
Old Military Road, 91, 92
Old Orchard Inn, 313
Olean, 132
"Old Green Lady", 225
Onchiota, 141
100 Views of the Adirondacks, 137
Oneida, 215
Orebed Trail, 142
Oregon, 179
Ortloff, George Christian, 135
Osborn Lake, 202
Oseetah Lake, 157
O'Shea, Peter V., 141, 144
Os-ten-wanne, 113
Ostertag, George, 270, 395
Ostertag, Rhonda, 270, 395
Oswegatchie River, 203, 207, 255

BOULDERS BEYOND BELIEF

Otne-yar-heh, 113
Outside Magazine, 219
Overlook (boulder), 323
Oxbow, 203
Ozisik, Metin, 9
Ozonia, 190

P

Pack, Charles Lathrop, 386
Pack Commemorative Rock, Charles Lathrop, 386, 386 (photo), 387
Pack Demonstration Forest, 387
Pack Lake, 387
painted rocks, 28
Paint Mine, 377
Paint Mine Boulders, 375–378, 376 (photo), 377 (photo)
Paint Mine Brook, 376
Palmer, Gwen, 389
Panther Mountain, 232, 346, 347
Patriot Navy of the East, 211
Patriot War, 211
Paul Smiths, 162
Peace Sign Rock, 167
Peaked Mountain, 282, 283
Peaked Mountain Boulders, 282–284, 283 (photo)
Peaked Mountain Brook, 283
Peaked Mountain Lake, 283
Peep at Luzerne, 368
Peninsula Trail, 224
Perched Rock, 54, 54 (photo)
perched rocks, 23
Peregrine Falcons, 42
Perils of Pauline, 159
Perkins Clearing, 356
Perry, Clay, 45, 193, 196, 213, 294, 389
Peter, Captain, 162
Peter's Rock, 162
Peters Rock, Captain, 162
Petty, Bill, 98
Pharaoh Lake, 394
Pharaoh Lake Wilderness, 288, 289
Pharaoh Mountain Wilderness Area, 285
Phelps, Ed, 84
Phelps, Orson Scofield "Old Mountain", 84,
86, 315
Phelps Trail Boulders, 83–86, 84 (photo)
Picture Rock, 165 (photo)
Picture Rock, Canada Lake, 396 (photo)
Piercefield, 163
Pierces Corners, 202
Pigeon Lake Wilderness Area, 267, 268
Pig Rock, 28, 358, 358 (photo), 359
Pilot Knob, 310, 311
Pine Lake, 331, 335
Pine Lake Boulders, 330, 331
Pines, The, 313
Pinnacle Boulders, 322, 322 (photo), 323
Pinnacle Pullout Boulders, 323
Pinnacle Restaurant, 323
Pinnacle, The, 183–185
Pirate (boulder), 307
Piseco, 344
Piseco Lake, 344, 346
Pisgah Mountain, 136
Pitchoff Mountain, 92, 94, 97, 98, 100–102
Place Names of Franklin County, 146, 162
Plymouth Rock, 28
Podskoch, Martin, 186
Pohqui, 42
Point-of-Rocks, 46
Poke-O, 42
Poke-O-Moonshine, 41, 41 (photo), 42
Poke-O-Moonshine Boulder, 41–43, 42 (photo), 43 (photo)
Poke-O-Moonshine Campground, 42
Pond Mountain, 264
Ponte de Dios, 293
Poole, Carol Payment, 146, 162
Porter Mountain, 88, 102, 105
Porter Mountain Boulder, 105, 106
Porter Mountain Trail, 88
Porter, Noah, 105
Porters Corners, 316
Port Henry, 55
Port Kent, 46
Possons, Charles H., 302
Post Office (rock formation), 46
Potash Mountain, 368
Potash Mountain Boulder #1, 367, 367 (photo), 368

418

Potash Mountain Boulder #2, 368, 369, 369 (photo)
Potash, The, 368
potholes, 27, 28, 56 (photo), 57, 201–203, 206, 208, 209, 217, 237, 238, 291–293, 294, 302–304, 356, 364, 397
Potter, Joel E., 295
Pottersville, 22, 28, 295, 296
Pratt family, 259
Precambrian Greenville marble, 193
Preston, William, 259
Prison Boulder, 328, 329, 329 (photo)
Puffer Pond Basin, 395
Puffer Pond Trail, 395
Pulpit Pothole, 203
Pulpit Rock (Ausable Chasm), 46
Pulpit Rock (Lake Placid), 134, 135
Pulpit Rock (Oxbow), 201–204, 202 (photo)
Punch Bowl (pothole), 44
Putnam, 277
Putnam Farm Road, 374
"Putt", 277
Putt's Monument, 277–279, 277 (photo), 278 (postcard)
Putt's (talus) Cave, 279
Pyle, Howard, 210
pyramids, 30

Q
Qattasa Sinkhole, 152
Quarterly, The, 190, 191, 207, 209
Quebec Brook, 188
Queer Lake Trail, 268
Quinn, Joe, 9

R
Railroad Notch, 105
Rainbow Falls (AMR), 74
Rainbow Falls (Ausable Chasm), 45
Rainbow Falls (Tooley Pond Road), 166
Rambles to Remarkable Rocks, 34, 315
Randorf, Gary, 104, 137, 138
Ranger School Trail Boulder, 176, 177
Raquette Falls, 225
Raquette Lake, 249
Raquette River, 162

Rathbone, Ellen, 222
rattlesnakes, 309
Ray Brook, 130
Rayonier, 164
Red River, 255
Reids Rock, 299
Remsen Falls, 255
Resting Rock, 54, 55
Reuben Wood Rock, 170–172, 171 (photo)
Revolutionary War, 92, 292, 295, 315
Reynolds family, 304
Reynolds, Jeanne, 143
Rich Lake, 223
Rich Lake Boulder, 222–224, 222 (photo)
Rich Lake Trail, 222, 224
Ripley's Believe it or not, 181
riprap, 333
River Reflections: A Short History of Morristown, New York, 208
River Rolls On, The, 215
Rivezzi, Rose, 175, 345
Roadside Boulder, 351, 352
Roadside Geology of New York, 40, 119, 122
Roaring Brook Boulder, 69–71
Roaring Brook Falls, 70
Roaring Brook Trail, 66
Robbins, Edythe, 394
Rockachusetts, 33
Rock & River, 92
rock city, 131
Rock City Park, 132
Rock Garden Trail, 109
Rock of Gibraltar, 61, 62
"Rock of the Pines", 215
rock overhang, 52
Rock Pond, 231,
rock profiles, 19, 25–27
rock-shelters, 27, 85, 290, 336, 338
Rock, The, 387
rock tripe, 388
Rocky Peak Ridge, 50
Rogers Co., 121
Rogers, Donald, 98
Rogers, Emma, 259
Rogers, Robert, 306
Rogers Rock, 306, 307

Rogers Rock Boulders, 305–307
Roger Rock Campground, 306, 307
Rogers, Roy, 259
Rogers Slide, 304, 306, 307
Rondaxe Fire Tower, 264
Rondaxe Mountain, 264
Rookie (boulder), 324
Roosevelt, Franklin D., 125
Roosevelt, John Ellis, 261, 262
Roosevelt, Theodore, 261–263
Roosevelt Rock, 260
Roost Beef (boulder), 238
Rooster Comb Mountain, 80
Rooster Comb Rock, 79, 79 (photo), 80
Rosetta Stone, 156, 156 (photo), 157
Roth, Will, 157
Round Mountain, 62
Round Mountain Boulder, 26 (photo)
Round Pond, 59, 64
Round Rock, 52
Routes and Rocks of the North Country, 202
Ruggesteinen Balanced Rock, 23
Russell, 209

S

Sabael, 237
Sabattis, Peter, 162
Sacandaga Campground, 348
Sacandaga Park, 312, 313
Sacandaga Reservoir, 313
Sacandaga River, 313, 348, 354, 366
Sacandaga River, East Branch, 348
Sacandaga River, West Branch, 339, 342, 348, 349
Sacandaga Valley, 313, 315
Sachs Trail, 80
Saddleback Mountain, 137
Saddleback Mountain Boulder, 25 (photo)
Safari Hobbit (boulder), 373
St. Amand, Joseph M., 194, 397
St. Lawrence County Historical Association, 190, 207, 209
St. Lawrence River, 207
St. Regis Falls, 399
St. Regis Lake, Lower, 162
Saint Regis Mountain, 149

Saint Regis Mountain Boulders, 147–150, 148 (photo), 149 (photo)
Saint Regis Mountain Fire Tower, 147 (photo)
Saint Regis River, 149, 162
Saint's Rest, 335
Saint's Retreat, 335
salt spring, 214
Sam's Point, 307
Sanford, Justin, 65, 310, 339, 343
Santa Clara Conservation Easement Tract, 184
Saranac Lake, 129, 136, 149, 159
Saranac Lake 6-ers, 129
Saranac River, 142, 159
Saratoga County, 362
Saratoga Springs, 313
Sargent Pond Trail, 229
Satellite (boulder), 132
Saugerties, 256
sawmill, 295, 319
Sawteeth, 143, 144
Sawyer Mountain, 232–234
Sawyer Mountain Boulder, 231–233, 232 (photo)
Sawyer Mountain, Little, 233, 234
Scarface Mountain, 129, 130
Scarface Mountain Boulder, 128–131
Schaefer Boulder, Paul, 381, 381 (photo), 382
Schaefer, Carl, 379
Schaefer, Paul, 379, 381, 382
Schaefer Trail, 379
Schaefer Trail Boulders, 378–381, 379 (photo)
Schaefer, Vincent, 379
"sketching the Mt. Jo Trail", 108
Schmid, Walter, 257
Schneider, Paul, 373
Schofield, Josephine, 109
Schoharie Valley, 338
Schroon, 286
Schroon Lake, 285, 286, 296
Schroon River, 385
Schul, Leslie, 325
Scusa Access Trail, 272
Sea stack, 179
Seaver, Frederick J., 162
Second Brother, 82
Second Pond, 157

BOULDERS BEYOND BELIEF

Second Pond Boat Launch, 159
Second Pond Boulders, 155–157, 155 (photo), 156 (photo)
Second Pond Flow, 381
Sedimentary rock, 20, 21
Sehlmeyer, Joanne, 368
Sehlmeyer, Richard, 368
Sentinel Rocks, 84
Sentry (boulder), 373
Sentry Box, 46
Sentry Rock, 371
Setting Pole Dam, 163
Seventh Lake, 251, 252, 254
Seventh Lake Boat Launch & Fishing Access, 251, 253
Seventh Lake Mountain, 250
Seventh Lake Trail, 251
Seven Wonders of the World, 30
Severance Hill, 285
Severance Hill Boulder, 284–286, 285 (photo)
Sevey Corners, 166, 171, 177, 179
Seymour, Louis "Lewey", 236, 356
shale, 21
Shawangunks, 34, 38, 307
shelter cave, 147, 242, 325, 364, 365
Shelter Rock, 94, 95
Sherman Mountain, 339
Sherman Mountain Balanced Rock, 339, 340
Ship's Prow, 242
Shoebox Falls, 60
Shorey Short Cut Trail, 137
Siena College, 66
Silver Lake Mountain, 140, 141
Simms, Jeptha Root, 341
Sinclair Falls, 166
sinkhole, 151, 152
Sixmile Creek, 144
Six Nation Indian Museum, 141
Sixth Lake, 252
Skylight, 9
Slack, W. R., 304
Slant Rock, 85–87, 86 (photo)
slate, 21
Sleeping Turtle, 173
Sleep Inn, 383
Sliding Rock Falls, 144

Sliding Rock Trail, 144
Sloppy (boulder), 323
Smith, Alfred E., 226
Smith, Paul, 162
Snowy Mountain, 232, 237–239
Snowy Mountain Boulders, 237–240, 237 (photo), 238 (photo)
Snyder, Charles E., 271
Solitary Rock. 58, 58 (photo)
South Bay, 144
South Colton, 180, 182
South Glens Falls, 389, 391
South Schroon, 287
Southside Trail, 84
South Woods, 399
Spain, 194
Spectacle Lake, 342
Speculator, 28, 351
Speculator Tree Farm Tract, 356
Spiritualists, 196
Split Rock Bay, 394, 395
Split Rock, Charles Lathrop, 386, 387
Split Rock: Flatrock Mountain, 275, 275 (photo), 276
Split Rock: Hague, 300–302, 300 (postcard), 301 (photo)
Split Rock: Harrietstown, 145, 146, 145 (photo), 146 (photo)
Split Rock: Keene Valley, 80–82, 81 (photo)
Split Rock: Lewey Lake, 235, 235 (postcard), 236 (photo)
Split Rock; Pharaoh Lake, 394
Splitting Headache (boulder), 371, 371 (photo) 374
Sprite Creek, 321
Square Boulder, 345–347
Squaw Bonnet Mountain, 238
Squaw Brook, 239
Squaw Brook Boulder, 239, 240
Stagecoach Rock, 97–99, 97 (photo)
Stager, Curt, 162
Stallion Boulder, 343, 343 (photo), 344
Stamford, Connecticut, 304
Stand-alone Boulder, 91, 91 (photo), 93
Stark, 177
Star Lake, 143, 399

Star Lake: Images of America, 399
Starmer, Tim, 148, 228, 361, 394
State University of New York (SUNY) College of Environmental Science & Forestry, 176, 223
Steps (boulder), The, 280
Stewart Landing, 321
Stewart Pond Bridge, 366
Stewart Rapids, 166
Stink Lakes, 338
Stoddard, Seneca Ray, 45, 303
Stoltie, Annie, 139
stone, 21
Stoner Lake, 338
Stoner Lake, Little, 338
Stoner Lake, West, 338
Stoner Lodge, Nick, 320
Stoner, Nick, 173, 338
Stone, Robert, 20
Stoner's Cave, 172, 173
"Stonish Giants", 113
Stony Creek, 362, 394
Stony Crest Island, 211
Street, Alfred Billings, 101, 113
Strobeck Rock, 334, 335
Stuff: the absolute true adventures of men, women and critters, 302
Subterranean (boulder), 276
Sucker Brook, 171
Sugar River, 217, 218, 277
Sugar River Falls, 218
Sugar River Unique Bedrock, 217, 218
Suitcase (boulder), 333
Summit Boulder, 104
Summit Rock, 111, 113, 115
Sunday Rock, 28, 180–183, 181 (photo), 182 (illustration)
Sunday Rock Association, 180
Sunrise Mountain, 52
Sunrise Trail, 52
SUNY College of Environmental Science and Forestry, 176
Super Slab, 132
Swamp (boulder), 132
Swamp Thing (boulder), 276
Sweet Pea (boulder), 132

Sword of Damocles, 384
syenite, 97, 98, 301
Sylvester, Nathaniel, 126
Syracuse Post Standard, 151

T
Table Rock, 46
tafoni, 238
Tahawus, 111, 114
Talcotville Falls, 218
Tales of Jayville New York and the North Country, 194, 397
Tales of the Empire State, 210
talus, 22, 51, 64, 69 (photo), 187, 242, 267, 268, 271, 279, 289, 341
talus caves, 27, 68
Taylor, Jenny, 99
Taylor, Peter, 99
Taylor Pond Management Complex, 42
tectonic caves, 27, 242
Tenant Creek Falls, 352
Thacher Park, John Boyd, 315
Thendara, 269, 275
Third Brother, 82
Thirteenth Lake, 283, 381
Thomas, Captain E. E., 141
Thomas, Sally, 181
Thurman, 374
Tibbitts, George F., 354
ticks, 37
Tongue Mountain Range, 309
Tongue Mountain Range Boulders, 310
Tongue Mountain Range Trail, 396
Tooley Pond, 168
Tooley Pond Boulders, 166–168
Tooley Pond Mountain, 177
Tooley Pond Road, 166
Torture Rock, 382
Tory, 315
Tory Cave, 315
Tory Rock, 314–316, 315 (photo)
"Touchy Sword of Damocles" (TSOD), 111
Tower of Power (boulder), 332, 333
Trailhead Boulder, 123
Trailside Boulder, 91, 93, 94, 104
Train, David Thomas, 311, 372, 373, 398

Transportation, Department of (DOT), 384
Trappers of New York, 341
Trauma (boulder), 373
Treadway Mountain Boulders, 399
Trim, Paula LaVoy, 399
Trithart, David, 175, 345
Trout Brook, 22, 293, 295, 296
Trout Brook, North Branch, 286
Trout Lake, 190
Troy, The, 389
Truesdale, Hardie, 137, 139
Tupper Lake, 206
Tupper Lake Boat Launch, 162
Tuscarora, 215
12 Short Hikes near Keene Valley, 79, 82, 139
25 Ski Tours in the Adirondacks, 257
Twin Falls, 166
Twin Pond, 59, 397
Twin Pond Brook, 59–61
Twister (rock), 65
Two Towns…Two Centuries, 143

U

Uncle Am's Rock, 204
Underground Empire, 195, 196, 213, 294, 389
Underground Railroad, 213
Underwood Railroad Bridge, 162
Uno's Chicago Grill, 383
Up Old Forge Way, 253, 264, 265
Upper Boulder, 65, 66
Upstate New York, 217
Urnaitis, Timothy M., 207
USA Today, 306
Utah, 28
Utowana, 249
Utowana Lake, 247, 249
Utowana Lake Boulder, 248–250, 249 (photo)

V

Valleyland Boulders, 84
Vall-Kill by Roosevelt Rock, 261
Van Benthuysen, Jacob, 295
Van Diver, Bradford B., 40, 119, 122, 202, 217, 218
Van Hoevenberg, Henry, 109
Van Laer, Scott, 19

Vaughn, Henry, 25, 301, 303, 390
Vermeulen, Jim, 341
Vermontville, 151, 152
View Restaurant, The, 304
Virginia, 28
Vrooman, John, 341
Vrooman Lake, 338

W

Wadhams, 55
Wadsworth, Bruce, 89, 100, 129, 130, 186, 221, 270
Wakely Mountain, 232
Waldheim, The, 261, 262
Wallface Mountain, 110, 111
Walton, Richard J., 271
Wanakena, 176
Ward, Elizabeth, 139, 319 (photo)
Warm-up Wall, 323
Warren County Historical Society, 382
Warrensburg, 313
Washburn Ridge, 287
Washer, Dick, 121
Washer, Josephine, 121
Washington, D. C., 384
Washington, George, 314
Watcher's Rock, 254
Waterfront Lodge Camp Mi-Wok, 254
Water Over the Fall: St. Regis Falls History, 399
Water Rock, 319, 320
Watertown, 397
Watson, Winslow C., 113
Wauwinel Island, 211
Weaverton, 374
Weber, Sandra, 86
Wechsler, Alan, 332
Weis Rock-shelter, 27
Wells, 348, 350–352, 365, 393
West Branch Boulder, Ausable River, 122, 123
West Branch Boulders, Sacandaga River, 347–349, 348 (photo)
West Branch Gorge, 349
West Branch Nature Trail, 122
West Flow, 144
West Lake, 321, 335
West Lake Trail Boulders, 334–336, 335 (Photo)

West Mill Brook, 140
West Mountain Ridge, 362
West Pond Rocks, 398 (photo)
Westport, 55
West River Trail, 73, 74, 77
West Turin, 217
Whale Rock, 59, 60, 60 (photo)
Whale, The (boulder), 371
Wheelerville, 318, 322
Whetstone Gulf State Park, 214
Whitaker Lake, 359
Whiteface Brook, 118
Whiteface Brook Boulders, 116–118, 117 (photo)
Whiteface Brook Lean-to, 118
Whiteface Brook Shelter, 116
Whiteface Brook Slide, 118
Whiteface Landing, 117, 118
Whiteface Mountain, 116, 118, 124, 125
Whiteface Mountain Summit Rocks, 124, 125
Whiteface Mountain Trail, 118
Whiteface Ski Center, 122, 123
Whiteface Ski Center Bridge, 122
Whiteface Veteran's Memorial Highway, 125
Whitehouse, 348
White Lake, 277
White Rock, 59, 60, 60 (photo)
White Rock Boulder, 325
White Rock Camp, 325
Wild Pines, 310
Wilkie Reservoir, 388, 389
Wilkie Reservoir Split Rock, 388, 388 (photo), 389
Williams, Donald R., 393
Williams, Stephen, 343
Willy's Cave, 172, 173
Wilmington, 28, 121, 123, 125
Wilmington Notch Falls, 123
Wilton, 107
Windfall Pond, 268
Wind Tunnel, 101
Wisconsin glaciation, 40
Wisell, Kurt, 283
Wisher, Brad, 304
Wishing Well, 294
Wood, Ellen, 323
Woodman, Tom, 79, 82, 88, 139
Wood, Reuben, 170
Worth, Town of, 399
Wright Peak (photo), 38

X

Xianren Bridge, 28

Y

Yale University, 105
Yorkshire, U. K., 23
"Yosemite in Miniature", 45

Z

Zander Scott Trail, 66
Ziegler, Dan, 105 (photo)
Zimmerman's Rock, 399 (photo)

Made in the USA
Middletown, DE
02 October 2023